BLOOD MONEY

ALSO BY PETER SCHWEIZER

*Architects of Ruin: How Big Government Liberals
Wrecked the Global Economy—and How
They Will Do It Again If No One Stops Them*

*Clinton Cash: The Untold Story of How and
Why Foreign Governments and Businesses Helped
Make Bill and Hillary Rich*

*Secret Empires: How the American Political Class
Hides Corruption and Enriches Family and Friends*

*Profiles in Corruption: Abuse of Power
by America's Progressive Elite*

*Red-Handed: How American Elites Get Rich
Helping China Win*

BLOOD MONEY

Why the Powerful Turn a Blind Eye While China Kills Americans

PETER SCHWEIZER

HARPER

An Imprint of HarperCollins*Publishers*

HarperCollins books may be purchased for educational, business, or sales promotional use. For information, please email the Special Markets Department at SPsales@harpercollins.com.

FIRST EDITION

Library of Congress Cataloging-in-Publication Data

Names: Schweizer, Peter, 1964– author.
Title: Blood money : why the powerful turn a blind while China kills Americans / Peter Schweizer.
Description: New York, NY : HarperCollins Publishers, [2024] | Includes index.
Identifiers: LCCN 2023043053 (print) | LCCN 2023043054 (ebook) |
ISBN 9780063061194 (hardcover) | ISBN 9780063061217 (ebook)
Subjects: LCSH: Elite (Social sciences)—Political activity—United States. | United States—Foreign relations—China. | China—Foreign relations—United States.
Classification: LCC HN90.E4 S33 2024 (print) | LCC HN90.E4 (ebook) |
DDC 305.5/20973—dc23/eng/20231128
LC record available at https://lccn.loc.gov/2023043053
LC ebook record available at https://lccn.loc.gov/2023043054

23 24 25 26 27 LBC 5 4 3 2 1

To Rhonda, with great love—
Thank you for everything.

Be so subtle that you are invisible. Be so mysterious that you are intangible. Then you will control your rivals' fate.

—Sun Tzu

When you want to help people, you tell them the truth. When you want to help yourself, you tell them what they want to hear.

—Dr. Thomas Sowell

CONTENTS

PART IV: LOOT A BURNING HOUSE (趁火打劫)

INTRODUCTION: VACANT EYES

> Here then was one of the great secrets of the war and of the world. . . . But hardly anyone would believe it . . . and almost all the great responsible authorities stood gazing at it with vacant eyes.
>
> —Winston Churchill, *The World Crisis* (vol. 2)

Americans were horrified in early 2023 when a Chinese spy balloon as tall as a twenty-story building drifted openly into US airspace and traversed the country from Alaska to South Carolina, following a flight path near US cities and major military installations. The balloon was finally shot down over the open waters of the Atlantic.[1]

Chinese officials claimed that it was a weather balloon that had gone off course. After early warnings and a delayed response in shooting it down, President Joe Biden eventually called the balloon's mission "unacceptable" and a "violation of our sovereignty."[2]

But less obvious and far greater looming dangers from China have also invaded the United States. Unlike the spy balloon, these invasions are killing Americans. Illegal weaponry, drugs, money, secret agents and bots to sow social chaos, and a deadly life- and economy-disrupting virus have all invaded from China. Yet most of our leaders choose to gaze with vacant eyes rather than expose and confront the danger.

Many people fear that a war with China may be coming. But the war is already here.

This is not a shooting war, with boots on the ground, fighters flying overhead, or navy destroyers pummeling the coastline. American soldiers and Marines are not dying on battlefields; cities are not being bombed. It is a war, nevertheless, with massive civilian casualties, that is decimating our social stability if not actual buildings.

Sun Tzu, the ancient Chinese strategist, posited that "the supreme art of war is to subdue the enemy without fighting."[3]

This ancient concept remains central to modern China's approach to war. Sun Tzu's words guide the minds of today's Chinese leaders. Since 2006, every officer, soldier, and sailor has been required to study Sun Tzu's book *The Art of War* as a textbook.[4] In keeping with this approach, China's official military strategy focuses on—in the Chinese leaders' words—going after the United States' "'soft underbelly' in terms of politics, economics, and the spirit and psychology of [its] people."[5] Chinese leaders have coined new terms such as "unrestricted warfare" and "disintegration warfare" to describe Sun Tzu's old strategy of winning without fighting.

For several years, the Chinese military and intelligence services have studied "disintegration warfare," which was "clearly building on Sun Tzu's ideas of deception, disruption, and subduing the enemy without fighting," said Admiral Fumio Ota, the former director of Japan's Defense Intelligence Headquarters. In 2010, the Chinese military produced a book entitled *Disintegration Warfare*, which featured Sun Tzu's "To subdue the enemy without fighting is the acme of skill" on the front cover.[6] The same quote is repeated ten times in the Chinese government's official "three warfares" strategy adopted in 2003.[7]

Deception is key to the strategy of fighting without appearing to fight. Sun Tzu also posited that "all warfare is based on deception," a phrase that is etched on the wall of the library at the Chinese military's command academy in Nanjing.

According to a textbook given to Chinese military officers, "Xi Jinping has emphasized that our state's ideology and social system are fundamentally incompatible with the West. Xi has said, 'This (incompatibility) decides it. Our struggle and contest of power with the West cannot be moderated. It will inevitably be long, complex, and at times extremely sharp.'"[8]

Complex, sharp, and deadly.

The lethal consequences of China's war are real—and amount to casualties greater than the United States has suffered in war in the past fifty years. In the past five years alone, hundreds of thousands of Americans have died as a result. The casualty count is in the millions and mounting daily. It is a complex strategy, a hydra of drugs, disease, propaganda, and illicit pistol parts, each contributing to social chaos and killing Americans. Beijing conceals its involvement, and our leaders fail to expose and confront it.

It is important to distinguish between the Chinese government, which is run by the Chinese Communist Party (CCP), and the Chinese people. In many respects, the Chinese people are already the regime's biggest victims. So when the term "China" or "Beijing" is used in this book, any indictment is of the Communist government, not the people of China or people of Chinese ancestry living in or doing legitimate business within the United States.

Perhaps even more shocking than Beijing's aggressions toward us has been the willful blindness of our political leaders. Rather than confronting the reality that Beijing is wreaking havoc on our soil, they focus on domestic policy minutiae. Why?

A simple part of the answer is corruption. Some of our leaders, who are named in the chapters that follow, have financial ties to the Chinese state and don't want to see the flow of money disrupted.

A more complex part of the answer is that acknowledging the truth of what China is doing would require our leaders to accept a profound paradigm shift and would force extremely difficult choices that would also dramatically disrupt the lives and livelihoods of elites from Silicon Valley to Wall Street; those who benefit from partnerships with Chinese government–linked companies very often finance the campaigns of our political leaders.

If Beijing is quietly killing us, how can anyone stand by and watch?

Like all human beings, those of our political class are creatures of habit and stick with what is easy. It is a lot easier to continue to do what they are doing and ignore facts that would radically reshape their approach to leading our country.

Some are perhaps truly ignorant of China's actions and intent, but most are aware of what China is doing and have chosen the path of least resistance, preferring the safe predictability of their ambivalence to the vigorous work of countering those bent on our destruction. In the chapters to follow, you will find out who they are and why they are doing nothing.

Once you focus your eyes on what China is doing to us, you will realize how detached from reality are the conversations in Washington and in much of the news media.

While we debate domestic politics to address the fentanyl crisis, the reality is that Beijing is deeply involved at every stage of the drug's production and distribution in the United States. And well-connected politicians have ties to some of the drug networks spreading this poison to America.

While we seek to heal the social division and minimize chaos in American life, we ignore Beijing's role in fueling divisions and even violence on American streets.

While our leaders debate the theoretical implications of TikTok being owned by a Chinese company, Chinese strategists have already held practical discussions about how to deploy it as a "cultural weapon" against the United States. In this book, we will follow that enthusiastic conversation and explore who in Washington profits from this arrangement both financially and politically.

While we debate the origins of covid-19 and the effectiveness of masks, school closures, and vaccines, we avoid confronting the fact that, intentional or unintentional Wuhan leak aside, China carried out a sweeping strategy during the height of the virus to maximize our death toll, while successfully imposing its political will on us in surprising and deceptive ways, with the complicity of US health leaders.

What you are about to read is based on close research of restricted Chinese military journals, Chinese corporate records, private emails from key American leaders, leaked documents from the Department of Homeland Security, the FBI, and other federal agencies, and internal communications from the Mexican military and law enforcement, as well as criminal court records in the United States. This book contains no unnamed or anonymous sources.

In the pages that follow, you will meet an American president who rarely challenges Beijing on anything, including the fentanyl poisoning of America, and whose family received $5 million from a businessman with links to a Chinese organized crime leader involved in the fentanyl trade. Indeed, some of that money appears to have flowed indirectly to Joe Biden himself.

We will meet a former American president who ignored the fentanyl crisis only to cash in with China shortly after leaving office.

We will meet a governor who invited Chinese organized crime networks into his state, including those neck deep in the illegal drug trade.

We will be introduced to a powerful congressional committee chairman who looked away from the deadly fentanyl crisis in his backyard, while having entanglements with numerous money-laundering operations based out of his own congressional district.

We will learn about how China shaped the covid crisis to maximize damage to the United States and how senior US health officials covered it up with the express purpose of protecting China.

We will uncover how Beijing is fueling violence in America's streets and which American officials turn a blind eye to avoid confronting China over its actions.

We will expose how America's response to the virus was, in part, influenced and manipulated by Beijing, leading to a higher death toll and the suspension of American civil liberties.

We will meet the American billionaire now living in China who is funding organizations sowing chaos in American cities.

We will explore the Beijing-connected organization supported by some members of the Alexandria Ocasio-Cortez–Bernie Sanders wing of the Democratic Party, steering a radical turn of the American Left.

We will expose how some of the biggest names in entertainment were paid to help to spread a Chinese spy app to millions of Americans.

We will uncover the Hollywood big shots who eagerly followed Beijing's marching orders and allowed their films to be turned into pro-China propaganda vehicles.

This book is divided into four parts, each assigned a relevant proverb from a classic Chinese strategic text. Chinese military and political officials still consider these texts and proverbs, much like those of Sun Tzu, to be highly instructive today. For example, a group of thirty Chinese generals has regularly hosted conferences on how to apply these classic texts to current affairs, and twenty-one Chinese generals have endorsed the publication of a nine-book series of these ancient texts to train the next generation of Chinese military officers and government officials.[9]

Employing deceptive practices to defeat an enemy without appearing to fight it is a common theme.

Each of these sections exposes the way China is waging war against the United States without seeming to wage war.

Part I, "Murder with a Borrowed Knife," reveals Beijing's comprehensive involvement by proxy in every step of the cartel operations responsible for the US fentanyl crisis. American political figures, either compromised by personal political or financial considerations and unwilling to do the heavy lifting to confront China, sit largely silent as hundreds of thousands of Americans die.

Part II, "Watch a Fire from Across the River," exposes the various ways in which Beijing surreptitiously sows and heightens social chaos in the United States—by arming criminal gangs, using radical proxies in the streets, and deploying social media bots to create even more anger and division. Again, our political leaders remain willfully ignorant of what is going on.

Part III, "Hide a Dagger in a Smile," reveals the way China is quietly and systematically using investments in not only "cultural products" such as TikTok but also Hollywood films and video games to penetrate the lives of America's youngest generations. Hollywood titans participate in these actions because they profit financially, and our political elites ignore them because they profit politically.

Part IV, "Loot a Burning House," reveals the myriad of ways in which China sought to maximize American casualties from covid and manipulate our leaders into imposing lockdowns, which became the largest suppression of civil rights during peacetime in US history. Our health care leaders hid information from us to protect their Chinese colleagues and themselves.

Part I

MURDER WITH A BORROWED KNIFE

（借刀杀人）

CHAPTER 1

The New Opium Wars

President Joe Biden sat facing China's president Xi Jinping, each at a separate table draped in blue cloth. It was November 2022, and the two leaders were in Bali, Indonesia. They conversed amid elaborate flower arrangements on the floor and American and People's Republic of China (PRC) flags standing in the background.[1] It was their first in-person meeting since Biden had been elected president.

The meeting lasted for more than three hours. President Biden came with a full agenda: Taiwan, the war in Ukraine, human rights, Tibet, and climate change.[2] One issue that he did not raise was fentanyl, which was not unusual. In all the recorded meetings and conversations President Biden and President Xi have had since 2021, the time spent on fentanyl has been almost nonexistent.[3]

Biden and Xi left Bali with no resolution of any agenda items. They did release a joint statement; the Biden White House noted that both leaders had agreed that weapons of mass destruction, specifically nuclear weapons, should never be used.[4]

But a different kind of Chinese weapon of mass destruction (WMD) is regularly exploding over the United States.

Some of its victims wander the streets hunched over like zombies, their brains fried. Others collapse on sidewalks, lie in a comalike state on the ground, or are seen "slumped over the steering wheels of cars in traffic."[5]

Hundreds of thousands have just dropped dead.

This lethal weapon is fentanyl, a synthetic opioid that in 2021 alone claimed more than 67,000 lives—that is, more than American combat deaths in the wars in Iraq, Afghanistan, and Vietnam combined.[6] Fentanyl is now the leading cause of death of Americans under the age of forty-five.[7] It has killed more Americans in a single year than were killed in the atomic bombing of Nagasaki.[8]

All evidence points to fentanyl being intentionally deployed. Fentanyl is being covertly and systematically aimed at the citizens of our country by a major foreign power—the most lethal peacetime attack in human history.

Most people who die of fentanyl poisoning ingest it unintentionally; it is laced into other illegal drugs, such as marijuana or cocaine, without their knowledge.[9] Many victims believe that they have purchased an FDA-approved drug such as Xanax or Vicodin, when in fact the product is a counterfeit pharmaceutical laced with fentanyl.[10]

Some victims, such as the musical artists Prince and Tom Petty, are famous, but most pass briefly through the news, to be remembered only by their devastated families and loved ones.[11] Make no mistake: remembered or not, these casualties blight our communities—even "good neighborhoods." About half of the people who die from fentanyl overdoses are young and of military age. As one former US government official has put it, "This is the equivalent of removing two or three divisions of Army or Marines off the rolls every year."[12]

A group of West Point cadets traveled to Fort Lauderdale, Florida, for fun and sun over spring break. Four cadets picked up what they thought was cocaine, but it was laced with fentanyl. All four soon went into cardiac arrest. Three other people apparently tried to administer CPR, but in the process they exposed themselves to fentanyl and also needed to be hospitalized. Thankfully, all seven involved survived.[13]

"There's never been a drug like fentanyl before. For street drugs, this absolutely destroys anything else in terms of lethality and danger," warned Josh Bloom, a senior director of chemical and pharmaceutical research at the American Council on Science and Health.[14]

Jim Crotty, a former deputy chief of staff at the Drug Enforcement Administration (DEA), calls fentanyl "the most pernicious, the most devastating drug that we have ever seen."[15]

Even the Mexican drug cartels, hardened and seemingly indifferent to human suffering, have a fearful respect for fentanyl. They call it El Diablo, "The Devil."[16]

It's little wonder that in 2019, some senior officials at the US Department of Homeland Security asked for fentanyl to be classified as a "weapon of mass destruction."[17]

How did the most dangerous drug ever created become a household word, and scourge, in America?

Not by accident, but by deliberate design. Beijing's hand can be found in every stage of the poison's spread in North America.

Some people might be aware that the precursor chemicals of fentanyl come from China. But, as we will see in the next three chapters, Beijing's complicity in America's fentanyl crisis is far more strategic than the mere export of chemicals. Our national leaders have access to materials that would make them fully aware of this. Based on leaked US national security documents, Mexican government hacked emails or correspondence, and Chinese corporate records, we know that the fentanyl operation is under Chinese control from start to finish, including:

- Production of the basic chemicals needed to make it (precursors)
- Creation of fentanyl and counterfeit pills in both Mexico and the United States
- Distribution of the deadly drug within the United States
- Facilitation of drug cartel financial transactions, and even money laundering
- Facilitation of communications networks used by the cartels to operate without detection in the United States

Indeed, we will show that some of the people involved in running these drug networks have positions of considerable power in the Chinese government or the CCP. Fentanyl shipped through Mexico is a "borrowed knife" for China that can be wielded against Americans while the country claims that it is not their weapon.

What makes this story even more troubling is that many politicians in the highest ranks of *our* government have access to this evidence but have remained strangely silent about China's deep and direct involvement in unleashing this menace. They have chosen to be willfully ignorant—complicit by indifference. They have what Churchill called "vacant eyes."

Many of their names will be familiar: President Joe Biden, Senator Mitch McConnell, Congressman Adam Schiff, former president Barack Obama, and California governor Gavin Newsom, among others. Despite the easily available, compelling evidence of Beijing's involvement, most of our leaders carefully avoid holding China to account.

Our investigation shows that some US political and business leaders are working or investing with known members of the drug networks poisoning Americans. Apparently, the money is just too good. Compromised by commercial opportunities that benefit them or their close allies and hiding behind the excuse of not wanting to "disrupt" the US-China relationship, they effectively allow open season on Americans and sabotage our future generations.

Chinese military officers have acknowledged using drug warfare against the United States for *decades*, pushing first heroin, then methamphetamine, and currently fentanyl into the United States with ever-increasing lethality. And consistent with military escalation, there are plans to deploy even more potent drugs as weapons.

In the 1990s, two senior Chinese military officers analyzed the power of the US military extensively and concluded that it was futile for Beijing to try to match it. Instead, in a book called *Unrestricted Warfare*, they suggested the use of creative strategies to defeat the United States. Just weeks after it was released in 1999, CCP officials seized all copies of the book and removed it from circulation. Apparently, they were not angry with the authors, who would go on to have stellar careers, one retiring as a high-ranking general, the other as an influential professor in Beijing. Rather, the officials must have preferred that the contents of the book not be publicly acknowledged. *Unrestricted Warfare* might have disappeared completely from the public eye but for the fact that a copy was smuggled out of China and translated into English.[18]

Unrestricted Warfare proposed that Beijing deploy a series of nonmilitary weapons that would reimagine the tools of warfare and redefine the battlefield with "out of the box" strategies. Nothing was too extreme as far as the authors were concerned. As they revealed, "The first rule of unrestricted warfare is that there are no rules, with nothing forbidden."[19]

One of the more shocking ideas was using illegal drugs as "drug warfare."[20] The authors described a plan to export and distribute illicit drugs in America, cause death, a health crisis, and social mayhem, and generally tear at the country's social fabric.[21] A few US military strategists have noted the threat. In 2014, the United States Army Special Operations Command issued a "Counter–Unconventional Warfare: White Paper" declaring that China's method of conducting warfare against the United States included "drug warfare."[22] Others in the US government have drawn the connection as well. One report from the Naval War College stated, "China is complicit in pushing fentanyl into the United States in an effort to destabilize, undermine and weaken the fabric of America's social and political systems."[23]

"America could be attacked without anyone realizing the attacks were happening," another former military officer observed. The strategy would be "Death by a thousand razor cuts (with some looking self-inflicted)." In 2014, John Poole, a Marine combat veteran and security consultant, essentially predicted the fentanyl crisis that was about to hit the country. "The internal 'disaster' that some PRC officers have advocated through drug warfare correlates with U.S. law enforcement concerns of what might follow a narcotics deluge," he wrote in a journal for intelligence and special forces professionals. "Basically, an influx of illicit drugs would result in an increased number of addicts who would engage in theft to secure the money for their next 'fix.' Street combat would intensify as gangs vied for neighborhood control, and larger payoffs would further compromise the political and criminal justice systems."[24]

Sound familiar? America's total number of overdoses would reach a new high nearly every year after that prediction.[25]

Most lawmakers in Washington have chosen to ignore the frightening implications of *Unrestricted Warfare*. Reframing Communist China as a commercial and global "partner" has been too enticing— and lucrative.

Drug warfare has a special resonance among Chinese leaders. During the nineteenth-century Opium Wars, Imperial China was the target and the Chinese people the victims. Introduced to China during the seventh century, opium contributed to a national tragedy for the country more than a millennium later. British merchants, including the British East India Company, commercialized opium in China, making it inexpensive and readily accessible to Chinese people. The company became "the world's first drug cartel."[26] The company soon controlled nearly all of world production.[27] One American involved in the poisonous trade was Warren Delano, Jr., the grandfather of future president Franklin Delano Roosevelt. As far as Delano was concerned, it was a "fair, honorable, and legitimate trade."[28]

Opium addiction devastated the Chinese people: at one point, an astonishing 25 percent of the population was using, if not hooked on, opium.[29] Chinese officials tried several times to halt the trade, but Great Britain always responded with force, sending in the powerful Royal Navy to keep the Chinese market open to opium. Many critics in Great Britain, including William Gladstone, later a Conservative British prime minister, regarded the so-called Opium Wars as "unjust and iniquitous."[30]

Communist Chinese officials today believe that the opium trade was not just about British merchants making money but was in fact an "attack by stratagem" designed to drug their country into submission.[31] There is no question that the drug trade had a deleterious effect on China: at the beginning of the nineteenth century, before the opium arrived in large quantities, China was the largest economy in the world. After decades of opium addiction, the country found itself "on its last legs."[32]

The damage done by the opium trade casts a long shadow in China. Even today, military officials express outrage about the way Great Britain's Opium Wars reduced China to a minor power. They regard the opium trade as "national drug trafficking activity on probably the grandest scale in recorded history."[33] Communist Party officials insist that this history never be forgotten. Shortly after Xi Jinping became the country's leader, he led fellow members of the Politburo to a cultural exhibit exploring Chinese progress since the Opium Wars called "The Road to Revival."

"Every Chinese schoolchild knows that the modern drive for wealth and power is, at root, a means of avenging the Opium Wars and what followed," noted the *Economist*. "How the conflict is remembered still matters very much."[34]

From the perspective of President Xi and the Communist Party, what better means of rising to power and avenging the Opium Wars than by turning the tables against the Western world that it blames?

For Xi, advancing one's national interests—to the detriment of others'—with a poisonous weapon is not only legitimate, but also patriotic. A few years ago, he had a sixty-ton granite statute, complete with surrounding gardens, built to honor his father. Barbara Demick compared it to the Kim Jong Un cult of personality. "The optics look straight out of North Korea," she reported in the *Los Angeles Times*.[35] Xi's erecting the monument was to be expected—by all accounts he clearly admires his father and the way he lived his life. In one formative story of his father's life, the fourteen-year-old boy and some classmates decided that their teacher was a counterrevolutionary. So they tried to poison him.[36]

* * *

The current fentanyl crisis has effectively been more than fifty years in the making. For decades, Communist China has been involved in the international illegal drug trade and intimately connected to the drugs flooding into the United States. And for decades, many of our leaders have remained silent, favoring commercial deals over accountability.

In 1951, just two years after the birth of Communist China, the CCP was deliberately pushing opium and heroin into Japan.[37] Advancing into the United States was not far behind. A year later, large amounts of heroin coming from the People's Republic of China arrived in New York and San Francisco harbors. Fortunately, they were seized by US authorities.[38]

General Matthew Ridgway had commanded the famed 82nd Airborne Division during World War II and later became the commander in chief of US forces in Japan. In 1952, he wrote in an official report, "Investigations of arrests and seizures in Japan, in 1951, proved conclusively that the Communists are smuggling heroin from China to Japan and using the proceeds to finance party activities and obtain strategic materials for China."[39]

In 1955, the US Senate held hearings on the matter. Richard Deverall testified. He had served in the US Army during World War II and then become an organizer for the American Federation of Labor. He was the union's Asia representative, which meant spending long periods in Japan, meeting with workers and Japanese government officials. He noticed the rise in drug use and addiction not only among the Japanese public, but also among American GIs stationed in the country, and investigated. In his testimony before the Senate, he confirmed that Beijing was aggressively involved in "the dirty narcotics business" and "has as one of its principal targets the country of Japan."[40] Indeed, by the early 1950s, Chinese opium exports accounted for a large portion of the opium sold in Japan.[41]

Other reports emerged that Beijing was actively looking for partners to sell drugs in the West. During the nineteenth century, one of the most successful distributors of opium in China had been Jardine, Matheson & Company, a Hong Kong–based British export-import company run by two Scotsmen. It was said that the firm's partners "made their careers exporting tea from China but made their *fortunes* importing opium" to China.[42] In the 1950s, the CCP approached the company with a lucrative export proposal. "Today it is the Chinese, or rather their government, who offer tons and tons of opium to the firm of Jardine and Matheson [to sell to the West]," explained William Jardine, a descendant of the founder who in 1957 was running the firm. "But we refuse."[43]

Highly regarded senior US military officers also saw Beijing's hard push into the drug business. Retired Marine Corps lieutenant general Victor Krulak was a commanding officer in the Pacific. He had fought heroically in World War II. From his perch, Krulak had seen plenty of intelligence about Beijing's involvement in the drug trade. The Chinese Communists "do want hard money and opium is probably China's greatest export staple," he explained in 1972.[44]

In July 1958, Frank Bartholomew, the president of United Press International, covered a massive drug bust in Switzerland involving diplomats and counterintelligence agents. Authorities had been tipped off about the rising number of financial transactions involving Beijing's illicit drug traffic to Europe, and the article quoted a source as saying that the activity was "for the dual purpose of helping finance the heavy costs of the spy organization and inflicting on the Western countries an intensifying problem in narcotics. The money runs into incredible figures." Swiss officials had seized heroin from China worth $30 million to $50 million.[45]

By the early 1960s, Chinese narcotics exports to the United States had intensified. "Narcotics officials report that opium from Red China is being channeled into the United States at several major ports," reported the *Tampa Times* in 1962. "Miami is one."[46]

Beijing's weaponization of drugs against the West became especially systematic in the jungles of Vietnam. Communist China supported the Communist insurgents not only with guns and ammunition but also with another powerful weapon to deploy against American fighting men: heroin. CCP leaders even bragged about it.

In 1965, Chinese foreign minister Chou En-lai was in Egypt for meetings with President Gamal Abdel Nasser, an occasional ally of Beijing. Chou was the second most powerful man in China after Mao Tse-tung, and he had a secret to share:

At present U.S. servicemen are experimenting with opium eating and we are helping them in this respect. We have already grown the best quality opium especially for them. . . . Do you remember those days when the Westerners forced sales of opium on us? Today we will pay them in their own coin. We will use opium to shatter the morale of the U.S. troops in Vietnam and the effects on the United States will indeed be beyond prediction.[47]

In fact, Beijing "devoted vast tracts of farmland in the southwestern province of Yunnan and the northwestern provinces to poppy growing." The product was then sent to countries like Vietnam and Japan to be targeted at US troops.[48]

A bipartisan group in the US Senate took Beijing's weaponization seriously and confirmed that what Chou En-lai had bragged about was in fact happening. The Senate heard testimony from General Lewis Walt, a four-star Marine general who had served in World War II and received two Navy Crosses for heroism. He had also seen combat in Korea. He had later become the assistant commandant of the US Marine Corps and was sent to Vietnam to investigate the drug problem. He testified:

In June of 1970, immediately after our Cambodian incursion, South Vietnam was flooded with heroin of remarkable purity—94 to 97 percent—which was sold at the ridiculously low price of first $1 and then $2 a vial. If profit-motivated criminals were in charge of the operation, the price made no sense at all—because no GI who wanted to get high on heroin would have batted an eyelash at paying $5, or even $10. The same amount of heroin in New York would have cost

$250. The only explanation that makes sense is that the epidemic was political rather than economic in inspiration—that whoever was behind the epidemic wanted to hook as many GI's as possible, as fast as possible, and as hard as possible.

General Walt noted that the distribution of heroin to American GIs was being carried out with military-like precision. "Everyone was agreed that the operation appeared to be highly co-ordinated and centralized," he explained to the Senate, and that "the heroin was sold in the streets in plastic vials of similar manufacture." They were not just some drug dealers trying to make money. "Why, if the operation was criminal in origin, did they sell stuff that was 94 to 97 percent pure, when people manage to get high in New York on 10-percent heroin? Why didn't they dilute it?" US intelligence concluded that the heroin epidemic among US service members was linked to Chinese trafficking of narcotics.[49]

The US Senate even sent staffers to South Vietnam to investigate and confirmed what General Walt had reported, especially the substance's lethal purity.[50]

Chou En-lai's claim to Nasser came true—and with devastating effect. Drugs proved to be a very potent weapon to deploy against Americans. By 1971, US drug casualties in Southeast Asia were mounting.[51] And not surprisingly, the morale and readiness of US forces in the region dropped dramatically. Indeed, in 1971, Congressman Robert Steele reported that the Richard Nixon administration was increasing the rate of troop withdrawals from Vietnam in part because of the high rate of heroin addiction among GIs.[52]

* * *

Though the "French connection" for heroin dominated the US market and American imagination in the early 1970s, in New York City, detectives also eavesdropped on a "Chinese connection" on US soil. In 1973, heroin in plastic bags was seized in New York, leading to the arrest of twenty members of a narcotics ring. Frank Rogers, the New York City narcotics prosecutor, declared, based on taped phone conversations, that there was a direct "Chinese connection." Brooklyn district attorney Eugene Gold added that this was "clear and substantive evidence we have that mainland China and Hong Kong (a British colony) are being used as a means of getting heroin into the United States." He noted that "The boss of the smuggling ring" was "an important Chinese national" who "confers with top government officials" in Beijing.[53]

Beijing's involvement in the international drug trade and specifically the targeting of Americans sparked some concern in Washington, DC, among both Democrats and Republicans. Yet Dr. Stefan Possony, a military strategist at the Hoover Institution at Stanford University, noticed that despite the extensive evidence of Beijing's involvement in the drug trade, many in Washington had become silent on the subject due to a growing desire for warmer ties with Beijing. "Beginning in the early 1960s, the subject, which originally had attracted great attention, became an 'unsubject,' to paraphrase Orwell," he wrote.[54]

With the arrival of the Nixon administration in January 1969, doing business with China became a real possibility. The prospects of huge commercial opportunities in the closed economy with the largest population in the world enticed many.

The Nixon administration brought other pressures to bear, working to dismiss or hide evidence of Beijing's complicity in the drug trade. In 1972, columnist Jack Anderson wrote in the *Washington Post* that the Nixon administration was distributing documents that were "unusually conciliatory" in tone toward the Communist Chinese, including claims that Beijing was not involved in the narcotics trade.[55] His reporting was echoed by the syndicated columnist Paul Scott, who was one of the best-connected reporters in the nation's capital at the time. Scott had been wiretapped by the CIA a decade earlier because his sources were so good and his reporting so detailed.[56] Scott reported that Nixon's push for better ties with Beijing meant that discussions about the Communist involvement in the drug trade were now strictly forbidden in the federal bureaucracy. "Government officials must not reveal any information of heroin traffic from China or the direct involvement of the Peking [Beijing] government," he wrote.[57]

At the time, the Pentagon was flying reconnaissance planes over Southeast Asia to identify poppy fields in countries such as Laos and Burma. But the overflights of Burma—Beijing's ally and a notable producer of opium—were halted at the request of Secretary of State Henry Kissinger, specifically to avoid damaging the United States' relations with China.[58]

CHAPTER 2

China's Foot Soldiers

When US government officials do acknowledge that drugs are coming into the United States from China, rather than holding the Chinese government to account, they seem to place all the blame on Chinese organized crime groups, known as triads, for the illegal drug production and distribution. But triad business is effectively CCP business. In 1982, the Chinese Communist Party made peace with the triads. By effectively joining forces, they turbocharged the quantity of illicit drugs bound for the United States, achieving both profits from and sabotage of its chief rival. The story would not be complete, however, without also acknowledging the US bankers and politicians who are complicit in the win-win.

On May 23, 1982, Chinese leader Deng Xiaoping sat down with two immensely wealthy Hong Kong tycoons, Li Ka-shing and Henry Fok, for a civic peace summit. Both were enormously successful investors in real estate and finance, and also known to have links to the triads. The cooperation Deng proposed was simple. Over the course of the next several decades, Hong Kong industrialists and triad leaders would demonstrate allegiance to the CCP, and the CCP would allow them to operate largely unfettered in Hong Kong. In one speech Deng opined that some triads were "good" and "patriotic." The triads kept their criminal drug trafficking overseas and performed certain favors for the Communist Party with the leadership's blessing. Cooperation would be run through the Communist Party's United Front Work Department, which is used to promote the Communist Party overseas. As we will see, several Chinese nationals working with the United Front Work Department became major players in the drug trade.[1]

Henry Fok was described by Beijing as a "patriotic capitalist," but he was suspected of having triad links, and his son was arrested in the United States for arms smuggling."[2] Fok, who died in 2006, lived a luxurious life traveling the world on his private 747 aircraft. He had a second one just for his staff. Among his many homes was one "in the middle of the China Sea, reachable only by boat or helicopter."[3] He made his money early in life smuggling goods during the UN embargo during the Korean War, later hooking up with a notorious gambling tycoon and alleged triad member nicknamed "Devil King." Among Fok's holdings was a large stake in a casino whose VIP rooms were run by the triads.[4]

The other tycoon at Deng Xiaoping's peace summit, Li Ka-shing, was perhaps the biggest single economic player in Hong Kong. Some believed that 30 percent of all the companies on the Hong Kong stock exchange were controlled by Li.[5] There are numerous examples of close ties between Li Ka-shing and Chinese triads. In 1997 two Canadian intelligence agencies (the Royal Canadian Mounted Police Criminal Analysis Branch and the Canadian Intelligence Service Analysis and Production Branch) compiled a draft report called "Sidewinder," which analyzed the connections between Chinese businesses in Canada and triad members. According to the draft report, the triads had been collaborating with Hong Kong tycoons and Chinese government officials. The bulk of the case studies in the report involve Li Ka-shing's business empire and its operations in Canada. Indeed, of the eleven specific cases of Hong Kong tycoon and triad collaboration, nine involve businesses owned or directly linked to Li. At the same time, Li was a close friend and business partner with the late Stanley Ho and Cheng Yu Tung, for example, each of whom "[were] known to be associated to many documented triads," according to a Canadian intelligence memo. Li Ka-shing has done numerous deals with both in locations from Canada to Singapore. Li has also been business partners with triad-linked Henry Fok and with Malaysian billionaire Robert Kuok, who did real estate deals with Burmese heroin traffickers Lo Hsing Han and Steven Law.[6]

Li's ties to a Western investment bank are also well established. Goldman Sachs earned hundreds of millions of dollars in fees from Li's business deals.[7]

The effects of the evolving peace between the CCP and the triads yielded results. By the close of the 1980s, the Chinese triads controlled 60 percent of the heroin coming into the United States.[8]

Yet between 1989 and 1993, the George H. W. Bush administration continued to insist—against all evidence—that China was cooperating with the US government to combat the international drug trade. In 1992, then senator Joe Biden, who was serving his fourth term and was the chairman of the Senate Judiciary Committee, convened hearings on drug trafficking and China. He noted that "China has become a major trafficking route for heroin and opium" and expressed concern that "China is poised to become the lynchpin of the heroin trade." He criticized the George H. W. Bush administration for doing "far too little to combat this dangerous development."[9]

Biden was correct in his criticisms, but somehow, in his rise to vice president and now president, his public resolve on this matter changed dramatically, as we will see.

The effective merger between the Chinese state and criminal drug syndicates underscores the military interests inherent in their drug-trafficking ventures. For example, in 1994, the Thailand office of the International Criminal Police Organization (Interpol) received a tip that methamphetamines were being produced *inside* Chinese military barracks "under the supervision of a general." Interpol tracked the shipment quietly, and when the cargo arrived in the Philippines, police were "able to inspect two Chinese ships and seize 150 kg" of the drugs. The police arrested thirty-three Chinese nationals, including five soldiers. One was a People's Liberation Army (PLA) captain.[10]

Not surprisingly, Chinese law enforcement has provided little help when it comes to the triad-controlled drug trade. In the 1990s, Tao Siju, the minister of public security, opined that "as for organisations like the triads in Hong Kong, as long as these people are patriotic . . . we should unite with them." Indeed, Tao himself did just that. China's top cop opened a nightclub in Beijing called "Top Ten" with businessmen known to be leaders of the triads.[11] Chinese intelligence services were also happy to work with the triads, likely using them in valuable human intelligence operations.[12]

Even the brutal reputation of the triads became an asset for Beijing. Sun Yee On is a particularly violent gang that requires new members to drink a mixture of blood and rice liquor while kneeling before a Taoist altar. When a man tried to open a decorating store in an area the gang claimed as their "turf," he was chopped up in broad daylight with a ten-inch butcher's knife as staff members and customers looked on.[13] When senior CCP officials travel overseas, they sometimes rely on Sun Yee On members to protect them.[14]

***

Fujian, a rugged southern coastal province of mainland China, is the base of operations of much of the triad activity and was reportedly the birthplace of the triads.[15] It just so happens that CCP chairman Xi Jinping spent seventeen years in Fujian, longer than anywhere else as a party boss, serving as acting governor between 1999 and 2002.[16]

In the early 2000s, Xi was a rising star in the Communist Party, with a powerful father. It was in Fujian that he met his wife, Peng Liyuan, a gifted singer. She sang to Chinese troops "fresh from the Tiananmen Square massacre."[17]

Fujian has been notorious for not only how openly the triads and cartels operated but also how much they enjoyed the protection of local Communist Party and government leaders. Organized crime figures received "political protection" and "managed to escape detection" in the province, according to an official Canadian report published by the United Nations.[18] Violent criminal gangs such as Fuk Ching operated openly in Fujian, extending their reach into California, Hawaii, North Carolina, Massachusetts, and New York City.[19] During Xi's tenure as a leader in Fujian, organized crime figures lived openly in the province. For example, the head of the Green Dragons Gang of New York did so despite the United States having issued a warrant for his arrest on murder charges. "Naturally Fujian authorities cannot seem to find him to extradite him," reported Nicholas Kristof and Sheryl WuDunn of the *New York Times*.[20]

In 2009, the US Department of Justice (DOJ) Organized Crime Drug Enforcement Task Forces noted that criminal gangs from Fujian were a major source of heroin flowing into New York and New Jersey.[21] Speaking specifically of Fujian, the DOJ has noted that many drug-trafficking cases in the United States lead back to China, specifically that "gang members flee to China when sought by American law enforcement."[22] Of course, Chinese law enforcement officials rarely cooperate—nor did Xi.

The triads were even part owners of Fujian Changle International Airport. What sort of government allows a drug-selling crime organization to own part of an airport?[23] Perhaps a government that gains from criminal exports.

At least one member of President Xi's family has possible ties to organized crime. A cousin of Xi's was a person of interest in an Australian government investigation looking into a "money-laundering front company" that helped "suspected mobsters move funds in and out of Australia." The cousin, a Communist Party member, had previously been a member of the Chinese People's Armed Police. When asked about the allegations, the Chinese Foreign Ministry dismisses them as "groundless accusations based on rumors" meant to "smear China."[24]

"The entire political system in China is predicated on corruption, complicity and cover-up, and it is virtually impossible to rise through the ranks if you are not corrupt or at least complicit in the system," said Jorge Guajardo, who served as Mexico's ambassador to China from 2007 to 2013. "If you are not corrupt, the system boots you out."[25]

Of course, Xi was not booted out. He rose to the top.

Further intertwining the triads with state interests, Chinese officials allowed triad-linked businessmen such as Li Ka-shing to take leadership positions or equity stakes in the government's sovereign wealth fund, the China International Trust and Investment Corporation (CITIC).[26] Soon other tycoons with triad ties joined the investment fund's ranks. Alvin Chau, connected to the 14K triad, became an officer of CITIC. He was eventually expelled from Australia due to his "extensive organized crime connections."[27] At CITIC, such triad businessmen work closely with senior officials at the Chinese Ministry of State Security.[28]

In the 1990s, US policy toward the CCP drug traffickers remained soft. Virtually every major financial player in the United States wanted to do business with CITIC, regardless of CITIC's complicity with the triads, which were sabotaging the United States with illicit drugs.

In 1997, senator John Kerry published a book called *The New War: The Web of Crime That Threatens America's Security*, calling out the Chinese government for its ties to organized crime, which were specifically threatening US security. Kerry, who was a member of the Senate Foreign Relations Committee at the time, wrote that China was a central hub for of the international drug trade, quoting estimates that more than $200 billion was the "yearly Chinese earnings from drug production, smuggling, and distribution."[29] He accurately noted that Chinese triads were at the center of the global international drug trade.

But then Kerry changed.

He remained on the Senate Foreign Relations Committee for more than a decade after he wrote his clarion call, but strangely went silent. As we will later see, when the CCP and the triads emerged as a key supplier of fentanyl to the United States and after Kerry became secretary of state, he appears never to have publicly pressed Beijing on the subject. He did write a letter to the United Nations, asking it to restrict the sale of fentanyl worldwide.[30]

It is worth noting that while Kerry was calling out China for its involvement in the drug trade, he was also taking trade delegations to the country. "What's suddenly happening is the (Chinese) market is reaching a critical mass," Kerry said as he visited with thirty company executives from fifteen companies. "In certain sectors, it's take-off time." The purpose of the trip was "To open doors, to connect, and to sell." Soon after the release of his book, he stopped talking about it.[31]

CITIC proved to be the CCP's ticket to crippling US policy on the drug problem, inking deals with American financial firms and moving in the highest corridors of power. In February 1996, CITIC chairman Wang Jun met with President Bill Clinton and others in the White House. Even when CITIC officials became publicly enmeshed in shocking illegal activities in the United States, officials in Washington seemed prepared to look the other way.[32]

One alleged triad member funneled money to Bill Clinton's reelection campaign. The so-called Chinagate scandal is often fuzzily recalled as an instance of Chinese officials trying to curry favor with the Clinton team. Less well remembered is that a major source of those funds was a shady businessman named Ng Lap Seng, who, according to FEC filings and other reports, was believed to be a member of the Shui Fong triad.[33] Shui Fong was also involved in the international drug trade.[34]

The clublike relationships developing among Chinese Communist leaders, Chinese organization crime, American financiers, and US political officials were perhaps best epitomized by a dinner aboard a yacht called *Monkey's Uncle* in Hong Kong.

**

The Goldman Sachs yacht pulled slowly away from the Causeway Bay Typhoon Shelter in Hong Kong and moved through the dark waters of the bay. It was early October 1997, and a small group of powerful individuals gathered to discuss how they might work together to make money in Hong Kong, including through investments in a new Hong Kong airport. Guests included high-ranking CCP officials, triad-connected businessmen, Goldman Sachs investment bankers, and US secretary of commerce William Daley.[35]

Imagine an American firm or senior government official meeting with overlords of the Mexican drug cartels. Would the US secretary of commerce sit down with Sinaloa cartel affiliates to discuss opportunities for American businesses? The standards regarding China were very different, no doubt because the scale of profits in mainland China distorted the Americans' sense of priorities, even at the expense of US security.

**

By the turn of the millennium, the triads were slowly moving out of the heroin trade into something even more lucrative—and dangerous. Synthetic drugs—methamphetamines, for one—were promising a wide market.

Chinese authorities promised the Clinton administration that they were making "special efforts" to control the production of the chemicals that went into those drugs, but production continued apace. Elements of the Chinese government, far from trying to control the production of these illicit drugs, were actively promoting their production. The French government–backed drug investigative agency Observatoire Géopolitique des Drogues claimed in a 1998 special report that "such large quantities of these substances could only be produced and transported by soldiers of the People's Liberation Army." It pointed out that the Chinese military controlled a chemical and pharmaceutical conglomerate called 999, which included "400 factories" producing the stuff.[36]

Despite paper promises to Washington, the People's Republic of China was becoming the "world's largest producer of ephedrine," said the French agency, which was then used to synthesize "illegal amphetamine-type products" that were headed largely for the United States and Europe.[37]

One of the most economically viable synthetic drugs that emerged was fentanyl. Drug dealers like to lace other drugs with it because it is relatively cheap and produces a rapturous high. But it is also potent—it is "thirty to fifty times stronger than heroin"—and therefore exponentially more dangerous.[38]

Fentanyl became a sharpened "borrowed knife."

Fentanyl was first developed in 1960 by a Belgian scientist and was prescribed primarily for patients who were recovering from painful surgeries. The US Food and Drug Administration approved fentanyl for legal, prescribed use in 1968, after which it had a limited use in hospitals. But when the patent expired in 1981, its production and distribution on the black market proliferated. Its street names were "China Girl" or "China White."[39] Fentanyl was increasingly mixed with other drugs, from marijuana to street-produced Adderall.[40] Between 2005 and 2007, the DEA attributed more than a thousand deaths to illegally manufactured fentanyl. By the 2010s, mortality rates skyrocketed.[41]

Chinese companies began selling fentanyl openly, in English, on the internet. American dealers could place an order and make payments through PayPal, and the Chinese supplier would ship it directly to them through the mail or a parcel service such as FedEx. It happened on the internet's dark web, but it also happened out in the open. According to one investigation, 40 percent of those offering to sell fentanyl and mail it to people in the United States were officially registered companies in China. Alibaba, China's equivalent of Amazon, became a source for drug sales, according to US federal court cases.[42] They were out-in-the-open sales, not just on the dark web.[43] Beijing did not show concern despite the mounting body count in the United States.

Fentanyl websites operate freely in China. Even though the Communist government routinely shuts down websites that it does not approve of for a variety of reasons, when it comes to closing websites selling fentanyl, it has not cracked down "to any serious degree."[44]

Chinese Customs and the State Post Bureau are well known for screening every letter and package sent from or to China. The goal of this practice is to maintain control and prevent "harm" from being done to the country, but with fentanyl shipments to the United States, they seem unable—or unwilling—to screen and seize the packages. According to the Drug Enforcement Agency (DEA), "China is the primary source of fentanyl and fentanyl-related substances trafficked through international mail and express consignment operations."[45]

Clearly, the People's Republic of China is a surveillance state: officials closely monitor the flow of people and goods into and out of China, including fentanyl shipments. The Chinese police have, notoriously, few restraints on their conduct. They "disappear" people, arrest bloggers without warrants, kidnap billionaires, and imprison human rights activists.[46] They relentlessly pursue drug dealers operating *inside* China. If Beijing wanted to "disappear" the country's fentanyl exporters, it would. But it doesn't.

To avoid detection by the US Postal Service or package delivery firms such as FedEx, Chinese fentanyl manufacturers mislabel their packages to conceal the contents, describing them as a food substance or glue. The Chinese state punishment for mislabeling shipments of fentanyl? "Civil penalties and small fines." Offenders face no criminal charges.[47]

The flood of drugs sent through the mail from China launched the US fentanyl epidemic. First responders, such as paramedic Peter Canning in Connecticut, were astonished by what they were seeing. He noted that the DEA had distributed a booklet called "Fentanyl: A Briefing Guide for First Responders" that in his words instructed "emergency personnel" to "check the scene for packages from China" before treating a person who is dying—for fear that the responders might be harmed.[48]

When Customs and Border Protection (CBP) and the US Postal Service improved their identification of packages arriving from China that contained fentanyl and other drugs, Chinese companies began transshipping the drugs through other countries. "Shanghai, China is a major exporter of fentanyl to the U.S. and shippers are known to transship to avoid detection," noted prosecutors in one fentanyl case. So the shippers started shipping the drugs via Dubai and other intermediary locations instead.[49]

Clearly, China was weaponizing fentanyl against the United States. However, quantities were still limited by parcel services. Then a solution emerged: Instead of shipping fentanyl incrementally through the mail, why not mass-produce it in Mexico?

* * *

The Chinese triads began forging relationships with the Mexican drug cartels and quickly became business partners with them.[50] The cartels started to mix fentanyl with their heroin. Fentanyl production proved to be so lucrative that "El Chapo," the infamous head of the Sinaloa Cartel, quickly shifted from producing heroin and cocaine to fentanyl.[51]

From the perspective of the Chinese triads and their allies in Beijing, routing the drugs through Mexico not only made logistical sense but also provided Beijing a measure of plausible deniability. The borrowed knife. The drugs were coming from Mexico, not China, right?

A similar operation, but on a smaller scale, occurred north of the border in Canada. Chinese triads established laboratories along the US border in British Columbia to produce fentanyl in Canada, smuggle it into the United States, and ship it abroad.[52]

Most of the pharmaceutical ingredients needed to produce the synthetic cocktail known as fentanyl are produced in China. In the northern city of Shijiazhuang, west of Beijing, chemical companies churn out such ingredients. A highly militarized city boasting some eleven military facilities including several command schools, military hospitals, and medical facilities, it is also a government-designated national development zone. So the companies producing the fentanyl chemicals get tax credits.[53] Some 40 percent of the production of this chemical comes from this city alone. Wuhan, now synonymous with covid-19, is another big production center of fentanyl components.[54]

In Mexico, the cartels rely on a long list of Chinese companies to provide the precursor chemicals. The Mexican news outlet Infobae published a list of sixty-four Chinese companies that it had concluded were major suppliers to the Sinaloa Cartel and the Jalisco New Generation Cartel (CJNG) in Mexico. Several of the companies listed in the database were state owned, and several more were politically connected.[55] Xuyang Biotechnology Company describes itself as "a production and sales LLC (wholly state-owned) specialized in producing and exporting Pharmaceutical Intermediates. . . . We own six subsidiary [sic] and we enjoy tax exemption privileges."[56] Another company, Skyrun Industrial Company, is also state controlled, specializing in "developing, producing and handling raw pharmaceutical material and intermediates." Many of the top leaders of the company are Communist Party members.[57]

Usually, the public discussion about China's involvement with our fentanyl crisis ends here: China profits from selling and shipping the precursors from China to North America. But the country's involvement is far deeper and includes every link in the fentanyl chain from production to distribution, money laundering, and cartel communications.

***

Fentanyl precursors produced in China are shipped to Manzanillo, Mexico, a major port with two scenic bays northwest of Mexico City. US officials believe that 90 percent of the fentanyl precursors arriving in Mexico from China come via this port. It's little surprise that the port is a "crucial entry point for fentanyl and methamphetamine precursor chemicals" into the United States.[58]

Manzanillo is by no means the only port in Mexico serving as a conduit for fentanyl. In 2019, Mexican authorities found a stunning twenty-three tons of fentanyl aboard a ship that had arrived from China in the Mexican port of Puerto de Lazaro Cardenas. That is enough to kill more than 11 *billion* people.[59]

But Mexican companies don't run these ports; a Chinese company does. The international terminals at both ports are controlled and operated by Hutchison, which is largely owned by Li Ka-shing, whose ties to the Chinese triads were documented previously. The company also enjoys a close working relationship with the Chinese government and military, and major shareholders include the American financial firms BlackRock and Vanguard.[60] Hutchison also operates other ports around the world, including several others in Mexico.[61]

With Hutchison running the international terminal, Manzanillo has also become a conduit for the shipment of arms to terrorists and criminal gangs working in Mexico and the United States.[62] The company has been flagged by US officials over the years because of problems with smuggling—and not just the weapons being run through Manzanillo. When Hutchison wanted to run a port in the Bahamas, US Embassy officials were worried, citing "U.S. agencies' concerns about possible smuggling attempts through the terminal," according to State Department cables. The US Department of Defense issued an intelligence assessment in October 1999 concerning Hutchison's shipping facilities being used to "facilitate the movement of arms and other prohibited items into the Americas."[63]

In Mexico, Hutchison controls not only the international terminals at several ports but also the railroad terminal that sends railcars from Manzanillo to central Mexico and then north to Kansas City, Missouri. The fact that the railroad terminal is under Chinese control means it is "open sesame" for drug shipments, according to a report by the US Army War College.[64] One particularly successful Chinese businessman living in Mexico allegedly became the largest supplier of chemicals for the Sinaloa cartel. According to court filings, he procured some fifty tons of methamphetamine precursors from a Chinese pharmaceutical company and supplied them to the cartel. When he was arrested in Mexico, the Shanghai-based businessman had a secret room in the house stacked high with cash—some $207 million—as well as military weapons.[65]

Some Mexican leaders saw what was happening and raised the subject with Chinese government officials of fentanyl chemicals being shipped into Mexico in vast quantities to be turned into drugs and shipped north to the United States. But the Chinese officials were predictably uninterested in doing anything about it. "They just didn't see what was in it for them to look into their own industries exporting these chemicals," noted former Mexican ambassador to China Jorge Guajardo. "In all my time there, the Chinese never showed any willingness to cooperate on stemming the flow of precursors into Mexico."[66] In fact, Chinese officials claimed that they couldn't find "*any* scheduled precursor chemicals trafficked to Mexico" by Chinese companies. Really?[67]

In northern Mexico, some two thousand Chinese nationals meticulously work to import the ingredients that produce fentanyl. How these two thousand Chinese nationals ended up in northern Mexico to work with the cartels remains unexplained.[68]

Once the fentanyl is synthesized, it is pressed into pills to be smuggled across the border. The pills need to look like real prescription drugs. Who do you think provides the pill presses?

Chinese companies have been smuggling pill presses illegally into the United States, mislabeling them as machine tools or other items or sending them disassembled to avoid detection.[69] The destination is drug dealers and criminal gangs[70] for the "mass production" of street drugs.[71] Now Chinese companies send large quantities of pill presses to Mexico, too, including the metal cast dies to imprint pills with counterfeit numbers such as "M523" and "10/352," which are the markings of real oxycodone pills. In other words, these Chinese companies are helping dealers produce counterfeit and illegal street drugs.[72]

In April 2020, the DOJ sent out an alert to law enforcement agencies with a blunt headline: "Chinese Pill Presses Are Key Components for Illegally Manufactured Fentanyl." In the document, which was obtained by the author, the DOJ noted the "relatively moderate pricing" of $1,000 per pill press—essentially at cost. Why are Chinese companies not charging a huge markup to sell the pill presses to the drug cartels? The DOJ also noted that the "ambiguous export regulations in China allow traffickers to use vague manifest descriptions to describe pill press machines to avoid scrutiny from U.S. Customs and Border Protection (CBP) personnel."[73] Chinese pill press manufacturers are required by US law to alert the DEA when they ship pill presses to the United States so federal authorities can track those who might be illegally producing drugs. But the Chinese companies simply ignore the law—with devastatingly lethal consequences in America. And Beijing does not punish them for doing so.

There is apparently no law in China regulating the sale of pill presses, "making them easily accessible to drug traffickers," according to an internal DEA report obtained by the author.[74] Pill presses in a variety of sizes are readily available for purchase on Chinese English-language websites.[75]

*　*　*

China's contribution to the current US fentanyl crisis is more than lax law enforcement and does not end with the production of this poison. "There is no question there is interconnectivity between Chinese organized crime and the Chinese state," noted Frank Montoya, Jr., a former chief counterintelligence official at the Office of the Director of National Intelligence. "The [Chinese Communist] party operates in organized crime–type fashion. There are parallels to Russia, where organized crime has been co-opted by the Russian government and Putin's security services."[76]

The Zheng drug syndicate, or cartel, operated a large fentanyl distribution ring in the American Midwest and bragged to drug dealers that it could openly "synthesize nearly any" narcotic, including fentanyl. In 2018, the DOJ indicted the cartel leadership in China. But despite arrest warrants, China allowed the cartel's leaders to continue to live freely in Shanghai.[77]

An important player in the Zheng drug syndicate was a Chinese Canadian scientist named Bin Wang. On the surface, Wang operated as a legitimate businessman out of a nondescript warehouse in Woburn, Massachusetts, just north of Boston. Wang sold chemicals to National Institutes of Health (NIH) research projects. The building complex featured a paper-shredding company and a dry cleaning company. The space he occupied had previously housed a "monster paintball" company.[78]

Behind the legal facade, Wang was running a Zheng syndicate narcotics distribution hub. Wang's companies received parcels from China with narcotics smuggled within bulk shipments of legitimate chemicals from Wang's Chinese companies. The fentanyl and other drugs were then separated into individual parcels for his US distributors. Wang advised his employees to "heat seal" the fentanyl into "foil bags"; falsely label the parcels with the name of safe, legal chemicals; then ship them across the United States.[79]

After the Zheng network was broken up by US law enforcement, Wang was indicted and charged with ten crimes. He received a sentence of six years in prison.[80]

Wang's case exemplifies the symbiosis between drug cartel members and the Chinese government. While distributing fentanyl in the United States, Wang worked for Beijing to create a computerized platform to track chemical shipments worldwide, which meant flying to China monthly, in part to meet with Chinese government officials to discuss his progress.[81] Wang was also the head of the Nanjing University Alumni Association for the Boston area. Although the association sounds innocent enough, it functions as if it is a United Front group and uses its US-acquired knowledge to serve Beijing's technological needs.[82]

Operating out of the same Woburn, Massachusetts, warehouse was another organization with interesting government ties (and name) called the Chinese Antibody Society. According to court filings, this group, which had been launched, in the words of the Chinese government, "by China and for China," also worked to collect intellectual property to be sent back to China.

All this is to say that Wang was not your typical drug trafficker. Given his CCP connections, his drug trafficking could be seen as an extension of his duties to the state.

Similarly, Canadian authorities busted a fentanyl-importing and -exporting ring that included individuals who were members of the Chinese People's Political Consultative Conference (CPPCC).[83] A United Front group, the CPPCC is a "political advisory body" and a central part of the CCP's system of rule. The organization is chaired by a member of the Politburo Standing Committee of the Chinese Communist Party.[84] "CPPCC members are not 'ordinary' citizens, but are Party-state political operatives with special duties, obligations, and responsibilities to the regime," said Daniel Garrett, a former US government national security official.[85]

Suspected triad members involved in the drug trade populate the CPPCC. Ng Lap Seng, the triad member who funneled money to the Bill Clinton campaign in 1994, was a member.[86] Stanley Ho, a gambling magnate and resort owner in Macau, also served as a member of that organization, even though he had alleged ties to both 14K and Sun Yee On, triads that distribute drugs in the United States.[87]

Wan Kuok-koi, aka "Broken Tooth Koi," a leader of the 14K triad, was involved in the drug syndicate activities of that organized crime outfit while also sitting on the CPPCC. Wan openly acknowledges that the drug trade is a weapon to be used against the United States, with an ambition to unite Chinese organized crime syndicates around the world "in support of Beijing and against the U.S." After the United States sanctioned him for his drug trade involvement, the Chinese government even gave him an award at a March 27, 2021, ceremony in Beijing.[88]

But Beijing's involvement goes even deeper.

Mass production, distribution, and sales of fentanyl in the United States require a secure means of communication to circumvent surveillance by US law enforcement. Enter a Canadian company called Phantom Secure, which advertised a completely secure communication technology. A cartel favorite for years, Phantom Secure offered custom-modified mobile devices such as BlackBerrys and smartphones, plus a service to delete all data in the event of a user's arrest. According to federal authorities, "Phantom Secure's devices were specifically designed, marketed and distributed for use by transnational criminal organisations, specifically those involved in drug trafficking." What made these devices especially secure was that the servers that stored client communications were in China-controlled Hong Kong or Panama. Phantom Secure chose those locations knowing that officials in neither country would cooperate with international law enforcement.[89]

Eventually, in 2018, the FBI and its Canadian and Australian counterparts shut down Phantom Secure, arresting its senior executives for helping drug cartels. It is interesting to note that the company and its CEO had seven US bank accounts, as well as accounts in Canada, Ireland, Singapore, the United Arab Emirates, China, and Hong Kong.[90]

Chinese organized crime figures involved in the drug trade also speak openly on WeChat, a Chinese messaging app. WeChat is operated and owned by Tencent, a Chinese tech firm with close ties to the Chinese military and intelligence service. The Chinese government regularly monitors the app to suppress political dissent. But when it comes to drug trade chatter, it looks the other way. "It is all happening on WeChat," said Thomas Cindric, a retired DEA agent from the elite Special Operations Division. "The Chinese government is clearly aware of it. The launderers are not concealing themselves on WeChat."[91]

Besides secure communications, drug cartels also need to launder their money.

Some of the Mexican cartels' most successful and proficient launderers are Chinese and use Chinese state banks to do their dirty work. In the United States, Chinese nationals living across the United States from Virginia to Illinois to Oregon have been arrested in recent years for laundering money for drug cartels.[92] This pattern suggests a much larger system, especially considering the other established aspects of Chinese national alliance in the illicit drug trade.

In May 2012, law enforcement officials received early indications of the drug supply network and the role of Chinese banks when they made moves in five states as part of Operation Dark Angel. They arrested twenty people, including the leader of a drug network based in Mexico. US federal agents noticed that he was, curiously, wiring cash overseas, including to "banks in China." Typically, in the past, cartels had worked with banks in South America or the Caribbean. The presence of Chinese banks was new—and different.[93]

Chinese banks are highly regulated and controlled by the government. Yet in a leaked Department of Homeland Security (DHS) report obtained by the author, the cartels shifted to Chinese money laundering because of "their low fees" and "their ability to transfer monies rapidly to many regions in the world."[94]

According to another internal Drug Enforcement Administration (DEA) document also obtained by the author, "Mexican drug traffickers use Chinese citizens living in the United States for money laundering and thus deliver their earnings south of the border." In Oregon, officials found three Chinese citizens who had transferred millions of dollars of cartel money into more than 251 Chinese bank accounts while handling more than three hundred cash deliveries across the United States from Los Angeles to Boston.[95]

Or consider the recent case of a Chinese American gangster named Xizhi Li, a successful money launderer who moved street money into large bank accounts that cartel leaders could convert into assets such as "yachts, mansions, weapons, technology and bribes to police and politicians." Li enjoyed close association with Chinese government officials and the Communist Party elite. He worked through a web of contacts from Latin America to Chicago, China, Los Angeles, and New York.[96]

Li grew up in a Mexican border town before migrating to Southern California and becoming an associate of the 14K triad. He fathered children with a Chinese woman but married a Mexican American woman, with whom he also had kids. He soon got into the drug business, smuggling cocaine out of Mexico. His approach to money laundering was simple and straightforward: a cartel would contract with him to launder some $350,000—an amount that would fit comfortably into a suitcase. He would give it Mexican pesos that he had stored in a safe house, minus his commission fee. He would then sell the dollars to wealthy Chinese clients who were looking to get hold of US currency. Li even had an association with a senior Chinese military official. To sell the dollars, he would have the wealthy client transfer the equivalent amount of money into bank accounts that he controlled in China, a process called "mirror transactions." He didn't use obscure banks for those transactions; rather, he used the most politically connected banks in China: the Industrial and Commercial Bank of China and the Agricultural Bank of China, which are state controlled. Somehow the Chinese state didn't seem to notice—or care. The quantity of money involved was enormous. Li had dozens of couriers operating from California to Georgia. In Chicago, two of his couriers handled more than $10 million over a seven-month period.[97]

The DEA eventually caught up with Li, and he was tried and convicted. But what struck US investigators was the fact that his network had been able to operate freely in China without Beijing's intervention. Like others in the drug trade, Li's henchmen had used WeChat to communicate. Again, the app is known to function as a Chinese "government monitoring tool."[98]

Beijing undoubtedly maintains strict controls on the flow of money to and from mainland China. Yet China-based companies and organizations are "taking a central role in global money laundering" when it comes to the flow of fentanyl. Cartel profits are routed to China and then back to Mexico. "Most contact with the banking system happens in China, a veritable black hole for U.S. and Mexican authorities."[99] Indeed, "China's willingness to cooperate internationally in anti–money laundering operations . . . remains limited."[100]

One method used to launder large sums of money is employing thousands of Chinese students on education visas in the United States to pick up suitcases of cash and then transfer them for money laundering, with the money then routed through WeChat and Chinese banks.[101] As one DEA official put it, "I can't emphasize this enough, the involvement of the Chinese has really complicated all of these schemes."[102]

Admiral Craig Faller led the US Southern Command, which oversees all US military operations in Latin America, for three years. He testified before Congress in 2021 that Chinese money launderers are "the 'No. 1 underwriter' of drug trafficking in the Western Hemisphere." He observed that the Beijing government was "at least tacitly supporting" those money-laundering activities. After all, China possesses "the world's largest and most sophisticated state security apparatus. So there's no doubt that they have the ability to stop things if they want to. They don't have any desire to stop this." Indeed, the Chinese government uses these money-laundering networks to funnel money to United Front groups in the United States and other countries.[103]

CHAPTER 3

Willful Blindness

When Japanese planes bombed Pearl Harbor, FDR responded quickly, speaking to the nation within twenty-four hours and declaring it a "day of infamy." He squarely blamed the attacker. China's attacks through fentanyl are deadly but deceptive, and our leaders remain largely silent. When deaths from fentanyl are mentioned, they frame them as evidence of a drug crisis, not a foreign attack.

Phase one of the fentanyl attack began when Barack Obama was president. Obama's public views about China when entering office were benign, even naive. As he explained in 2009, there are "some in China [who] think that America will try to contain China's ambitions; some in America that think there is something to fear in a rising China. I take a different view. I believe in a future where China is a strong, prosperous, and successful member of the community of nations; a future when our nations are partners out of necessity, but also out of opportunity."[1]

Obama also came into office wanting to deemphasize the war on drugs. In 2009, he removed the drug czar, the director of the Office of National Drug Control Policy, from his cabinet, diminishing that voice on a variety of foreign and domestic policies.[2] He also deemphasized drug fighting in his foreign policy. Burma, a long-known center of the international drug trade with Chinese involvement, saw economic sanctions removed by the Obama administration in the name of supporting democratic reforms in that country. It was a stunning move. According to Gibson Dunn: "It is rare for an active sanctions regime to be terminated in such a comprehensive fashion." It was now possible for some entities in Burma, many linked to the international drug trade, to move their assets more freely around the world. Whatever the administration's well-intentioned motive in removing the sanctions, the end effect was to bolster the international drug trade.[3] And the international drug trade thrives on product sold in the United States.

Notably, some of Obama's largest financial supporters needed warm ties between the United States and China for their ventures to work. Jeffrey Katzenberg, the CEO of DreamWorks Animation, was reportedly Obama's largest fundraiser for his 2008 election and 2012 reelection campaigns. In Part III, we will explore the close relationship between DreamWorks and the Chinese government. The DreamWorks partnership in China was a result of an agreement negotiated by then vice president Joe Biden during the Obama administration.[4] Indeed, Katzenberg would become the cochairman of the Joe Biden 2024 campaign as well.[5] In short, powerful figures in Washington and their wealthy Hollywood backers have strong financial interests in maintaining smooth relations with Beijing.

Obama was also the intended beneficiary of a Chinese influence operation in 2012, when $800,000 was illegally funneled into his reelection campaign through straw donors.[6]

By 2016, Obama was less naive and China much bolder. In September, Obama went to Hangzhou, China, for a meeting of the G20. When other foreign heads of state arrived—from Russia, India, Brazil, and many other countries—China granted them the typical red-carpet attention at the airport. But when Air Force One pulled up to the airport terminal, Obama was not provided with a staircase or red carpet. Instead, he was forced to exit from the rear of Air Force One via an exit in the plane's belly that is seldom used by US presidents.

"These things do not happen by mistake," said Jorge Guajardo, Mexico's former ambassador to China. "Not with the Chinese." He added, "It's a snub. It's a way of saying: 'You know, you're not that special to us.'" Susan Rice, Obama's national security advisor, was "baffled and annoyed" by the incident. Obama told reporters that "none of this detracts from the broader scope of the relationship."[7]

That "broader scope" now included fentanyl, a mounting problem that the Obama White House appeared determined to ignore, at least as far as exposing China's role in the crisis.

The Obama administration knew by 2016 that America was in the middle of a street fentanyl crisis. Between 2013 and 2017, more than 67,000 Americans died of overdoses—more than the number killed in the Vietnam War. The vast majority of the overdoses were of fentanyl. Health care experts petitioned Obama to declare a public health emergency. "Fentanyl was killing people like we'd never seen before," said Derek Maltz, a former agent in charge of the DEA's Special Operations Division in Washington. "A red light was going off, ding, ding, ding."[8]

The Obama administration knew that fentanyl precursors were coming from China, and with great fanfare in President Obama's last year, the administration announced an agreement with Beijing to restrict the export of fentanyl-related chemicals coming to the United States. It would result in "reducing the supply of fentanyl" in the United States, the White House promised.[9] But nothing changed. The chemicals kept coming in increasing quantities. The illicit fentanyl supply exploded. And the death toll continued to climb.

As mentioned earlier, Obama's secretary of state, John Kerry, did not raise the matter in any serious way with Beijing. His sole action appears to have been writing that letter to the United Nations and asking it to ban the sale of fentanyl.

Those on Capitol Hill were no better. In 2016, Senator Pat Toomey of Pennsylvania introduced a bill to cut the Chinese source of fentanyl. But he could not find a single senator to cosponsor his bill.[10]

In January 2017, just before leaving the Oval Office, President Obama issued a report on the drug crisis in the United States. "The dramatic increase in the availability and use of heroin and fentanyl is a national security, law enforcement, and public health issue, and it has become the highest priority illicit drug threat to the Nation," the report declared.[11] Those words were correct but empty. It was not enough of a priority to confront China over its central role in the crisis.

In the ensuing months, Susan Rice spoke optimistically about China's growing cooperation with the United States on the fentanyl issue. "For several years," she noted, there had been "in-depth cooperation and dialogue on counternarcotics [with China]," and we were now seeing China "crack down on the fentanyl threat."[12]

But that was an illusion. Rice completely misread the problem of fentanyl and the international drug trade, declaring that fentanyl "is not only killing far, far, far too many Americans, but is also one that will destabilize China if left unaddressed, so we have a mutual interest in this."[13]

In fact, the fentanyl crisis was not "destabilizing" China; it was strengthening China relative to the United States.

The "crackdown" she promised never came. In fact, exports of precursors continued to grow.

The body count in America continued to rise. The year Obama left office, fentanyl deaths in the United States jumped by a whopping 50 percent, to almost thirty thousand. The number might actually have been higher because some state coroners did not provide specific drug identification on the death certificate.[14]

Enforcing the issue with China would have been challenging and disruptive for President Obama and his postpresidential plans. In late 2017, Obama was back in China, a little more than a year after the plane incident. This time he was ready to cash in. For former US presidents, making highly paid appearances in China has always been a nice source of revenue. It doesn't matter if they are Democrats or Republicans. Obama might have recently signed a $60 million book deal just months after leaving office, but that did not deter him. How much he made appearing at the Global Small and Medium-Sized Enterprises Summit in Shanghai is unknown; there is no disclosure requirement. But it was undoubtedly a nice payday. At the event, involving thousands of Chinese attendees, it cost $900 to shake his hand and a cool $40,000 to have a picture taken with him, according to Chinese state media.[15]

Since leaving office, former president Obama has remained almost completely silent about China's involvement in the fentanyl crisis.

In 2017, the Donald Trump administration echoed the previous administration's concerns about fentanyl deaths—not China's culpability. During Trump's first year in office, something very unusual happened in US history: Americans' overall life expectancy declined. A major contributing factor was the mounting toll of fentanyl deaths.[16]

Assistant Secretary of State Kirsten Madison called the opioid crisis "the most 'severe *drug crisis*' the U.S. has ever faced." (Emphasis added.)[17] In October 2017, President Trump declared the opioid crisis in general to be a national public health emergency under federal law and directed all government agencies to fight the crisis. It was an important shift in domestic resources.[18]

But no one seemed to want to call it a war.

The Trump administration publicly pushed Beijing on the supply of fentanyl to the United States, becoming the first to do so explicitly. Its bold approach seemed to yield some results when President Xi promised to act and declare fentanyl a controlled substance.[19] "What [Xi] will be doing to fentanyl could be a game changer for the United States," Trump predicted on his return trip from the G20 summit in Argentina.[20]

Of course, it didn't work out that way. Chinese state-media went on the attack. Only days after the fentanyl deal between presidents Trump and Xi was announced, the Chinese government–run Global Times argued that the problem was a result of Americans' decadent demand for drugs and explained that China did not have a fentanyl crisis. Global Times even claimed that white Americans were more susceptible to fentanyl than "other ethnic groups" were.[21] This is, of course, the precise opposite of how China talks about the Opium Wars. In that case, it was the fault of the suppliers, not the customers. In this case, to blame the drug producers, the distributors, and the money launderers would be to blame themselves.

Beyond the Beijing spin, the realities remained the same. The chemicals used to make fentanyl continue to be exported from China, often by state-linked companies headed by politically connected executives. The chemicals arrive at port facilities in Mexico controlled by Chinese companies, are mixed by Chinese chemists based in Mexico, and are turned into fentanyl-laced pills on Chinese-supplied pill presses. Chinese triad networks continued to be involved in distribution, and the drug money was laundered through Chinese state banks.

In 2019, after the Trump-Xi agreement, a leaked document from the Department of Homeland Security came to a dismal, if predicable conclusion: "There is no indication that China took extra steps to strengthen its counter-fentanyl capabilities."[22]

Officials in the Trump administration followed the well-trodden path of believing that China was interested in helping the United States overcome its fentanyl crisis. General Robert Spalding, who joined the National Security Council in the Trump White House, witnessed the naiveté firsthand. He understands how Beijing operates. He speaks Mandarin and has served at the US Embassy in Beijing. While in the Trump White House, he asked the acting director of the Office of

National Drug Control Policy about fentanyl coming in from China. "We're cooperating with the Chinese government to bring the makers of the drugs to justice," the director confidently told the general. Spalding warned him that the CCP was not actually cooperating, regardless of what they were telling him.[23]

Unfortunately, Spalding got it right.

Trump's agreement with Xi did nothing to stem the tidal wave of fentanyl. Matthew Donahue, the deputy chief of operations and chief of foreign operations for the Drug Enforcement Administration, described in March 2021 how "an unlimited and endless supply" of fentanyl chemicals kept "coming from China to Mexico."[24] Around the same time, China's National Narcotics Control Commission smoothly cautioned that US-China cooperation on fentanyl-related investigations and prosecutions remained "extremely limited."[25]

***

The fentanyl epidemic has not spared wealthy areas such as Burbank, California, where at least seven high school students have overdosed on fentanyl.[26] The situation is so bad that the Burbank Unified School District, like many others around the country, started requiring schools to stock up on naloxone, a drug to contain the effects of a fentanyl overdose.[27] In 2022, two men were arrested in Burbank with a hundred thousand counterfeit oxycodone pills laced with fentanyl.[28] Nineteen-year-old TikTok influencer Cooper Noriega was found dead in a Burbank park with fentanyl in his system.[29]

Burbank falls within the district of California congressman Adam Schiff, one of the most powerful and influential elected officials in America. A former prosecutor, Schiff has been in Congress since 2000, rising to serve as the chairman of the secretive and powerful House Intelligence Committee between 2017 and 2023. From his perch, Schiff had responsibility for, among other things, US national security. Schiff has been outspoken on numerous national security threats, but not when it comes to fentanyl, even though fentanyl deaths in the Los Angeles area rose by a stunning 1,208 percent from 2016 to 2022.[30] If you go to the Intelligence Committee's webpage that describes its work under his tenure, the word "fentanyl" yields no results. That is to say, the Intelligence Committee under his leadership, by its own account, did *nothing* on a topic that the Obama administration had declared a threat to our national security in 2017. A search of Schiff's congressional webpage yields a lone mention of "fentanyl," a brief reference to a single piece of legislation.[31]

Fentanyl is clearly not a priority for Schiff.

Voters in his district have noticed the silence. "According to the United States Attorney's office for the Southern District of California in San Diego, more deadly Fentanyl is being seized by border officials in San Diego and Imperial counties than at any of the nation's 300 plus ports of entry, making this federal district an epicenter for Fentanyl trafficking into the United States," one constituent noted in the *Glendale News-Press*, a local paper. "The city of Glendale is about a two-hour drive from our southern border and California Rep. Adam Schiff's district since 2013. Not surprisingly, on Dec. 31, 2022, we received another piece of mail from the Congressman's office with no reference to the Fentanyl crisis. Congressman Schiff often writes in the local newspapers without reference to the Fentanyl problem in his district."[32]

In contrast, Schiff was outspoken on the far, far less dangerous outbreak of monkeypox, demanding more action on a vaccine, even though it has killed no one in the United States at the time of this writing. Schiff also gave numerous interviews on CNN, MSNBC, and other news outlets about the Ebola virus, which at the time had killed just one American.

Why Congressman Schiff has little to say about the deadly fentanyl crisis is an abiding mystery. Part of the reason may be that raising the issue might cause undue attention to his financial connections to individuals involved with criminal networks in Southern California, many of whom are tied to money laundering and the drug trade.

Encompassing Hollywood, Burbank, and Glendale, California, Schiff's congressional district has long been a hub of organized criminal activity. Beginning in the early 1990s, the *Los Angeles Times* and other newspapers in the region began reporting on the rise of Armenian gangs in the district.[33] These gangs, not to mention those from Central and South America and China, are involved in all kinds of violent crime, including drug trafficking, gunrunning, murder, extortion, and white-collar crimes such as money laundering.

Some of Schiff's work in the state senate, before he was elected to Congress, fueled financial crimes in his district. One bill related to Medi-Cal created a gateway for considerable fraud, which an organized crime syndicate in his district seized upon, perpetuating the largest Medicaid fraud case in history at the time. California business leaders warned Schiff about the fraud they were witnessing, but he appears to have ignored it. In 2010, four hundred FBI agents executed a massive investigation and arrested seventy Armenian mobsters. The criminals ran 118 phantom clinics, many of them in Schiff's district.[34] The ringleader, Armen Kazarian, lived in Schiff's district.[35]

Once in Washington, Schiff opposed legislation that would have cracked down on criminal money-laundering networks. In 2005, a bill was introduced onto the House floor to expand the role the federal government would have in fighting gang violence by creating "an anti-racketeering statute similar to the one used against the Mafia dons to prosecute criminal street gangs." But Schiff opposed the bill.[36] Armenian organized crime continued to expand in Schiff's district, and his connections to some of the players involved are concerning.

In 2017, Schiff established a joint fundraising committee with California senator Barbara Boxer called PAC for a Change. One of the largest donations—$95,000—came from the head of a sketchy firm located in Schiff's district called Allied Wallet.[37] The company was run by Andy Khawaja, an executive who would come under investigation by federal authorities and whose business was tied to money laundering, with a major footprint in China.

Money also flowed to the campaign in other ways. Schiff's congressional campaign took in at least $36,000 in donations from executives at Allied Wallet. Another $16,100 came from Khawaja, and two additional $10,000 contributions came from two other executives of the company. While Schiff was accepting those donations, it was publicly known that Allied Wallet had been under FBI investigation. It was not the first time: in 2010, Allied Wallet had been forced by federal authorities to forfeit $13 million for its involvement in an illegal gambling scheme.[38] At the time Schiff accepted donations from the executives, the company was being investigated for its ties to "illegal pharma" companies around the world.[39] Khawaja threw a lot of money around, clearly in search of political access. During the 2016 presidential campaign, he first backed Hillary Clinton and then switched to Donald Trump.[40] In the case of Schiff, he clearly gained access. On October 16, 2016, Khawaja and Schiff sat down for a private meeting with Saudi prince Salman bin Abdulaziz Al Saud in Beverly Hills.[41]

Allied Wallet made money processing credit card payments for "'high-risk' online retailers that traditional financial institutions avoid." They included criminal organizations "that apparently break the law in underhanded and odious ways."[42]

Allied Wallet also had a partnership with a Chinese company called China UnionPay, which Chinese triads used to launder money. China UnionPay is a Chinese state-owned entity with close ties to the CCP and a card brand that "is often seen as an arm of Chinese state policy."[43] UnionPay has been used by organized crime groups and drug traffickers all around the world, including the Chinese triads.[44] Allied Wallet seemed to function "as a sort of credit card processor for fraudsters, swindlers, and rip-off artists bilking the public out of more than $100 million."[45]

Schiff has other interesting donors and friends besides Allied Wallet.

Arthur Charchian is a Glendale, California, lawyer who was involved in a money-laundering scheme.[46] Charchian is the head of Southern California Armenian Democrats and a Schiff booster.[47] Shortly after Schiff introduced legislation on the Armenian genocide, another Armenian, gang leader Pogos Satamyan, donated $10,000 to the Democratic Congressional Campaign Committee.[48]

In 2019, Democratic megadonor Ed Buck was charged with drug trafficking and "operating a drug house." Buck was a donor to Schiff's campaign and a social acquaintance as well.[49]

Openly pressing for aggressive action to deal with the Chinese-linked fentanyl networks might lead to open discussions of money-laundering networks operating in the United States and raise some difficult questions for Schiff.

Schiff represents a congressional district that is at the heart of the American entertainment industry, including the cities of Burbank and Hollywood. Hollywood titans who finance his campaigns rely on access to the Chinese market for a sizable portion of their profits. From his earliest national elections, Schiff received the backing of entertainment industry titans such as Jeffrey Katzenberg and Steven Spielberg.[50]

Their partner at DreamWorks, David Geffen, promised to raise however many millions of dollars were needed to defeat his opponent in 2000.[51] As we will see in Part III, these titans have deep, abiding, and lucrative ties to the Chinese government that they do not want disturbed. DreamWorks has modified films for American audiences at the request of the Communist Chinese government, pushing CCP propaganda both subtly and not so subtly.

Taking aggressive action against China for its fentanyl activities could disrupt these relationships.

Schiff is not alone for strangely avoiding the topic of China's involvement in fentanyl. Congresswoman Alexandria Ocasio-Cortez represents the Bronx and Queens, and those communities have also been shattered by fentanyl overdoses.[52]

And yet Ocasio-Cortez, who serves as the vice ranking member of the powerful House Oversight Committee, has been weirdly silent on fentanyl and China's role. Her congressional website yields plenty of mentions of her passionate work on topics like taxes and gun control, but there is not a single mention of fentanyl as of this writing.[53]

* * *

Joe Biden was outspoken in 1992 when it was exposed that Beijing was involved with the heroin trade. The then senator from Delaware showed initiative in calling out the Communist leadership for its illicit activities. But now with the far more deadly fentanyl crisis, he has grown silent. Granted, he made some noise about the subject during the 2020 presidential campaign, promising to "make fentanyl a top priority in our dealings with China," but as we saw earlier, according to officially released notes of the conversations he has had with President Xi, he has not raised the subject with the Chinese president as of this writing.[54]

When the so-called monkeypox virus emerged in 2022, the virus received "czar" status in the White House, even though, at the time, it had not claimed a single American life.[55] Fentanyl gets no "czar" status at 1600 Pennsylvania Avenue. And China has not been called to account.

In late 2022, the Biden administration named twenty-two countries as being transit points for drugs or producers of drugs. One country not on the list? China. In announcing his administration's drug strategy, Biden could only promise, "We will look to expand cooperation with China . . . to disrupt the global flow of synthetic drugs and their precursor chemicals."[56]

Biden's secretary of state, Antony Blinken, has made excuses for Beijing, absurdly arguing that some of the precursors arriving in Mexico from China have been shipped by accident. He cautiously added that mentioning precursor shipments from China was "not about pointing fingers."[57]

Though sometimes promising to help stem the flow, China has never cooperated on fentanyl, nor is its involvement accidental. This is a war.

When Joe Biden delivered the State of the Union address in 2023, he talked about fentanyl, acknowledging the stigma associated with substance abuse, and called for better substance abuse services. In other words, he treated it as a conventional drug problem. So he promised more drug detection machines and more inspections of cargo. What he never mentioned was Beijing's hand in the matter.[58]

President Biden has been remarkably quiet in discussing China's involvement in the drug trade; he does not challenge its leadership about their conduct. Why might that be? As I recounted in *Red-Handed*, members of the first family received some $31 million in deals from a small group of Chinese businessmen with deep ties to the highest levels of Chinese intelligence.

However, some of these businessmen who funneled money to the Bidens have ties to the fentanyl trade, including $5 million from a Chinese national who was a business partner with a notorious triad leader. This cash flow connects the Bidens with Chinese triad associates.

One of the largest sources of money flowing from China to the Bidens came from a mysterious Chinese tycoon named Ye Jianming, the chairman of CEFC China Energy Company. Joe Biden's son Hunter Biden had a close working relationship with "Chairman Ye," as he called him. Hunter explained in emails to his business partners that he spoke with Ye on a "regular basis" and that "we have a standing once a week call as I am also his personal counsel (we signed an attorney client engagement letter) in the U.S." He also said that he was helping Ye "on a number of his personal issues" including unspecified "sensitive things."

Ye showered the Bidens with money. He gave Hunter a three-carat,

$80,000 diamond. In July 2017, his company gave the Biden family a $5 million, interest-free, forgivable loan. (The email notes that the loan is not just to Hunter but to the "BD [Biden] family.") There were other cash transfers, too.[59]

Ye is from Fujian province, the hotbed of triad activity in China. While sending the Biden family millions of dollars, he was also business partners with the former leader of a Chinese triad called the United Bamboo Gang (UBG). His name is Zhang Anle, but he is more commonly known by the name "White Wolf." Ye and White Wolf set up the Shanghai Zhenrong Petroleum Company together.[60] White Wolf's gang, UBG, also has a "partnership" with Mexico's Sinaloa Cartel and helps them in the production and distribution of fentanyl in the United States. UBG helped to turn "the Sinaloa Cartel into the King of Fentanyl," according to a Mexican investigation of the cartel.[61]

White Wolf had been arrested and convicted in the 1980s on drug-trafficking and racketeering charges in the United States.[62] The UBG is involved extensively in the international drug trade, having sold heroin in the United States for decades. As one government report stated, "It is believed the gang is active in several U.S. cities, including Chicago, Honolulu, Houston, Miami, Phoenix, and various California cities. The UBG has built up a sophisticated network capable of supplying members with guns, narcotics, and fraudulent identifications."[63] White Wolf also has close ties with the Beijing government; senior Communist Party officials call him "Big Brother."[64] The fact that a Chinese businessman who showered millions on the Bidens is partners with a crime syndicate partnering in the distribution of fentanyl into the United States might be shocking enough. But there is more.

Hunter Biden also received $1 million from one of Ye's executives, Patrick Ho, who was charged and convicted in the United States on bribery charges at the United Nations.[65] Ho was working on a bribery scheme run in parallel with alleged Chinese triad member Ng Lap Seng, who was convicted of similar charges. The Shui Fong triad is tied to the drug trade.[66]

Hunter Biden also worked with CITIC, some of whose members have triad links. The extent of their dealings is not clear. Hunter met with CITIC executives while his father was vice president, hoping to do business with them. He apparently gave them a signed copy of his father's 2009 book.[67] In turn, when CITIC was interested in the possibility of a Universal Theme Park in China, they approached Hunter Biden's firm to arrange a meeting with Comcast executives.[68]

There are other ties in Biden world as well. Hunter Biden's attorney, Abbe Lowell, has represented a variety of well-known American clients from New Jersey senator Bob Menendez to members of the Trump family. But he was also a legal representative for Ng Lap Seng.[69] Lowell has also represented Qin Fei, who is accused of being a Chinese intelligence officer, and Lum Davis, who pled guilty to illegally lobbying for the Chinese government.[70]

The problem of conflicting personal ties when it comes to confronting China on fentanyl extends beyond the Biden family to members of his administration. And so does the silence.

In early 2023, Deputy Secretary of State Wendy Sherman spoke about the fentanyl crisis, but she did not talk at all about China's role in it. Instead, she described the scourge vaguely as a global health issue. "Global health is another area in which we all need to work together, and the issue of fentanyl is not just a counter-narcotics issue," she said. "It is a global public-health issue, a huge global public-health issue."[71]

Why won't Wendy Sherman call out China on its central role in the fentanyl crisis? In 2021, she became the United States' second highest diplomat after leaving her post as a counselor for a consulting firm, the Albright Stonebridge Group (ASG), which has deep ties to Beijing. According to ASG's website, China is the "firm's largest single country practice," with offices in both Beijing and Shanghai. Sherman's firm also boasts "former high-level" Chinese officials as members of the firm. "We work to create allies within the Chinese system."[72]

It's hard to call out "allies" within the Chinese system for their involvement in the international drug trade. It's a repeated pattern. Americans continue to die, and many US officials seem to have decided that the value of alliances within the Chinese government outweighs the value of American lives and security.

John Kerry, now Biden's special envoy for climate issues, has Biden's ear on several important issues. The two are, among other things, longtime Senate colleagues. Decades ago, Kerry spoke strongly about Chinese involvement in the drug trade. Now when it comes to China, he prefers to focus on climate change issues. Apparently, pressing China about its complicit drug-related conduct in the United States—and *actual* deaths it has caused—would interfere with his attempts at a climate change agreement—and *theoretical* future climate-related deaths.

Pressing Beijing over fentanyl could also damage the Kerry-Heinz family investment portfolio. The family's fortunes are tied up in considerable investments in mainland China, including major stakes in Hillhouse China Value Fund ("over $1 million"), Tiger Global LP ("over $1 million"), and Teng Yue Partners ("over $1 million"), among others.[73] These numbers may be significantly understated in Kerry's financial disclosures. Teng Yue Partners, for example, which is "focused on public and private equity investments in China" has a $5 million minimum investment requirement on most of its funds.[74] The firms in which Kerry's family is invested are also deeply tied to the Chinese government establishment. The chairman of Hillhouse, Zhang Lei, is closely aligned with Beijing and is involved in numerous United Front organizations. He has also invested in companies blacklisted in the United States and has put his personal wealth to work in causes supported by President Xi.[75]

The Biden administration has, on several occasions, announced financial sanctions against fentanyl networks. But the results are minimal because they don't affect the big players and the Chinese institutions that help the cartels operate. And China thumbs its nose at the United States.

China's ambassador to the United States, Qin Gang, absurdly insists that his country is not involved in the fentanyl trade. The ambassador proudly stated that since 2019, "not a single criminal case has been opened in China that involves the manufacturing, trafficking and smuggling of fentanyl-related substances."[76]

Like a murderer mingling with onlookers at the scene of his crime, Beijing mocks America for the fentanyl crisis. Hua Chunying, a spokeswoman for the Chinese Ministry of Foreign Affairs, posted on social media a series of messages declaring that "China won't become the U.S." At one point, she wrote, "China does not allow the drug problem to haunt the nation and kill 100,000+ per year."[77]

***

It's not just fentanyl.

They appeared to be ordinary California homes in quiet, sometimes upscale, residential neighborhoods. But the 130 houses were, in fact, involved in a massive illegal marijuana-growing operation. Dozens of Chinese nationals purchased the homes in Sacramento, the state capital, with money wired from criminal gangs in Fujian province, China.

US federal officials, who had been tipped off about unusually high utility bills in the homes, eventually figured out what was going on. "This was a large-scale operation, with millions of dollars coming into the US from China," recounted Cindy Chen, an assistant special agent in charge at the IRS. The *Los Angeles Times* said that "nearly half of the 21 people charged were Chinese citizens." The money and people involved were part of another front on the drug war. Federal officials seized 61,000 marijuana plants and 441 pounds of processed dope when they broke up the operation.[78]

In short, organized Chinese networks are moving into the American illegal marijuana business. And it's not just happening in Sacramento.

In Seattle, money from mainland China was used to purchase properties in the Puget Sound area to grow illegal marijuana.[79] In Oklahoma, law enforcement officials say that 75 percent of the illegal marijuana operations they've shut down are connected to "Chinese investors and Chinese organized crime."[80] In San Bernardino County, California, authorities served a stunning 2,100 search warrants and seized more than $1 billion in processed cannabis and marijuana plants. Again, Chinese nationals were bringing money from the mainland and purchasing property in which to set up massive illegal dope operations, this time in the Chino-Ontario area in California. "My best estimate is probably 97% to 98% of all of our indoor marijuana cultivations are run by Chinese nationals," said Sergeant Rich Debevec of the San Bernardino County Sheriff's Marijuana Enforcement Team.[81]

In the small, rural state of Maine, according to a leaked U.S. Border Patrol memo, there are estimated to be 270 illegal marijuana operations owned by Chinese nationals growing more than $4 billion worth of the drug. The state's entire congressional delegation has asked the DOJ to shut them down.[82]

The marijuana these operations produce is highly potent, roughly three times as strong as the illegal marijuana sold in the 1990s.[83] And illegal marijuana is increasingly being laced with fentanyl.[84]

* * *

Despite all the evidence, Beijing denies that it has anything to do with the fentanyl trade and feigns offense that the United States is blaming it for an American cultural problem. In other words, it would have the world believe that the fentanyl problem is evidence of a weak American society, a demand problem rather than a supply problem. Somehow, based on the denial narrative that it has created, it would have the world overlook the fact that this particular drug is the product of an international supply chain that stretches from Chinese factories to the American heartland.

* * *

Even in the beautiful state of Kentucky, there have been record levels of drug overdose deaths, fueled largely by fentanyl.[85] But like so many fellow members of the DC elite, Kentucky senator Mitch McConnell has never made China's role in fentanyl a priority, despite the body count.

In 2019, McConnell, the leader of the Republicans in the US Senate, was asked by the *Washington Post* what he had done to deal with the fentanyl crisis. His home state has been particularly hard hit, just like Adam Schiff's congressional district in California. McConnell's office told the paper that he had "taken meaningful steps to address the opioid crisis, including holding roundtables in his home state." He had also "led an effort in 2015 and again in 2018 to address opioid addiction in pregnant women."[86]

Like other national leaders, Senator McConnell has been strangely inactive and ineffective in holding China's leaders to account for what they have done to the American people. Aggressively dealing with the fentanyl crisis requires calling out and confronting the main force behind its creation and distribution: China's leadership. For McConnell, that means putting his family's finances at risk.

McConnell's family, through his father-in-law, is financially beholden to the Chinese government. As I have recounted in previous books, the Chao family runs an international shipping business that is heavily dependent on the good graces of the Chinese government.

The family businesses, Foremost Group and its subsidiaries, do considerable work with some of the companies named in this book, including Hutchison Port Holdings, which operates ports around the world and as we've shown, has been the subject of concern for decades about smuggling activities. The family's dependence on Beijing's favor for the operation of their business is real. Were Senator McConnell to take action that angered the Chinese leadership, they could effectively destroy the Chao family business overnight.

* * *

It is not just our leaders in Washington who have proven to be remarkably silent on this deadly matter. In California, Governor Gavin Newsom has also had trouble indicting China when talking about fentanyl. Three times as many people died in San Francisco of fentanyl and other drug overdoses than officially died of covid-19.[87] Fentanyl deaths have skyrocketed in California, up by more than 2,100 percent since 2016.[88] Yet fentanyl gets remarkably little of Newsom's attention. In April 2023, he was asked by a San Francisco resident, "Hey Gavin, tell me whatcha gonna do about the fentanyl epidemic?" Newsom responded, "What should I do, J.J? You tell me what we need to do. That's why I'm here" and walked away.[89]

Newsom has a history of shielding the CCP from legitimate criticism while cultivating commercial ties with China. In 2008, when Newsom was the mayor of San Francisco, the Olympic torch relay for the Beijing Olympic Games was expected to run through the Bay Area. Earlier torch relays in London and Paris had been met by human rights protestors, which had deeply embarrassed Beijing. So Newsom executed an intricate "fake-out," changing the torch relay route at the last minute, leaving thousands of protestors and supporters at one end of San Francisco while the torch passed through the other side of town. The protestors were furious, as were Bay Area leaders from Newsom's own political party. "Gavin Newsom runs San Francisco the way the premier of China runs his country—secrecy, lies, misinformation, lack of transparency, and manipulating the populace," declared Aaron Peskin, the president of the San Francisco Board of Supervisors, who represents Chinatown. "He did it so China can report they had a great torch run."[90]

While Newsom was protecting China's image from protests against the torch relay, he was launching ChinaSF, an ambitious effort to make the Bay Area the "premiere [*sic*] U.S. gateway for Chinese companies expanding into the North American market."[91] Newsom's former communications aide, Darlene Chiu Bryant, became the organization's longtime head.[92]

ChinaSF was highly favorable to the Chinese entities involved: any investment they made in an American company would grant them intellectual property rights in China for the technology developed. It "would involve U.S. companies handing over their secret formulas."[93] But many of the Chinese companies and businessmen that were involved in ChinaSF and benefited from the program had ties to Chinese organized crime.

Newsom's Chinese partner in the venture was Vincent Lo, who served as cochairman of ChinaSF and president of the Council for the Promotion & Development of Yangtze. The council signed a memorandum of understanding with the Bay Area Council on behalf of Chinese partners.[94]

Lo has links to the CCP, as well as alleged connection to the triads. In the 1990s, Lo's company reportedly hired triad members to provide "canteen and security services" on his building sites on construction projects around Hong Kong. His company first confirmed the practice, but then Lo denied it.[95] Lo also backed a Hong Kong politician whose associates were accused of soliciting support from triad members.[96] At the same time, a prominent businessman accused Lo's companies of "sending armed thugs" likely linked to Chinese triads to forcibly take over his luxury villa complex in suburban Beijing. Lo's company denies the claim.[97]

Lo and his brother also sit on the board of the Real Estate Developers Association of Hong Kong, whose leadership is populated with developers linked to the triads.[98]

Why did Newsom partner with an individual with all these alleged triad connections? Lo and his family secured large deals in the Bay Area with help from Newsom's ChinaSF. Lo and his business associates acquired the iconic Bank of America Center in San Francisco.[99] ChinaSF championed development projects carried out by Lo's family, including the 555 Howard Street project in the Bay Area, which is tied to the California High-Speed Rail project long championed by Governor Newsom.[100]

Other triad-connected businessmen benefited, too.

In 2010, Newsom announced that he was bringing the headquarters of a Chinese energy company called GCL-Poly to San Francisco.[101] The company was partly owned by a subsidiary of China Poly Group, a company with "intimate ties" to the Chinese military.[102] In fact, in the 1990s, the company had been implicated in a plan to smuggle thousands of fully automatic machine guns into the United States and has been tied to "sketchy dealings with third-world dictators and arms traders" around the world. China Poly is also said to work "hand and glove" with Chinese organized crime figures: according to one report, triad-linked Stanley Ho once "spent millions" to acquire an object of tremendous propaganda value for the company.[103] Why would Newsom's ChinaSF green-light such a company's moving into San Francisco?

Newsom also touted the success of bringing Chinese propaganda outlets to the Bay Area. When ChinaSF arranged for *China Daily*, a government-controlled newspaper, to set up its West Coast office in San Francisco, Newsom issued a statement welcoming the news. He touted it as a success, even though the paper is owned by the Central Propaganda Department of the Chinese Communist Party.[104]

At the same time, Newsom announced that a Chinese energy company called Trina Solar Company would be setting up an operation in the Bay Area. The company was later embroiled in controversy when an American competitor's CEO alleged that it was likely receiving support from the People's Liberation Army via hackers who were stealing intellectual property from competitors and giving it to the company.[105]

Newsom's links to the Chinese triads go well beyond ChinaSF. Mayor Newsom worked with a San Francisco businessman named Allen Leung and reappointed him as chairman of the Chinatown Economic Development Group. But Leung was no ordinary businessman; he was the dragonhead of the "ominous" Chee (variously "Ghee" or "Gee") Kung Tong, "transpacific incarnations of criminal Triad gangs originating in China." Members of his gang were involved in the drug trade. Leung was brutally murdered in 2006.[106]

Mayor Newsom also had a fishy history with Leung's successor, Raymond "Shrimp Boy" Chow, an organized crime leader in San Francisco's Chinatown. Chow had been arrested and gone to jail numerous times. In 1978, he was convicted of armed robbery and spent seven years in jail. In 1986 he was convicted of assault with a deadly weapon and served three more years in prison.[107] But Chow was no ordinary criminal; after his release, he worked for leaders in the Wo Hop triad. In the 1990s, he went to prison yet again, this time on federal firearms charges, but was released early for cooperating with the DOJ. Controversy ensued when Shrimp Boy took control of an organization that the mayor's office was funding. Public outrage in the Asian community in San Francisco led Newsom to cancel the contract.[108] The grant was withdrawn, but there seemed to be no animus with the mayor. Chow later posted a photo of himself with then lieutenant governor Gavin Newsom on his Facebook page.[109]

Shrimp Boy was a "dragonhead" of the Chee Kung Tong and a head of a triad crime syndicate including Wo Hop To.[110] In 2016, Shrimp Boy was charged with a total of 162 counts of racketeering, aiding and abetting the laundering of drug money, and other offenses and was found guilty of murder. Among those crimes was his apparent involvement in the killing of Leung.[111]

Shrimp Boy's lawyers argued that the prosecutor in his case, who had been appointed by Newsom, culled "political figures out of the prosecution." Those who skirted criminal charges, according to the lawyers, included individuals "appointed, connected, extremely closely associated with" Gavin Newsom and other political elites.[112]

One of Shrimp Boy's collaborators was Keith Jackson, who had important ties to Newsom as well. Mayor Newsom had appointed Jackson to his 2003 transition team. Jackson was a "fixture in the hallways of City Hall" during Newsom's tenure, recalled Aaron Peskin. Shrimp Boy partnered with Jackson because he "has a lot of political influence and can do 'inside deals' with the City." Jackson had been hired as a consultant by Newsom's cousin Laurence Pelosi for a massive real estate project that was important to Newsom. But Jackson had a very dark side. While the FBI was investigating Shrimp Boy, its agents were introduced to Jackson, who claimed that his son ran a $50,000-a-week drug business. Jackson was later charged in a murder-for-hire scheme and a gunrunning deal involving Shrimp Boy and the Chinese triads. Those charges were dropped as part of a plea agreement.[113]

In August 2021, Governor Newsom addressed a gala for the Chinese newspaper *Sing Tao Daily*.[114] He was effusive with his praise of the news outlet, especially the "leadership team at Sing Tao Daily for your dedication to journalistic integrity and for providing balanced news stories to Chinese Americans and beyond."[115] In context, the comments are curious because the paper has demonstrated a strong pro-CCP tilt in recent years.

As governor, Newsom has been reluctant to support even rudimentary initiatives designed to contain China's activities in California. In 2022, the California State Legislature passed with strong bipartisan support a bill that would ban the sale of agricultural land in California to foreign governments, with a primary focus on China. Newsom vetoed the bill.[116]

Perhaps part of Newsom's motive over the years has been financial. He sells his wines in both mainland China and CCP-controlled Hong Kong.[117] In recent years his wife has been a shareholder in several Chinese companies, to the tune of potentially hundreds of thousands of dollars.[118]

Californians have died by the tens of thousands because of fentanyl produced and distributed by China. But calling out China for its involvement in the fentanyl trade is not something Newsom appears remotely interested in doing. A broad national conversation dealing with Chinese organized crime, which is intimately involved in the drug trade, would raise uncomfortable questions for Newsom. And politicians like to avoid discomfort.

In March 2023, Governor Newsom stood near the Mexican border and outlined his "master plan" to deal with the fentanyl crisis. The strategy included elements such as deploying the National Guard to seize fentanyl supplies, conducting overdose prevention efforts, raising awareness about the dangers of drugs, and holding the "opioid pharmaceutical industry accountable."[119] Somehow Newsom's comprehensive plan overlooked holding Beijing accountable for its involvement in every step of this scourge.

At the end of October 2023, Governor Newsom traveled in China, visiting six cities over the course of a busy eight days. According to Newsom's office, the purpose of the trip was "to advance climate action, economic development and tourism, and to combat xenophobia."[120] Since Newsom is not a US federal official and simply a state governor, the trip was organized by the Chinese People's Association for Friendship with Foreign Countries, an "affiliate" of Chinese intelligence.[121]

Beijing gave Newsom superlative treatment. He was granted a coveted meeting with President Xi in the Great Hall of the People, the first US governor to do so since 2017. In an unusual move, Newsom was allowed to sit side-by-side with the Chinese leader, a sign of respect. When US Secretary of State Tony Blinken had visited earlier in the year, Blinken sat opposite Chinese officials while Xi was in the center—a position of superiority. This elevation of Newsom caused one Chinese writer to explain that this was a good will gesture by China to the US, but it was also recognition of Beijing "having a 'long-term investment' in him [Newsom]."

What transpired during the meeting is not fully known. As the two met, the Chinese media was allowed to enter the Great Hall of the People, but the American media was blocked.[122]

In public, over the course of his week-long stay, Newsom had nothing critical to say about Beijing, but he did admonish both Republicans and Democrats back home "to tone down their criticisms of China," according to the *San Francisco Chronicle*.[123]

Newsom's office says that he brought up the subject of fentanyl with Xi in the context of "China's role in combating the transnational shipping of precursor chemicals," implying the shipments were somehow occurring independent of the Chinese government.[124] Hong Kong media wrote that Newsom "mentioned the fentanyl crisis in the United States" to Xi but did not elaborate.

"These were honest conversations," Newsom later explained, but quickly added "no fingers were being pointed. And the overriding purpose was around a substantive desire to engage and a need and desire to reconcile our differences."[125]

Based on California's fentanyl death rate, approximately 116 Californians died of the opioid during his visit to China, the country that played a central role in the production and distribution network of the drug.

For Newsom, it appears that honestly addressing the fentanyl crisis by dealing with China's central role in the crisis might disrupt his political and financial security. He is an especially prominent case of fentanyl crisis blindness, as the governor of the only state that borders both the Pacific Rim and Mexico, but other state leaders around the country take the same posture. Do they fear damage to their political careers by taking on China? Economic retribution, whether personal or state interests, or both? In any case, the risk of losing another hundred thousand American lives over another year of inaction certainly outweighs the political benefits they receive from closing their eyes.

Drug warfare is real. It is a powerful weapon that has been deployed against the United States. It has caused untold casualties. Politicians find it convenient to focus on the blast caused by the fentanyl missile while ignoring from where the missile was launched—Beijing.

Drug warfare against the U.S. is effective because it targets the Achilles' heel of a free country. Americans are "free" to pursue happiness. Subverted, this becomes an excuse to turn to illicit drugs for recreation or escape from reality. Drug warfare also works because it provides Beijing with deniability. The Chinese government has deployed it through a third country, Mexico. This is its "borrowed knife." Its leaders are also working to distance themselves further from culpability as Chinese nationals move fentanyl precursor–manufacturing operations to India.[126] They have also calculated that our politicians' pursuit of self-interest will lead them to remain willfully blind.

But more drug weapons are on the horizon. Carfentanil is a drug used to sedate large animals such as elephants. It is also being shipped from China and showing up in North America. Canadian officials intercepted a kilo of the drug in Vancouver. That single kilo would have been enough to kill everyone in Canada; with enough left over to depopulate both Sweden and Finland.[127]

There is also xylazine, also called "tranq," a veterinary tranquilizer that is now being sent from Chinese companies to drug cartels and producers in Mexico and the United States. The drug is authorized only to be used on animals; but dealers mix it into fentanyl to save money. You can buy it online from Chinese suppliers. Users can develop bizarre medical conditions: purple blisters on their skin, along with white patches encircled by red rings. As with fentanyl, people often don't know they are taking xylazine.[128]

"A kilogram of xylazine powder can be purchased online from Chinese suppliers with common prices ranging from $6–$20 U.S. per kilogram," said the DEA. "At this low price, its use as an adulterant may increase the profit for illicit drug traffickers."[129]

"To fan the flames of hate and division," reasons Frank Montoya, a former FBI official. "The Chinese have seen the advantages of the drug trade. If fentanyl helps them and hurts this country, why not?"[130]

But fentanyl is not the only WMD that Beijing has deliberately unleashed on the United States.

Part II

WATCH A FIRE FROM ACROSS THE RIVER

（隔河观火）

CHAPTER 4

Arming Criminals

Paul Kutz, a fifty-three-year-old accountant, was minding his own business near a Marriott hotel in Poughkeepsie, New York, when a masked gunman burst into the hotel in an attempted robbery. The gunman eventually let loose with a barrage of bullets, spraying thirty rounds from his modified Glock handgun. Rounds struck Kutz in the heart, lungs, and liver—killing him.[1]

Tamara O'Neal, a physician at Mercy Hospital in Chicago, was on duty when her ex-boyfriend showed up in the emergency room. Angry over their canceled engagement, he fired thirty rounds from his modified handgun, killing her, a pharmacy technician, and a police officer. Police returned fire and shot the gunman in the chest before he turned the gun on himself.[2]

Whether in a hotel, hospital, school, or city street, the chatter of machine-gun fire is the sound of unrest and destruction. It had been a relatively rare occurrence since the tommy guns of Depression-era gangsters. Only recently have the menacing noise and horrid bloodshed returned, courtesy of a small illegal device—shipped en masse from China to the United States—that converts a Glock handgun into a machine gun. "They're coming in in boxes from China, by the thousands, and very hard to stop," said Cook County, Illinois, sheriff Tom Dart.[3]

America is seemingly at war with itself, with violence, social division, and the resulting chaos on the rise. But there are important accelerants that are helping to turn sparks into an inferno. The Chinese strategy of unrestricted warfare involves using unconventional methods to weaken the United States, including, as we saw in Part I, drug warfare. But unrestricted warfare also involves undermining a country's "national will, values, and cohesion."[4] The ability to destabilize a rival country from within is a powerful weapon. This strategy—"Watch a fire from across the river"—has deep roots in Chinese history.[5] More recently, the Chinese government has adopted a strategy of wearing down its enemies from within by exploiting existing disagreements and divisions. This shocking notion has been well established by the Communist leadership. In 2013, a book produced by the Chinese military called *The Science of Military Strategy* noted that good strategy includes going after an enemy's "'soft underbelly' in terms of politics, economics, and the spirit and psychology of his people."[6]

Beijing actively works from "across the river" to exacerbate social chaos and violence in our country. Our leaders often appear completely oblivious to this intentional strategy. Let's begin by looking at how China is putting illegal weapons into the hands of felons and criminal gangs across the United States.

The gadgets started arriving in the United States in large quantities in 2018—packages containing small metal squares about the size of a penny. But these small devices have an outsize effect: they convert standard Glock handguns into fully automatic weapons capable of firing twenty rounds per second. It's an ingenious if horrific strategy: a small, inexpensively manufactured apparatus married to a handgun that is plentiful and legal, turning it into a potent, illegal machine gun. Auto sear switches, or Glock switches, as they are called, are illegal in the United States except for use by law enforcement personnel and a select group of others who must obtain a federal license requiring an extensive criminal background check. As a result, criminals in the United States looking for more firepower purchase them illegally from China.

These small devices, which are also illegal to own in China, are openly produced and advertised on Chinese websites for sale to Americans. Not surprisingly, as with drugs, Beijing has shown little interest in cooperating with US officials to stem the flow. As a result, America's cities increasingly sound like war zones.

In 2019, ShotSpotter, a gunshot detection technology deployed in 130 American cities, detected four hundred total incidents of machine-gun fire. In 2021, the same cities experienced 5,600 incidents—an increase of 4,200 percent. In Minneapolis, there were just five incidents of machine-gun fire in 2020. In 2021, there were seventy-eight—a rise of over 1,400 percent.[7] That same year, a stunning 80 percent of the cities using ShotSpotter experienced automatic gunfire.[8]

Federal officials believe that the proliferation of auto switches is one of the main reasons that mass shootings (those including four or more fatalities) have become more common in Chicago and, by extension, in all American cities.[9]

Though some illegal auto switches are made on 3D printers in the United States, the vast majority on the street are a result of the "flood of the devices into the U.S. market from China," according to the Bureau of Alcohol, Tobacco, Firearms and Explosives (ATF).[10] The metal machine-tooled switches from China are widely recognized as being of much higher quality than the plastic versions made domestically with 3D printers.[11]

In Los Angeles, the LAPD says, the switches on the street are shipped predominantly from China.[12] In 2019, more than two hundred packages containing the devices from China were intercepted at Los Angeles International Airport.[13]

Those looking to purchase the switches from China don't have to look far. You can buy them openly on English-language websites operated by Chinese companies. They advertise "Glock Pistols Select of Switch Full Auto for All Models Glock all Generations." The website Made-in-China, which says it is "connecting buyers with Chinese suppliers," offers switches made by numerous manufacturers, many of which offer bulk discounts.[14] You could, at one point, also find them on China's e-commerce site Alibaba.com, the Amazon of China, and buy them in plain view.[15] Or the companies might mask the device by advertising a switch for an airsoft gun that fires tiny plastic BBs, but the device also works on a real handgun.[16] The advertisements are written in English.

In contrast, Alibaba bans the sale of items "related to sensitive political issues."[17] It demonstrates meticulous control of commerce at China's bidding. Auto sear devices are illegal to sell inside China, and Alibaba certainly complies with that law.

Chinese companies also use US websites to market the switches. One site, Wish.com, is "known for trafficking illegal gun parts," according to a US attorney, has listed Chinese auto sear switches for sale.[18] Some ambitious

Chinese companies have even set up pages on Facebook advertising their product—pages that remain active as of this writing. In Chicago, the Crime Gun Intelligence Center, a joint project of several federal government agencies including the DOJ, identified a website in China, CBTForce .com, that listed the devices for sale. The website has a Facebook page as of this writing in March 2023.[19] The switches can also be found for sale on Instagram, Facebook, and Twitter.[20] The Crime Gun Intelligence Center estimated in 2019 that some 2,500 people in the United States had "acquired one or more" of the switches from just that one Chinese website.[21] Who knows how high that number is now.

As US law enforcement officials have become better at identifying switches arriving through the mail from China, producers in China have switched tactics. Now switches are increasingly shipped to Mexico and then smuggled across the border into the United States, eventually ending up in the hands of gangs, felons, and drug dealers.[22] At the same time, drug cartels in Mexico are starting to manufacture the devices themselves, using machines provided by Chinese companies.[23]

This is a strikingly similar replay of the Chinese government's strategy with fentanyl: when US authorities successfully began blocking shipments sent from China via mail or parcel, Chinese sellers switched to a land bridge in Mexico to continue supplying these devices to criminals in the United States. This is "delivery saturation around the United States," warned the Department of Homeland Security in an internal memo obtained by the author, with a map showing that distribution is concentrated in major cities including Los Angeles, San Francisco, Chicago, Detroit, Miami, Washington, New York, and Philadelphia.[24]

A man in Milwaukee referred to as "Luckyy Rich" on the packaging bought twenty switches from Alibaba.com. "Everybody who is in the streets of Milwaukee is looking to purchase Glock auto-sears to install on their firearms," he told federal officials after he was arrested.[25]

In a suburb south of Chicago, federal agents arrested two men who had 117 of the switches and were selling them. They had imported the switches from China.[26]

In southern Illinois, a teenager was arrested in 2023 for thirty switches he had purchased from China and was apparently intending to sell.[27]

Nicholas Bell of Minneapolis allegedly ordered a package of twenty-one switches from China in the hope of selling them. Fortunately, his package was intercepted by US authorities, and he was arrested and charged.[28]

In Philadelphia, US customs officials intercepted a package with twenty switches made in China.[29]

How is it that a device that is highly illegal in China is openly advertised for sale in English and ends up on our streets, not China's, in large quantities?

"These kind of switches make a whole class of weapons particularly lethal," said former ATF agent David Chipman. "These are really catered to criminal and extremist buyers and owners."[30]

These tiny metal switches, made in China, promise nothing but mayhem on American streets. "We're seeing Glock switches used all over the place," said East Baton Rouge, Louisiana, district attorney Hillar Moore, "whether it's murder, attempted murder, witness intimidation . . . shooting up in a neighborhood or shooting up houses." His office has seen more than eighty cases in the past two years involving switches on guns used to commit crimes.[31]

According to ATF, the number of switches seized by law enforcement officials investigating crimes jumped by a startling "570% during a period of 2017 to 2021, compared to the previous five years."[32]

When the Mongolian Boys Society, an Asian biker gang, decided to shoot up a rival's backyard assembly in Fresno, California, they used a modified, automatic Glock; their act of revenge killed four and wounded six.[33]

Robberies, assaults, and murders are now regularly facilitated by auto sear switches.[34] In an internal 2020 memo, the Miami Police Department warned of "the prevalence of machine guns used in recent shootings," noting "many of these devices are made in China."[35] "Auto sears are everywhere on the street right now," commented Jefferey Boshek, a twenty-one-year ATF veteran. "They're one of the scariest things we've dealt with since I became an agent."[36]

As with the fentanyl trade, when it comes to the illegal weapons and parts trade, the Chinese government appears complicit. Chinese authorities appear to have made little effort to stop online sales. They also seem unmotivated to stop the deceptive production and distribution practices that are used to evade US authorities. The Chinese manufacturers often falsely label the devices as made in Austria by Glock, even though the gun manufacturer has no involvement whatsoever in their illegal production.[37] To ship them to the United States, the Chinese companies obscure the contents of the packages, listing "multitool switches" or "handcrafted finished pieces" on the package.[38] As we saw in relation to fentanyl distribution, falsifying customs forms to sell illegal items to Americans is not a serious crime in China. The penalty is a small fine with no jail time.

By the end of 2020, the ATF had traced some 2,500 people in the United States who had ordered the devices from China.[39] Still, when US officials identify a company in China exporting illegal switches to the United States, the company often simply creates a new website and keeps sending them.[40] US officials have subpoenaed PayPal records to get the buyers' information; Chinese authorities do not cooperate.[41] For this reason, US authorities are focusing on the buyers in the United States, rather than the producers in China.[42]

Beijing takes advantage of the rising incidence of machine-gun fire on American streets, which it helped create, to promote America's cultural decline. China's official news agency publishes stories about the rise of illegal machine guns in the United States thanks to auto sear switches. But the articles fail to mention the key fact that the switches originate in China and are deceptively shipped here.[43] For example, in a piece published in November 2022, the Chinese government news agency reported that in Chicago the switches were fueling "deadly violence" in the Windy City and that machine-gun fire was becoming common, without making any connection to the Chinese role in the problem.[44]

Auto sear switches are not the only weapons-enhancing technologies that China is clandestinely exporting to the United States. Another highly regulated technology, the firearm suppressor (aka silencer), is being smuggled into the United States as well. According to federal authorities, beginning in 2019, there was a "huge influx" of illegal suppressors being shipped to the United States from China. Owning a suppressor, if it is legal in your state, requires a federal license. As with firearms, felons cannot legally own them. But these clandestinely imported Chinese suppressors enabled criminal gangs and drug cartels in America to get around those requirements and buy them in large quantities. And over the next three years, federal officials traced an astonishing 42,888 suppressors arriving from China.[45] Those were only the devices they traced. How many more got through?

As with the auto sears, Chinese suppliers have openly advertised their products—in English—on websites hosted on Chinese servers. They even advertise them on Alibaba.[46] Again, there is no real Chinese market for them since possession of a firearm or a suppressor is strictly illegal in China. To ship them to US customers, Chinese suppliers obscure the contents of the packages. "They're labeled as machine parts," said Robert Hammer, the special agent in charge of the Seattle field office of Homeland Security Investigations. "They're labeled as metal tubes. They're labeled as cans. But never have they been labeled as a firearm silencer."[47]

Suppressors can be very helpful for a criminal enterprise, diminishing noise and limiting gun recoil. Drug traffickers, extremists, and violent gangs eagerly seek them. So they end up in the hands of felons such as Allen Seamster in Utah, who obtained a suppressor from China. When authorities raided his home, they found the suppressor, illegal firearms, and methamphetamines.[48] Drug dealers in San Francisco have bought suppressors as well.[49]

* * *

In June 2020, with violent protests on the rise, cities such as Louisville, Kentucky, were on edge. As events began to unfold, federal officials announced that "10,800 assault weapons parts" that had been sent illegally from Shenzhen, China, had been seized by customs officials.

It was not the first time. In 2019, officials at the Long Beach Seaport in California uncovered some 53,000 illegal gun parts in three separate shipments from China. In 2018, according to US Customs and Border Protection (CBP), it had seized thirty-one illegal gun parts shipments from China. In 2019, that number rose to seventy-eight. In 2020, it seized 5,300 illicit gun parts shipments.[50]

What exactly is going on?

To those who track such matters, the events were highly disturbing but also not surprising. Beijing has a long history of engaging in questionable gun sales around the world to nefarious "regimes and nonstate actors."[51] US government officials have often complained that China does not provide information that will enable officials to track the flow of Chinese arms globally, something that other countries such as the United States provide regularly.[52] Likewise, China has on numerous occasions tried to smuggle weapons illegally into the United States and Canada. The intended recipients were criminal gangs in America and separatist groups in Canada.

In 1992, Tommy Fok, the son of Henry Fok, was arrested for trying to smuggle fifteen thousand AK-47s into the United States. After pleading guilty and spending eighteen months in jail awaiting trial, he was released with time served and returned to Hong Kong.[53] In 1996, the Chinese companies Norinco and Poly Technologies tried to smuggle two thousand fully automatic machine guns into the Port of Oakland, California. The weapons were seized by US officials and became the largest seizure of machine guns in US history. Poly was controlled by the children of some of Beijing's most powerful leaders, and the guns had likely been shipped by the Chinese state-owned shipping company. Senior executives in the companies were implicated and charged by the US Justice Department. The leadership of the company seemed to embrace the attempted sale. Chinese executives knew that the guns were going to be used by criminal gangs and extremist groups in the United States—but they didn't care. As the US attorney in California put it, the act was a direct challenge to "the sovereignty of the United States."[54]

The Clinton administration seemed to shrug off the provocative act, perhaps eager for closer ties and the commercial deals that would follow. "I don't see why this needs to complicate U.S.-China relations at all," declared State Department spokesperson Nicholas Burns.[55]

In the 1990s, Canadian authorities confiscated "large quantities" of Chinese-made AK-47s that had ended up in the hands of militant Native tribes, especially the Mohawks. Norinco was once again the manufacturer.[56]

The Chinese Communist government strictly controls the production of gun parts.[57] Yet, as previously mentioned, US officials have had a hard time getting Chinese officials to shut down the manufacturers that are illegally exporting gun parts to the United States. Though there are international agreements in place to trace individual firearms, China does not generally participate in them, and US leaders have largely given them a pass. As Dr. Ted R. Bromund of the Heritage Foundation reported, "China even managed to work into the international tracing agreement a loophole that exempts it from putting serial numbers on its firearms." He added, "When U.N.-appointed experts report uncomfortable facts about China's arms trafficking, China gets them fired."[58]

The influx of auto sear switches, suppressors, and weapons parts from China continues. In just the first quarter of 2023, officials seized 106 illegal suppressors at Dallas Fort Worth International Airport alone.[59] In December 2022, US officials in Michigan indicted seven men for procuring switches from China. "These devices are an emerging threat to our communities, our children, our law enforcement officers, and anyone who stands in the path of their indiscriminate spray," said US attorney Mark Totten.[60] In 2022, the ATF announced a 500 percent increase in the confiscation of auto sear switches around the country. Cities such as St. Louis continued to devolve into war zones. In 2021, the ATF reported 66 incidents of full auto gunfire. The next year, there were 339. Well over a third occurred in St. Louis County.[61]

What are our leaders doing to counter this? The answer is: nothing.

No American president appears to have brought this up with Beijing in his consultations with President Xi. President Biden has pressed for gun restrictions on ordinary Americans but has never publicly discussed this problem, where criminal elements are gaining access to machine guns courtesy of Chinese manufacturers' illegal shipments.

But the problem is not just in the White House. "With two of the top six busiest cargo airports in the country, Kentucky is on the frontlines in the fight against illegal 'Glock switches,'" reported WHAS-TV in Louisville. Many of the devices are shipped through those cargo airports and distributed throughout the United States. But they stay in Kentucky, too. In 2022, ATF reported an 800 percent increase in the devices found in the Bluegrass State compared to 2021.[62] Who knows how many others went undetected?

Yet Senator McConnell, who lives part-time in Louisville, has been silent on the subject. Holding China to account, exposing and denouncing its conduct, should be expected, but he has so far done none of those things.

On the rare occasion when American politicians have brought up the switches, they don't mention China's culpability or demand any accountability from Beijing. In 2021, senators Amy Klobuchar and Cory

Booker wrote to Attorney General Merrick Garland to express their concerns about the devices. Did they ask to confront China to stop their clandestine flow into American cities? Did they call out the CCP for its conduct? They asked only that the DOJ "take immediate action to work with local law enforcement to prevent the use and proliferation of these devices," which was already happening. Though China's role as a supplier was noted, there was no mention of holding Beijing to account—or taking any action in response.[63]

When eleven senators introduced a bill to tighten the already tight restrictions on owning the device in the United States, there was no recourse or action proposed toward China. The bill simply recommended that the DOJ develop a strategy to deal with the explosion in the number of devices. They are already strictly illegal; the source of the problem is their production in China and distribution in the United States.[64]

In 2022, fourteen US states announced that they were backing a Mexican government lawsuit against American gunmakers. The lawsuit alleged that the gun manufacturers were spurring violent crime in Mexico—even though the lawsuit presented no evidence that the gun manufacturers were shipping guns illegally or that laws were being broken.[65] Yet none of these states has publicly taken China to task for trafficking illegal weapons technologies that are falling into the hands of criminal gangs operating in the United States. US political leaders are more focused on going after American gun manufacturers producing a legal product for millions of Americans than cracking down on Chinese companies catering to and further weaponizing criminal gangs in the United States.

Gun control advocates focus their attention on taking away semi-automatic "assault rifles" from law-abiding citizens—supposedly to control crime. But they have been silent about China's providing felons and criminal gangs with illegal devices that transform ordinary pistols into automatic weapons. Perhaps there is little political value in raising this issue, but it would seem to be a place where gun control advocates and Second Amendment advocates could find common ground. The question is, why does no one in Washington seem to care?

President Biden has confronted China about Chinese weapons killing Ukrainians. During a video conference call with President Xi in 2022, Biden had said: "I'm not threatening you. But if Chinese weapons are killing Ukrainians—or China is trying to unravel sanctions, the consequences for your relations with us, and the Europeans, not just with the governments but with the private sector, are going to be profound. You don't want to do this." But one must ask: Why has Biden never issued such a warning over fentanyl, or over weapons enhancements illegally shipped into the United States from China—both of which are killing Americans?[66]

Imagine if the roles were reversed: if China were being inundated with American-made products that were creating carnage in cities across the country. What if the devices were being sold openly on American ecommerce websites and shipped with deceptive labeling to felons and criminal gangs in China? And all the while, Washington was doing little to stem the flow. Would Beijing simply treat it as a "local law enforcement" issue? Would Chinese leaders be silent when meeting with US officials? Would they be silent in the media? More likely, they would aggressively challenge the US government about its conduct. If this were true, one must ask: Why would China's leaders be more willing to stand up *to* America than our leaders are willing to stand up to them *for* America?

As with drug warfare, Beijing justifies inciting US civil unrest in general with the narrative of China's own "Century of Humiliation." In the nineteenth and early twentieth centuries, its propagandists argue, Western powers weakened the country by supporting factions, arming various groups, and paying off corrupt officials.[67] As the historian Piers Brendon observes, the Century of Humiliation "is a period etched in acid on the pages of Chinese student textbooks today."[68] In the same way that it flipped the Opium Wars of the nineteenth century and created the Fentanyl Wars of the twenty-first century, Beijing now works to create a Century of Humiliation and weaken the United States by fomenting division by putting weapon-enhancing technologies into the hands of felons and criminal gangs, but also fueling social division on US streets. The Chinese Communist Party is also aggressively trying to tear Americans further apart by fueling division in cyberspace, as we shall see next.

CHAPTER 5

Magnifying Social Chaos

Black smoke curled upward from a brick building in downtown Houston, Texas, dispersing into the hot July sky. Chinese diplomats were burning documents in the building's courtyard. When the Houston Fire Department arrived to douse the flames, the firefighters were denied entry.

Just a day earlier, the Chinese consulate on Montrose Boulevard had been ordered to close by the US State Department for activities involving espionage and theft of intellectual property.[1] But that was not all; members of an elite People's Liberation Army unit based at the consulate had been recruiting and radicalizing Americans under the guise of promoting the Black Lives Matter protests and riots that had engulfed the country.[2]

The callous killing of George Floyd by police officer Derek Chauvin on May 25, 2020, near Minneapolis, Minnesota, sparked peaceful protests against police brutality and involved hundreds of thousands of earnest Americans nationwide. But violent riots also ensued, justified by the idea that the United States is fundamentally flawed and institutionally racist. A 2020 Chinese military report obtained by the author reveals that Beijing sees our mounting social chaos and division as a national weakness, noting that "the intensifying political rivalry is depleting the energy of the U.S."[3]

During the summer of 2020, America was ablaze. From the end of May through late July, there were 574 riots, 624 confirmed acts of arson, 97 police vehicles set on fire, more than 2,300 incidents of looting, 28 deaths, and more than 16,000 people arrested for crimes associated with protests. More than two thousand cops were injured in the rioting. In all, thirteen police officers were shot, and nine were struck by cars.[4]

Though the violent protests of 2020 are now history, the Chinese campaign to sow violent division in the interest of precipitating American decline remains very much alive and active. Beijing's agents, both Chinese military officers and members of American extremist groups that pledge allegiance to the CCP, have actively worked to promote racial division, civil unrest, and violence in America—online and in the streets.

Racial diversity is one of America's greatest strengths and a hallmark of American exceptionalism. Perhaps this is why Beijing is so intent on subverting racial harmony. When the Chinese military updated the "PLA Political Work Regulations" in 2003, they included "Three Warfares" to be used: "Public Opinion Warfare, Psychological Warfare, and Legal Warfare."[5] The Three Warfares speak to a strategy of destroying enemies from within by exploiting their problems and steering unrest within rival countries during peacetime. This is targeting the "soft underbelly" of America.

The CCP strategy of exploiting race relations is not new, even as the specific tactics have changed with technology. During the 1960s, the American civil rights movement peacefully brought together millions of Americans seeking to dismantle corrupt, discriminatory laws and practices and bring about racial reconciliation. But there were also far more radical, militant elements involved in the national debate about race relations, including the Black Panther Party. The Panthers were not reformers; they were revolutionaries. And Communist China saw them as potent allies who could further divide the United States and serve as a "revolutionary force."

For Black Panther Party leaders such as Huey P. Newton, Communist China was their ideological home, a place they believed best represented their political ambitions. It was, after all, Chinese communism that had radicalized them. "My conversion was complete when I read the four volumes of Mao Tse-Tung to learn more about the Chinese Revolution," Newton wrote.[6]

Newton and others made pilgrimages to Communist China, where they were greeted and encouraged by high-ranking Communist Party officials. They were energized by the Communist country—even if the bloody Cultural Revolution was still going on. "Everything I saw in

China demonstrated that the People's Republic is a free and liberated territory with a socialist government," Newton wrote, apparently missing the mass incarcerations, arrests, and killing of political opponents taking place around him. Beijing even offered him political asylum during the visit. He politely declined.[7]

For Mao, an alliance with American black radicals made strategic sense. "We should support whatever the enemy opposes and oppose whatever the enemy supports," he said, as a core strategic principle.[8]

In 1968, after the assassination of Martin Luther King, Jr., the CCP organized a protest in China, and Mao issued "a new clarion call to all the exploited and oppressed people of the United States to fight against the barbarous rule of the monopoly capitalist class."[9] Never mind that the CCP was far more aggressively oppressing its own people, minority groups especially, in its own country.

"China's support for the black liberation struggle precedes BLM; and is rooted in the revolutionary internationalism of its founder, Mao Zedong," wrote the academic Joe Pateman, who is sympathetic to both black radical movements and the Chinese government. Mao "provided theoretical guidance for several radical black liberation movements and figures in the USA, especially from the 1950s to early 1970s." Mao made several statements in support of African American revolutionaries, and that spirit remains among some of the Beijing elite. In his "Statement Supporting the American Negroes in Their Just Struggle Against Racial Discrimination by US Imperialism," he railed against the imperialist system. He explained that black Americans had a hard time voting. Never mind that there is no real free voting in China.[10]

Mao clearly saw racial division in the United States as an opportunity to gain a foothold of power against Washington. "The speedy development of the struggle of the American Negroes is a manifestation of sharpening class struggle and sharpening national struggle within the United States," he declared.[11] On another occasion he called the black community "an extremely powerful revolutionary force," intimating the potential for it to be deployed for the benefit of Beijing.[12]

After Mao's death in 1976, the Chinese leadership became less vocal in support of US radical black movements. That was partly because the black radical movement itself was in decline and partly because Beijing's priorities toward the United States started to shift. Beijing was eager to strike deals with the United States to boost China's prosperity. Even in economic cooperation, however, the Chinese never lost focus on political rivalry. Deng Xiaoping, the reformist leader who took over after Mao, told his colleagues that it was a good strategy to "hide your strength, bide your time."[13]

The time came in 2013, when a series of high-profile cases, including the deaths of Trayvon Martin in Florida and Michael Brown in Ferguson, Missouri, triggered widespread protests and rioting. As millions of Americans sat glued to their TV screens and watched the protests and violence unfold, many assumed that, in each case, the people they were seeing were local activists. In fact, though Black Lives Matter (BLM), named after the #BlackLivesMatter movement that followed Martin's death, is the organization that gets most of the media attention, activists with pro-Beijing ties did much of the heavy lifting for the violent protests that erupted.

One of the key organizers of protests in Ferguson was Montague Simmons, the leader of the Organization for Black Struggle (OBS) in St. Louis, twenty miles southeast of Ferguson. However, he later confessed that many of the people in the streets of Ferguson had not been Missouri locals; they had been brought in from out of town. As he explained during a presentation in New York, some ten thousand out-of-state activists had been brought in to participate in protests.[14] Simmons also had some other interesting ties; in addition to being involved with OBS, he was reportedly a member of Liberation Road, an offshoot of a secretive pro-Beijing organization called Freedom Road Socialist Organization (FRSO).[15] The left-wing author Max Elbaum wrote a definitive history of the radical movement. In it, he acknowledged that FRSO has a long history of taking "their cues from Beijing."[16]

FRSO has a tight organizational structure designed to maintain both control and secrecy. "Small Units" of three to seven people meet every week. "Districts" incorporate areas involving numerous Small Units; Districts meet once a month. A national governing board maintains discipline and charts the organization's focus.[17] In 2010, the FBI raided the homes of several FRSO leaders on allegations that they were providing "material support for terrorism." Charges were never filed.[18]

Beginning with Ferguson, FRSO activists played an important role in the next half decade in pushing protests toward violence. More moderate protest leaders, perhaps needing their energy, never called them out for their ties to Beijing. Instead, they readily accepted them as good-hearted comrades in arms.

Spontaneous large protests are a rarity. While a single brutal event might serve as a catalyst of people's anger, large protests generally require organization, leadership, and planning. People need to know when and where to show up for a mass gathering to gain traction—and, in the twenty-first century, media coverage has to be arranged.

Veteran organizers such as Brian Becker stoked the flames to try to make the protests more militant. Becker, the national director of something called the ANSWER Coalition, is also a member of another secretive Beijing-tied group called the Party for Socialism and Liberation (PSL). Becker cast what was happening in Ferguson as a "rebellion" not just a protest.[19] And PSL activists would play an important role in organizing protests that became violent over the next half decade.

In Ferguson, PSL was also on the streets, distributing flyers proclaiming "There can be no peace with this system! . . . The Party for Socialism and Liberation stands with those in the streets—they have every right to rebel. . . . the system is criminal . . . The cops are the real gangs."[20]

In 2007, Becker had demanded that activists recognize that "it is the responsibility of all revolutionaries and progressive people to resist the imperialist offensive and offer *militant political defense of the Chinese government.*"[21]

As Becker led numerous protests in the United States condemning police brutality, he simultaneously defended China's police brutality ("on steroids"). In 1989, the Chinese military and police gunned down thousands of peaceful protestors in what became known as the Tiananmen Square Massacre. Becker called it "the massacre that wasn't" and vigorously defended the regime's brutal conduct.[22]

Communist Chinese propaganda has highlighted Becker and his work. In one interview with Global Times headlined "China's Socialist Goals a Source of Inspiration to Those Who Seek a Humanist Alternative: Anti-War Socialist," Becker is quoted as declaring his deep admiration for Beijing.[23] Indeed, when he was not leading violent protests in the United States on racial matters, Becker appeared on Chinese stated-owned media criticizing the United States and defending the Chinese regime. The

US military buildup constituted a threat, he said. But when Beijing builds up its military, it is a purely defensive matter.[24]

Carl Dix is an East Coast radical who descended on Ferguson to connect the struggle to the bigger picture—in his mind—of police brutality reaching "genocidal proportions" in America.[25] Dix, a cofounder and spokesman of the Revolutionary Communist Party, went to distribute fliers, calling the police officer involved in the shooting a "murdering pig" and encouraging mass civil disobedience, refusing to condemn protestors who had thrown bottles at the police. At one point, he was arrested.[26] He, too, was quoted in Chinese state media.[27]

Dix is what one might call a professional protestor. He later moved on to organize a series of protests in New York City and led a march to Rikers Island, a jail holding many maximum-security prisoners, demanding that the facility be closed down.[28] In celebration of Mao's hundredth birthday, Dix recalled that he had been inspired to join the movement by the examples of Mao and the Black Panthers.[29]

Beijing seized the opportunity to criticize the United States after the Ferguson riots erupted, arguing that racism in the United States was common and American culture was in decline. *China Daily* opined that it was "often shocking for foreign visitors to walk into a community or a public school in the US and feel that racial segregation, which is illegal, still exists somehow in reality."[30]

China's State Council Information Office, a propaganda unit within the PRC, annually publishes a "Chronology of Human Rights Violations of the United States." In the 2016 version of its also annual corollary, "Human Rights Record of the United States," it claimed that there was "worsening racial discrimination" in the United States and that clashes between the police and black suspects "were reminiscent of the past racial terror of lynching."[31] Incidents of racial discrimination were not uncommon, the Chinese government said. In fact, "racial discrimination is normal in the US" and "a permanent part of the American landscape."[32] This from the regime whose treatment of the Uyghur population has been called "crimes against humanity and possibly genocide."[33]

"Under the leadership of the Communist Party of China," wrote Joe Pateman, "the Chinese state has displayed unwavering solidarity with BLM, by giving the movement extensive coverage and support in its official media and government statements."[34] Given its own egregious human rights record, Beijing's interest in the struggles of Black Americans is not humanitarian, and it is certainly not to encourage reconciliation. Beijing sees American racial division as an opportunity to insert its influence and magnify the damage it causes. During that tumult, it saw the opportunity arise again. While the ashes of the Ferguson riots were still warm, Beijing was learning how to shape the public debate in the United States by organizing and steering protest movements. To see the pattern, it helps to consider how it has played other race cards.

In 2016, tens of thousands of Chinese Americans took to the streets in cities across America to protest the arrest and conviction of Peter Liang, a Chinese American NYPD officer who had become involved in the accidental shooting death of Akai Gurley when a bullet ricocheted off a wall. He was charged with manslaughter. Activists in the Asian American community began holding events, claiming that his arrest was an example of discrimination against Asians and alleging that he was being treated more harshly than a white police officer would be in a similar situation. Though many of the organizers were simply concerned Americans, Beijing's hidden hand of influence may have lurked in the shadows. While many organizers dismissed perceived media suspicions that the campaign had "Chinese liaisons," other organizers grew to believe "that some activists were bribed by the Chinese government to co-opt the campaign."[35]

One organizer based in California named Sidney established himself as the "*de facto* General Director" of the campaign. But soon concerns emerged "that his activities were backed by China." In Asian-American online group chats it was charged that "the initiator of the Liang campaign was invited by the Chinese Embassy to have dumplings." Sidney denounced the claims as "absurd," but was ultimately removed from the leadership to prevent him "and other self-appointed leaders from being used as the conduit to channel in the Chinese state's agenda."[36]

Two years later, in 2018, six to eight thousand Chinese students held a massive counterprotest in San Francisco. It turned out to be an organized propaganda stunt. They had been bussed into the city by Chinese intelligence officers likely working out of the PRC's consulate in San Francisco. They arrived to disrupt pro-democracy and anti-CCP rallies that had been organized by Tibetans, Uyghurs, and others.[37]

* * *

The night after the world saw the nine-minute George Floyd arrest video, a crowd descended on the police precinct where the officer had worked. The precinct was vandalized, along with dozens of other buildings. Over the next three days, the precinct was set ablaze, and hundreds of businesses were looted and burned throughout the Minneapolis metropolitan area.[38] In an awful confluence of Chinese influence, George Floyd had both fentanyl—and the covid virus—in his system at the time of his death.[39]

Over the ensuing weeks and into the summer, Americans around the country came together to protest what they had witnessed. But there were also organized efforts by radical groups to turn the protests violent. The secretive, Beijing-tied FRSO and PSL played important roles in lighting the fuse. There was also an extensive online campaign executed directly from China to heighten emotions and anger.

Less than a year earlier, in October 2019, FRSO had celebrated the seventieth anniversary of the victory of the Chinese revolution. To FRSO, the revolution meant that the Chinese people had "embarked on one of the most wondrous processes of social transformation ever known, creating a socialism with Chinese characteristics. In doing so they have changed the world as they have transformed China." FRSO officially declared that the "'American Century' . . . is over now." The future was Beijing. "Long Live the Peoples Republic of China!"[40]

The goal in the summer of 2020 was not just protest but violence and property destruction—with Chinese characteristics. As Jess Sundin, the wife of FRSO political secretary Steff Yorek, explained just weeks after the Minneapolis protests began, "I want to be absolutely clear as an organizer—what I did most of the last three weeks was organize rallies . . . and marches—those night demonstrations, the emptying of the Police Department, the emptying of Target and other majors stores . . . is absolutely tied to, connected to, and part of the movement." She denied that the violence had been started by Antifa or other anarchists. It was instead organic to their protest. She was particularly pleased about the burning of the police station: "I can't tell you the joy it brought all of us to see the Third Precinct destroyed."[41]

The world joined Beijing in watching the "fire burning from across the river."[42] As its members incited violence, destruction, and division in US cities, it is no coincidence that FRSO was also lauding Beijing. "The Communist Party of China was founded with around 50 members," it tweeted on July 1, 2020. "Through decades of struggle the Party led the revolution to victory in 1949. Today the Party leads the People's Republic of China in building socialism."[43]

Mick Kelly, a Minneapolis-based leader of FRSO with responsibility for its "international relations," echoed Beijing's refrain that American culture is in decline and the People's Republic of China is ascendant.[44] "Quite a few leaders of Freedom Road Socialist Organization have traveled to China, some many decades ago, and we look forward to building a closer relationship with the CPC [Communist Party of China]," he explained in an essay commemorating the hundred-year anniversary of the CCP. His essay was published by the government's publishing house and included in a collection titled *A Century of the Communist Party of China, Statements from 100 Foreign Communists*. "Marxism-Leninism has done great things for the people of China," he wrote. "It will do the same for the American people."[45]

In China, party officials watch closely when social protests and riots take place in the United States, and they specifically track the role that FRSO plays. The Center for Marxist Parties in Foreign Countries of CCNU is a Wuhan-based organization that serves as an intelligence service for the CCP on events overseas and regularly reports on those involving allied movements and parties. The organization reported on its Chinese-language website that "Research members of the center provide dozens of research reports on the development of the international Communist movement to the General Office of the Central Committee of the Communist Party of China and the International Liaison Department of the Central Committee of the Communist Party of China." (Author's translation.) These details were omitted from the English-language website.[46] The center regularly monitors FRSO's activities. For example, the center claimed in a report that in the summer of 2020 FRSO became an umbrella for dozens of unorganized groups, including BLM.[47] The center tracks and reports approvingly on FRSO activities to party officials in Beijing.[48]

FRSO pledges its support for the Chinese Communist Party. "Dear

Comrades," begins a message FRSO sent to the CCP in 2022 at the Twentieth National Congress of the Communist Party of China.

> Freedom Road Socialist Organization congratulates the leadership of the Communist Party of China, with Comrade Xi Jinping at its core, for the great successes achieved at the 20th National Congress. . . .
>
> Socialist China is an example to oppressed people everywhere who yearn for a better future. Again, congratulations on a successful 20th Congress. The CPC is truly a great political party that has proven its ability to do great things.
>
> Long live the Communist Party of China!
>
> Long live the unity between the people of China and the people of the U.S.!
>
> With fraternal greetings.[49]

The violent protest model FRSO employed in Minneapolis was copied across the country. A little more than a week later, by June 8, an estimated $2 billion in property damage had been caused across the country, at least 96,000 members of the National Guard had been mobilized in thirty-four states, and two hundred cities had curfews in place.[50] Some of the violence was spontaneous. But many of the violent protests included members of FRSO and PSL activists. And those radical Beijing-linked groups were just getting started.

In Jacksonville, Florida, protests became violent in late May, when police and first responder vehicles were attacked, and dozens of violent protesters were arrested. The chief of police declared it "a riot."[51] On June 6, a large crowd started gathering in the city in what was dubbed "one of the largest civil rights protests in Jacksonville history." Certainly, most people attending wanted a peaceful protest, but a previous protest had turned violent. The Jacksonville Community Action Committee had been founded and was run by an activist named Michael Sampson. Sampson was also a member of FRSO.[52]

When rioting engulfed Kenosha, Wisconsin, in August 2020, FRSO was there, too, leading protests. The group even has a chapter there.[53]

It was the organized nature of so many of the protests that aroused suspicion. Anonymous flyers appeared around the country in places such as Rhode Island, encouraging people to engage in violent criminal activity because of the George Floyd killing. Rhode Island State Police colonel James Manni said that the FBI was trying to determine "whether it was someone from outside Rhode Island or whether it was a foreign government." "Given the way it played out, it's hard to believe it was not organized," said Providence mayor Jorge Elorza.[54]

***

FRSO was not the only pro-Beijing group behind protest violence during the summer of 2020. Just four days after the death of George Floyd, three groups in San Francisco, Boston, and New York, all sharing the name "Chinese Progressive Association" (CPA), joined the call to protest, signing onto an open letter that told Chinese Americans to resist "assimilation into whiteness." "In this painful moment, we ask our Asian communities to choose our shared liberation," the letter said.[55] When it came to the protests growing in 2020, CPA San Francisco leaders called for solidarity with protestors, arguing that the US "police system" was "unjust" and racial minorities needed to stick together.[56]

According to renowned Australian academic and author Clive Hamilton and Mareike Ohlberg of the German Marshall Fund, in their international bestseller, *Hidden Hand*, the CPA is "known to be a united front group."[57] CPA San Francisco, like the other CPA groups, was set up as "left wing and somewhat militant" and Maoist in its orientation.[58] They have sent delegations to Beijing and generally toe the line.[59]

It is impossible to quantify exactly how many of the violent protests were due to the influence of CCP-linked groups. But it is clear that these Beijing-aligned groups and the CCP were cheering them on. The People's Republic of China "has a distinctive system that blurs the lines between classical espionage, clandestine operations, and influence-seeking."[60] The United Front is a government-run umbrella organization that steers other organizations to advance the interests of the CCP around the world. As we will see, some United Front groups played an important role in stirring up protests in the United States in 2020 and to this day. President Xi calls these groups "magic weapon[s]" that will help Beijing achieve global superiority. "We must consolidate and develop the most extensive patriotic united front . . . and maximize all forces that can be united," he explained in a speech at the Nineteenth Party Congress.[61]

CPA San Francisco's leadership also has ties to other Marxist organizations. Michelle Foy, who is the finance and administration director at CPA San Francisco, is also a member of Liberation Road.

The CPA has forged ties with the Chinese Communist government while at the same time hiding its ideological leanings from the American public. CPA San Francisco leader Alex Tom organized programs to bring progressives in the United States closer to China. "We built relationships with people in the [Communist] Party," Tom recalled. A key ally in his work was the Chinese government's Ministry of Education. CPA San Francisco leaders also traveled to China, apparently at the government's expense.[62]

Alex Tom is more open than other CPA leaders about his ties with Beijing. "China has had a very important role in funding left experiments," he said on one occasion. ". . . And we have a relationship with the Chinese Embassy. I've had various conversations with them about our positioning."[63]

Another founder of the CPA was Harry Wong, remembered by friends as a "communist fighter."[64] Wong opened a bookstore in San Francisco called People's China, where he sold Chinese government and CCP literature. He was said to be "a firm believer of Mao and socialist China."[65] Among his most important agenda items was working hard to secure closer ties between Beijing and Washington—a key goal of the CCP.[66] And a major focus of the CPA was establishing "China support," meaning pushing the policy positions of the Chinese government.[67]

When riots erupted in the Twin Cities shortly after George Floyd's death, a Washington, DC, activist leader named Eugene Puryear went to Minnesota to get involved. Puryear was in the middle of things, appearing on Chinese state media and talking about racism in America.[68]

Puryear had been organizing protests in Washington, DC, for years. He gained some fame in the movement when, in 2015, he confronted DC mayor Muriel Bowser over her plan to hire more police officers. What Bowser had thought would be a simple press conference turned into a spirited argument, "intermixed with Black Lives Matter chants" led by Puryear and his team.[69] After the riots in Ferguson, Puryear helped form a group called #DCFerguson.[70]

Puryear is also a leader in the previously mentioned PSL.

From Minneapolis, Puryear headed to Philadelphia. Before a "massive crowd" there, he declared, "This isn't a riot. It's an uprising! It's a rebellion! And successful uprisings and rebellions become REVOLUTIONS." He stoked the narrative of oppression with comments such as "The cops draw their lineage from the slave patrols," and he encouraged the crowd to "stay in the streets and make this country ungovernable."[71] It was "Three Warfares" messaging in its purest form.

Protesters organized by PSL at one point shut down a major road in Philadelphia. "No good pig in a racist system!" they chanted. "All power to the people! All power to the people! No power to the pig! No power to the pig!"[72] Puryear later traveled the country speaking to (and on behalf of) BLM groups.[73]

Allegiance to the Chinese regime, not improving the lives of actual people, seems to motivate his rhetoric. When he is not denouncing hopelessly racist America, Puryear speaks and writes of the glories of the CCP. He authored a book called *Shackled and Chained: Mass Incarceration in Capitalist America*. In it, he condemned what he regards as widespread police brutality in the United States.[74] And brutality in Communist China? He has a strangely different view about police brutality there. When the Chinese military and police descended on Tiananmen Square in 1989 and slaughtered thousands of civilians? That mass brutality was justified because those peaceful protesters were "a counterrevolutionary effort."[75]

On his podcast, Puryear often pairs American racism with the predictable CCP narrative of America's inevitable cultural decline. He dedicated one episode to addressing "Why China Will Win: Capitalism Inherently Collapses."[76] Criticisms of China's human rights record, Puryear argues, are "warmongering propaganda."[77]

Many radical activists who do not express public support of communist China are still products of Beijing's influence on America's streets. As Professors M. L. R. Smith and David Martin Jones from the prestigious Department of War Studies at King's College in London noted, many of these activists are fueled by Maoist ideas, which provided "the ideological wellsprings that have inspired the growth of cultural warfare in the West." With riots and violence, they noted "Maoism's most fruitful influence in the West consists in its cultural and intellectual bearing on activists who do not necessarily appreciate or have any deep understanding of Mao or Maoism, but see themselves as progressive anti-imperialists, or emancipatory social justice or human rights warriors."[78]

* * *

Whereas hundreds of thousands of Americans protested peacefully during the summer of 2020, Beijing-tied groups were among those looking for violent action. On July 3, 2020, a mob of six hundred people descended on a Denver-area police station. The protest had been organized by members of the pro-Beijing PSL. They surrounded the Aurora Police Department's District 1 station and barricaded it for more than seven hours, preventing officers from leaving. Four PSL members were arrested and charged with inciting and engaging in a riot. The charges were later dropped by prosecutors.[79]

Weeks later, when locals in Denver put together a pro-police rally, PSL members showed up to disrupt the event. The PSL mob first chanted loudly—and then violence ensued. PSL's Lillian House defended their conduct, saying that "most demonstrators did not engage in violence" and that "the majority of the crowd was simply making noise." Nick Rogers, the president of the Denver Police Protective Association, observed that the violence had been so bad that a Denver SWAT lieutenant believed that people might have been killed had the police not been present.[80]

In China, officials were watching the proverbial fire burn from across the river—a fire they were surreptitiously stoking with hopes of building an inferno. Officials at the Center for Marxist Parties in Foreign Countries of CCNU were monitoring and reporting on the activities of the PSL in Denver and sharing that information with senior party officials.[81] They track the organization regularly.

In October 2020, when locals in Denver had a rally in opposition to "BLM, Antifa and related Marxist associations," leftists held a "BLM-Antifa Soup Drive," where, some speculate, soup cans were hurled as weaponry. In a previous clash at a pro-police rally, PSL members had reportedly attacked rallygoers and even struck one event organizer with a skateboard.[82]

PSL was also "behind some of the largest demonstrations" in Philadelphia, according to the *Philadelphia Inquirer*. PSL organizers did not want reform; instead, they demanded that the police department be abolished. "How do you reform a system that is broken?" PSL organizer Mecca Bullock asked the crowd.[83]

Though the *Philadelphia Inquirer* described the role that PSL was playing in organizing violent protests, it failed to inform its readers about PSL's close ties to Beijing or the organization's defense of more extensive and widespread police brutality in China.

In Boston, a large crowd gathered to protest the death of a woman at the hands of the police. Leaders of the PSL pushed it further, calling the police "pigs" and leading the crowd of hundreds in chanting "No good cop in a racist system."[84] Boston-area newspapers breathlessly covered the event. Again, as with the other news outlets reporting on events organized by the PSL, they never informed their readers about the group's foreign sympathies.[85]

In Madison, Wisconsin, PSL leaders called for the release of all inmates from Dane County Jail and organized "phone and email campaigns to pressure local officials."[86] They had earlier demanded that the city "abolish policing structures." When rioters smashed businesses and looted them that summer, a local PSL leader defended them. According to PSL leader Sawyer Johnson, the destruction and theft were "rooted in grief and anger and pain and hundreds of years of oppression." He added, in words that echoed those of Puryear and others around the country, "These young folks are not rioting; they are leaders of an uprising. They are the leaders of a rebellion."[87]

There was an organized protest at the home of the local prosecutor, who was handling a case involving several looters. Protesters with a generator and speakers used a bullhorn to harass and call him "racist" in a clear effort at intimidation. Johnson had earlier called those same two looters "Black revolutionary activists."[88]

Even in tiny Westville, Indiana, population just over five thousand, PSL was among groups who organized a protest demanding the release of all inmates from the Westville Correctional Facility.[89]

In Alaska, PSL activists showed up "at most Black Lives Matter protests."[90]

* * *

Though Beijing-aligned left-wing groups clearly contributed their share of chaos on America's streets, Beijing seems to have also planted fire-starters on the Right.

A man arrived in the United States in December 2014 with elite credentials, gobs of money, and a remarkable story to tell.[91]

Guo Wengui, aka Miles Guo, aka Miles Kwok, aka Ho Wan Kwok, said he was fed up with the Communist system and eager to expose vast corruption among the Chinese government elite. Outspoken and brash, the former member of China's aristocracy was now willing to name names while calling for the overthrow of the Chinese Communist Party.

In China, Guo had lived in central Beijing in a lakeside estate worth some $230 million, with a separate barracks for his guards. Dining with Communist Party nobility and building lavish hotels, he had befriended Western dignitaries such as former US secretaries of state Henry Kissinger and George Shultz.[92] Tony Blair, a former prime minister of Great Britain, had been a friend since 2008.[93]

His ties that mattered most, however, were with the much-feared Ministry of State Security (MSS), China's foreign and domestic spy agency. Ma Jian, the vice minister, was his close ally and friend. Guo would later testify in a New York civil trial that he had "worked closely" with the MSS when he lived in China and that the ministry "occupied a whole floor in his hotel," the Beijing Tongzhou.[94]

His financial trajectory in China was straight up—like a rocket—until Vice Minister Ma was arrested on bribery charges, the by-product of a factional dispute with other Chinese officials. Guo then fled to the United States.

He bought a $68 million penthouse in Manhattan's exclusive Sherry-Netherland residential hotel with a panoramic view of Central Park. His letter of introduction to the co-op association had come from Tony Blair. "Miles is honest, forthright and has impeccable taste," Blair wrote to the co-op board.[95] The Chinese government noisily demanded that Guo be returned to China to face corruption, bribery, money-laundering, and even rape charges. Guo denied culpability. The Chinese government often makes such charges against political opponents, whether true or not.[96]

Guo began doing in the United States what he'd done in Beijing: making the right high-level political contacts. In 2017, he joined Mar-a-Lago, President Donald Trump's Florida club,[97] and began making public appearances. When he was scheduled for a press conference at the Hudson Institute in Washington, DC, Chinese Embassy officials tried unsuccessfully to cancel it. There was also a reported cyberattack on Hudson's computer network prior to the event.[98] The storyline—superrich CCP insider switches sides—was irresistible.

At the Hudson event in October 2017, Guo met one of the most powerful and influential voices in American politics: Steve Bannon, the head of the Trump 2016 presidential campaign, who had left his White House post as President Trump's senior strategic advisor just a couple of months earlier.[99] (Full disclosure: Bannon was a cofounder of the organization I now head, the Government Accountability Institute, and served as its chairman from 2012 to 2016.) Bannon continued to voice his public support for Trump and advocated taking a hard line against Beijing.

The two men joined forces. With Guo's money and Bannon's vision, they became involved in an array of media platforms and two non-profits to spread their message, including numerous Guo media channels on YouTube and a myriad of social media accounts. According to leaked contracts, Guo signed Bannon up for at least $1 million per year for "strategic consulting services," beginning in August 2018. Bannon also joined the board of Guo's nonprofits the Rule of Law Society and Rule of Law Foundation.[100]

Bannon himself launched a podcast called *War Room*, which has a large and devoted audience. Guo sometimes appeared as a guest, or Bannon would tout his work on air.[101]

In June 2020, with a fleet of airplanes buzzing overhead carrying banners, Bannon and Guo were standing on a boat in front of the Statue of Liberty to proclaim the formation of the "Federal State of China," a new government of sorts to bring freedom to mainland China. Bannon proclaimed Guo to be "the George Washington of the new China." Followers of the movement would be "citizens." The two even displayed a new blue national flag for China.[102]

With his media channels operating, Guo started to promote his businesses as an investment opportunity. Targeting primarily anti-Communist

Chinese living around the globe, his pitch was simple: make money *and* bring down the CCP. Guo even claimed that those who invested with his enterprises would "get political asylum" once the federal government became aware of their motivations and efforts. There was also a cryptocurrency exchange, and even a fashion line. "Each unique G Fashion collection is an exhibition of state-of-the-art craftsmanship applied to sartorial concepts," he declared.[103] The volume of investment money Guo collected was enormous—more than $1 billion.[104]

But although Guo proclaimed his hostility to the CCP, some of his actions seemed designed to undermine the very movement he claimed to support. Through his media outlets, he pushed conservative-seeming critiques to the extreme. When conservatives raised questions about the effectiveness and safety of covid vaccines, the GNews website proclaimed that the vaccines were "a continuation of the biochemical war" by China. He falsely claimed that there are seventy Communist Party members on Pfizer's board of directors.[105] His views were hyperbolic forms of legitimate concerns being raised by conservatives.[106]

"The CCP wants to gain control of all aspects of the world, and the Jews are in their way," Guo opined when discussing the covid vaccine. He noted that "The American economy is in Jewish hands. Many of the 3000+ fund managers on Wall Street are Jews. Vaccines hurt Jews the most. . . . The world internet is overwhelmingly in Jewish hands."[107] The stories would begin with a grain of truth—but then head off in an outlandish direction, often in ways that seemed to undermine the side Guo claimed to be supporting.

In the fall of 2020, the Hunter Biden laptop story began circulating among media outlets after it had emerged from a Delaware repair shop, and publications such as the *New York Post* began verifying the contents of the hard drive. But Guo's news outlets, including GTV Media, began making fantastical and false claims about the laptop. On September 24, 2020, a GTV Media executive claimed that Chinese sources had sent the company "three hard disks" of material on Hunter Biden. That proved to be false: the material had come from the laptop left at the repair shop. But the false claim served to fuel speculation that the laptop was foreign disinformation. The laptop contained a treasure trove of suitably damning information about the Biden family's financial dealings in China, Russia, and Ukraine, but Guo's outlets focused on salacious and sometimes false stories. They claimed to have photos of Hunter Biden sleeping with underage girls—also false and not on the laptop.[108] "[Guo] took fake photographs and claimed they came from Hunter's laptop," recalled Jack Maxey, a former *War Room* cohost who worked with Bannon and Guo on the project.[109] Maxey and another colleague, Vish Burra, quit *War Room* because they were troubled by the deceptions and believed that Guo's actions were distracting from the larger, more important story of Biden family corruption contained on the laptop.[110]

Why would Guo's media operation work make exaggerated claims that only raised doubts about the damning Hunter Biden laptop?

A curious intersection of relationships between Guo and Hunter Biden might provide the answer. Recall that Guo's sponsor in China was Ma Jian, the vice minister of the MSS. Well, that same Ma Jian was also a business partner with the Chinese executive who arranged Hunter Biden's ownership stake in a Chinese government–backed private equity firm in China called BHR Partners.[111] Exactly what this intersection means is not clear—but it raises some troubling possibilities.

In July 2021, yet another Guo vehicle was launched: a social media app named GETTR. Headed by senior Trump campaign advisor Jason Miller, GETTR promised to be a free speech social media platform. Some 4.5 million users signed up in the early months.[112] A Chinese influence operation designed to plant pro-Beijing propaganda in the media began running accounts on both GETTR and Gab.com, another right-oriented social media site.[113]

The fact that Guo was financially behind GETTR was obscured. He announced that he was an advisor to the company, and Miller acknowledged that Guo was one of the company's "international consortium of investors" through his family's foundation.[114] The level of control and direction that the Chinese billionaire had over the operation of the platform would only later become clear.

Guo, with help from Bannon, was building a powerful conservative media dynamo. But there were curious signs that did not align with his claim to be a dissident fleeing from the Chinese secret police. There was a dark, sometimes hidden part of his operation that raised serious questions about his true allegiances.

In the 1920s, the Soviets ran an intelligence effort called Operation

Trust that penetrated the anti-Soviet movement in Europe by establishing a fake anti-Soviet organization called Monarchist Union of Central Russia. By ostensibly becoming a member of the opposition, the Soviets could identify and root out their most effective opponents. It was a remarkably successful operation.[115]

Was something similar going on with Guo? Though he spoke about his opposition to the CCP, his actions were hardly oppositional. He used his media empire to foment "mobs against other opponents of the Chinese Communist Party."[116] He released a "hit list of dissidents," many of whom had spent decades fighting the Beijing regime, by claiming "without evidence [that] they are spies from the Chinese Communist Party (CCP)."[117]

In 2020, Louis Huang, a cofounder of a Chinese human rights group in Vancouver, Canada, was beaten up by two men who were reportedly sent by Guo.[118]

Bob Fu, a well-known Texas-based Chinese human rights leader and head of a Christian organization called ChinaAid that supports religious freedom in mainland China, was the subject of protests and physical threats by Guo's supporters. Guo called Fu a "fake pastor" and a Chinese Communist spy.[119] In eleven videos distributed on his YouTube channel, according to a lawsuit filed by Fu, Guo asked his "comrades" to "converge to Midland, Texas to find Bob Fu and kill him. This is the time to test your loyalty and ability."[120]

Fu is a longtime pastor at a church in Midland and a highly respected critic of the CCP. Yet followers of Guo began appearing outside Fu's home on October 4, 2020, passing out accusatory flyers.[121] "I have no other choice but to conclude and believe that someone from the regime asked him to carry out this campaign against me and other dissidents," Fu said.[122]

Guo activists gathered in the street in front of the house of a California-based anti-CCP activist for days, hurling verbal threats.[123]

In Princeton, New Jersey, a Guo-linked mob surrounded the home of a Chinese democracy activist and cursed at his school-age daughters. The protestors stayed outside the home for two months.[124]

Even Chen Guangcheng, the world-famous "barefoot lawyer," who had a harrowing story of fleeing from the Chinese government and had long been working against the CCP, was a target of Guo.[125]

Though Guo proclaimed himself to be a dissident, he regaled people with stories about his friends at the Ministry of State Security. In one journalist's trial testimony about Guo, she claimed that one "business associate" of Guo was "in charge of hunting down the Chinese dissidents" in the United States. He had mentioned the pal, Dzhang Yue, to her, and she testified that "there are several people right here in New York City who were arrested or interrogated or tortured by Mr. Dzhang."[126]

Guo continued to maintain communication with "lots of high-ranking officials" from the MSS, even though he was supposedly a fugitive renegade living in the United States, according to court testimony.[127] In 2017, he gave a live interview with the US government's Voice of America about corruption in China. Right after the interview, he told a colleague that he "spoke to someone who's [a] high-ranking official in the intelligence—in the Chinese intelligence." Apparently, the official wasn't upset, because Guo himself "appeared quite happy."[128]

Some dissidents who met with Guo complained that he appeared more interested in "bargaining with the [Chinese] government about his properties in China" than fighting Beijing.[129] That certainly seemed to be the case when Guo sat down in 2017 with senior officials from the MSS in his New York City penthouse. Liu Yanping, a deputy minister in the MSS, arrived at his home with some colleagues. Guo's wife made and served dumplings. The conversation was likely cordial—and transactional—because some of Guo's assets had been frozen in China.[130] We know the details of the conversation because it was recorded—and Guo has admitted in a civil court case that the quotes below are accurate.

"Let's get this thing over with," the deputy minister said at one point. "Why have [so] many cases? Besides it's not a big issue. I calculated your assets. After you pay the debts, you'll still have some assets left."

"The conditions of your capital and asset[s] are still very good," he reassured Guo. The two discussed "solving the matters" between the CCP leadership and Guo.[131]

Guo's views of the CCP seemed much more ambivalent in the presence of his visitors than his public, anti-party rhetoric. "I have never said I'm against the party, neither have I said that I love the party, but I hope I will be given a reason in the future not to go against the party. I hope one day I can close my Twitter account and go back to my normal life without speaking up in videos."

Guo explained that his dispute was not with the CCP or President Xi but with a faction of the party that had arrested his business partner Ma Jian.[132] But he also said that he wanted to work with the CCP to root out corruption within the party. "I want to report to the central committee in the spirit of supporting President Xi's anticorruption campaign."[133] At one point, the spymaster asked Guo if they could resolve matters and if he was "still willing to make contributions to our nation." Guo responded, "Of course, I'm very willing to do it, if conditions allow me to do so."[134] Those were strange comments by a supposed opponent of the Chinese Communist Party.

At the meeting, Guo signed a letter pledging loyalty to President Xi. He later claimed that he had made the pledge under duress.[135] When the delegation finally left, he walked them out of the building.[136]

There are other clues indicating that Guo may not be exactly who he claims to be. Some of the people he surrounded himself with had curious ties as well; William Je, a China-based investor, has been described as Guo's "money man."[137] But Je had the sort of political connections one would not expect from someone working with a dissident of the regime. He was a former member of the Chinese People's Political Consultative Conference (CPPCC), an important advisory body established by the CCP. Members are screened for their political reliability. When Guo was asked during a New York civil case whether he knew Je, he initially pleaded the Fifth. He eventually admitted that, in fact, he knew Je. When asked about Je's affiliation with the CPPCC, Guo again pleaded the Fifth.[138]

Je was also a member of a United Front group called the Hong Kong Chongqing Friendship Federation. United Front groups, as discussed earlier, are designed to carry out the work of the party overseas.[139] It was also revealed that Je's investment fund was another part owner of the conservative social media company GETTR.[140]

Why would Guo work with someone so closely wedded to the party? Why would Je associate with Guo? It was a strange partnership that seemed to make no sense.

Though Guo's erratic attacks and messages sowed chaos on the

Right and raised questions about what he was ultimately up to, the backdoor workings of the media operation raised red flags about his ties to the Chinese mainland and the CCP.

A look behind three of the Guo channels reveals that the master "recovery" email address and phone number are a Chinese email account at QQ.com and a Chinese mainland–based phone number. The QQ.com domain is run by Tencent, a Chinese media tech company closely wedded to the Beijing regime—hardly an appropriate tech partner for a dissident operation. The administrator accounts have direct links to mainland China, and administrators of two other channels work alongside mainland-based administrators. The mainland China phone number was certainly monitored by the Chinese government.[141] Why on earth would a dissident television network use those as its contact email address and phone number?

And yet, officials in China were also running a sophisticated cyber campaign online against both Guo and Bannon, using bots and fake accounts to attack them.[142]

Meanwhile, at the social media company GETTR, Guo fired the entire cybersecurity and IT staffs and replaced them with a tech team that communicated in Chinese. It was Guo's move, done independently of the CEO. "Jason Miller played no part in the decision, it was all Guo," a former executive at the company told the *Washington Examiner*.[143]

Though Jason Miller was the CEO and face of the company, Guo still exerted his control. According to leaked communications, when the chief technology officer, Joe Wang, was caught in a deadline dispute between Guo and Miller, Guo asked him, "Do you obey Jason or me?"

"I obey you," Wang wrote back.

Ken Huang, another executive at the company, piped up, "Mr. Guo, of course we all obey you."[144]

In March 2023, Guo was arrested by federal officials on fraud charges, including allegations that he had bilked investors out of more than $1 billion. When authorities arrived at his 9,000-square-foot apartment, they found a fire burning inside.[145] A search of his three New York City area residences found a cell phone scrambler "designed to defeat government wiretaps," twenty-nine cell phones, seventeen computers, and forty-three USB drives. Also on the scene: gold pins with "symbols of the Chinese Communist Party."[146]

Most of the investors who were ripped off were anti-Communist Chinese. Does someone in mainland China have their names? Are the data of those who used GETTR secure? Is Guo a dissident . . . or a spy? A hustler playing both sides? Or simply a con man?

"The evidence at trial does not permit the Court to decide whether Guo is, in fact, a dissident or a double agent," US district court judge Lewis Liman wrote in a decision in a civil case involving Guo. "Others will have to determine who the true Guo is."[147] What can be determined, however, is that Guo sowed distrust and thus chaos. He financially harmed and threatened those with whom he professed to be allied, whatever his motivations were, and that had to delight Beijing.

CHAPTER 6

Destabilizing Democracy

It is not clear exactly when they arrived at the Chinese Consulate in Houston, Texas. A contingent of Chinese intelligence professionals from the Second Department of the People's Liberation Army, an intelligence unit, landed in the United States sometime in the first half of 2020. They posed as academics under so-called J-1 research visas, never disclosing their affiliation with the Chinese military. Working with technicians from Huawei, a Chinese military–linked technology company, the intelligence officers were identifying and targeting Americans they hoped would get involved with at least the peaceful protests, if not the violent riots. They posted "customized" videos to TikTok instructing Americans how to organize protests and riots. In fact, PLA officers were on US soil, working to weaponize big-data technology to promote division and violence in the United States.[1]

In July, the US government demanded that the Houston consulate be closed, precipitating the burning of documents in the courtyard and the Chinese officials' departure. Later, US officials spoke openly about how the consulate had been involved in stealing American technology and spying.[2] But they were largely silent about the role those Chinese intel officers played in steering protests in order to foment violence. When asked about it in one forum, all that Assistant Attorney General John Demers from the DOJ's National Security Division said was that he could not discuss the matter in detail, describing it only as a "covert foreign influence" effort.[3]

Why the silence? Is it because the George Floyd protests were considered sacrosanct by the political and media class? That made them a perfect target for exploitation by China.

If the PLA unit had gone undetected, how effective could it have been in stirring up further division in the United States? Were—and are—there other similar units operating undetected elsewhere in the United States?

Paul Dabrowa, an artificial intelligence expert and biohacker, testified before the Australian Senate in 2020 about the way intelligence professionals manipulate the public through social media:

> The first thing to remember is that persuasion (or propaganda, a term popularised by Edward Bernays in the 1920s) need not persuade the majority of the public to be effective. It's enough to persuade just one per cent of the population to destabilise a democracy effectively with protests, rioting and a collapse in institutional trust. So the question that really needs asking is how hard is it to radicalise one per cent of the public with modern, weaponized forms of persuasion?
>
> The answer is dangerously easy.[4]

The Chinese Communist government has long been intrigued by how social media could be used to sow unrest in other countries. *The Science of Military Strategy*, the regularly updated manual produced by China's military, said in the 2015 edition, "Since the beginning of the 21st century, cyberspace has been used by some countries to launch 'color revolutions' against other countries . . . [through] behind-the-scenes operations using social networking sites such as Twitter and Facebook as the engine, from manufacturing network public opinion to inciting social unrest."[5]

The Chinese military personnel sent to Houston were probably connected to Base 311, the home of a secretive Chinese military unit named simply 61716. The unit is situated outside the city of Fuzhou in southeast China. Unit 61716 is the tip of the spear for Chinese information warfare initially against Taiwan but also the United States, with responsibilities including the implementation of the Three Warfares strategy. To review, Three Warfares adopts the approach that by using "media or public opinion warfare, psychological warfare and legal warfare," Beijing can wear down its enemies from within, exploiting differences and divisions within countries. Little is known about this top secret base, its true structure and function; it is shrouded in mystery. But it is known that research at the facility includes a focus on "political polarization" in America.[6]

In 2020, as American cities burned, Beijing boldly and publicly backed the protestors, amplifying their actions and statements. "Growing Global Support for US Protests over Killing by Police," blared *China Daily* on June 8.[7] The newspaper had earlier published a cartoon titled "Racism Kills" depicting a police officer wearing a Ku Klux Klan hood labeled RACISM sitting on the back of the Statute of Liberty.[8]

Chinese state-owned media outlets disseminated other cartoons that were shared by the Chinese state-owned television network showing an American covid vaccine center with a young Asian standing in front. "By the way, is there also a vaccine for racism?" he asks the doctor. In another instance, Global Times published a cartoon with the Statute of Liberty holding a gun, towering over a tiny cutout figure marked "Asian" with a target on its chest.[9]

Back in the 1960s and early '70s, the Chinese Communist Party worked aggressively to exploit racial differences in America by supporting black radicals such as the Black Panthers. Recently, a Chinese journalist floated the idea of renewing the public alliance that Mao had had with the Black Panther Party but with the new generation of black radicals. Chinese government officials bragged about the work that Beijing had done over the decades to support and encourage the black radical movement in the 1960s and '70s. "Black leaders like Du Bois and Huey Newton visited China in the late 1950s and 60s," wrote one Chinese journalist on Twitter. "Imagine Washington's reaction if China invites BLM or Antifa leaders to Beijing today or Chinese officials meet them in DC during the ongoing protests like US official did [with Hong Kong activists]."[10] Indeed, as the *Washington Post* acknowledged, the most vocal support for the BLM movement from Asia "came from the representatives of Beijing."[11]

* * *

Laura Daniels, Jessi Young, and Erin Brown were furious about the racial injustice in America. All of them went on Twitter to express their views. Spencer Taggart's Twitter account featured a photo of a white man with a beaming smile and a description of himself: "Husband, Dad & Teacher—Passions = Strategy, Vision, Christ, Family, Speaking, Consulting, & Growth." Taggart worried about the "tearing of American society," and said that "American society is in deep division." His tweets were retweeted by people such as Gretchen Robinson, April Sutton, and Erica Jones, adding to the chatter in general about the inevitability of an American "civil war," claims that "America is broken," and predictions of "the imminent collapse of American society."[12]

Similar tweets do often come from Americans concerned about the social fissures they see. But Laura Daniels, Jessi Young, Erin Brown, and Spencer Taggart and some of his retweeters were not Americans; they did not exist at all, except in the imagination of someone in China—or someone acting on behalf of Beijing. All of the accounts were fake. And there were thousands of others strategically constructed to fan the flames of division in the United States.[13]

For Chinese military strategists, divisions in the United States mean opportunity. After all, their goal is to "Sow discord in the enemy camp . . . to perplex, shake, divide, and soften the troops and civilians on the opposing side."[14] But they also want to do more than create division and anger; they want to erode American pride and create disgust—because while "anger drives people to the polls; disgust breaks up countries."[15]

Chinese state media continue to flood the internet with messages of the decline of the United States, with its "deepening social divisions, and the worsening racism." Indeed, it is on the "verge of collapse."[16]

***

During the Cold War, the Soviets also tried to exploit racial tensions as a weapon against the United States, but they were not particularly good at it. Part of the problem was their lack of understanding of American culture. The other problem was that they were limited by their tools. They had to use flyers and forgeries in their attempt to pit Americans against one another.[17] They never had a powerful tool like social media. Today, Chinese military intelligence units utilize social media as an important tool in creating political—and therefore social—divisions in the United States.[18]

As protests mounted across the United States in the summer of 2020, Twitter deleted an incredible 170,000 accounts linked to a Chinese government influence campaign, including accounts tweeting about George Floyd and other divisive issues. One tip-off was the fact that the tweets were overwhelmingly posted during business hours in Beijing. The organizers of the influence campaign worked to increase engagement on their tweets to "boost them to the top of Twitter's search for specific hashtags." Analysts said that "This allowed the campaign to effectively drown out organic activity on that hashtag for a period of time."[19]

China's president Xi had vowed to "retake the Internet battlefield." The operation was now fully under way.[20]

With unrest in the United States growing, Beijing looked to build a digital fire with messages about the injustice of America and her inevitable decline. They didn't create fake stories; they simply amplified the most radical and extreme positions that had the potential to tear at America's social fabric. They pushed conflicting messages, supporting BLM *and* pro-police messages. Generally, they shared content about explosive topics that had first appeared in the *New York Times* or on MSNBC. "The point was not to take a side but rather to boost divisiveness by amplifying competing, emotionally-charged viewpoints."[21] Chinese officials call this tactic "borrowing mouths to speak": amplify stories that make the point you want to make, rather than trying to make that point yourself.[22]

Beijing clearly saw the success Russia had had by creating fake accounts back in the 2016 election. Russian operatives had created fake BLM accounts that were so convincing that some, such as those of the fictional activist Luisa Haynes, accrued fifty thousand follows. More astonishingly, Luisa's tweets were quoted by *Time*, *Wired*, HuffPost, and *USA Today*.[23] Those fake Russian accounts were among the top accounts retweeted on racial justice matters. They played to both sides, left and right, working to further polarize American society. They targeted BLM and LGBTQ audiences with extreme messages and gun rights audiences on the political Right.

Even Jack Dorsey, then the CEO of Twitter, was duped by a fake Russian BLM account. "Crystal Johnson," an account highly active in a heated social media war over racial justice and police shootings, tweeted,

"Nobody is born a racist." Dorsey retweeted it as well as another by "Crystal."[24]

Beijing clearly learned from Moscow. In 2013, a Chinese official named Wu Riu wrote in a secretive military journal about how psychological warfare over social media could "subdue the enemy without fighting." That seems like a bold claim, but the author listed several methods, including "creating information chaos" and "exaggerating the conflict of interests within the enemy camp."[25] China is now carrying out that strategy. It got off to a slow start building a covert presence on social media, but soon its fake accounts began to accumulate followers and reach "heavyweight influencers."[26]

Cybersecurity firms found hundreds of accounts set up by Chinese state-linked actors that were made to look like ordinary Americans talking about a variety of controversial topics, from gun control to race relations. The campaign included accounts on Facebook, Twitter, and YouTube and had the potential to create social movements. Beyond chatter, they directed people to protest the US government's response to covid and racial matters. The posts by this "army of fake Twitter accounts" were often shared by state media and even Chinese diplomats, exposing them to "millions of viewers."[27] If Beijing-aligned activists stirring up violence in the streets was the "ground war," this was the "air war."

The end goal of both was to sow panic, fear, and distrust of the American government. During the summer of 2020, with BLM protests mounting, Twitter accounts started sharing posts with the hashtag "#dcblackout" with claims that Washington, DC, was going to experience a blackout on both the internet and mobile phone networks, carried out by the federal government to control the population. The news was fake, but Chinese accounts pushed it aggressively and managed to create a brief spasm of alarm in the nation's capital.[28]

In the spring and early summer of 2020, YouTube discovered and banned nearly 2,600 channels linked to Beijing. The company vowed to undertake an "ongoing investigation into coordinated influence operations linked to China."[29] The full extent of the campaign cannot be known. Though some of the networks were discovered and deleted, regarding videos specifically, "many more remain to be discovered," warned cybersecurity officials.[30]

Russian state social media accounts worked in tandem with Chinese influence operations; and Chinese officials amplified Russian disinformation online, creating a psychological loop designed to exacerbate American tensions. Pro-Kremlin media outlets such as Sputnik and RT were among the top media sites retweeted by the Chinese government media accounts.[31]

* * *

Money is needed to sustain disruptive groups fanning the flames of dissent, both on the ground and online. Though having funds flow directly from Beijing to radical activists in the United States would leave blatant fingerprints, financial support can sometimes take a more circuitous route. This is in keeping with Beijing's strategy of plausible deniability. Watching the fire burn from across the river means creating the impression that you never actually crossed the river to ignite, fuel, or stoke the conflagration.

The American billionaire Neville Roy Singham is a mysterious figure who made his fortune in part due to his ties with Communist China. Singham now lives in China and has emerged as a key funder of radical groups in the United States, including those that push violent protests in the United States and stick to a strict pro-Beijing script.

Singham grew up in Jamaica and Detroit and as a young man adopted Communist ideological views, joining the League of Revolutionary Black Workers (LRBW). From early adulthood, he had an affinity for the CCP.[32] LRBW was "heavily influenced by Maoist thought," and, as he wrote to colleagues later in life, "I have been following China since I was 14 years old. The Chinese and Cuban revolutions defined my generation's attraction to liberation and socialism."[33]

Singham attended Howard University and then, despite his Maoist views, started a software consulting business, eventually naming it Thoughtworks, based in Chicago. He also became a "strategic technical consultant" for Huawei, the Chinese military–linked tech company, beginning in 2001. It is unclear when the arrangement ended; some say in 2008, but Singham's friends say the collaboration between Huawei and his firm continues.[34] Huawei is a major contractor to the PLA, and its mission includes serving as a central component of the Chinese military's communications infrastructure. Huawei's opaque organizational structure hides the company's ownership. While Huawei claims to be employee-owned, researchers scrutinizing the company have concluded that its "trade union committee" ownership stake is effectively a fig leaf for CCP control.[35] Numerous countries, including Australia, New Zealand, the United Kingdom, France, Japan, and the United States, view Huawei as a national security threat.[36] The exact work that Singham did as a "strategic technical consultant" to that company wedded to the Chinese military-industrial complex is not clear. Thoughtworks eventually opened an office in Beijing. In 2010, it held its Software Development Conference in China's capital city.[37]

For Singham, the job was not just work; he was on a mission. He praised Venezuelan dictator Hugo Chávez, declaring that the country he ruled (with an iron fist while starving his people) was a "phenomenally democratic place." Singham loved the Chinese model, finding it superior to America's. "China is teaching the West that the world is better off with a dual system of both free-market adjustments and long-term planning," he told *Fortune* magazine in 2008.[38]

But what does this have to do with sowing social unrest in the United States?

In 2017, Singham sold Thoughtworks to a London-based investment firm called Apax Partners.[39] Though Apax is often described as a British investment firm, the reality is not so simple. Apax is partly owned by the Chinese government's sovereign wealth fund, the China Investment Corporation.[40] With an office in Shanghai, Apax also has considerable investments in mainland China, courtesy of its ownership structure and partnership with the Chinese government, which provides it opportunities to make favorable deals in the Communist country.[41]

The sale of his software consultancy to the Beijing-backed Apax was a financial boon for Singham. Some report that it made him a billionaire. There was a certain hypocrisy in the financial fortune he acquired by selling his software company. "As a socialist I believe the world should have access to the best ideas in software for free," he had once said.[42] Of course, you don't build a personal fortune by giving your best ideas away for free.

Singham now lives in Communist China and is connected to several companies there, including Shanghai Luoweixing, in which he invested

$20 million, and Gondwana Foods, into which he poured $32.5 million. He also represents a company called Shanghai Shinong Company.[43] He appears to be well connected with political authorities, due to his "many contacts with the Chinese state."[44] In one email to friends, he explained that Li Bo, a well-known Chinese academic, is "a very good friend of mine here [in China]." Li works with the Guancha Syndicate, a media outlet regarded by the nonprofit organization Reporters Without Borders as a "Chinese propaganda outlet."[45] Singham's ties to the regime are so substantial that he was reportedly invited to attend the Chinese Communist Party Congress.[46]

While enjoying his affluent life and connections in Beijing, Singham has poured more than $100 million into organizations driving the protest movement in the United States. According to the chief scientist at Thoughtworks, Martin Fowler, Singham sold the company so he could fund his "activist work": radical pro–Communist Chinese causes.[47]

The primary vehicle is an entity he established called People's Support Foundation, which, according to corporate records, listed $156 million in assets and no liabilities. The People's Support Foundation has a track record of putting tens of millions of dollars into organizations with a "pro-China bias."[48]

The foundation lists Singham's love interest, Jodie Evans, as the president. They were married in 2017.[49] We will see that Evans, a longtime activist and a founder of CODEPINK, works to promote the causes of the Chinese state.

Singham has pumped money in congressional races, funding Congressman Pramila Jayapal to the tune of $17,800 in campaign contributions, with thousands more to Ilhan Omar and Barbara Lee.[50] Wife Jodie Evans has given tens of thousands as well.[51] In addition, it is Evans who has the connections in Washington. For decades, Evans has been a major player in the nation's capital, where she meets often with US policymakers. Evans was a close aide to California governor Jerry Brown, serving as his director of administration. In 1991, she ran his presidential campaign.[52]

Evans is firmly convinced that China is the future and that America is jealous of Beijing's economic successes. "Today the U.S. elite are obviously terrified at the tremendous economic success of China," she said, and "China is not threatening the U.S. militarily." The real problem is the United States: "China's success stands in the way of U.S. domination of the world."[53]

CODEPINK sponsors events such as China and the Left: A Socialist Forum, designed to counter critics of Beijing on the political left in the United States.[54] The Chinese military and government-run media often quote CODEPINK approvingly.[55]

CODEPINK launched a campaign called China Is Not Our Enemy; its supporters lobby members of Congress, arguing that the United States should take a conciliatory tone toward Beijing. Criticisms of Beijing's harshest policies, even the internment of the Uyghurs, is not tolerated. "Our concern is that it is being used as a tool to drive the U.S.'s hybrid war on China," she said, "instead of a human rights issue that needs to be addressed as such." On a video podcast, Evans featured a guest who argued that the idea that Beijing is engaging in genocide is "farcical" and a "total lie."[56]

CODEPINK cosigned a letter in the summer of 2021 arguing for a softer US policy toward China in the name of aiding climate progress. More than forty groups signed the letter calling for an end to the "dominant antagonistic approach" in the relationship between the United States and China.[57]

According to tax records, Singham's largest financial commitment is to a New York project called The People's Forum.[58] The organization acknowledged its gratitude to Singham on Twitter, referring to him as a "Marxist comrade."[59] The two coexecutives of the People's Forum, Claudia De La Cruz and Manolo De Los Santos, are members of the Party of Socialism and Liberation (PSL), which we met earlier.[60] Recall that PSL leader Brian Becker demanded that party members offer a "militant political defense of the Chinese government."

The People's Forum seeks to "strengthen and unify social movements of working class and marginalized communities" and is "fostering collaboration" between what amounts to radical groups.[61] The People's Forum serves as a platform for both BLM and radical so-called antifascists. For example, when the PSL protestors were arrested in Denver for barricading a police department, the People's Forum came to their defense and organized a worldwide protest.[62]

So, in brief, an American Marxist now living in China, who made his wealth by selling his business to an investment firm partly owned by the Chinese government, is now connected to well-known efforts to support violent protestors and other radical groups in the United States.

Singham also donates to organizations such as the Alliance for Global Justice, which has reportedly been involved in funding several Antifa groups, and sponsored trips to revolutionary sites in China for activists from the United States.[63] The Alliance for Justice funds a myriad of pro-CCP groups such as Popular Resistance, which defends the Chinese government's actions at Tiananmen Square and decries any reference by the West to the massacre as an "imperialist agenda."[64]

From his perch in Communist China, Singham funds researchers and activists to defend Beijing from critics of its most heinous crimes. One of Singham's employees is Vijay Prashad, formerly a professor at Trinity College in Hartford, Connecticut, and now a senior fellow at the Chongyang Institute for Financial Studies in China. Prashad has likewise downplayed the Uyghur genocide, saying, "The Uyghur situation, like so much else, is exaggerated in the Western press. . . . I am also not predisposed to believe the dross that appears in a Western press."[65] In another instance, Prashad went even further when he seemed to defend China's treatment of the Uyghurs. "That's the price that people pay," he said in an interview. "You can't preserve some cultural forms and alleviate or eradicate absolute poverty."[66] (Prashad maintains that he has "always been opposed to any form of colonialism and genocide.")

Singham's funding of Chinese propaganda has not gone unnoticed. In India, a money-laundering investigation involving the media company led the government's Directorate of Enforcement to Singham. It argued that Singham was sending money to PPK NewsClick Studio to push a pro-Beijing narrative, with sources in the Directorate alleging that Singham was associated with the propaganda arm of the Communist Party of China.[67] (Singham has denied the allegations.)

Similar claims, which Singham denies, have been made regarding his funding of media outlets in South Africa.

Singham also funds something called BreakThrough News, which includes Eugene Puryear and Brian Becker, the activists we met earlier trying to radicalize protests, as anchors.[68]

* * *

CODEPINK and Singham's People's Forum work closely with a "cryptic" organization called Qiao Collective to steer the American Left toward a more pro-CCP position.[69] The mysterious group professes to speak for Chinese students and ethnic Chinese living in the United States but refuses to condemn human rights violations committed by the Chinese government; it uses quotation marks when referring to freedom in the United States.[70]

Academic scholars have tracked the Qiao Collective's social media accounts and noted that the "most overrepresented words and emoji in the description of users following Qiao all have a connection to Communism." They also noted the close interaction between Qiao and "Chinese state-aligned accounts" online. As they wrote, "Qiao's funding and background is not transparent, which has led to some suspicion about their potential proximity to the PRC government."[71]

What is so important about this mysterious group? The Qiao Collective draws support from "many" of the "top leadership" of the Democratic Socialists of America (DSA), a political organization with a large following (approaching one hundred thousand members in the United States) that also wields considerable political power. Prominent members of the organization include US representatives Alexandria Ocasio-Cortez, Ilhan Omar, Cori Bush, Jamaal Bowman, and others in state chambers. Senator Bernie Sanders, though not officially a member, is well regarded by the DSA and has been publicly supportive of the group's goals.[72]

DSA manages to straddle the divide between being left wing and seemingly pro-Beijing while also being well positioned inside the Washington establishment. Beijing also sees the organization as useful in its goal of sowing dissension and divisiveness in the United States. The organization is unsparing in its condemnation of the US political system, regarding both the Senate and Electoral College as "undemocratic."[73] But the organization has little critical to say about the dictatorial regime in Communist China.

During the Cold War years, the old DSA was somewhat anti-Communist, particularly when it came to the Soviet Union.[74] But its present-day heir has increasingly tilted pro-Beijing. In 2019, when the Chinese government banned "Hong Kong's largest independent labor organization," a member of DSA's International Committee proposed putting out a statement to condemn the act. A straw poll found that by a three-to-one margin, the committee preferred to remain silent.[75] The US government's shutting down a labor union would lead to an outcry. But when the Chinese government does it, there's no apparent concern. As one DSA member put it, "The reaction from some DSA leaders is best described as gleeful." Some veteran activists in the DSA have noticed the pro-Beijing shift. "Within and outside DSA, many on the Left have aligned themselves with the Communist Party of China (CPC)," noted *Tempest* magazine.[76]

When the DSA released its political platform for 2021, it made clear that it resisted any efforts by the United States that might keep Beijing's influence at bay. The DSA wants all foreign US military bases closed.[77]

Beijing is, of course, thrilled by the evolution of the DSA. State-controlled media describe the DSA as emerging "as the 'New Communist Movement' of young activists inspired by Mao Zedong in China, as the Soviet-aligned Communist Party USA, declined."[78]

The fact that the Communist Party USA (CPUSA) is small and ineffective has been noted by CCP officials, who see the DSA as an imperfect substitute but an attractive one. China's Center for Marxist Parties in Foreign Countries of CCNU regularly features domestic and foreign analysis of the DSA and notes the growing size and influence of the organization. The Wuhan-based body approvingly notes the role that both Bernie Sanders and Alexandria Ocasio-Cortez have played in swelling the DSA's ranks.[79]

Beijing understands the CPUSA is not going to gain much traction anytime soon, but the DSA has power and influence. In one analysis, the Center points out that although the CPUSA and DSA are both "socialist parties," the Communist Party has a "relatively weak foundation" and it has "undoubtedly a long way to go before it can form a broad influence in the United States." But the Chinese government sees the DSA as a fertile ground for cooperation.[80]

Still, another post by the Chinese organization approvingly quotes a CPUSA official as saying that "the Democratic Party's dominance by big capital" means that it is an "imperfect instrument" to advance Marxist goals, but "an imperfect vehicle is still a vehicle." It mentions both Sanders and AOC as politicians who have resisted Big Capital's hold on the party to advance socialist goals.[81]

The CCP delights in using the work of organizations such as the DSA for its own benefit. "Using foreign strength to propagandize China" is the idea that when foreigners make statements beneficial to Beijing, it is a particularly potent form of propaganda. As previously noted, Chinese government officials sometimes refer to it as "borrowing mouths to speak."[82] DSA leaders don't seem to mind being dummies for this sort of political ventriloquism.

On January 10, 2023, a resolution was introduced in the House of Representatives to establish a Select Committee on the Strategic Competition Between the United States and the Chinese Communist Party. The resolution received overwhelming bipartisan support. But sixty-five members of Congress voted against it, including DSA-affiliated (or policy-aligned) representatives including Cori Bush, Pramila Jayapal, Alexandria Ocasio-Cortez, Ayanna Pressley, and Rashida Tlaib.[83] Even the appearance of representing US interests in relation to China seems too much for these members.

So when the Strategic Competition Committee held its first hearings in February 2023, the event was interrupted almost immediately by members of CODEPINK, who held up signs during testimony reading CHINA IS NOT OUR ENEMY and STOP ASIAN HATE. They were escorted from the room, but their message was clear: you are not even supposed to talk about the challenges presented by the CCP.[84]

Following the committee hearings and the protest, Jodi Evans sat down for an interview with the Chinese government's Global Times. "I find very racist the way China was dealt with in the hearing and the way China is dealt with in the media," she declared. "There is not much that is human, rational, or respectful in any of the ways that they talk about China." She complained about "how gullible the United States electorate is" when it comes to China.[85]

**

Fanning the flames by Beijing continues today, well after the 2020 protests and riots ended. ULTRA MAGA BELLA Hot Babe had something to say. With 26,000 followers during the US midterm elections, she attacked Barack Obama as a "lizard person." On the other hand, someone named Salome Cliff made clear on Twitter that Trump was "persecuting minorities." These accounts and many others were, of course, fake.[86] As the 2022 midterm elections approached, Chinese information operations began "aggressively targeting the United States" with efforts to "sow division both between the U.S. and its allies and within the U.S. political system itself."[87]

The Chinese approach is better and more sophisticated than Russia's approach—even though Russia gets most of the attention in Washington. "You might think in terms of the Russian intelligence services providing bursts of bad weather," said Ken McCallum, the director general of MI5, Britain's internal intelligence agency. "China is changing the climate."[88]

One would think that Beijing's ties to groups promoting violence in American cities and its online influence campaign would draw serious attention from official Washington. But its efforts have been largely ignored. During the Trump administration, officials such as Secretary of State Mike Pompeo and Director of National Intelligence John Ratcliffe spoke openly about Beijing's influence campaigns. But most DC elected officials and appointees remained more interested in Russia's futile efforts to sow dissent.

The brutal January 2023 killing of Tyre Nichols by five black police officers in Memphis, Tennessee, led to protests and vigils across the United States. Though many people took to the streets to lament the death of Nichols and to question why such police brutality took place, it is no surprise that the pro-Beijing PSL used it as an opportunity to push a more extreme message and even engage in acts of violence.

In Atlanta, PSL leaders "guided" protestors downtown, according to the *Atlanta Journal-Constitution*. They wanted the police to be defunded and the money to go to social groups instead.[89] In Boston, PSL members gathered. "No good cop in a racist system," they chanted. "No justice, no peace."[90]

PSL organized nearly thirty protests across the United States, including in New York City, Detroit, Austin, Anchorage, San Francisco, San Diego, Asheville, Chicago, Philadelphia, and Rhode Island.[91] The message was not reform; it was complete destruction of American police forces. "We must dismantle this (police) system and turn it upside down" was the message from PSL organizers in Boston.[92] In New Haven, Connecticut, a PSL rally called to "Abolish the Police."[93]

In New York City, BLM leader Walter "Hawk" Newsome led a boisterous crowd including PSL members who became violent, jumping on police cars, smashing windows, and attempting to hit police officers. "No justice, no peace, kill these killer police," the crowd chanted. Crowd members held signs that read DOWN WITH PIGS and DEFUND THE NYPD. "F**k peace!" said Newsome. "We ain't never taken violence off the f**king table."[94]

In Atlanta, violent protestors burned a police car. PSL was there in force.[95]

Plenty of Americans enabled those efforts. When activists from Beijing-allied groups such as FRSO and PSL organize protests and encourage violence, the news media cover the events but never mention the broader agenda or foreign ties of the organizations. They instead present their members as idealistic American activists. Likewise, other liberal and leftist organizations appear all too willing to work jointly with them, turning a blind eye to their deeper destructive agenda. And politicians in Washington seem to be cowed into silence, unable to isolate the organizations from the broader movement.

One of the most divisive issues in America today is the debate over trans rights. Here, too, you see the hand of these Beijing-linked organizations and financiers. For PSL, the trans movement has become a central part of the radical Marxist movement. "The revolution will not be gender-conforming," stated one article that examined the substantial number of trans members of the PSL.[96]

These pro-Beijing groups see the trans movement as a powerful force to advance their pro-Beijing agenda and push to further radicalize the movement. "The unity of our movements terrifies them," they explain. Regarding attacks on the trans movement: "These are attacks that serve the interests of the capitalist class." Regarding linking black radical movements, the anti-police movement, and socialism: "The ability to link all of those things together is extremely, extremely dangerous to the capitalist order."[97]

Beijing-based Roy Singham's organizations have also funded and organized efforts to push the LGBTQ movement further into the American public debate via an event titled Becoming Numerous: Legacies of Queer and Trans Rebellion.[98]

Curiously, the trans movement in the United States has attracted the interest not only of Singham but also of Joseph Tsai, the billionaire cofounder of Alibaba. Alibaba is essentially a state-controlled entity in China. But it has made Tsai quite rich. He has poured millions of dollars into trans causes and research in the United States. In July 2021, the Joe and Clara Tsai Foundation launched the Wu Tsai Human Performance Alliance with a commitment of $220 million.[99] One of the initiatives is the Wu Tsai Female Athlete Program at Boston Children's Hospital, which serves as a Wu Tsai Human Performance Alliance "innovation hub." The Female Athlete Program's definition of female "includes transgender females as well as those assigned female at birth."[100] The director of the Female Athlete Program, Dr. Kathryn Ackerman, is a proponent of transgender athlete inclusion.[101]

Boston Children's Hospital, which hosts the Wu Tsai–funded research, faced a backlash in 2022 over its first-of-a-kind "Center for Gender Surgery that performs mastectomies on teenagers as young as 15, as well as since-deleted wording on the hospital's website that claimed teens as young as 17 can get vaginoplasties."[102] One of the hospital staffer's controversial claims is that "a good portion of children do know [their gender identity] as early as seemingly from the womb."[103]

Another center Tsai has funded at Stanford University is heavily involved in trans research, advocacy, and activism.[104] The same institute held a book club event to promote scientist Ben Barres's book *The Autobiography of a Transgender Scientist*.[105]

Though Singham, Tsai, and the two pro-Beijing groups push for trans rights in the United States, one place they don't push them is in China. In that country, adults who transition live much more precarious lives because civil liberties in general are limited. The Chinese government has limited LGBTQ appearances on television and in films, arguing that the depiction of those subjects is damaging to the country. The Chinese government views LGBTQ as "an evil foreign influence that prevents young people from marrying and having children" and bans "effeminate men" on television, among other depictions that could be seen as pro-gay.[106] Social media companies have shut down accounts on the LGBTQ topic. Indeed, LGBTQ groups "often don't officially register with authorities" because they will not be approved.[107]

But FRSO, PSL, Singham, and Tsai have not publicly criticized the Chinese government for its conduct. Do they support LGBTQ rights or simply see them as a cynical weapon to wield and with which to divide the United States?

On November 4, 2023, three hundred thousand protesters converged in Washington to denounce Israel's response to the brutal terrorist attacks by Hamas that had claimed fourteen hundred civilian lives almost a month earlier. The event shut down major portions of the nation's capital and a now familiar cast of characters and interested parties where at the epicenter. Event organizers included People's Forum, PSL, and CODEPINK, joining with Palestinian rights organizations. The massive crowd heard from Eugene Puryear and Brian Becker of the PSL, as well as Vijay Prashad and Layan Fuleihan from the People's Forum. The crowd chanted "From the river to the sea, Palestine will be free," a call for the complete geographical elimination of Israel. Some protestors surged toward the White House, pouring red paint on the fence around 1600 Pennsylvania Avenue.[108]

The Washington march was only the most visible of a drumbeat of actions taken to target Israel by these organizations that are Chinese-aligned, and sometimes funded by China-based sources.

The Anti-Defamation League (ADL) identified Beijing-tied PSL as "one of the primary organizers of dozens of anti-Israel protests across the country." PSL members not only defended Palestinians; they also approved of the Hamas terrorist attacks on Israeli civilians. At a PSL co-sponsored protest in New York City, a speaker explained that "resistance is not terrorism." In Anaheim, California, at a protest co-sponsored by PSL, a speaker celebrated this "moment where Hamas is taking control, they're resisting."[109]

In mid-October, two thousand protestors had taken over Copley Square in Boston to demand an end to all US aid for Israel. The crowd also chanted "From the river to the sea, Palestine will be free." PSL was one of two organizers for the event.[110]

These actions taken by these groups aligned perfectly with Beijing's policy line. Communist China has long supported the Palestinian cause, and that did not change even with the brutal terrorist attacks. China does not consider Hamas a terrorist organization. Foreign Minister Wang Yi, in the shadow of the attacks, would not condemn Hamas.[111] Chinese tech giants Baidu and Alibaba even began excluding the name "Israel" from their online maps. Baidu explained this was only because

Israel was such a small country, but reporters noted that Lebanon's name did appear—even though it had half the landmass of Israel.[112]

When California high school students in mid-October walked out of their classrooms in solidarity with the Palestinian cause, the Chinese Progressive Association helped sponsor the event. "This is not an open-air prison," one speaker explained of Gaza. "It is a concentration camp."[113]

China-tied FRSO implicitly lauded the Hamas killing of women and children, explaining, "The Palestinian resistance is dealing a heavy blow to the Israeli apartheid state. The decades of oppression, humiliation, and callous cruelty by the occupiers of Palestine are being answered in the only language oppressors truly understand."[114]

One FRSO event perhaps best illustrates how these organizations' support for China and Hamas are intertwined. In October 2023, FRSO leadership held an event in Minneapolis to celebrate the anniversary of the Chinese revolution, and to "show what the peoples' movements today can learn from them." The celebration concluded with a brief but enthusiastic rally for the "Palestinian freedom fighters."

"When I hear people calling for a complete ceasefire, I think 'No that's not quite right,'" said FRSO member Meredith Aby. "Because we only want one side to stop fighting." She concluded her remarks by chanting "From the River to the Sea!," a cry that calls for the elimination of the state of Israel. And the audience shouted back "Palestine will be free!"[115]

The People's Forum, funded by China-based Roy Singham, organized protests in New York City and elsewhere, to "stand with the people of Palestine, who have the right to resist apartheid, occupation, and oppression."[116]

Manolo de Los Santos, founder director of the People's Forum (and a PSL member) echoed the views of many in his celebratory mood in the wake of what Hamas had done: "The people have broken out! The heroic resistance of the Palestinian people is an example to all revolutionary movements." Los Santos later told National Public Radio that he would not "criticize any part of Hamas's" brutal attack on civilians.[117]

Beyond protests and some outbreaks of violence, these groups also began pushing for "direct action" at "political offices, businesses, and workplaces that fund, invest, and collaborate with Israeli genocide and occupation." Dubbed "Shut It Down for Palestine!," the plan is to "co-ordinate planned disruptions" in the words of People's Forum. Joining them was CODEPINK, PSL, and others.[118]

It was a remarkable replay of the violent and disruptive days of 2020 when the cause had been different—but the end results are the same: tumult, social divisiveness, and chaos. It was like fanning a small flame, and then watching the fire burn from across the river.

The United States has its dividing issues and problems—but China is happy to fan the flames. Much of that work is being done by groups that meet with CCP officials, are tracked by Chinese Communist intelligence, and receive funding from China. Devices supplied by China arm American felons and extremists with machine guns and wreak havoc in the United States.

Our leaders are silent and absent.

Part III

HIDE A DAGGER
IN A SMILE
（笑里藏刀）

CHAPTER 7

A TikToking Bomb

"Russia will bomb Sweden," said the voice on the TikTok video. "Why, Russia? I don't want to die," continued the panicked voice. Russian forces were soon going to invade, claimed another voice on a different TikTok video. Other clips parroted the threat. "Now comes the war. Prepare food and warm clothes."[1] TikTok's algorithm, which determines what people see, made sure that those videos were popping up on the screens of young children, not adults, in Sweden. Widespread panic followed.

"My 11-year-old was extremely frightened yesterday and asked whether there was going to be a war soon," one Swede reported. Parents described how their children were too anxious to sleep. Teenagers were calling government offices "anxious about an impending invasion." The Swedish government's hotline for kids was reportedly flooded with calls.[2]

Who planted these TikTok videos remains a mystery. But how they went viral is indisputable: the Chinese government ultimately controls TikTok and therefore its algorithms.

Regardless of who produced the videos, the psychological effects of the videos on young TikTok users were real, immediate, and profound, revealing the power of the Chinese app that has become the most popular platform in America. With just a few videos, TikTok was able to alter the psychological state of many people. And this is only one anecdote. Even a cursory review of the evidence suggests that the Chinese-built app is a perfect tool to manipulate and "weaken another country's morale."[3]

Halfway around the world in Los Angeles, doctors at UCLA are seeing a strange surge in neurological cases at their clinic. Young girls are experiencing "twitching, verbal outbursts, involuntary repetitive movements, and sounds." In the past, the doctors reported seeing one or two such cases a year, but they are now seeing ten to fifteen cases a month.[4]

What is going on? Researchers call it a "mass sociogenic illness." This is not an illness spread by a biological virus, but rather a "psycho-digital" one. Some professionals call it "TikTok tics," since the malady is a result of spending hours on TikTok, causing overstimulation, then a "nervous system disturbance" manifested in bizarre behavior.[5]

The United States is facing a hydra of Chinese information weapons specifically targeting our children. Unlike Cold War propaganda, videos of military parades, or glorious pictures of Chairman Mao, the new propaganda may not seem political, nor is it simply intended to persuade or misinform. It is highly sophisticated, designed to influence the brains of the younger generation, with profound effects. It is a dagger pointed at our children, hidden behind the smile of TikTok. In the Chinese Communist view, you can run from it—but you can't hide.

The Chinese military and Communist Party officials have thought deeply and written extensively about waging "cognitive warfare" on the United States. The CCP sees apps such as TikTok, video games, and movies as powerful weapons to wage psychological warfare against the West. "Even the last refuge of the human race—the inner world of the heart—cannot avoid the attacks of psychological warfare," they wrote in *Unrestricted Warfare*.[6] Unfortunately, they have found willing accomplices among some of the most powerful people in American politics and entertainment. Those national leaders continue to turn a blind eye to the challenge, refusing to acknowledge what Beijing is doing.

Despite its links to the Chinese propaganda apparatus, TikTok has thrived with the help of American celebrities and thought leaders who are either ignorant or ambivalent about TikTok's true nature. The first celebrity to sing its praises was the late-night talk show host Jimmy Fallon. "There's a really cool app I've been getting into lately called TikTok," he told millions of Americans watching his show. "Do you guys know that?" The in-studio audience sat in silence—most people watching on television likely did, too—because they had never heard of TikTok before. "If you don't have it, download it," he instructed. What Fallon didn't tell his audience was that he—not *The Tonight Show* itself—had forged a partnership with the Chinese company and created a series of TikTok "challenges" designed to grow interest in the app. The daytime talk show host Ellen DeGeneres soon followed with an equally glowing account on her show.[7] The rapper Cardi B, for a large fee, posted some videos on TikTok—to no great effect, but it did lend her name to the platform.[8] None of those celebrities seemed to weigh the gravity of being used to encourage Americans to download a potential Chinese spy app. How much money they were paid is not known.

Celebrities weren't alone. Major American institutions jumped in to work with TikTok. In 2019, for example, the NFL announced a multiyear content partnership with TikTok.[9] One wonders what conversations were had besides "Show me the money!" As we will see, politicians also lined up to use it.

TikTok is an app produced and managed by a Chinese company called ByteDance. Since its introduction in 2017, it has become the most powerful and revolutionary communication platform for reaching young people around the globe. With close to a billion users all over the planet, it has penetrated the heart of America's culture, becoming a central part of the lives of our children and young adults. The Chinese government does not permit the app in its country. There, a separate ByteDance product called Douyin is used. On its surface, TikTok is a friendly app that features silly dance videos, stunts, pranks, and lip-syncing videos. Behind the closed doors of Chinese military and intelligence services, however, we will see that officials are giddy about their ability to steer our children's minds with TikTok and the other products China peddles to the West.

The average American using TikTok spends eighty-two minutes a day on the platform, triple the time the average user spends on Snapchat or Twitter, twice what the average user spends on Instagram or Facebook.[10] TikTok's big break came with the covid pandemic, when bored Americans of all ages, sitting in their homes during lockdowns, turned to the novel app for entertainment. (We will learn in Part IV that China pushed America toward lockdowns.) Between January and March 2020, the number of monthly active users of the app jumped by 45 percent.

"An extra 13 million people got hooked on TikTok across the United States," wrote Chris Stokel-Walker in his book *TikTok Boom: China's Dynamite App and the Superpower Race for Social Media*, "enough to fill a state the size of Illinois." In March 2020, Americans spent 134 million hours on the app. The average user opened it "at least eight times a day."[11] After the pandemic receded, most users never left the app. They were hooked—by design.

The addictive quality of TikTok is remarkable, even when compared to other apps such as Facebook or Instagram. Dopamine is a neurotransmitter that plays a significant role in human motivation. Accomplishing a task triggers dopamine, giving users a feel-good sense of fulfillment but also a craving in their brain for more of those good feelings. It is well documented that substances such as alcohol and nicotine can increase dopamine levels, even if we have not accomplished anything. Gambling can also create a dopamine high.[12]

TikTok is a digital dopamine supermachine.

Aware of TikTok's addictive potential, the Chinese Communist Party (CCP) recently tasked party members to "strengthen the connection between the media and the audience, and *construct channels that the masses cannot live without*." (Emphasis added.)[13]

And of course, TikTok fits that description.

* * *

In August 2013, at the Communist Party's National Propaganda and Ideology Work Conference, President Xi explained China's need to have more sophisticated propaganda. Innovation, he said, was in order: "[We] must meticulously and properly conduct external propaganda, innovating external propaganda methods, working hard to create new concepts, new categories and new expressions."[14] As he directed in 2016, the year before TikTok was launched, "Wherever the readers are, wherever the viewers are, that is where propaganda reports *must extend their tentacles*." (Emphasis added.)[15]

A year later, TikTok emerged.

Though many Chinese technology companies are located in Shanghai, the country's center of commercial power, ByteDance is comfortable in China's capital city, the seat of Communist political power. The company is located near the massive headquarters of China's Ministry of State Security (MSS), which is convenient given that ByteDance, while streaming billions of videos onto the screens of our children's telephones via TikTok, is also spearheading an artificial intelligence infrastructure project run by the Chinese intelligence service.[16]

ByteDance is not just a participant in but also a cofounder of the Beijing Academy of Artificial Intelligence, created in November 2018—months after TikTok was launched—by the government along with two of China's top universities.[17] The academy is headed by a former Byte-Dance senior executive and falls within China's civilian-military fusion, which means whatever technologies it develops will be applied to the Chinese military.[18] This could help explain that although ByteDance has offices around the world, it keeps the vast majority of the software engineering operations in its Beijing headquarters.[19]

Like any other enterprise in China, ByteDance has a Communist Party committee inside the company that imposes party discipline. At ByteDance, the party committee happens to be headed by the firm's editor in chief, who, as the title implies, helps control who sees what in the company's feeds around the world. Members of the committee gather regularly to study speeches by Chairman Xi and "pledge to follow the party in technological innovation."[20] "This arrangement helps the party, which also means the state, to monitor what happens in private companies," said Professor Feng Xiang of Tsinghua University. "In return [they] can claim some kind of help from the government."[21] In short, ByteDance is not simply an entertainment company; it is wedded to the Chinese Communist Party military-intelligence-industrial complex.

The genius of TikTok lies in its algorithm's ability to push highly addictive, personalized content. It determines what the eyes of America's children see, and thus how their brains are conditioned. Because every TikTok feed is unique, there is no way of knowing what each person is seeing. That gives the app tremendous stealth power to shape or distort public opinion, the specifics of which are untraceable, at least by us.[22]

TikTok gives the user few choices about views; those decisions are made largely by the algorithm. Whereas Facebook and Twitter allow you to pick who and what to "friend" or "follow" to determine what information you are fed, TikTok chooses for you. According to the Chinese

Propaganda Ministry, the algorithm that powers TikTok has the same source code as apps offered in mainland China that are used to control and monitor the domestic population.[23] "TikTok's algorithmic design makes it an ideal tool for disseminating CCP propaganda," said law professor David Sloss.[24]

The powerful algorithm, designed to keep audiences glued to their phones, is not only a company secret—it is also a *state* secret. The Chinese government has designated it as a "national security asset."[25]

ByteDance AI engineers partnered with researchers from Peking University to craft the algorithm.[26] Peking University is one of the most elite institutions in China. Its four major military research laboratories make sure that work done at the school is integrated into the Chinese military-industrial complex.[27]

To addict users, the TikTok algorithm gathers enormous amounts of information about them to craft a detailed profile of who they are. "When you gaze into TikTok, TikTok gazes into you," said Eugene Wei, a Silicon Valley investor and engineer who has worked as a product chief at Amazon and Flipboard.[28]

The all-seeing eye of TikTok censors and controls political content. Leaked "moderation" documents from TikTok justify the company's removal of content about Hong Kong, Tibet, and Tiananmen Square due to "real-world harm," and therefore moderators mark such content and ban it from feeds.[29] (In response to reporting on these documents, TikTok claimed that the guidelines were no longer or had never been in use.) The company can censor or "disappear" both users and videos or create them through "'shadow accounts' operated by company employees posing as regular users" to push desired content.[30]

Just as the company punishes users who might express solidarity with those being oppressed by the Chinese government, some users suspect that it rewards those who support the CCP. One TikTok user in Texas posted a clip playing China's national anthem and called President Xi "my president." The number of his fans spiked from two thousand to nearly ninety thousand.[31] (ByteDance denies that TikTok rewards pro-China content.)

ByteDance censors articles critical of the Chinese government and the Communist Party in its subsidiaries around the world.[32] That a Chinese-owned company would censor political stories is hardly surprising. Less well understood is how TikTok's algorithm can be "tuned" to distribute information that can move public opinion on a level of informational control with societal impact. This tuning can allow the app to be used for "data weaponization."[33]

Exhibit A: the constant video feed. If the algorithm is as purposeful as it seems to be, it is certain that users receive persistent messaging concomitant with CCP goals. It has long been recognized that repetition is a key component in persuasion and psychological influence.[34]

Paul Dabrowa is an artificial intelligence expert in Australia and cofounder of an AI firm. He previously founded a company to commercialize technology developed for the National Aviation and Space Administration (NASA) and has studied propaganda and persuasion as part of his academic work. During testimony before the Australian Senate, he explained that the TikTok AI "has the capacity to create a user-specific profile of individuals' fears and anxieties, learning which stimuli are likely to trigger desired responses and behaviours. It could then utilise addictive principles and implement stimuli that compel young adults to spend hours scrolling on their phone, purchase products, or join political movements."[35]

The fact that Dabrowa mentioned young adults and the incidents from Sweden to Los Angeles involve teenagers is not a coincidence. Exhibit B: from its earliest days, TikTok has focused on getting direct access to this demographic—purposely bypassing parental involvement or even awareness.

ByteDance has positioned TikTok as a "parent-free" platform for young people and has marketed it as such—"a playful space for underage users," according to three scholars in their study of the company.[36] Unlike Instagram, Facebook, or Twitter, "nosy" parents or adults cannot monitor their children's feed.[37] Naturally this appeals to kids, even very young users: one-third of Americans on TikTok could be under the age of fourteen.[38] So the Chinese-state actor ByteDance, through TikTok, is influencing the emotions and perceptions of our children and grandchildren, not simply in the passing way troubling videos alarmed children in Sweden but on a consistent, daily basis—over years. Said Dabrowa, "Over time, in the same way that a cat can be taught to play the piano, your child can be subconsciously taught to associate positive emotions with whatever Tik-Tok desires, all the while shielded from parental oversight."[39]

The CCP and the military have done a lot of strategizing about how best to accomplish this level of control. They recognize that it must be highly personalized—"precision communication"—to work best. It is "1 key for 1 lock," meaning that to persuade a group, they need to make their propaganda messaging unique to each member of that group.[40]

Chinese military officials have big dreams for using not only apps like TikTok but also video games and Hollywood films to manipulate the attitudes of young people in the Western world. This is not hypothetical. They are quite clear about their goal of changing American society to conform to their image. Don't take my word for it. Read what key Chinese strategists have written in restricted military journals.

Colonel Dai Xu is a professor at the People's Liberation Army (PLA) National Defense University (PLA-NDU), China's most important military academy. And like the Ministry of State Security, PLA-NDU is near ByteDance headquarters in Beijing.[41] Dai wrote that the real battle between the United States and China is "information-driven mental warfare" and compared apps such as TikTok and social media platforms to a "modern day Trojan Horse." The internet, he said, is a "deformed domain shaped by the interweaving of people's minds and the main form of power competition between nations."[42]

Another leading Chinese PLA strategist, Zeng Huafeng of the National University of Defense Technology (NUDT), wrote of a cognitive, or mind, war on the United States, and proposed how to defeat us without firing a shot. NUDT works with ByteDance on national artificial intelligence projects involving the Chinese military.[43] Zeng defines the "cognitive space" as "the area in which feelings, perception, understanding, beliefs, and values exist" and argues that this is where the battle can be won. To that end, he said, Beijing must use "information and popular spiritual and cultural products as weapons to influence people's psychology, will, attitude, behavior and even change the ideology, values, cultural traditions and social systems." According to Zeng, these cultural tools, including apps, video games, and films, should be used to "target individuals, groups, countries, and even people around the world."

Stop and contemplate what these two prominent strategists in China are saying about the "cultural products" we invite into our homes and minds: they are to be used to steer people's psychology and change their values and cultural traditions. Zeng argues that Beijing can win "mind superiority" through:

- "Perception manipulation" via propaganda, by changing how people look at the present
- "Cutting off historical memory" by warping their views of their own country's past so people will be open to changing their values
- "Changing the paradigm of thinking" by targeting people to change the way they view problems and thereby changing their beliefs
- "Deconstructing symbols," by getting people to reject certain traditional symbols and thereby modifying a nation's identity[44]

But here is the kicker: *"The ultimate goal is to manipulate a country's values and achieve strategic goals without an actual overt military battle."* (Emphasis added.)[45] Sun Tzu could not have said it better.

Manipulating values? Warping people's views of their country's past to change their values? Modifying a nation's identity? (Does this sound familiar?)

The key, these and other strategists believe, is to be intentional but not too overt. Chinese propaganda experts call it "subconscious messaging."[46] Listen to how they advocate for a soft touch to influence young people in the West to "conceal" their real message:

With regard to Western audiences, we need to conscientiously filter the content of communication, finding more points of resonance and common ground . . . even in the case of positive propaganda we also need to be adept at "softening" the content. For example, using stories to convey things, "translating" viewpoints into stories, and concealing them in stories, . . . we should adopt open and emotional methods.[47]

Propaganda is most effective when it "can be directed to 'impressible persons,'" they write.[48] The best way to do this is not with blatant political messages but with entertainment. "Entertainment is the main motivation for Generation Z content consumption," said Peng Zhengang, the deputy director of the Propaganda Department. By better understanding those they mean to propagandize, the CCP can "explore effective communication strategies and paths, [and] improve the ability to set agendas."[49]

Strategically, it is important for propaganda to be stealthy, slipping insidiously past targets, who will ideally not even know they are being targeted. As Chinese military officers put it, using AI and algorithms to drive apps such as TikTok enables them to reach "different audiences and make even more international audiences see our PLA reporting *and think that they chose the content.*" (Emphasis added.)[50]

Chinese propagandists also recognize that young Western people may easily discern and discredit themes or messages from one source but not when that theme or message comes from many sources. They compare this phenomenon to "multiple voices in a choir. Each communication subject sings its own melody." The key is to simulate a community—a peer group—as TikTok does. "Content control is becoming more important," said analyst Liu Ying, noting that "emotional incitement . . . can affect public opinion more than facts and truth."[51]

Emotional content offers a powerful mechanism to mask propaganda. A Chinese government-funded study of "digital propaganda and opinion manipulation in social media platforms" explained that "emotional content can easily lead the audience to have the illusion of 'independent thinking' and attribute irrational emotions to 'righteous indignation' or 'empathy,' which intensifies the value of delusion."[52]

What message will that chorus sing? Its members speak freely among themselves of their motive. Their goal is to "strengthen the overseas promotion of the Communist Party of China and guide the international community to form the correct [view of the Communist Party and of China]," Shen Haixiong, a deputy minister and senior propagandist, observed.[53]

Propaganda requires continuous messaging to be effective, hence the constant video stream that is the hallmark of TikTok.[54] One PLA propaganda journal stated, "Younger PLA propagandists increasingly realize the popularity of short videos online, and TikTok is the best example of this so far."[55]

This online propaganda is a "highly concealed propaganda method" noted a Chinese government study on online manipulation, and as a result "its effect can far exceed traditional propaganda." They argue it is so powerful that "it can even affect the social stability and political security of a target country or region."[56]

For Chinese propagandists, TikTok is also perfect because it represents what they call "computational propaganda." The recommendation algorithm subverts "the traditional news information content selection and distribution model," providing the CCP with information control. The algorithm "guides users'; cognition to be gradually strengthened in the repeated information push, so that public opinion can be promoted."

The evidence is clear: Chinese psychological warfare strategists have Americans, particularly young Americans, in their crosshairs. They believe that not only are young people easier to influence but the effects of the propaganda messaging are longer lasting.[57] The Chinese government is devoting serious amounts of resources to understanding how to manipulate young users. The Communist government recently opened an external propaganda office to target Generation Z audiences overseas.[58]

Chinese propagandists also see social media tools such as TikTok as a way to sway elections in the United States and around the world. One official wrote that Beijing should "exploit big data analysis, AI processes, bots and astroturfing, grasp the different personalities of voters and realize large-scale guidance of public opinion and changing their [political] orientation."[59]

"The crumbling of a regime always starts in the realm of ideas," declares a Chinese military textbook discussing the need to use online media to win the propaganda war. "Political upheaval and the toppling of a regime could occur in a single night. But changing the way people think is a long-term process. Once the front lines of human thought have been broken through, other defensive lines also become hard to defend." The book goes on, "The battle for 'mind control' happens on a smokeless battlefield. It happens inside the domain of ideology. Whoever controls this battlefield can win hearts. They will have the initiative throughout the competition and combat." The authors even quote President Xi: "When it comes to combat in the ideology domain, we don't have any room for compromise or retreat. We must achieve total victory."[60]

***

"Building a community is very similar to running a country," said Alex Zhu, the onetime CEO of TikTok. "In the early stage, building a community from scratch is like you just discovered a new land. You give it a new name, and if you want to build an economy you want to build population and you want people to migrate to your country."[61]

Digital utopia or dystopia?

TikTok says that this effort is all about allowing its audience to "experience new perspectives and ideas." But exactly who drives these perspectives and ideas?[62] More than 130 Communist Party members hold management positions at ByteDance.[63] And when the company hires content reviewers, it gives priority to CCP members.[64] Furthermore, ByteDance populates senior management positions with people who have previously served in the Chinese propaganda apparatus as members of state-run media organizations, which fall under the direct authority of the Chinese Communist Party. More than twenty such veterans have senior responsibilities as company directors, presiding over entire departments. More than sixty appear to have remained in the employment of Chinese state media while working for ByteDance. At least three hundred employees have ties to Chinese state media.

This might explain why TikTok encourages creators on the platform to push "positive energy," a phrase adopted by President Xi of China when discussing pushing a positive message about Communist China.[65]

The chairman of ByteDance China is Zhang Lidong, widely considered the second most important person in the company after ByteDance's founder, Zhang Yiming. Zhang Lidong worked as a reporter and editor in chief at a state-run newspaper.[66]

The ByteDance director of government affairs previously worked for *People's Daily*, the central paper of the Chinese Communist Party. On a LinkedIn profile, the person describes their work at the paper as having "analyz[ed] the reading habits of Internet audiences and the identity characteristics of mainstream party media audiences." Further, they claimed that "'without violating the party's propaganda policy, [they] actively carr[ied] out special news planning' with local government offices."[67]

Chen Lin, the vice president for products at ByteDance, oversees tweaking the company's algorithm to refine what people see across all company products. At an April 2018 ByteDance Communist Party Committee meeting, he explained that the apps should not just give the users what they want but also "highlight socialist core values."[68]

An editorial director for ByteDance simultaneously serves on the editorial board of the China News Service, which is controlled by the United Front Work Department of the CCP. She is also on the board of a publication called *China Weekly*, which is run by the Central Committee of the Communist Youth League.

In yet another instance, an international operations manager at ByteDance is reportedly also the "chief editor for international news" at a website called Beijing Time. Beijing Time, according to its own website, "builds a media communication platform for Beijing's patriotism education base for the Beijing Municipal Party Committee Propaganda Department."

A total of twenty-four employees at ByteDance and TikTok previously worked at *People's Daily*, the official mouthpiece of the CCP. ByteDance has a senior executive whose job is to coordinate with the Chinese state media (i.e., the propaganda apparatus) so that they work effectively together. The deputy general manager of ByteDance is "responsible for the formulation of the cooperation strategy between the company and the central [state] media" and "cooperate[s] with partners in content planning, data mining, product interaction, business, etc."[69]

Clearly, the digital land where America's children frolic is a Chinese state version of *The Truman Show*.

Beginning in early 2023, ByteDance executives started exerting even greater control over TikTok as high-level executives from ByteDance started taking increasing responsibility and control for TikTok's operation. The moves concerned some US-based TikTok employees who complained to US managers to no avail.[70]

Beyond the troubling ties of the senior executives running ByteDance is the fact that the company is required by law to be a component of the Communist Party's propaganda agenda. In December 2019, new internet censorship rules issued by the government tightened restrictions on "'negative' content" and required media companies such as ByteDance to promote posts that reflect "Xi Jinping Thought" and "core socialist values" as well as increase the "international influence of Chinese culture."

The new law requires social media companies to "ensure that the algorithms undergirding their apps promote CCP propaganda."[71]

The founder of ByteDance, Zhang Yiming, presents himself as just an entrepreneur, insisting that he is not a Communist Party member and maintaining that his company would never turn over information to the Communist Chinese government. "Even if we get such a request," he said, "it is impossible" for us to comply.[72]

However, Zhang must know that the CCP is in charge. He ran a humor app in China that got into trouble with the government for its bawdy, off-color jokes. He was quick to fall in line. "I earnestly apologise to regulatory authorities, and to our users and colleagues," he wrote in an online statement reminiscent of the self-denunciation confessions that were common during the Maoist era of China. "Since receiving the notice yesterday from regulatory authorities, I have been filled with remorse and guilt, entirely unable to sleep. . . . Our product took the wrong path, and content appeared that was incommensurate with socialist core values, that did not properly implement public opinion guidance—and I am personally responsible for the punishments we have received." He went on to say that the problems with the service were a result of "a weak [understanding and implementation of] the 'four consciousnesses' [of Xi Jinping]." He pledged that going forward, for his companies, including ByteDance and TikTok, "technology must be led by the socialist core value system." And he promised "further deepening cooperation with authoritative [official Party] media, elevating distribution of authoritative media content, ensuring that authoritative [official Party] media voices are broadcast to strength."[73]

He also noted that it is important to "integrate the right values into technology and products," as defined, of course, by the Communist Party.[74]

Chinese government propaganda outlets work seamlessly on TikTok's platform. MediaLinks TV, a DC-based Chinese subsidiary, runs several accounts on TikTok for the Chinese government. But these accounts are not identified as such by TikTok. In the months before the November 2022 midterm elections, one account called NewsToks (@newstokss), ran dozens of videos attacking American politicians, mostly Republicans. "[Senator Ted] Cruz, [Texas Governor Greg] Abbott Don't Care About Us," ran the title of one video. [Senator Marco] Rubio Has

Done Absolutely Nothing," blared another. One video questioned Joe Biden's campaign promises and suggested that he was manipulating voters. The accounts received 8.3 million views on TikTok.

Eight million views on TikTok is the tip of the iceberg—a glimpse of China's state propaganda apparatus working below the surface to influence and divide Americans, in this case during an election. The accounts also ran polemics on abortion, guns, and racism.[75]

TikTok can boost whomever or whatever it wants on its platform, anonymously. For the former Chinese state media executives who populate the leadership of ByteDance, this is the tactic known as "borrowing mouths to speak." As the former editor in chief of *China Daily* allowed in 2016, "We have always attached great importance to 'borrowing a mouth to speak' and used international friends to carry out foreign propaganda."[76]

Chinese psychological warfare specialists have a special interest in "borrowing mouths to speak" to young Americans. Liu Liming, writing for the Chinese military's psychological warfare publication, recommended that Beijing should "actively cultivate a group of media outlets and think tanks with small audiences that are 'grey' and peddle falsehoods, and establish a database of negative topics and conspiracy theories" to thwart one's "adversary, with a special focus on targeting younger Western audiences' distrust of mainstream media, politicians, and even values."[77]

ByteDance desperately wants Americans to believe that it is not a Chinese company. In 2020 (updated in 2021), TikTok distributed a memo within the company entitled "TikTok Master Messaging," concerning public relations with the American media. First: "Emphasise TikTok as a brand/platform." Next: "Downplay the parent company ByteDance" to "downplay the China association."

In 2021, the company circulated employee guidance to address questions about "China/ByteDance Ownership." "TikTok is a global company," the spin claimed, obscuring Chinese control. "The app is only for users aged 13 and over, according to our terms and conditions," the memo stated, obscuring the reality that a full third of the platform's users could be fourteen or younger. "Therefore, in relation to our users, we may speak of *young people*, but not of *children*." (Emphasis added.)[78]

***

College sophomore Kate Fields described the effect of TikTok on an entire generation: "I get stuck in a rut of scrolling for hours through things like TikTok. When I go to complete a task that takes longer than a few seconds, I can't make myself do it because I no longer have the patience to achieve the task."[79]

TikTok is severely damaging the cognitive abilities of America's youth. The phenomenon is known as "TikTok brain." A stunning 50 percent of TikTok users say that watching longer videos, such as movies, now feels stressful. Focusing on reading a book or doing homework has become harder.[80] Heavy TikTok users develop addiction signs: nervousness, irritability, anxiousness, and severe sadness when deprived of the app.[81]

"The app provides an endless stream of emotional nudges, which can be hard to recognize and really impact users in the long run," argued Marc Faddoul, a codirector of the digital rights group Tracking Exposed. He warned that heavy use "can have a serious impact on your mental health."[82]

TikTok can also warp a person's sense of time. "We flick through the videos one after the other one after the other," said Lazaros Gonidis, a researcher at the University of Kent in Great Britain. "And then without realizing, we have spent an hour or two, instead of spending 10 minutes." But because of its addictive nature, "when they're doing something else that prevents them from using TikTok—let's say they're stuck in class, and they have to listen to a teacher talking for an hour—it may seem to them longer and more boring than it actually is."[83]

TikTok users are finding it increasingly difficult to concentrate; for young people this is a particularly troubling problem since their prefrontal cortex, the part of the brain responsible for attention, memory, and impulse control, is still developing until the age of twenty-five.[84]

"I have seen firsthand how TikTok's appeal can turn to significant and potentially deadly mental health problems in our youth," said the clinical psychologist Alan Blotcky.[85] TikTok can also reportedly influence the personalities of heavy users, promoting narcissism.[86]

TikTok has also been linked to mass events of youth vandalism and other antisocial behaviors. A "devious licks" challenge prompted San

Francisco area public schools to shut bathrooms across the city because it was encouraging rampant vandalism.[87] In rural South Dakota and other locations, people following a "TikTok challenge" loosened the lug nuts on car wheels, a dangerous act that could lead to tires falling off.[88] Then there was the "skull-breaker challenge," which resulted in serious head injuries.[89]

Because TikTok is hyperpersonalized—no feed is the same—the platform can magnify US social divisions. Indeed, TikTok's feed may be the worst for providing divisive content.[90] It has become a useful avenue for groups looking to encourage violent attacks within the United States. Because the algorithm shows content from accounts that users may not even follow, this could aid extremists in evading TikTok's modest content moderation efforts. For example, during the riots of 2020, TikTok's algorithm spread videos explaining "how to sabotage railroad tracks; methods to interfere with the U.S. National Guard during riots" and even "how to access the White House through tunnels."[91]

The problem of social media's effects on the human mind extends beyond TikTok, of course, and includes Facebook and other platforms. What makes TikTok different is the control the app has over its users. Facebook and Twitter allow control of the user's feed and a choice of what and who are seen—not so with TikTok. Most videos a user sees are posted by unknown people but selected for that user by the algorithm. And TikTok is not interested in allowing independent academic researchers to study the effects of its app on its users. Facebook and Twitter have cooperated with academic researchers. But when Professor Filippo Menczer of Indiana University proposed collaboration on research into TikTok, he was told, "Absolutely not." "At least with Facebook and Twitter, there is some level of transparency but, in the case of TikTok, we have no clue," Professor Menczer said. "Without resources, without being able to access data, we don't know who gets suspended, what content gets taken down, whether they act on reports or what the criteria are. It's completely opaque, and we cannot independently assess anything."[92] In other words, this Chinese government–linked firm is saying "Trust us." A stunning array of people in Washington seem prepared to do just that.

Beijing is aware of the psychological and emotional problems caused by TikTok. That is precisely why the version of TikTok offered in China is very different from the version people see in the United States and the rest of the world. In China, TikTok is called Douyin; the differences are more than just the name.

If TikTok is mental cotton candy, the Chinese version is "spinach." Douyin and TikTok are similar in their design and share a common algorithm. But Douyin features a large library of videos addressing educational topics as well as content related to professional life. The algorithm discourages these on TikTok in the United States.[93]

"In [China's] version of TikTok [Douyin], if you're under 14 years old, they show you science experiments you can do at home, museum exhibits, patriotism videos and educational videos," said Tristan Harris, a cofounder of the Center for Humane Technology and a former design ethicist at Google. "And they also limit it to only 40 minutes per day. Now they don't ship that version of TikTok to the rest of the world. So it's almost like they recognize that technology's influencing kids' development, and they make their domestic version a spinach version of TikTok, while they ship the opium version to the rest of the world."[94]

The talk show host Joe Rogan is characteristically even more blunt in his assessment. "China's version of TikTok celebrates academic achievements and athletic achievements. . . . What are we doing on TikTok? Kids are f**king dancing. They're screaming about veganism and how blue their hair is."[95]

Not only does this have psychological effects, but it also warps the aspirations of young people in America in the long term. Harris pointed out that in surveys of preteens in the United States and China, American kids say that their "most aspirational career" is to be a "[social media] influencer." In China it's to be an astronaut. "Again, you allow those two societies to play out for a few generations, I can tell you what your world is going to look like," he warned.[96]

It's not just professionals like Harris who notice the stark differences. Consumers who operate on both platforms notice it, too. "My Tik tok feed (South East Asia) is filled with teenagers doing stupid things," said Jiawen Cheong from Singapore. "My Dou yin feed is filled with self-improvement, photography, travel, calligraphy, life hacks, trivia, interesting new products, and of course, cute dog/cat videos."[97]

The fact that dumbed-down content rules in America and the rest of the world but in China the content is educational is by strategic design. "Any content that improves personal skills and contributes to overall growth in everyone's life can be regarded as 'pan knowledge' content" in China, and therefore gets a boost, noted one Chinese digital advertising company. This type of material accounts "for 20 percent of the total broadcast volume on Douyin." The US version has much more emphasis on songs and entertainment.[98] As a result, "educational content is one of the most viewed categories of Douyin videos," says Creators Network, a platform for social media content creators. "As opposed to the more comedy-focused content that TikTok users trend [in the United States]."[99]

The Chinese government has decreed that it wants restrictions on how long children can be on Douyin in its country, and ByteDance has been "particularly aggressive" in responding to the government's requests. The solution: blackout hours. So the app is closed in China between 10:00 p.m. and 6:00 a.m.; it has built-in breaks; the company also adds a five-second pause between videos and inserts messages such as "Put down the phone"; and, as allowed, time limits are enforced.[100]

**

"Delete TikTok now," read the message from the supersecretive hacking organization known as Anonymous; "if you know someone that is using it, explain to them that it is essentially malware operated by the Chinese government running a massive spying operation."[101] Anonymous has gone after the KKK and the Russian government, along with corrupt businesses and governments.[102] As for TikTok, Anonymous knows how much data it gathers from its users, including address books and photos from telephones on which the app is installed.[103] It collects an "abnormal" amount of information, "as much as half a megabyte—or 125 pages of typed data—in less than 10 seconds." And "researchers have also discovered that TikTok was accessing the contents of smartphone clipboards—where users might paste sensitive information like passwords—every few seconds, which one Israeli researcher calls 'very concerning and very rare.'"[104]

Beyond the data on users' phones, TikTok collects their "faceprints" and "voiceprints." That means it can catalog the unique resonance, intonation, rhythm, and pacing of a user's voice. It also captures a user's visual "faceprint," meaning that it collects digitally recorded representations of your face.[105] Notably, the broad collection of much of this data "has nothing to do with the actual function" of the app, according to German IT experts. ByteDance has also "built back doors" and "spy functions" to enable the massive, secretive collection of data.[106] That data makes it easier to manipulate you—without your knowledge. Chinese researchers in the study about digital propaganda and opinion manipulation say that the collected data allows propaganda to be targeted "so as to guide the attitude and opinions of the audience."[107]

The company claims that it keeps them on servers in the United States or Singapore and uses them only to give users a better experience on TikTok. But BuzzFeed News obtained audio recordings of internal meetings at TikTok revealing that American user data were regularly being accessed by the company's engineers in China. "'Everything is seen in China,' said a member of TikTok's Trust and Safety department in a September 2021 meeting."[108]

Australian senator James Paterson confirmed that Australian user data, despite also being stored in the United States and Singapore, was accessible in mainland China.[109]

TikTok likes to make a big deal of having moved its company servers to Texas and Singapore; they are no longer physically located in mainland China. But the geographic location doesn't matter because the data can still be accessed from mainland China. And in fact, TikTok makes clear to anyone using the app that it has the right to share data with other parts of its corporate group, and that means ByteDance in China.[110]

The problem goes beyond TikTok. China's TCL Technology produces television sets for companies such as Walmart, Best Buy, Costco, and Target. *The Ellen DeGeneres Show* and the Call of Duty video game series each count it as a corporate sponsor and partner. Never mind that in 2020, it was revealed by the US Department of Homeland Security that the company had "incorporated backdoors into all of its TV sets exposing users to cyber breaches and data exfiltration." The company could hack the data as Americans were in their living rooms and surveil them, sending their images and conversations to China. When the breach was exposed, TCL claimed that it had fixed the problem with a patch—without notifying anyone. (Trust us, they said.) Meanwhile, neither of TCL's partners—*The Ellen DeGeneres Show* or Call of Duty—seemed to care. "This is a full-on back door," said one researcher. "If they want to, they could switch the TV on or off, turn the camera and mic on or off. They have full access."[111]

In the summer of 2020, concerns over TikTok came to a head when the Trump administration declared TikTok to be a national security threat. The White House issued an executive order to force the sale of TikTok to an American company. The order pinpointed the problem: "TikTok automatically captures vast swaths of information from its users, including Internet and other network activity information such as location data and browsing and search histories."[112] The Trump administration was not alone in its concerns. In a rare show of bipartisanship, Senator Chuck Schumer of New York and Senator Tom Cotton of Arkansas requested a national security review of TikTok before Trump issued his executive order, arguing that the app represented "a potential counter-intelligence threat."[113]

As a result of these concerns, in 2020 the US military, Wells Fargo, the state government of Nebraska, and others banned their employees from having TikTok on their work phones, and many more have since done so.[114]

Big American investors in TikTok's parent company, ByteDance, began meeting with Trump officials to try to prevent the forced sale—but the meetings appeared to go nowhere.[115] There was clear movement in Washington toward action on TikTok—but then it ground to a halt.

Chinese propaganda officials were confident that the TikTok ban would go nowhere. As one official confidently explained in a military journal, "Since 2020, the subtle changes in Sino-US relations and the activity of TikTok have made the United States unable to stop it, anxious and dependent on it."[116]

In early June 2021, newly elected president Joe Biden rescinded Trump's TikTok order to force a sale and replaced it with an open-ended order calling for greater investigation.[117] In Washington, sometimes the best way to avoid action is to commit to studying the problem. Biden's hesitancy was intriguing. Just months earlier, during the height of the 2020 election, the Biden campaign had demanded that all staff members remove TikTok from their phones, citing security concerns.[118] If he thought it was such a security risk for his staff, why wouldn't he want to protect the American people?

Biden's executive order to study TikTok would drag out settling an official American policy for years and buy ByteDance critical time. No doubt, one of the big reasons for Biden's retreat from the forced sale was the array of powerful American investors who had an ownership stake in ByteDance and also happened to be big donors to the Biden campaign and the Democratic Party.[119] Firms such as Sequoia Capital, KKR, General Atlantic, and the Carlyle Group own large stakes in ByteDance. The earliest US investor was the Susquehanna International Group, a "secretive" investment firm based near Philadelphia. "Susquehanna is like a black hole," one financial professional told the *Wall Street Journal*. "There's no light that escapes."[120] A forced sale would be potentially disastrous for these investors; they clearly wish to maintain their profitable status quo.[121]

Susquehanna has a sizable stake in ByteDance, about 15 percent. The head of Susquehanna, Jeff Yass, personally owns about 7 percent of the company. Yass is a heavy giver to libertarian and conservative causes, especially the Club for Growth, which supports limited government. Since 2010 Yass has contributed some $61 million to the organization. Club for Growth has come out against a ban on TikTok. Yass has also supported libertarian politicians like Senator Rand Paul of Kentucky, donating some $24 million of his political action committees and campaigns since 2015. Senator Paul strongly opposes a ban on TikTok.[122]

Sequoia, the fabulously successful tech investment firm with offices in both California and China, was also an early investor in ByteDance. Sequoia China is estimated to own a 10 percent stake in the company. Sequoia has significant ties in China, with a large office in Beijing. Neil Shen, who founded Sequoia China, has connections to the Chinese government, serving as a member of the National Committee of the Chinese People's Political Consultative Conference. Sequoia China also employed the daughter of a CCP Politburo member.[123] Sequoia has political connections in Washington, too. Its senior policy director served as a member of President Biden's transition team. And Chairman Michael Moritz, a partner at the firm, gave millions to Democratic Party–linked PACs such as American Bridge 21st Century (AB PAC) and the Lincoln Project, which helped get Biden elected.[124]

Other large financial firms also have ties to ByteDance. In 2019, the Chinese company received a $1.3 billion loan from a consortium led by Morgan Stanley, Goldman Sachs, Bank of China, and China Merchants Bank's Wing Lung Bank.[125] The Carlyle Group, another politically connected investment firm, bought a $150 million stake in ByteDance in 2020. The firm's cofounder David Rubenstein is a close ally of President Biden, and the first family has made numerous visits to Rubenstein's expansive Nantucket mansion.[126]

These American financiers, and others, became aggressive lobbyists for ByteDance. "Yiming always knew that having an ally in the U.S. was necessary," one executive told the *Australian Financial Review*.[127]

While financial backers were meeting with US officials to protect their interests in ByteDance, and celebrities continued to push the app with no questions asked, ByteDance hired an army of lobbyists to work the corridors of official Washington.

Though many people might be hesitant about representing a Chinese company intent on spy craft and producing propaganda aimed at American kids, plenty on both sides of the aisle in the nation's capital are happy to take their money. Many of those on the payroll of ByteDance and its US subsidiary, TikTok, have serious government experience. Of the forty lobbyists ByteDance hired in 2022, only four had not been in government service. The list included at least two former US senators and at least two former members of the House of Representatives.[128]

Senate majority leader Chuck Schumer's former trade counsel, Stacy Ettinger, was part of a lobbying team hired by ByteDance. So, too, were former aides to House speaker Kevin McCarthy and former House speaker Nancy Pelosi. ByteDance also brought on a former top aide to Al Gore and a former assistant secretary of commerce in the George W. Bush administration.[129] This strategy might as well be christened "No lobbyist left behind."

Perhaps the most effective TikTok lobbyist was David Urban, a key player in Trump's 2016 win in Pennsylvania. After the campaign, Urban was rumored to be in consideration for White House chief of staff.[130] Instead of joining the administration, he continued to work as a lobbyist. In 2020, he served as an advisor to the Trump reelection campaign.

Urban had experience lobbying for suspicious Chinese firms. He worked on behalf of ZTE, a Chinese tech firm that was investigated by the US Justice Department on a myriad of issues.[131] The firm had been fined more than $1 billion for evading the US trade sanctions against Iran and North Korea. In April 2018, the administration announced new measures effectively blocking US companies from selling equipment to ZTE—a crippling blow to the company.[132]

TikTok and its lobbyists tried to obscure the details of their lobbying efforts. A Chinese company or its American affiliate must file a disclosure report under the Foreign Agents Registration Act (FARA). This is required of anyone lobbying on behalf of a foreign government or company, which TikTok certainly is. FARA reports are far more detailed than regular lobbying disclosures. Filing under FARA requires much greater transparency about with whom the lobbyists meet, what journalists they may be trying to influence, and publicity campaigns they are funding. But TikTok's lobbyists did not file under FARA.

"It's time TikTok lobbyists register as foreign agents," declared Senator Marsha Blackburn of Tennessee. When other Chinese companies such as Hikvision failed to file under FARA, the Department of Justice went after them.[133] The Biden Department of Justice has had nothing to say in the case of TikTok.

Beyond the lobbyists, there are American officials who are "advising" ByteDance and TikTok in various capacities. David Plouffe, Barack Obama's campaign manager for his successful 2008 presidential run and later a senior advisor to President Obama, signed on to help TikTok CEO Shou Zi Chew interact with members of Congress on Capitol Hill. So, too, did Jim Messina, Obama's 2012 campaign manager and later deputy White House chief of staff. Tony Sayegh, a senior advisor to the Trump White House, got involved in the effort because he worked for one of ByteDance's investors.[134] In 2020, Vishal Disawar worked for Joe Biden's presidential campaign as the digital organizing platforms director. TikTok later hired him as its global program manager to focus on "integrity issues related to misinformation, elections, and impersonation for all content types including user generated content and state affiliated media."[135] It also hired Isabelle Frances Wright, who had previously worked for Jim Messina, to be TikTok's global election integrity policy lead.[136] One of TikTok's communication directors is a former communications director for Congressman Adam Schiff of California.[137]

To date, neither the Biden administration nor the US Congress has done anything of substance to address this threat aimed squarely at our children. In 2022, a law was passed to ban the app on US government phones;[138] several states including Florida, Wisconsin, South Dakota, North Carolina, and others have banned TikTok on state government phones because of privacy and security concerns.[139] But what about our young people?

Years of inaction by our political leaders stand in sharp contrast to the actions of other governments with fewer resources than our own. For example, when the obvious threats from TikTok first emerged in the public debate, the government of India was quick to ban the app completely. TikTok was "prejudicial to [the] sovereignty and integrity of India, defence of India, security of state and public order," it declared. TikTok lost two hundred million users overnight.[140]

The move was widely seen as necessary in the world's most populous democracy. "Deep penetration of Chinese platforms in an open democracy like India makes its future election processes vulnerable to outside interference and manipulation," one digital industry analyst observed.[141]

In the United States, our ability to defend ourselves and our children from this obvious threat has been paralyzed. Major American financiers want to protect their investments. Major and minor celebrities are eager for the revenue they can generate on the platform. Some political advisors see an advantage to be gained by staying on the app—despite its dangers. "Right now TikTok can be a valuable weapon," said Bradley Beychok, a cofounder of the political action committee American Bridge 21st Century, "especially since Republicans have run away from it for political reasons. You wouldn't want a tool like that to be taken off the shelf." As one Democratic consultant told the *Wall Street Journal*, "Especially among Gen Z voters, it is the dominant platform. If we're going to turn out young voters . . . we've got to have things they actually like and do." Banning the device before the 2024 election would be "politically insane."[142]

During the 2022 midterm elections, the Democratic Party made a concerted effort to court TikTok influencers for its get-out-the-vote effort. The influencers met with party officials who provided them with details about the midterm election battleground map and even outlined key congressional districts they hoped to sway. They even provided "effective messaging strategies." The DNC paid some of them retainers for meeting with politicians in Washington, including former president Barack Obama.[143]

American politicians fear a backlash not only from Beijing but also from young voters who are hooked on the app. "It would be the most unpopular thing Congress has done in decades to somehow ban TikTok," GOP strategist Eric Wilson told the *Journal*. "I don't think given the average age of members of Congress that they understand how engaging TikTok is as a news source."[144] Given what we know about the CCP's propaganda efforts on the platform, this reality should compel immediate action by US policymakers.

Congresswoman Alexandria Ocasio-Cortez came out against banning TikTok, declaring that it "doesn't feel right" in part because other social media companies collect data, too.[145] She never addressed the fact that because TikTok is controlled by the Chinese state, it represents a very different challenge than that of an American tech company. She also expressed no concerns about the propaganda and social manipulation aspects of the platform. Later it was revealed that the Hispanic Caucus Foundation, where she sits on the Advisory Council, received a $150,000 contribution from ByteDance. And a TikTok lobbyist sat on the organization's board of directors.[146]

Congressman Adam Schiff lamely advises his own children to be "careful about your private data if you use TikTok on your phone" because it "may not be secure." But he opposes a ban and has himself embraced TikTok, even during his tenure as a member of the sensitive House Intelligence Committee, despite ample warnings from the American intelligence community about the threat that it represents and his advice to his own children.[147] During the 2022 midterm elections, Schiff requested a meeting with executives from the Chinese-owned company to discuss their approach to controlling "election disinformation." What he had in mind was domestic, not Chinese, disinformation.[148]

California governor Gavin Newsom has expressed no concerns about TikTok and has embraced the platform as a tool to spread his political messages. For security purposes, President Biden banned the use of TikTok on federal devices and more than thirty states have done the same. Newsom remains a prolific user of the platform, not only for political messaging but also videos of his family participating in TikTok stunts.[149]

In Washington, conscientious leaders on both sides of the aisle continue to ring alarm bells—even if actions to address the problem go nowhere. President Trump first raised the issue. Republican senators Marsha Blackburn, Tom Cotton, Marco Rubio, and Rick Scott have demanded that aggressive action be taken.[150] On the Democratic side, Senator Chuck Schumer has pushed for a detailed national security review.

Senator Mark Warner, a Democrat from Virginia, who was a tech entrepreneur before he went into politics, warned, "If your kids are on TikTok . . . the ability for China to have undue influence is, I think, a much greater challenge and a much more immediate threat than any kind of actual, armed conflict." As he noted, "The level of code in TikTok is exponentially higher, for example, than the lines of code in Facebook." The app can never be "fully safe" while that code is controlled in China.[151]

The Chinese leadership is vigorously fighting to defend TikTok from being banned in the United States because they know what a valuable tool it is. "The one who wins the platform wins the world," said Professor Shi Anbin, a propaganda analyst at the elite Tsinghua University. The fact that the app is under attack in the United States "fully demonstrates that whoever can attract young people will control the future."[152]

TikTok is only one app. ByteDance has created another called CapCut that enables content creators to produce videos. The Biden White House used the app to create catchy videos of President Joe Biden and former president Barack Obama in March 2023, even though ByteDance's TikTok is officially banned from White House devices.[153]

CHAPTER 8

Digital Entertainment

The enormous video game market presents another opportunity for Chinese companies to use "cultural products," as Chinese psychological warfare experts call them, to target Americans. Like TikTok, video games can be highly addictive conveyor belts of propaganda that also collect enormous amounts of user information. They are designed to mimic slot machines by offering a variable reward system that feeds the brain's desire for rewards. Twenty years ago, the largest video game companies in the world were in the United States, Japan, and Europe. Now China owns many of them.

In March 2021, ByteDance acquired Shanghai Moonton Technology, a studio that owns *Mobile Legends: Bang Bang*, a popular mobile phone game.[1]

One of the biggest players in the world gaming market is Tencent, a technology behemoth in China that was started with seed money from the Chinese intelligence services. Tencent, when it's not designing video games, works with the Chinese military to enhance its artificial intelligence (AI) capabilities in warfare. It owns the biggest and most successful video game companies in the world. Beginning in 2011, it made a big push into the US gaming market by acquiring a stake in Activision Blizzard (in 2022 Tencent tried to sell it to Microsoft, but the sale was blocked on antitrust grounds by the federal government). Tencent also bought Riot Games and Epic Games, among others.

Tencent has invested in more than eight hundred firms, including "Activision Blizzard, Ubisoft, PUBG Studios parent company Krafton, PlatinumGames, FromSoftware and Marvelous Inc."[2] Tencent's international video game push comes with the active support of the Chinese government.[3]

Riot Games, which is 100 percent owned by Tencent, is best known for *League of Legends*, which is played by tens of millions of Americans every year. The company's terms of service allow it to transfer data to whomever they want. They also make clear that the company complies with local laws—which in the case of China means sharing those data with the government whenever it wants to.[4] China's 2017 Cybersecurity Law requires companies such as TikTok and Tencent to store their China-generated data on Chinese government–owned servers. Any data transferred from the United States are also open to control by Beijing.[5]

Tencent also owns 40 percent of US-based Epic Games, the producer of *Fortnite*, which, as of 2020, was the most played video game in the world.[6] Epic Games is a private company controlled by Tim Sweeney, the company's founder. Sweeney said that Tencent does not have access to player data, but there is no disclosure requirement because the company is not publicly traded. Epic Games' terms of service, however, include a statement that the company has no liability for any form of data transfer to other parties, including foreign governments.[7] "Epic Games has a history of data security violations," wrote the data security specialist Aynne Kokas.[8]

Epic Games pays dozens of celebrities such as John Cena, LeBron James, Ariana Grande, and Bruno Mars large fees to incorporate their likenesses into their games.[9]

Tencent also owns a majority stake in Supercell, the producer of *Clash of Clans*.[10]

As with TikTok, the people who are playing these games are in general young: 60 percent of the people playing *Fortnite* are eighteen to twenty-four years old. These platforms are about more than game play; they have become communication forums where players connect socially. *Fortnite* has even hosted live concerts, during which people interact with fellow gamers.[11] Chinese companies' domination of the video game market translates into access to and influence over young people.

"China has several ways it can take its ideals to the world through games, and build a new kind of global power," warned Abishur Prakash, a cofounder of the Center for Innovating the Future.[12]

"Communication determines influence," reads one CCP textbook on propaganda. "Whoever has advanced means of communication and strong communication ability will be able to spread cultural concepts and values widely."[13]

Vey-Sern Ling, a senior analyst at Bloomberg Intelligence, believes that Chinese games have so deeply penetrated American culture that there is little chance they will ever be banned. "I doubt there is the political willpower to keep [American] kids from their *LoL* [*League of Legends*], *Fortnite* or *Brawl Stars*," he said.[14]

There is also the problem of data. The data threat posed by video games might be even greater than for TikTok. Gamers must usually provide their real names and payment information to the Chinese companies. They might also have to include a date of birth. If they chat with other players, they generate voice samples that can be stored and used for "deep fakes" that can fool their friends and family.[15]

What the Chinese government might do with these data is unclear, but the possibilities are troubling. Data are needed for algorithms and AI to work effectively—the more data, the better. "Tencent is well-positioned to contribute Chinese AI tools for military use because of the vast scale of its data-gathering practices, which enhance its AI expertise," wrote Kokas.[16]

Showa American Story is a popular role-playing video game starring Choko, a teenage gun-toting hero. The game is designed and produced by NEKCOM, based in Wuhan, China, and is set in the United States, which has become "an unofficial colony of Japanese economics and culture." In an interview with the Chinese nationalist website Guancha Syndicate, NEKCOM founder Luo Xiangyu noted the fact that the game is told from a "unique Chinese perspective," which is also in line with the CCP's propaganda goals. "We wanted to do something that was centered on the popular culture of the 1980s with a lot of American and Japanese culture," he said. "But we wanted to approach it from our own Chinese perspective." This means that the game is told through "the Chinese interpretation of other subjects." The game is widely played in the United States on PlayStation 4 and the online gaming service Steam. Guancha News declared in a headline, "Chinese Team Develops Game About 'Japanese Culture Colonizing America':

Telling the Chinese Story Well Does Not Necessarily Mean Telling Chinese Stories."[17]

The CCP sees video games as "national cultural exports" that can "create high-quality national style games to tell the Chinese story well and spread the voice of China well."[18] In one section of a cadet handbook on "The Role and Mission of External Propaganda Work," the party says that to "tell a good Chinese story" is the first step of effective propaganda work. To be clear, what it means by the phrase is, in its own words, "why Marxism 'works,' [and] why socialism with Chinese characteristics is 'good.'" It also means praising "the CCP's governance of the country."[19] To that end, the CCP runs game forums in China attended by all the major video game producers to discuss how to enhance their propaganda work inside video games. These events are organized by something called the China Audio-Video and Digital Publishing Association, which is tied to the Central Propaganda Department of the Communist Party.[20]

The CCP is counting on video games to influence young people in the United States and elsewhere. "Video games [are] one form of media that the party recognizes is highly attractive to young audiences in China, but particularly overseas," wrote Devin Thorne, an analyst at the Insikt Group. "And the question that we see work units under the Central Propaganda Department actively researching is how to disseminate Chinese culture—as curated by the party, obviously—and Chinese policies into video games."[21]

Genshin Impact is a fantasy role-playing game produced in Shanghai, China. The game is enormously popular with teens in the United States, ranking in the top ten on Apple Store downloads of adventure games.[22] The company behind the game is miHoYo, which boasts a CCP Party Committee. "The propaganda value that has been highlighted in party state media in relation to Genshin Impact's popularity overseas is that it's transmitting Chinese culture, particularly traditional Chinese culture," Thorne said. "It's sort of packaging that in a very fun and engaging way that's going to draw audiences in."[23]

Like TikTok, Chinese video game companies are at the beck and call of the Chinese government and intelligence services.

CHAPTER 9

The People's Republic of Hollywood

The Chinese Communist Party Propaganda Department has a foothold of influence in the United States not only through TikTok and video games but also through Hollywood, the quintessentially American industry.

Pretty much every major Hollywood studio now has coproduction and investor relationships with—and is therefore influenced by—Chinese companies. This includes some of the biggest names in entertainment. Huayi Brothers Media, Perfect World Pictures, and TIK Films "appear to be the primary conduits with which the PRC is funneling money and influencing the content that appears in the films that result from these co-productions." They have deals with famous Hollywood studios such as Universal Pictures, the Tyler Perry Company, Summit Entertainment, Miramax, New Line Cinema, DreamWorks, Lionsgate, Legendary Pictures, Warner Brothers, Amblin Entertainment, Team Downey, Apatow Productions, and more.[1] Some of these companies, such as Lionsgate, have numerous deals with several Chinese companies. Paramount has eight such deals in place.[2]

Coproduction deals mean that the Chinese companies involved help finance the high cost of big Hollywood film productions and help distribute the films in China. These coproduction deals also make the entire production legally accountable to the Central Propaganda Department of the CCP, meaning that the CCP assumes the right to determine what is included in a film and what is not and, more subtly, the inclusion of messaging designed to advance the interests of the Party.[3]

Some Hollywood executives and stars seem especially willing to embrace Beijing's messaging. Take, for example, the Russo brothers, Joe and Anthony, who have directed some of the biggest hits in recent years, including *Captain America: The Winter Soldier, Captain America: Civil War, Avengers: Infinity War,* and *Avengers: Endgame.* Subversive political themes abound in their Hollywood blockbusters. "We're not interested in a blindly patriotic interpretation of the character [Captain America]," noted Joe Russo. "We're much more interested in a deconstructed, subversive interpretation of the character. You can't have a character called Captain America without examining what that means."[4] *Captain America: The Winter Soldier,* was called by one reviewer a critique of "the post-Snowden US landscape of state surveillance and counter-terrorist overreach."[5]

Though critical of the United States as a surveillance state, the Russo brothers miss the irony of going into business with the biggest surveillance state on the planet: China. When Beijing decided to make a nationalistic action movie called *Wolf Warrior 2,* the brothers were happy to help it increase the quality of the film. *Wolf Warrior 2* charts the success of a heroic Chinese military officer who takes on evil Western mercenaries. One promo poster for the film showed the hero giving the middle finger with a patch that read I FIGHT FOR CHINA in English. The tagline below read, "Anyone who offends China, no matter how remote, must be exterminated."[6] The film idealizes the CCP and the Chinese government. Some have compared it to *Rambo,* but this is not accurate.[7] Though *Rambo* was patriotic in terms of its love of country, it was also highly critical of the US government and American bureaucrats. Some of John Rambo's biggest battles were with his own government. The same cannot be said of *Wolf Warrior 2,* which only praises the Chinese government (specifically, its positive work in Africa as compared to the United States' failures) and also pushes foreign policy such as the Belt and Road Initiative.[8] Indeed, the film elevates Chinese government bureaucrats to superhero status. No wonder Chinese embassies held screenings with receptions for the film.[9]

The Russo brothers provided advice on the film and introduced the Chinese director "to some of our relationships in the business, like a stunt team." They also arranged "a bunch of meetings . . . with some of the top-tier visual effects houses in the U.S."[10] and lined up the American actor Frank Grillo to play the villain in the film. According to Grillo, the Russo brothers' involvement helps make Chinese propaganda films competitive in global markets.[11]

The Russo brothers set up a film company in Los Angeles called AGBO, which they described as a "progressive film studio."[12] In 2018, AGBO received a $250 million investment from one of China's largest film companies.[13] They also set up a start-up studio with offices in Los Angeles and Beijing called Anthem & Song in what the *Hollywood Reporter* called "a hush-hush deal." The plan was for the brothers to produce Chinese-language films.[14] The brothers explained that they were turning to the Chinese film business because there is "no independent scene" in the United States anymore. The Chinese film industry is, of course, far less independent than the industry in the United States.[15]

Few people in Hollywood are willing to go quite as far as the Russo brothers, but others such as Steven Spielberg and Jeffrey Katzenberg are happy to do cofinancing deals with Chinese companies, which means that their films are subject to the scrutiny of the CCP Propaganda Department. Katzenberg wields enormous power not only in Hollywood but in Washington, DC, as well. He recently pledged that he would provide "all the resources" needed for Joe Biden to win reelection in 2024. And he has the resources to do it.[16]

Beijing casts a longer shadow on Hollywood productions than you might think. Of the one hundred highest-grossing movies released between 2014 and 2018, forty-one had Chinese investors.[17] Particularly popular are the science fiction and action genres, which allow the films to construct new, dystopian worlds that speculate about societal demise.[18]

Films are ideal for spreading propaganda because audiences expect to be entertained and thus let their guard down. Big blockbusters such as *Mortal Engines*, *Transformers: Age of Extinction*, and *Pacific Rim: Uprising* were all produced by American studios and financed with Chinese money. Many of the main characters are Chinese. In *Pacific Rim*, a California pilot named Jake is living a "hedonistic" lifestyle in the Golden State, when he is arrested early in the film. To avoid jail time, he agrees to travel to China to train pilots. As the story progresses, he learns that his selfishness is the problem and that he feels fulfilled by contributing to the defense of the Pacific Rim.[19]

Ethnic Tibetans are not so welcome in these films. When Marvel began work on the superhero movie *Doctor Strange*, they changed one of the central characters to avoid offending Beijing. The Ancient One, who was Tibetan in the comic books, was changed to Celtic. One of the film's writers later admitted that they had removed Tibetans from the film to avoid crossing the Chinese government.[20]

Hollywood blockbusters coproduced by Chinese companies and intended for release in the Chinese market also have far fewer dark-skinned stars than those released solely in the United States, including a lot of Hollywood blockbusters. According to a study conducted by professors at the Johns Hopkins Carey Business School, "Chinese society's aesthetic preference for lighter skin can be linked to the more frequent casting of pale-skinned stars in films targeting the Chinese market."[21]

The content of films is changing, too, with the plotlines often involving American characters being aided by technologically or intellectually superior Chinese characters. In films such as *The Martian*, starring Matt Damon, a stranded American astronaut is rescued by the Chinese government courtesy of a top secret rocket booster technology that it provides to NASA.[22] In *The Meg*, a main character is a Chinese marine biologist who draws upon her knowledge of sharks to deal with the massive creature. Both films were, of course, coproduced with China.[23]

Perhaps the easiest way to illustrate the escalation of CCP themes injected into storylines is to track the evolution of the children's films *Kung Fu Panda*, *Kung Fu Panda 2*, and *Kung Fu Panda 3*. The first *Kung Fu Panda* was made by Katzenberg's DreamWorks Animation without financing from Beijing. It depicts a martial arts bear named Po who worries whether he can rise to the challenge of the kung fu legends. He eventually believes in himself as an individual and defeats the enemy. In *Kung Fu Panda 2*, the story continues as a mentor helps Po find his unique strength and peace to vanquish the enemy—despite the enemy's superior technology.

But the film became less of an irreverent comedy and offered a "reverent tribute to Chinese culture." At the time, DreamWorks announced plans to construct a $330 million studio near Shanghai. Katzenberg sat down with Yu Zhengsheng, the chief of the Shanghai CCP, who encouraged him to produce "cultural products" that would help China's image. The new studio would, of course, be majority owned by Dream-Works' Chinese partners.[24]

Kung Fu Panda 3, cofinanced by China, has a very different message. Po no longer focuses on himself as an individual but instead focuses on the collective, encouraging the villagers to take up arms in an animated "people's war" against the antagonist. In short, collective Eastern values slowly replace the more individualistic Western values throughout the course of the series.[25]

In 2019, DreamWorks released another animated film called *Abominable*, about a group of teenagers trying to save a Yeti. The film, which was cofinanced by China's Pearl Studio, featured a map of China that included the Communist government's territorial claims in the South China Sea, which didn't even figure into the plot. The so-called nine-dash line makes territories claimed by Vietnam, China, Taiwan, and the Philippines strictly Chinese territory.[26] Some might wonder: Does the fact that this territorial claim is mentioned in a children's film matter? Gregory Poling, the director of the Asia Maritime Transparency Initiative, believes that it does. "If you do slap a nine-dash line on say Dream-Works movies that get localized and distributed around the world, it does I think send a subtle message that (the) default world view should be that the nine-dash line is real and legitimate," he said.[27]

In 2020, Pearl and DreamWorks partnered on another children's animation project, *Over the Moon*. The film is a paean to Chinese technological prowess; the main character expounds extensively on an advanced high-speed rail system being built by the government.[28]

Steven Spielberg has also become cozy with Beijing over the years. In 2016, he allowed Alibaba—which we have seen is largely state-controlled—to buy a stake in his company, Amblin Entertainment.[29] Necessarily, his company works closely with state censors to ensure that his films meet with their approval. Spielberg was not always so willing to play ball with Beijing. In 2008, he ducked out of a project connected with the Beijing Olympics because he was concerned about the Chinese government's involvement with human rights violations in Darfur.[30] How times change.

The Walt Disney Company's 2020 remake of *Mulan* was coproduced by the China Film Co-production Corporation, and the Central Propaganda Department had to approve the script.[31]

The politics of producing children's entertainment is enormous in China. The film *Despicable Me 2* was denied distribution in China because, it was rumored, the minions too closely resembled former CCP secretary general Jiang Zemin.[32] (Chinese authorities denied the rumors, insisting that the film had not been submitted for censorship approval.)

Films cofinanced with Chinese production companies show a consistent pro-Beijing tilt.

In 2016's *The Great Wall*, starring Matt Damon and Willem Dafoe and produced by Legendary Pictures and Universal Pictures, European travelers on the Silk Road flee behind the Great Wall of China after suffering a brutal attack by a monster. They end up fighting alongside Chinese soldiers to defeat the beast. In a central scene from the film, one of the Europeans sits down with a Chinese commander, and they discuss their lives. The Chinese commander notes that although the Europeans are mercenaries fighting for money, she—with great moral superiority—is fighting for the safety of her people.[33] The film, which was directed by the Chinese government's "officially ordained film-maker," was produced by a Chinese studio, whose parent company's chairman explained in 2016 that part of his role in life was expanding China's "soft power" around the world through film.[34]

The World War II epic movie *Midway*, starring Woody Harrelson and Nick Jonas, among others, was produced by Summit Entertainment with funding from China. Although a story about the US Navy's victory over the Japanese Navy in the decisive battle in 1942, the film goes out of its way to add a subplot that is not about the naval battle but highlights how much China suffered during the Second World War, with ample mention of how it helped defeat Japan. Chinese state media noted that the funding had given China a bigger role in the action film.[35]

The zombie blockbuster *World War Z*, starring Brad Pitt, was a global hit. Produced by Paramount Pictures, its plot was changed by studio executives to avoid upsetting Beijing. In one scene, the main characters believe that the virus that is causing people to turn into zombies originated in China. The scene was cut.[36]

In the film *Skiptrace*, starring Johnny Knoxville and Jackie Chan and distributed by Saban Films, an American witnesses a murder in China and is tracked down by a Chinese detective named Benny to testify at the murder trial. The American is depicted as a selfish "lowlife," while Benny is a completely honorable man. The American eventually realizes that Benny has his priorities straight and follows his example.[37]

In the remake of *The Karate Kid*, starring Jaden Smith as Dre, the main character at first finds himself in a decaying, dirty, and dangerous Detroit. But when he and his mother move to Beijing, they find it safe, clean, and orderly. The mother refers to China as a "magical place" that offers a better life than Detroit does. The film, produced by Will Smith, might have been called *The Karate Kid*, but since karate comes from Japan, in this film Dre learns kung fu, which comes from China.[38]

The film *Looper*, starring Emily Blunt and Bruce Willis and produced by TriStar Pictures, is set in 2044. The main character works and is paid in silver, but he cashes the money in for yuan, the currency of the People's Republic of China. At one point, he meets a time traveler who tells him, "I'm from the future . . . you should go to China." The film contrasts Kansas City with Shanghai, with the Chinese city clearly being superior.[39]

Universal Studios' *The Mummy: Tomb of the Dragon Emperor*, was coproduced by a Chinese film company, which meant changing the script. The producers cut from the script the imperialistic ambitions of the story's villain, a resurrected Han emperor, because apparently emperors were not imperialistic. (Huh?) "I could see how if you had a certain mindset you could misinterpret" the script, explained director Rob Cohen in defending the move.[40]

Transformers: Age of Extinction, starring Mark Wahlberg and produced by Paramount Pictures, fits the same pattern, with senior Chinese government officials coming off as results oriented and capable. In contrast, American officials are bumbling and generally incompetent. Like the others mentioned here, the film was cofinanced by Chinese companies.[41] It's part of a pattern in many of these coproduced films: "morally compromised or outright corrupt Americans" are defeated by Chinese heroes. In *Transformers*, an evil American, played by Stanley Tucci, is defeated by a Chinese woman named Su Yeming, who is working alongside Wahlberg.[42] The film is "a splendidly patriotic film," noted one reviewer in *Variety*, "if you happen to be Chinese."[43]

"These films implicitly endorse a view of China as benign, and to some extent even weaken the positional superiority of the U.S. vis-à-vis China, which, more than just being a passive victim of American folly, [China] assumes an active role in helping to right American-led wrongs," noted the scholar Chris Homewood.[44]

Part IV

LOOT A BURNING HOUSE

（趁火打劫）

CHAPTER 10

Social Engineering a Pandemic

In New York, refrigerator and freezer trucks arrived at hospitals empty, to be loaded up with dead bodies. The trucks would eventually head to crematoriums for the bodies to be burned.[1] In 2020, death and the fear of death were everywhere. In Houston, Texas, twenty-eight-year-old Dr. Adeline Fagan worked overtime trying to save lives. Like thousands of other frontline workers, she treated covid patients without wearing necessary personal protective equipment (PPE). She contracted covid and died.[2] It was not just a US problem; for most of 2020–2021, the virus cast a huge, ominous shadow over the entire planet. Millions of people died, and billions of people's lives were disrupted. It was the most disruptive global event since World War II.

The Chinese Communist Party (CCP) stands at the center of this pandemic. When the house began to burn because of the virus, the CCP took actions that amounted to looting the house while the world was fighting the fire. In some ways, our political class participated in the looting. And since those events, it has completely failed to hold Beijing accountable.

CCP leaders were quite clear that they saw the pandemic as an opportunity. Li Shenming, a deputy director of the Twelfth National People's Congress, wrote in the summer of 2020 about the pandemic, "Given the complicated international situation, the international struggles are entering an age of *unrestricted warfare* waged in all fields, directions and dimensions." (Emphasis added.) He explained that "it is China, in the final analysis, that is in control of this important period of strategic opportunity for development." The virus was "deeply revealing the decadent and declining nature of the capitalist system and values in the US. . . . The key lies in which country can outlast the other."[3]

Whether the virus emerged from a lab leak, which seems very likely, or was simply a natural occurrence, as some people continue to insist, Beijing manipulated the world. It conducted policies and actions that maximized the damage the virus would inflict. That in and of itself constitutes a bioweapon attack.

China also used the virus to advance its authoritarian system of government in the United States and democratic societies around the world. The pandemic brought what US Supreme Court justice Neil Gorsuch called "the greatest intrusion on civil liberties in the peacetime history of this country."[4] In short, Beijing manipulated the world's leaders into taking draconian measures to respond to the virus.

Yet our political leaders have overwhelmingly remained silent in the grim aftermath of the pandemic, having been outmaneuvered by Beijing. It would be as if, after the Pearl Harbor attack, our leaders had decided to go on as if nothing had happened. Only the death toll from covid has been far higher.

Exactly when the covid story begins is itself a mystery. In the fall of 2019, mounting evidence, largely concealed from the world, suggested that something was not right in Wuhan, China. In "late Summer and early Fall 2019," satellites detected a surge in the number of people in hospitals in Wuhan; the hospital parking lots were closer to capacity than usual, according to researchers at Boston University, Harvard Medical School, and Boston Children's Hospital. At the same time, searches for the terms "cough" and "diarrhea" in Wuhan jumped on Baidu, China's largest search engine. Cough and diarrhea are, of course, symptoms of covid.[5]

On September 12, 2019, the Wuhan Institute of Virology (WIV), which was conducting extensive research on viruses, quietly removed from the internet a database of 22,000 virus samples and their sequences that had previously been open access to scientists around the world.[6]

In October of that year, the International Military Sports Council Military World Games opened in Wuhan, with thousands of military athletes from around the globe participating. Some were stunned to find Wuhan a "ghost town," in the words of an athlete from Luxembourg.[7] Scores of athletes later reported getting seriously ill while at the games. One Canadian athlete recounted, "This was a city of 15 million people that was in lockdown. It was strange, but we were told this was to make it easy for the Games' participants to get around. [I got] very sick 12 days after we arrived, with fever, chills, vomiting, insomnia. . . . On our flight to come home . . . 60 Canadian athletes on the flight were put in isolation (at the back of the plane) for the 12-hour flight."[8]

By November 2019, three researchers from the WIV, all of whom had been working on coronavirus research, visited the hospital with symptoms consistent with what later became known as covid-19.[9]

The *South China Morning Post* later reported that internal Chinese documents claimed that the first covid-19 case had occurred somewhere near Wuhan on November 17. After that, up to five new cases had been reported per day through mid-December.[10]

By December 2019, people were becoming seriously ill in the United States and Europe. Blood samples taken from sick patients at the time and later retested confirmed that they had had covid-19.[11]

By the end of January 2020, the Chinese government blocked flights from Wuhan to the rest of China but allowed flights to leave it for the rest of the world.[12] Wuhan Tianhe International Airport had direct international flights to New York, San Francisco, Milan, Paris, Rome, Tokyo, Hamburg, Dubai, and many other international destinations.[13]

Perhaps someone in the United States should have noticed all of this. Chinese officials must have known by late December the lethality of what they had on their hands: a very dangerous and highly contagious disease. But Chinese laboratories "were ordered to stop further testing, destroy samples, and suppress the news to the fullest extent possible."[14]

The Chinese government not only made a critical decision to lie to the rest of the world but moved to corner the market on masks and other protective gear necessary to fight the virus. Beijing's policies maximized the damage covid-19 inflicted on the West. If Chinese authorities had declared a health emergency at the end of December, the global pandemic could have been slowed. In December, according to official figures, there were just a few hundred patients in Wuhan. By January 12, the number of cases exceeded fifteen thousand.[15]

Dr. Anthony Fauci, at the time the director of the National Institute of Allergy and Infectious Diseases (NIAID), said he learned about the outbreak in China on December 31, 2019, or in the "first couple of days" of January 2020.[16] Chinese officials reassured the world that the virus was not transmissible from human to human—something it now appears they knew was a lie.

Dr. Robert Redfield, then the director of the Centers for Disease Control and Prevention (CDC), received a phone call on January 3, 2020. It was his Chinese counterpart, Dr. George Fu Gao. Gao told Redfield that people had been getting sick after exposure to the virus at the wet market in Wuhan and no human-to-human transmission was taking place. A few days later, Gao admitted to Redfield that many cases were emerging that were not connected to the market.[17] Aware of the WIV and hoping to rule it out as a possible source, Redfield offered to send specialists to help investigate. Chinese officials didn't respond.

Also on January 3, China's National Health Commission ordered Chinese biolabs to destroy all samples of the virus, SARS-CoV-2, including those they had obtained from people already infected. Beijing also refused repeated requests from the World Health Organization (WHO) to give it access to the laboratory logs at WIV.[18]

Beijing aggressively silenced anyone in the country who talked openly about the virus. By January 1, eight people had been investigated by the police for spreading rumors about the disease, including medical doctors. In all, 254 people would be charged with the crime of spreading rumors in the first week of January 2020.[19]

At the same time, Chinese *imports* of critical PPE surged. According to a Department of Homeland Security internal intelligence memo obtained by the author, in the first month of 2020, Chinese imports of surgical face masks jumped by an astonishing 278 percent, imports of surgical gowns increased by a whopping 72 percent, and imports of surgical gloves climbed 32 percent.[20]

At the same time, China's *exports* of such critical medical supplies dropped like rocks into a pond. The export of surgical gloves and face masks plunged by half (48 percent each), and that of surgical gowns fell even further (71 percent); exports of intubation kits (56 percent), medical ventilators (45 percent), thermometers (53 percent), and cotton balls and swabs (58 percent) also dramatically declined.[21] If the American house is about to burn, Chinese officials must have thought, we may want to buy up all their fire hoses.

Beijing then worked to manipulate the trade data to obscure its actions. As the Department of Homeland Security stated in that internal intelligence memo, "In its communications, China intentionally concealed its trade activity by publicly denying it has ever imposed an export ban on masks and other medical supplies, combining its publicly released January and February trade figures to likely conceal the details of its import and export of medical supplies, and delayed release of key trade data, according to information from local press and a commercial trade data provider."[22]

On January 14, 2020, Chinese officials reaffirmed the lie that human-to-human transmission wasn't a danger. The WHO tweeted the same.[23]

On January 19, a thirty-five-year-old man showed up at a clinic in Snohomish County, Washington, just north of Seattle, with a fever and a cough. He had just returned from Wuhan. The following day, the CDC confirmed that he had the virus later known as covid-19, the first known case in the United States. Four days later, a woman in a Chicago hospital suffering from pneumonia became the second US-diagnosed case.[24]

PPE supplies were already pouring into China, a head start the country had obtained by lying to the world. On January 22, the WHO tried to pass a declaration of a Public Health Emergency of International Concern (PHEIC) to prepare the world for what was coming, but China blocked it. On January 30, the WHO voted again; China again tried to block the declaration but failed.[25]

Beyond the usual import methods, Beijing quietly activated a clandestine global network to procure masks and other supplies and send them to China. Thousands of United Front groups began aggressively buying critical supplies off retail store shelves in the countries where they lived, including the United States, Europe, Australia, and elsewhere, and shipping them to China. In Australia, the Border Force reported intercepting five "massive" shipments headed for China of "medical supplies, including masks and other personal protective equipment," that had been collected by United Front groups in Australia. That occurred just as Australia had begun scrambling for scarce masks.[26] In Canada, a Chinese businessman with possible ties to a money-laundering operation sent his private jet back to China with a load of PPE supplies. The

Chinese news agency Xinhua even praised the Chinese patriots "from dozens of countries on five continents [who] joined this invisible battle . . . they travelled day and night and raced against time to send back batches of scarce supplies to the motherland."[27]

In Japan, United Front groups gathered "520,000 masks in three days." The same was happening around the world from Toronto to Nairobi, from Buenos Aires to Milan. Canadian member of Parliament Erin O'Toole even went public with the report that Canadian intelligence believed that "United Front groups in Canada helped Beijing stockpile coronavirus safety supplies."[28] He was one of the few leaders who did.

At the end of January, as the world began reacting to the reality of the global threat, China managed to import some twenty million respirators and surgical masks in twenty-four hours.[29] At first, the Western world, oblivious to what was going on, generously sent China supplies. The European Union shipped nearly sixty tons of medical supplies to China, much of it from national strategic stockpiles. Beijing even asked that the supplies be shipped discreetly, lest it be somehow publicly embarrassed. "By contrast, when the pandemic arrived in Europe, the Chinese government made a big show of offering 'aid' to Europe—much of which actually came with a price tag."[30] By the end of February 2020, a stunning *two billion masks* had been shipped to China.[31]

In Washington, President Trump publicly thanked Beijing for its effort to "contain the Coronavirus," adding "on behalf of the American People, I want to thank President Xi!"[32] The Trump administration, apparently oblivious to the Chinese buying spree of critical medical supplies, transported seventeen tons of medical supplies to China in February and committed a total of $100 million to the effort.[33]

Later, US intelligence figured out what Beijing had been doing and spelled it out in a report titled "New Analytic Technique Indicates China Likely Hid Severity of COVID-19 from the International Community While It Stockpiled Medical Supplies": "We assess the Chinese Government intentionally concealed the severity of COVID-19 from the international community in early January while it stockpiled medical supplies by both increasing imports and decreasing exports," wrote Homeland Security intelligence analysts in that May 2020 memo. "We further assess the Chinese Government attempted to hide its actions by denying there were export restrictions and obfuscating and delaying provision of its trade data."[34]

At first, Dr. Fauci calmly reassured Americans that "This [virus] is not a major threat to the people of the United States and this is not something that the citizens of the United States right now should be worried about." Even after China admitted that the disease was transferrable from human to human, Fauci saw minimal risk for the United States. The Wuhan virus was "a very, very low risk to the United States," he said in a January 26, 2020, radio interview. He resisted the idea of a travel ban, telling US senators that restricting travelers from China was not a good idea. Redfield, he said, supported that position.[35] Within a matter of weeks, he moved from not supporting international travel restrictions to supporting a national stay-at-home-order.[36]

Rewind to October 31, 2019, when the Central Committee of the Chinese Communist Party gathered in the Great Hall of the People in Beijing. President Xi, in his remarks, envisioned a great clash coming between China and the West. The competition in political systems "is the most fundamental competition among countries," he wrote in a message published in China's top political journal, *Qiushi*. He exhorted the Propaganda Department to be prepared to "tell the good story about China's system at home and overseas. Constantly strengthen the persuasiveness and appeal of China's state system and state governance system." These systems, he emphasized, are "fundamentally based on Marxist principles."[37]

The global pandemic that soon followed hardly dampened that propaganda goal. With covid raging in China and moving to the shores of the United States, President Xi published a statement declaring that the Chinese government, rather than retreating in the face of the virus, would "exploit the pandemic" as a chance to expand Beijing's power on the global stage. He used a phrase that he would later repeat to leaders around the world: "We are promoting the concept of a Community of Common Destiny for All Mankind."[38]

What did he mean by that? It sounded friendly enough—idealistic, even unifying. But according to Chinese government officials, Xi's "idea of a Community of Common Destiny for All Mankind is a reflection of Marxist theory of the collective with a modern spirit." It means a "singular human collective," a twenty-first-century version of the "unified international proletariat."[39]

Xi saw an opportunity to weaponize the pandemic to advance China's ideological agenda. When the virus started to slam the United States, an occasion to advance Beijing's cause presented itself. In part, that was because of the equipment shortage that Beijing had helped engineer. It was the perfect moment to foist the Chinese form of governance onto the rest of the world.[40]

That Chinese form of governance was less than friendly in response to the pandemic: a brutal, police-enforced lockdown was enacted. Some people were forcibly locked in their homes with metal bars. Violators of the lockdown were publicly chained to metal posts.[41] Before the 2020 pandemic, forced lockdowns were widely seen in the West as being ineffective, damaging, even draconian. In 2017, in fact, the Centers for Disease Control and Prevention had issued guidelines for a "very high severity" pandemic, which they defined as one akin to the Spanish flu. The guidelines called for "*voluntary* home isolation *of ill persons*." (Emphasis added.) The "CDC might recommend voluntary home quarantine of exposed household members in areas where novel influenza virus circulates," it wrote. But it was voluntary, not mandatory. And it was voluntary for those who were *ill*. The CDC did *not* call for a forced lockdown for the general population during a pandemic.[42]

It had long been accepted that lockdowns and the severe disruptions they caused sabotaged the fight against pandemics. Dr. Donald Henderson, who was responsible for eradicating smallpox, explained to colleagues in 2006, "Experience has shown that communities faced with epidemics or other adverse events respond best and with the least anxiety when the normal social functioning of the community is least disrupted." Indeed, he and his colleagues went on, "There are no historical observations or scientific studies that support the confinement by quarantine of groups of possibly infected people for extended periods in order to slow the spread of influenza." He even cited a WHO working group that had concluded that "forced isolation and quarantine are ineffective and impractical." And given all that, "The negative consequences of large-scale quarantine are so extreme . . . that this mitigation measure should be eliminated from serious consideration."[43]

In contrast, lockdowns have long been enforced in China. While a quarantine requires the sick to stay at home, a lockdown requires everyone to stay at home. The practice has been common in China going back centuries.[44]

In the crucial days of the spring of 2020, American and European leaders abandoned its own medical wisdom and imitated the authoritarian policies of the Chinese police state. Within weeks, they imposed forced lockdowns throughout the Western world. Beijing lauded their doing so as an endorsement of its repressive measures.

What happened?

Beijing's hand loomed large in laying the groundwork for US leaders to embrace the Chinese model of keeping people in their homes.

In February 2020, the Imperial College in London issued a stunning report that received massive media attention. It sent many Western leaders into a panic. A research team led by Professor Neil Ferguson of Imperial College London used a computer model informed by flawed Chinese data to predict that two million–plus Americans and five hundred thousand British would die of covid—*unless something drastic was done*. The stunning report received massive media attention. Later, the former chief scientist for the European Centre for Disease Prevention and Control, Johan Giesecke, called Ferguson's model "the most influential scientific paper" he could recall. He also called it "one of the most wrong."[45]

In March 2020, Ferguson and his researchers at Imperial College London issued another bombshell report: China's brutal lockdowns were halting the virus! According to the report, China had "no new confirmed cases" of covid-19 transmitted from person to person—ostensibly because of the police-state lockdown. "This is an indication that the social distancing measures enacted in China have led to control of COVID-19," the research team claimed.[46] Ferguson concluded that the only "viable option" for Britain (and the world) was to follow was the model of "suppression" (like that being used in China).[47] But that conclusion was, in fact, flawed, given that it was based on unreliable data provided by the Chinese government.

The newspaper headlines shook world leaders and their advisors. President Trump was briefed in the White House on Ferguson's findings—reportedly, they "changed" his "demeanor."[48] Western political leaders quickly looked to imitate repressive China. What no one seemed to notice at the time was the curious ties that Imperial College London enjoyed with Beijing and Chinese involvement with the studies.

In October 2015, Imperial College London welcomed a very special visitor. Chinese leader Xi Jinping was on his only visit to London since he had achieved the party leadership, and among the few stops on his itinerary was a visit to that institution of higher learning. College president Alice Gast welcomed Xi with a glowing speech that celebrated Imperial College London's close work with the Chinese government. "Imperial College London strives to be just that, China's best academic partner in the west. . . . As China's top research partner in the UK, Imperial's academics and students benefit from collaboration on a daily basis," she told President Xi and the crowd in attendance. Interestingly, one of the areas of collaboration was "public health."[49]

Imperial College London was in rarefied company. The relationship continued, and in 2018, it was one of only two European colleges (none in the United States) to sign a "strategic academic cooperation agreement" with China's most elite college, Tsinghua University in Beijing.[50] Indeed, Imperial College also was the site of two major research centers that were sponsored by Chinese military-linked companies, whose work could "advance China's military ambitions." They were shut down by the British government in 2022.[51] When Ferguson and his team, which included Chinese researchers, put together their bombshell reports, they relied on data from Beijing.[52] Chinese misinformation embedded in those apocalyptic reports played to human fears, causing Western leaders to imitate the repressive Chinese state and forcibly lock their societies down.

Ferguson's reports were not the only vectors of deadly disinformation Beijing used to push Americans toward lockdowns. At about the same time that he released his reports, Dr. Clifford Lane, an assistant to Dr. Fauci, was dispatched to China as part of a WHO group investigating the virus.[53] Not surprisingly, the trip was choreographed by the CCP, which controlled what the delegation could see and to whom they could speak. As the delegation traveled between meetings and events, Western members of the team sat on one bus, Chinese doctors on the other. It was Lane's first trip to China, so he had no experience dealing with Chinese government officials or the CCP.[54]

Lane returned with an assessment of how China was handling the virus. "When we got there, the outbreak was already coming under control in China," he wrote to Fauci in an email, naively believing what CCP officials had told him. "The measures they put in place appear to be working. I think that they felt there were lessons learned they wanted to share with the rest of the world."[55]

How absurd are the Chinese numbers when it comes to reported covid cases? China, with 1.4 billion people, continually reported cases and death rates that compared more than favorably with those of much smaller, more remote countries.[56] The country of ground zero, no less.

Lane also reinforced what the Ferguson team had said and what Beijing wanted the world to believe: "From what I saw in China, we may have to go to as extreme a degree of social distancing to help bring our outbreak under control."[57]

Lane took the Chinese officials' word for the situation. In turn, so did Fauci. "Cliff went to China, and we wanted to find out what was going on there to see if there could be any lessons learned from what they were doing compared to what we're doing," he later testified under oath.[58] Interestingly, Lane never made it to Wuhan. Instead, he met with Chinese officials in Beijing and accepted their data and conclusion that "well-regimented" actions (mandatory lockdowns) were necessary.[59]

Chinese government officials, with their own political agenda, shaped Fauci's policy direction. On February 28, Fauci had written in the *New England Journal of Medicine* that the effects of covid "may ultimately be more akin to those of a severe seasonal influenza."[60] On March 9, he calmly advised that healthy people could go on cruise ships.[61] Less than a week later, he endorsed the idea of a national shutdown.[62]

On February 25, 2020, Donald McNeil, then a science and health writer at the *New York Times*, wrote Fauci an email comparing the Chinese and American responses to the virus:

In China, we in the media tend to report the horrors and the lockdown and the government's early lies. . . .

But the truth is that a lot of average Chinese behaved incredibly heroically in the face of the virus: 25,000 doctors and nurses went into Wuhan to help, knowing they might die. Average people gave up their stockpiles of masks so they could be shipped to Wuhan. Neighborhood committees brought food to thousands of little old ladies and checked on them every day, even as they asked them to stay behind their doors for fear of infection.

Meanwhile, in America, people tend to act like selfish pigs interested only in saving themselves. How can I hoard a mask? Where's my vaccine?

Clearly, McNeil's characterization of American's selfishness in contrast with Chinese heroics suggests a narrative with an agenda. And Fauci didn't appear to object to McNeil's characterization.

"You make some very good points, Donald," Fauci responded.[63]

Even before the United States, Italy fell into line with the authoritarian lockdown rhetoric. The leftist government in charge at the beginning of the pandemic had a history of cooperating with the Chinese Communist Party. In 2019, the Italian government had become the first G7 nation to join Beijing in the controversial Belt and Road Initiative.[64]

Italy's minister of health, Roberto Speranza, was a member of the left-wing Article One party. He later published a book titled *Perché guariremo: Dai giorni più duri a una nuova idea di salute* (Why We Will Heal: From the Hardest Days to a New Idea of Health) in October 2020, describing how lockdowns could be used to implement far-left ideas in the government: "I believe that, after so many years going against the wind, there is a possibility of reconstructing a cultural hegemony on a new basis." He also praised China for its covid response—and had no criticism of Beijing's handling of the virus. Indeed, he labeled China a "great protagonist" of our time.[65]

Once Italy announced forced lockdowns, Communist China was happy to offer guidance on how to implement repressive measures. On March 12, 2020, Chinese experts arrived in the country to help the government with the crackdown. "There are still too many people and behaviors on the street to improve," they instructed Italian officials.[66] Ninety percent of the country was closed by the third week in March. But the number of covid-19 cases kept rising.[67]

Italy now became the model for other Western countries, including the United States. If Italy could do it—why couldn't we?

The Trump administration issued guidelines for social distancing and encouraged people not to gather in groups. But with our federal system, it was up to state governors whether they wanted to implement forced closures. America's largest state, California, became the first to enact a mandatory statewide stay-at-home order.

In California, the lockdowns took on a strong-man pose. Authorities not only closed outdoor trails, they filled skate parks with sand. Sheriff's deputies in Los Angeles County even arrested a young man in Malibu for paddle boarding in the ocean.[68]

The next day Illinois followed suit. New York then announced a series of extreme measures, limited only because of a feud between Governor Andrew Cuomo and New York City mayor Bill de Blasio.[69] The rapid pace with which the United States abandoned its own protocols and embraced Beijing's model was remarkable. Even Professor Ferguson, who had gotten the ball rolling with his doomsday reports, was stunned by how quickly the United States slid into repressive measures. "I think people's sense of what is possible in terms of control changed quite dramatically between January and March," he said later. ". . . It's a communist one-party state, we said. We couldn't get away with that in Europe, we thought. . . . And then Italy did it. And we realised we could. . . . If China had not done it, the year would have been very different."[70]

A debate ensued in the United States about the constitutionality of mandates and enforcement—and whether they even worked. Beijing tried to tip the scales in favor of lockdowns. Chinese state media mocked those who disagreed with lockdowns as advocating "wash your hands" to prevent the spread of the virus. Twitter deleted some 170,000 accounts linked to Chinese bot campaigns, but many accounts continued to push propaganda meant to shame.[71]

South Dakota governor Kristi Noem closed schools for the remainder of the year but did not issue a stay-at-home order or close businesses. She was subjected to an online harassment campaign as a result. Other governors faced similar attacks that used similar enough language to have been driven by Chinese bots.[72] The Chinese government even bought ads on Facebook in praise of its response to the virus, without the usual disclaimer that Facebook requires of political and government-backed content.[73]

The fact that the Chinese authorities would invest money and effort in the United States regarding China's virus response is telling. It suggests that they saw enormous political value in American imitation of their tyrannical measures. In their narrative to the world, authoritarianism became the surest way to live; freedom, the fastest way to die. Steven Mosher quoted the editor of the CCP's Global Times: "Chinese government has adopted scientific and effective control measures. Loose political system of the U.S. allows more than 3,000 people [to] die of pandemic every day."[74]

The narrative worked. Officials around the United States began to adopt the Chinese practice of lockdowns and their enforcement through surveillance of the population. A Chinese drone company with deep ties to the Chinese military "graciously" donated a hundred drones to the United States as "disaster relief" to fight covid. Forty-three law enforcement agencies in twenty-two states received the drones, allowing them to monitor citizens to ensure that they complied with stay-at-home orders.

In Elizabeth, New Jersey, officials received five drones from China and used them to "Help combat people not following social distancing." The drones flew around the city and played messages from the mayor telling people to stay home. Local citizens were taken aback at the move. "We are trying to save lives, not be Big Brother," wrote the police department on Twitter. A major portion of the drones went to one state—California.[75]

In the city of Chula Vista, just outside San Diego, the police department rigged two drones with speakers and night vision cameras. "If we need to cover a large area to get an announcement out, or if there were a crowd somewhere that we needed to disperse—we could do it without getting police officers involved," explained a city police captain. The police department also planned to use the drones to inform the homeless population about covid.[76] Exactly how effective it would be to sneak up on an unsuspecting homeless person with a drone and chat at them through a loudspeaker was not mentioned.

Along with the lockdowns and the government-sponsored drones designed to monitor people, snitch lines were established for people to report their neighbors.[77] Students who failed to self-quarantine after returning to campus lost their housing money. Students could anonymously report fellow students who violated covid safety policies.[78]

The transition to Chinese-style lockdowns in the United States was facilitated by prominent US media outlets, which uncritically accepted China's claim that it had conquered covid by the early spring of 2020. Interestingly, media outlets have a history of skepticism regarding US government officials but accepted Communist officials in China at their word.

In March 2020, the *Washington Post* opined that "China's epidemic statistics suggest that its efforts have been effective."[79]

In August 2020, the *New Yorker* ran a piece titled "How China Controlled the Coronavirus."[80] Geremie Barmé, the Australian sinologist who coined the term "Great Firewall," compared the reporting to that of Walter Duranty, the infamous *New York Times* reporter who covered up Stalin's Ukrainian genocide.[81]

In November 2020, the esteemed British medical journal the *Lancet* ran a story about "China's successful control of COVID-19."[82]

In November 2020, the *Washington Post* claimed, "The U.S. has absolutely no control over the coronavirus. China is on top of the tiniest risks."[83] Around the same time, the *New York Times* reported, "U.S. says virus can't be controlled. China aims to prove it wrong."[84]

Of course, the world eventually discovered the obvious: China had not controlled the virus; it had covered it up and controlled the narrative.

From the earliest days of the pandemic, Beijing controlled the media message. On February 3, President Xi directed the Chinese media to report the country's response as "heroic." Three hundred government-paid reporters were sent to Wuhan and surrounding areas to "provide strong public opinion support."[85] Ordinary Chinese people who attempted to tell the world the truth were silenced. For example, Fang Bin, a businessman, disappeared on February 9 after releasing a video of corpses piling up behind a Wuhan hospital.[86]

By mid-March, reporters from the *New York Times*, the *Wall Street Journal*, and the *Washington Post* were expelled from the country.[87]

Western media amplified voices with curious pro-Beijing links uncritically. A key member of Britain's Scientific Advisory Group for Emergencies (SAGE) was Susan Michie. "Test, trace, and isolate system, border controls are really essential . . . social distancing . . . wearing face masks . . . We'll need to keep these going in the long term . . . I think forever," she declared. Michie was a fixture not only in the British media but also on CNN, breathlessly commenting on the need for Americans to get with the program and support government recommendations.[88] Michie, it should be noted, is not a microbiologist or medical expert but a behavioral scientist.[89]

Beyond her association with SAGE, Michie had another affiliation: she is a member of the tiny pro-Beijing Communist Party of Britain. In fact, she has been affiliated with the party for more than forty years. The Communist Party of Britain enjoys "fraternal" ties with the CCP in Beijing. When asked by a British reporter whether her political relationships influenced her views, she responded, "I've come on your program as a scientist . . . you don't ask other scientists about politics. So I'm very happy to speak about science which is what my job is, and to limit it to that."[90]

CNN never asked her about her political affiliations.

Lockdowns in the United States quickly became subject to political manipulation and control. As reported by CNN, hundreds of health care professionals wrote a letter supporting the Black Lives Matters protestors gathering in large numbers, which went against social distancing and lockdown rules. But they added, "This should not be confused with a permissive stance on all gatherings, particularly protests against stay-home orders. Those actions not only oppose public health interventions but are also rooted in white nationalism."[91] They never explained why rejecting lockdowns was a racist matter. Lockdowns enabled a chosen few—almost always Democrats—to exert control not only over people's daily habits but over who had the right to speak out. It was straight out of George Orwell's *Animal Farm*, except that in this case: All free speech is equal, but some free speech is more equal than others.

In Germany, the Federal Ministry of the Interior issued a paper that was widely influential in propelling the West toward lockdowns, calling for measures that were "preventive and repressive in nature" to control covid.[92] Among the paper's authors were German scholars with close ties to China, some of whom openly supported China's policies to control its own population. One of the authors, Otto Kölbl, had taught at a Chinese university and was researching "socioeconomic development in China." If that sounds innocent enough, his views were not. On his blog he described Hong Kong as "parasitic" because of its capitalist characteristics and praised the Chinese Communist Party for how it governed

Tibet.[93] Another author was Maximilian Mayer, who taught at several universities in China and was a research fellow at Renmin University. Mayer had previously been supportive of China's policies when it came to both foreign and energy policy.[94]

China also foisted on the United States and the world other measures that they claimed would help contain the spread of the virus and save lives—but had the opposite effect. Chinese officials explained in the early months of 2020 that perhaps the most effective way to treat severe covid patients was to put them on ventilators. It was "Chinese expert consensus" that ventilators should be the "first choice" for patients facing moderate or severe respiratory problems.[95] This led to panic buying in the United States, most famously epitomized by New York governor Andrew Cuomo. Short of ventilators, he gave an angry press conference on March 24, 2020, when the federal government only sent him four hundred. "What am I going to do with 400 ventilators when I need 30,000?"[96] China graciously stepped in and donated one thousand to New York City.

In the White House, Jared Kushner led an effort to procure one hundred thousand ventilators from domestic manufacturers in one hundred days.[97]

But the advice from China that set off the scramble and panic in the United States was not only wrong—it was dead wrong. Doctors in New York City and elsewhere quickly realized that ventilators did more harm than good. Studies showed that older patients put on ventilators had a 97.2 percent mortality rate. It is estimated that putting people on ventilators killed thousands of COVID patients in the United States.[98]

Throughout 2020, masks and other equipment were exceedingly hard to find in the United States, having been hoarded by Beijing. American health care workers, if they could find them at all, were using single-use masks for days in a row. Some medical professionals in other high-risk groups went without new masks for *months*. Some stitched together their own out of scraps of fabric. Many, such as Dr. Fagan in Houston, mentioned at the beginning of this chapter, died after exposure to covid due to a lack of on-the-job protection. In May 2021, the *New York Times* reported that more than thirty-six hundred first responders had died in the battle against the virus because of the lack of safety equipment.[99] Beyond masks, when it came to other personal protective equipment, the problem was "severe" in US nursing homes and added to the death count there.[100] Even as late as September 2020, 42 percent of nurses said they were still experiencing shortages of basic equipment.[101] Since early in the pandemic, the lack of equipment "endanger[ed] health workers worldwide," reported the WHO.[102]

Given the desperate demand, Beijing had leverage. It did not respond by donating supplies as the United States, Europe, and other countries had done for China in January. Instead, they sold the supplies back. More than 99 percent of China's 2020 exports of medical personal protective equipment were sold, not donated.[103]

Just as Beijing's media have been happy to report about machine guns on American streets without revealing that Chinese firms produce the auto sear switches that modified them, now, having worked to corner the market on medical supplies before alerting the world to the lethal virus it had unleashed, Beijing used the shortage of supplies as a symbol of American failure. Chinese media mocked the shortage of medical supplies as "a farce" and watched US government agencies in "a catfight for supplies."[104]

In early April, California governor Gavin Newsom proudly announced on national television that he had signed a $1 billion contract with a Chinese company to provide masks and other medical equipment for California health care workers. The contract was with BYD, a Chinese company with no experience in producing medical gear. However, among other things, it did build guidance systems for the Chinese military's missile program. BYD also had a history of hiring lobbyists to secure no-bid contracts—as was this one. When the contract terms were finally made public, it included heavily inflated prices. And when the masks arrived, federal inspectors rejected them for being subpar and unsafe.[105] None of this seemed to have bothered Newsom. When he traveled to China in October 2023, he visited a BYD factory, praising their products.

In April 2020, the British government crowed that it had secured three hundred ventilators from China. The ventilators were unloaded at a ceremony at a military air base in England. "I'd like to thank the Chinese government for their support in securing that capacity," said Michael Gove, a senior British government official. But British doctors who took delivery of the ventilators soon after warned that using them would cause "significant patient harm, including death." They were of poor quality and unusual design that the experienced doctors did not recognize.[106]

Dutch officials found that tens of thousands of masks procured from China were substandard. Spain and Turkey received tens of thousands of testing kits that didn't work. In Slovakia 1.2 million antibody tests imported from China were deemed worthless. They should "just be thrown straight into the Danube," declared the prime minister. Beijing generally responded to those problems by condemning those nations' ingratitude. As a condition of receiving the supplies, government officials were required to "publicly thank China in return for the shipments."[107]

Beijing's leverage of supplies was extremely helpful in tamping down the growing debate over the virus's origins and criticism of the way the CCP had deceived the world.

According to Secretary of State Mike Pompeo, President Xi told President Trump that "continued calls for accountability would jeopardize America's ability to receive PPE shipped from China." When Pompeo went public with his concerns about the virus's origins and the ensuing cover-up, Beijing complained—and Trump listened. "Shut the hell up for a while," the president reportedly told Pompeo.[108]

Trump was generally deferential to Beijing throughout the crisis, knowing that it had him at a disadvantage. For all his public bluster about the "China virus" and "kung flu," he privately told White House aides that if he were tougher on Chinese officials, they would be less forthcoming with information. So he remained uncharacteristically reticent in the face of Beijing's outrageous conduct.[109]

When other US officials challenged Beijing's conduct, the Xinhua News Agency claimed that China could cut off pharmaceutical supplies and plunge the United States into a "mighty sea of coronavirus."[110]

Chinese analysts saw the medical supply shortage as a means of fostering the growth of socialism in the United States. "The rich or famous have easy access to testing amid dire shortages of testing kits," reported Zhang Tengjun from the prestigious China Institute of International Studies, which advises the senior leadership of the Chinese Communist Party. "The continuous exposure of this phenomenon aroused the anger of the people and became the ideological basis for a new wave of democratic socialism [in the United States]."[111]

Beijing pushed the line further, arguing that lockdowns and suppressing civil rights in the United States were all about preserving rights. "When it comes to human rights," Chinese officials explained, "China prioritizes the right to live." It's not clear that government mandates of any kind saved lives. We do know that they made human suffering worse. One study by a lockdown opponent, a Danish professor, Christian Bjørnskov, looked at twenty-four European countries and found that "severe lockdown policies have not been associated with lower mortality."[112]

Another study by public policy scholars at the RAND Corporation and University of Southern California found that government closures and stay-at-home orders did not lower the death rate in either states or countries.[113]

Staying home caused a whole host of terrible outcomes. Half of cancer patients reportedly skipped their chemotherapy sessions. Organ transplant surgeries involving living donors dropped by 85 percent. Severe child abuse cases jumped by 35 percent. Suicide attempts by teenage girls skyrocketed some 50 percent.[114] Not to mention the dramatic negative effects the lockdowns had on education and low-wage workers.[115]

Some advocates of the lockdowns argued that they were important to calm citizens; that they would lessen public anxiety.[116] But studies demonstrated that they had the opposite effect, creating more fear. The primary driver of fear for many people became the simple fact that their governments had instituted lockdowns. "We found that people judge the severity of the COVID-19 threat based on the fact the government imposed a lockdown—in other words, they thought 'it must be bad if government's taking such drastic measures,'" reported one academic study.[117]

Lockdown advocates did not seem to worry so much about Americans' anxiety but rather the fact that they were not anxious enough. In late August 2020, Anthony Fauci told members of the White House Coronavirus Task Force that average Americans were not afraid enough. "They need to be more afraid," he said.[118]

Fear tactics pushed by Beijing drove our political leaders to seek solutions from Beijing. The American people were looking to their leaders for guidance—our leaders were looking to the CCP.

Beijing sought to prevail over, not work with, the United States.

Beyond its obfuscation of data about the virus and cornering of medical supplies, it actively worked to undermine US efforts to come up with medical treatments for the virus. Covid vaccines are now the subject of serious debate—about their ultimate effectiveness and, for many patients, their serious side effects. But in the early months of the covid outbreak, there was an earnest search for a solution. In early 2020, several biomedical research laboratories in the United States working on vaccine research were subject to online attacks.

Why would a foreign actor do such a thing? The FBI cybercrime section quickly identified the source of the malicious attacks as two Chinese nationals. They were no ordinary Chinese citizens. According to the Justice Department indictment, they carried out their work for Chinese intelligence under the cover of the Chinese Institute of International Studies, a known cover organization for Chinese spies. The two operatives targeted US facilities researching covid-19 vaccines or other solutions. Indeed, the attacks seemed precisely timed. In late January, the cyberattackers searched for vulnerabilities in a Maryland biotech firm that had announced less than a week earlier that it was researching a potential covid vaccine. A couple of days later, they went after a Massachusetts biotech firm researching a possible medical solution to covid. On February 1, they targeted a California biotech firm that had announced just a day earlier that it was working on a vaccine.[119]

Senator Rick Scott of Florida said that the Senate Armed Services Committee saw evidence that Beijing was attempting to sabotage America's vaccine development.[120] He alleged that they were not simply attempts to steal information but efforts to disrupt, or even destroy, research efforts designed to fight the scourge. The two Chinese nationals were indicted by the US Justice Department in 2020. Predictably, they have not been extradited by China to the United States.

Other Chinese government–affiliated hackers managed to steal $20 million in covid relief funds from the US government by setting up fake Small Business Administration loans and unemployment insurance funds in more than a dozen states. The US Secret Service considers the group behind the attacks, APT 41, to be a "Chinese state-sponsored, cyberthreat group."[121]

CHAPTER 11

A Cover-Up for China and Themselves

Why, of all the places on the planet, did Wuhan, China, become the epicenter of the global pandemic? From the earliest days of the crisis, some of America's most powerful health-care officials asked this question in private conversations.

Some of the answers raised serious concerns. Virologist Ian Lipkin from Columbia University warned Fauci in an email just weeks after the virus began, "Given the scale of the bat [coronavirus] research pursued there—that is to say at the institute in Wuhan—and the site of the emergence of the first human cases, we have a nightmare of circumstantial evidence to assess."[1]

Fauci acknowledged that understanding the exact origin of the virus was important: "The purpose of trying to determine the origin of an outbreak is to see what you can do, looking forward, to prevent it from happening again."[2] He was also very concerned about blaming China for the virus. He wrote in an email to a colleague about "Wild—wild speculations and accusations, you know, blaming the Chinese and talking about their [having released the virus] deliberately or accidentally— which certainly is a possibility."[3] His subsequent public talking points would lean much more on calling things "wild speculations" with very little mention of "certainly a possibility."

On another occasion, he said of correspondence with Jeremy Farrar, then the director of the United Kingdom's Wellcome Trust, that "he was afraid that people would be speculating and blaming people, blaming the Chinese, and—and that only will increase tensions and reduce cooperation."[4] Of course, Beijing was not really cooperating at all; it was hoarding supplies, lying about the number of cases, and hiding other data about the virus.

Fauci's lack of interest in the virus's origins seems to have been directly related to the concern that it would reveal China's culpability. On April 12, 2020, he received a long email from a colleague (name redacted) pointing to China's extreme lockdown measures and its fudging of the number of covid cases. Robert Redfield, the director of the Centers for Disease Control and Prevention, was copied. Fauci was not interested in discussing Beijing's responsibility. He responded, "Thank you for your note. . . . I can only say that I (and I am sure that Bob Redfield feels the same way) prefer to look forward and not assign blame or fault."[5]

This is the head of an organization that funded research in Wuhan to predict how the next coronavirus could start. However, when the Wuhan virus did emerge, he quickly lost interest in determining its origins.

Dr. Francis Collins, the director of the National Institutes of Health, shared Fauci's desire to protect China. He argued for settling the debate over the origins of covid and defeating the "voices of conspiracy" about a lab leak or a deliberate release because it was necessary to maintain "international harmony."[6] Another scientist, Dr. Ron Fouchier, was likewise concerned that further debate on the issue of the nature of covid would "do unnecessary harm to science in general and science in China in particular."[7]

Dr. Andrew Rambaut, who worked with other scientists to dispel arguments about a Chinese lab leak, was even more blunt. "*Given the shit show that would happen if anyone serious accused the Chinese of even accidental release,*" he wrote to his colleagues, "*my feeling is we should say that given there is no evidence of a specifically engineered virus, we cannot possibly distinguish between natural evolution and escape so we are content with ascribing it to natural process.*"[8]

The irony here is that some scholars in China believed that the virus resulted from a lab leak; they didn't see the truth as harming Chinese science. Two Chinese researchers working in Wuhan at the time—one at the School of Biology and Biological Engineering at the South China

University of Technology, the other at the Wuhan University of Science and Technology—investigated. They were blunt in their views, noting that the theory that the virus had spread from a bat being sold at a food market did not make sense and the market did not even sell bats. They quickly identified the research laboratories as the most likely place the virus originated from. They concluded, "The killer coronavirus probably originated from a laboratory in Wuhan. . . . Regulations may be taken to relocate these laboratories far away from city center and other densely populated places."[9]

The researchers were correct: an investigation by the Wuhan Center for Disease Control and Prevention in February confirmed that the so-called wet market did not even sell bats.[10]

The United States' appointed bureaucratic scientists seemed strangely determined to ally themselves with the CCP narrative—not with independent Chinese scientists. Collins was particularly interested in seeing the "naturally occurring virus" line become *the* conventional view. He emailed Fauci on April 14, 2020, asking, "Wondering if there is something NIH can do to help us put down this very destructive conspiracy [about an intentional release] with what seems to be growing momentum." Copied on the email was the U.S. National Institute of Allergy and Infectious Diseases (NIAID) deputy director Clifford Lane.[11]

Peter Daszak is the president of the EcoHealth Alliance, a nonprofit organization that works with local researchers around the world. The alliance served as a conduit to fund controversial research in China and other parts of the world. The US government, including Fauci's institute, funded the group. Daszak then sent those federal dollars to research laboratories around the world, including the Wuhan Institute of Virology. He was eager to steer discussions away from a possible lab leak for the benefit of his Chinese grant recipients. He signaled to the National Academies of Sciences, Engineering, and Medicine (NASEM), the Chinese Academy of Science, and others his ongoing discussion with colleagues to steer the debate away from a lab leak. "We discussed ways we could frame a future topic that would allow us to talk about some important issues around the 'natural history' of SARS-CoV-2, that might also be comfortable for our Chinese colleagues," he wrote.[12]

Daszak insisted that the virus had been naturally transferred from bats to humans. But in 2019, Daszak, Shi Zhengli (aka the Bat Lady), and others had released a report of a study in which they had taken blood samples of some 1,500 people between 2015 and 2017. They'd wanted to see whether people who lived or worked around bat caves might get coronavirus from bats. Would the disease transfer from bats to people? They had concluded that "this study suggests that bat coronavirus spillover is a rare event."[13]

After the emergence of covid-19, Daszak ignored his own report and offered a new narrative. "We can safely estimate that between one and seven million people are infected with bat coronaviruses each year," he wrote in June 2020. "Ignore the conspiracy theories: scientists know COVID-19 wasn't created in a lab."[14]

In July 2020, the WHO organized a committee to study the virus's origins. The US government submitted several respected names, including that of an epidemiologist from the CDC, for the committee. The WHO rejected the nominations; the only US representative would be Peter Daszak. The WHO investigation was more of a bureaucratic cover-up than a scientific investigation. The purpose and scope of the WHO investigation was "to identify the zoonotic source of the virus." In other words, the scientists would not even be going to take a serious look at the prospects of a lab leak.[15]

The WHO panel concluded by assessing the probabilities of the origin of the disease. They declared that the wet market scenario was "possible to likely" (even though no bats were sold at the market). Comically, they declared it "possible" that the virus could have been transmitted "through frozen food." A lab leak? That was "extremely unlikely."[16]

In early February, high-ranking public health officials tried to shut down the debate. A group of virologists published a letter in the *Lancet* on February 19, 2020. "We stand together to strongly condemn conspiracy theories suggesting that COVID-19 does not have a natural origin," they wrote. They declared that scientists "overwhelmingly conclude that this coronavirus originated in wildlife" and called on the public to stand with their Chinese colleagues fighting the disease. The letter was odd because it never really addressed the question of a natural virus escaping from the lab.[17] It purposely conflated every wild "conspiracy" with the simple idea of a worker making a tragic mistake.

The effort was organized by Fauci in a series of telephone calls and teleconferences. Fauci assembled a team to counter claims of a lab leak, and he curiously excluded from the conversation the head of the Centers for Disease Control (CDC) Robert Redfield, who happened to be a virologist. (Fauci is an immunologist.) Why would Fauci exclude him from these planning meetings? According to Redfield it was precisely because he believed that the lab leak was a possibility—and Fauci did not want that part of the conversation.[18]

Three days later, Fauci was at the White House for a press briefing of the Coronavirus Task Force. A reporter stood up and asked, "I wanted to ask Dr. Fauci. Can you address the suggestions or concerns that the virus was somehow manmade, possibly came out of a laboratory in China?"[19] Fauci responded by referring to the letter in the *Lancet*. "There was a study, recently, that we could make available to you, where a group of highly qualified evolutionary virologists looked at the sequences there and the sequences in bats as they evolve, and the mutations that it took to get to the point where it is now is totally consistent with the genome of the species from an animal to a human."[20]

He hoped that would settle the matter and take the heat off his colleagues in China. But the letter was hardly pure science. Its author was Daszak, who had also signed it. Though the letter stated that those signing it had "no competing interests," Daszak did.[21]

According to emails obtained through the Freedom of Information Act, Daszak tried to cover up his role in the letter. Under an email with the subject line "No need for you to sign the 'Statement' Ralph!!" Daszak wrote to University of North Carolina professor Ralph Baric, who had worked with Wuhan lab researchers on coronavirus gain-of-function research: "you, me and him should not sign this statement, so it has some distance from us and therefore doesn't work in a counterproductive way. We'll then put it out in a way that doesn't link it back to our collaboration so we maximize an independent voice."

Baric concurred, "Otherwise it looks self-serving and we lose impact."

Ultimately, Baric did not sign the letter, but Daszak did. When you scan the list of those who signed it, EcoHealth had employed or funded at least six of them.[22]

When the World Health Organization and the *Lancet* each established a committee to investigate the origin of the coronavirus, Daszak ended up on both. He was extensively quoted by Vox and other publications that attacked the lab leak theory. Hardly anyone seemed to notice his conflict of interest. When Jamie Metzl, a scholar who sat on the WHO's expert advisory committee on human genome editing, noticed, he wrote a letter to *Lancet* editor in chief Richard Horton mentioning the conflict. "I am not at all suggesting that he did anything wrong," Metzl wrote, "just that one of the possible origin stories includes him." The editor never wrote back.[23]

According to Daszak's emails, he seems to have drafted the letter at the request of the Wuhan lab. "You should know," he wrote to colleagues, asking them to sign the letter, "that the conspiracy theorists have been very active, targeting our collaborators with some extremely unpleasant web pages in China, and some have now received death threats to themselves and their families. *They have asked for any show of support we can give them.*" (Emphasis added.)[24]

Many who had expressed concerns about a possible lab leak had quickly rejected the idea without much change in the evidence. Why? Robert Redfield, the head of the CDC at the time, later said, "You have to question why someone flips his position within 72 hours and then gets a huge grant later. . . . Don't think they flipped their position without someone influencing them. . . . I think they flipped because it was in their personal interest."

As Senator Rand Paul wrote, both "Andersen and Daszak, by pliantly doing Fauci's dirty work, would ultimately be rewarded with millions of dollars in NIH grants just months after they led the public battle to discredit the notion that the virus might have originated in a lab."[25]

More than a year later, many of those who had signed the letter seemed to soften their previous emphatic—yet unverified—claim that the coronavirus transmission had not been caused by a lab leak. Sticking to their guns, but in a far less intrepid manner, they admitted, "Opinions, however, are neither data nor conclusions." Of course, the letter had served its purpose of steering the debate at a crucial moment.[26]

After his manipulations, Daszak was confident that his actions had deterred the Trump White House from exploring the matter of a lab leak. "I don't think this committee will be getting into the lab release or bioengineering hypothesis again any time soon—White House seems to be satisfied with the earlier meeting, paper in Nature and general comments within [the] scientific community," he wrote to Ralph Baric.[27]

Daszak also made excuses for his Chinese colleagues, who were deleting files and denying Western scholars access to sequences of the virus. "As you know, a lot of this work has been conducted with Eco-Health Alliance. . . . We do basically know what's in those databases," he explained, supporting his Chinese colleagues' hiding things from their counterparts in the West. In essence, he claimed to know what was in the data Chinese scientists had made unavailable, proclaiming "Nothing to see here!"[28]

In April, Peter Daszak emailed colleagues explaining that it was important that Chinese genome data about the virus *not* be released to the public. He offered no scientific reason to suppress the information; in fact, there wasn't one. Instead, his warning was about the "unwelcome attention" that would result.[29]

EcoHealth Alliance also resisted turning over its research to the US government—even though the federal government funded some of it. The NIH sent a letter demanding that it provide a sample of the sequenced coronavirus. Daszak responded by writing a protest letter attacking the government's request. "We don't want to hand those over to conspiracy theorists for them to publish and ruin and make a mockery of," he told *Nature* magazine in an interview.[30] For all of his involvement in the cover-up, Daszak was never asked by Congress to testify.

Fauci, Collins, and Daszak effectively covered for their Chinese colleagues in Wuhan, perhaps motivated by their naive belief that they were simply participating in a scientific endeavor. But the Wuhan Institute of Virology has an active Chinese Communist Party Committee. Researchers at the lab not only have their official duties, but many of them serve on Communist Party Propaganda Committees with names such as "[Communist] Party Branch of Research Center for Emerging Infectious Disease."[31]

Why is there a party committee at a research laboratory?

In fact, even the lab's Committee for Discipline Inspection exists for the "implementation of the party's line, policy, party discipline, relevant laws and regulations, and the institute's rules and regulations."[32]

Dr. Yuan Zhiming, the lab manager until late 2019, was a senior Communist Party official. Dr. Wang Yanyi, the director of the lab, in a 2021 New Year's speech pledged to "effectively play the role of a battle fortress of grassroots party organizations."[33]

Were US officials really so naive as to believe them? Or was their subterfuge in part because the research might implicate them?

***

On February 23, 2016, Peter Daszak sat with a group of health experts to discuss the possibility of a new pandemic. He described to the audience the work being done in China to alter bat viruses. That event—chilling in retrospect—was captured on C-SPAN. "So we sequence the spike protein . . . then we—well, I didn't do this work, but my colleagues in China did . . . you insert the spike proteins [into the backbone of the bat virus] . . . [and] you end up with a small number of viruses *that really look like killers.*"[34]

Daszak was referring to something often called gain-of-function research, which seeks to alter viruses to make them more lethal, ostensibly to prepare for possible future outbreaks. Researchers are essentially creating pathogens that don't exist in nature, like the bat virus engineering he described as having been performed at Wuhan. Dr. Fauci was generally supportive of gain-of-function research.[35] Critics consider it to be a dangerous game.

Researchers such as Professor Richard Ebright of Rutgers University thought the gain-of-function approach was dangerous. It was, he said, like "looking for a gas leak with a lighted match."[36] "The only impact of this work is the creation, in a lab, of a new, non-natural risk."

When researchers at the Wuhan lab helped create a version of covid from bats and placed them in mice, Harvard epidemiologist Marc Lipsitch was very concerned. This new creation brings "a unique risk that a laboratory accident could spark a pandemic, killing millions."[37]

"Really look like killers." Indeed.

Daszak was personally very familiar with the research at Wuhan. Beginning in 2005, Shi "Bat Lady" Zhengli and Daszak had together "led dozens of expeditions to caves full of bats, to collect samples and analyze them." Beyond joint research, Daszak and EcoHealth had been pouring money into Wuhan for years specifically for research on bat viruses.[38] As a result of that research, in 2017, Wuhan researchers had created a coronavirus that could infect humans. The research had been funded by Fauci's NIAID, the United States Agency for International Development, and the Chinese government.[39]

Who was monitoring those projects? Not the NIH, which, astonishingly, allowed EcoHealth Alliance to create its own oversight procedures on gain-of-function research in China.[40]

The research lab in Wuhan had been built by China under false pretenses. Originally conceived as a joint French-Chinese project, the French had helped construct the facility and fifty French researchers had been supposed to go to Wuhan to conduct research with their Chinese counterparts. That had never happened. And much of the construction, which was supposed to have been done by French firms, had been done by a company linked to the Chinese military. Once construction was completed, China took over the project.

"I am giving up the co-presidency of the BSL-4 because it is a Chinese tool," declared the French billionaire Alain Mérieux, who had participated in the lab's development. "It belongs to them even though it was developed with the technical assistance of France." French and American intelligence had long expressed concerns that the project would benefit the Chinese military. With the French now effectively excluded from the lab, no one was left to monitor its research.[41] The US State Department later declared that the lab had been engaging in "classified research . . . on behalf of the Chinese military since at least 2017." That is, shortly after the French had left.[42]

Another mystery: the lab was built with French assistance to accommodate 250 researchers. But there were only 38 researchers listed there.[43]

Beijing's secretive military goals for the lab did not deter Fauci, Collins, and other members of the US scientific establishment from funding work at the lab. There were even unusual secrecy provisions. For example, the memorandum of understanding (MOU) between the Wuhan lab and the Galveston National Laboratory in Texas required that each lab delete "secret files" upon the request of the other. In other words, if the Wuhan lab wanted something deleted, the Galveston lab had to delete it, too. And the definition of "secret" or "confidential" information was broad. "All cooperation and exchange documents, details and materials shall be treated as confidential info by the parties," the MOU read. The Galveston lab is a maximum-containment laboratory "focused on the study of highly infectious diseases and the development of medical countermeasures."[44]

There was also plenty of history when it came to virus leaks. In 2004, a SARS virus escaped from a Chinese lab, infecting eleven people. The lab was shut down, and the staff of two hundred had to be put into isolation.[45] In December 2019, there was a lab accident at another Chinese lab, this time the Lanzhou Veterinary Research Institute. Sixty-five lab workers were infected with brucellosis.[46]

In 2018, the US State Department expressed concerns about safety issues at the Wuhan lab. Officials who visited Wuhan sent cables back to Washington noting "a serious shortage of appropriately trained technicians and investigators needed to safely operate this high-containment laboratory."[47]

In the months before the 2019 outbreak, Chinese officials admitted that safety shortcuts were being taken at labs like the one in Wuhan. The director of the Wuhan lab at the time, Yuan Zhiming, complained, "The maintenance cost is generally neglected; several high-level BSLs have insufficient operational funds for routine yet vital processes. Due to the limited resources, some BSL-3 laboratories run on extremely minimal operational cost or in some cases none at all." He was also concerned about the lack of biosafety engineers to help run the labs.[48]

Daszak's work with the Chinese lab was particularly dangerous. Among the more troubling research projects EcoHealth funded was a 2015 project by Shi Zhengli of the Wuhan lab and the University of North Carolina epidemiologist Ralph Baric. The resulting research paper proved "that the spike protein of a novel coronavirus could infect human cells." It was a stunning revelation. The authors themselves realized just how dangerous their findings were, writing, "scientific review panels may deem similar studies . . . too risky to pursue." The study was supposed to alert the world of "a potential risk of SARS-CoV re-emergence from viruses currently circulating in bat populations."[49]

During the early days of the 2020 pandemic, Fauci held a private meeting with Baric but later denied really knowing him. According to Fauci's private calendar, on February 11, 2020, at 2:30 p.m., he had scheduled a "meeting with Dr. Ralph Baric." No one else was listed. But Fauci, when asked under oath in a civil case, was evasive about even knowing Baric. "I know of him," he said. "I wouldn't say I know him. I'm not sure. I may have met him at a meeting or not."[50]

We may never know if the coronaviruses the lab developed were also for military use. However, the *Journal of Defense Studies* reported in 2015, "China is capable of developing, producing and weaponizing, on the whole, some 40 anti-human pathogens and toxins either intact or genetically upgraded, if not largely engineered." The report also noted, "The PLA has been able to mask a potent, self-sustained biotechnological system for the research, development and production of biological weapons within civilian entities."[51] Of course, in the case of Wuhan, that scenario was at least in part made possible by the PLA-associated builder.[52]

That same year, James Clapper, then the director of national intelligence under President Obama, listed bioengineered pandemics as one of the biggest threats to national security in a report called "Worldwide Threat Assessment of the US Intelligence Committee" prepared for the Senate Armed Services Committee.[53]

China has expressed interest in the prospects of using biological weapons. "Modern biotechnology development is gradually showing strong signs characteristic of an offensive capability," declared Zhang Shibo, a retired general and former president of China's National Defense University. In 2017, the Chinese military's handbook *The Science of Military Strategy* included a new section on biology and mentioned using biological weapons for "specific ethnic genetic attacks."[54]

The notion of biological weapons runs deep in Chinese military thinking. In *Unrestricted Warfare*, the authors discuss how "man-made earthquakes, tsunamis, weather disasters, or subsonic wave and new biological and chemical weapons all constitute new concept weapons, and that they have tremendous differences with what we normally speak of as weapons." One of the most popular works in Chinese historical fiction is *The Romance of the Three Kingdoms*, in which the hero sells his rival poisoned grain to a create famine. Once the rival is weakened, he invades the rival and takes control.[55]

The Wuhan Institute of Virology has always insisted that it is focused on disease prevention. Unfortunately, that is what biological weapons researchers always say. The Soviets' Biopreparat, for example, claimed that its focus was to develop influenza preparedness. In fact, it was a bioweapons program.[56]

The ties between the military and the Wuhan lab are extensive.[57] In 2015, researchers at Wuhan and China's Air Force Medical University produced a chilling essay titled "The Unnatural Origin of SARS and New Species of Man-Made Viruses as Genetic Bioweapons." The authors included eighteen military scientists and weapons experts. The paper was startling in its conclusion: coronaviruses could be "artificially manipulated into an emerging human disease virus, then weaponised and unleashed in a way never seen before." They went further to predict that engineered viruses would lead to a "new era of genetic weapons." They even questioned whether such an attack with such a bioweapon could cause the "enemy's medical system to collapse." One of the paper's authors had worked extensively with WIV researchers, including coauthorship of twelve scientific papers.[58]

Yet when the virus emerged on the global stage and questions were raised about the possibility of a lab leak, Shi "Bat Lady" Zhengli became unglued. On February 2, 2020, she posted on WeChat, "I, Shi Zhengli, guarantee on my life that it has nothing to do with our lab. May I offer some advice to those people who believe and spread bad media rumors: shut your dirty mouths."[59]

The documented activities of other Chinese researchers validate suspicions about Chinese bioweapons programs. For example, in July 2019, two Chinese-born scientists were escorted out of Canada's National Microbiology Laboratory. It was reported that they had covertly smuggled samples of Ebola and other deadly viruses back to China. Observers noted that those deadly diseases did not pose a health threat to China.[60] Why did they want samples?

Shortly after the virus began to spread in January 2020, a PLA major general named Chen Wei was deployed to the Wuhan lab and took control.[61] Chen is an expert in biological weapons.[62]

Other elements of covid-19 made some scholars suspect that there might have been a lab origin. Scientists found that the covid virus's spike protein "binds the strongest" to human ACE2 receptors. That was surprising to researchers because a virus that starts in an animal and then jumps to humans "typically exhibits the highest affinity initially for its original host species."[63] But that did not appear to be the case here; the SARS-CoV-2 virus was extremely contagious to humans—far more than any other discovered in the past. The virus that slammed the planet in 2020 binds to human hosts at least *ten times* as tightly as other coronaviruses.[64] The SARS virus that first appeared in 2002, for example, infected fewer than ten thousand people.[65] The MERS virus in 2012 infected fewer than three thousand people.[66] The new virus that appeared in 2019 set off a global pandemic that infected hundreds of millions of people.[67]

Shockingly, in March 2018, researchers at EcoHealth Alliance, the Wuhan Institute of Virology, and the University of North Carolina, where Professor Baric taught, submitted a proposal to the secretive Pentagon research funding agency DARPA. In the proposal, they described their plans to perform gain-of-function experiments on a highly contagious SARS-related bat coronavirus in China. The proposal called for inserting furin cleavage sites into spike proteins of the virus, making it more infectious to humans. But DARPA rejected the proposal because it would involve gain-of-function experiments.[68]

According to acting NIH director Lawrence Tabak, EcoHealth had funded gain-of-function experiments in 2018 on the very same pathogens listed in the DARPA proposal. The experiments had been conducted at the Wuhan lab in 2018–2019 and administered by Fauci's NIAID as part of a project called "Understanding the Risk of Bat Coronavirus Emergence."[69]

It is a strange coincidence that less than a year later, a virus strikingly similar to the one described in the proposal to DARPA emerged in the city of Wuhan.[70]

Those who insist that the virus was completely natural and not altered in a lab argue that if the virus had been modified in a lab, they would have noticed "modification markers." And they have not seen any. But as early as 2005, American researchers were able to genetically modify coronaviruses without leaving any trace. Researchers at the WIV were able to do the same as early as 2016.[71]

Prominent international medical professionals said they had been afraid to raise questions about the lab leak. Some people consider Jeremy Farrar to be Great Britain's version of Anthony Fauci. A former professor at Oxford and director of the Wellcome Trust, he is now the chief scientist at the WHO. When the virus emerged on the world stage in late January, he was concerned by what he read. "In the last week of January 2020," he recounted, "I saw email chatter from scientists in the US suggesting the virus looked almost engineered to infect human cells. These were credible scientists proposing an incredible, and terrifying, possibility of either an accidental leak from a laboratory or a deliberate release. . . . It seemed a huge coincidence for a coronavirus to crop up in Wuhan, a city with a superlab." By his own account, Farrar acquired a burner phone, held "clandestine meetings," and had to keep difficult secrets. He contacted Anthony Fauci. They agreed "that a bunch of specialists needed to urgently look into it."[72] Apparently, they later dropped the idea.

"A bunch of specialists" never seriously took a "look into it." Why was there no serious investigation? Because powerful forces did not want an investigation.

We may never know where covid originated, and official Washington made sure of that. Thomas DiNanno, a senior State Department official, said that they were "warned not to pursue an investigation into the origin of COVID-19" for fear that they would "open a can of worms."[73]

Dr. Robert Redfield, the former director of the CDC, said he received death threats from peers after sharing his belief that the virus had escaped from a lab. One colleague said in an email that he should "wither and die." Others accused him of being racially insensitive—as if that had anything to do with the facts being discussed. Of the ordeal, he said, "I expected it from politicians. I didn't expect it from science."[74]

Alina Chan, a molecular biologist at the Broad Institute of MIT and Harvard University, has been outspoken about the need for further investigation of the lab leak theory. She looked at the early sequences of the virus and noticed that there was "very little evidence of mutation." Why did that matter? Because if the virus had jumped from animals to humans, as the wet market theory claimed, there should have been numerous visible adaptations.[75] But Chan, who is of Singaporean descent, has been accused of being a "race traitor" for pushing for more investigation.[76]

Other scientists were intimidated by the political implications of getting into the debate. "I suspect that this might even have led a part of the American scientific community to avoid addressing the question," said Professor Jacques van Helden of Aix-Marseille Université in France, "because expressing the possibility that the virus would result from a lab leak would have been perceived as support for Trump."[77]

Politics had infected medical science; believing that the virus emerged from a lab leak somehow meant you were supporting Trump or at least helping him in the 2020 presidential campaign.

Dr. David Asher, who ran the State Department's inquiry into the origin of covid, ran into stiff opposition. He discovered that "there is a huge-gain-of-function bureaucracy" in Washington.[78]

Matthew Pottinger, a former deputy national security advisor, noticed that there was a strong lobby of those within the federal government who did not want to look at the lab leak theory—who were, in fact, "predisposed" to its impossibility—because they were "conflicted," which "played a profound role in muddying the waters and contaminating the shot at having an impartial inquiry."[79] Those bureaucrats wanted to kill any investigation because they feared it could blow back on them, given their involvement with the research. Indeed, in December 2020, when US officials gathered at the State Department to hash out what to say about the Wuhan lab and the possibility of a leak, the director of the State Department's Office of the Biological Policy Staff in the Bureau of International Security and Nonproliferation, Christopher Park, told them not to make any statements that could "point to the U.S. government's own role in gain-of-function research." Park had personal reasons to avoid an international discussion about a lab leak; he had played a role in lifting the US government moratorium on funding gain-of-function research in 2017. DiNanno felt the concerns expressed "smelled like a cover-up, and I wasn't going to be part of it."[80]

It smelled like a cover-up because it *was* a cover-up. After the 9/11 attacks, the US government assembled a 9/11 Commission to figure out what had happened. Approximately three thousand Americans tragically died on 9/11.[81] Covid killed many, many more. Yet we have never had an accounting.

Dr. David Relman of the Stanford University School of Medicine called for a 9/11-like commission to be established concerning the origins of covid. But Fauci and others in the scientific bureaucratic establishment had no interest in doing so. "With every passing day and week, the kinds of information that might prove helpful will have a tendency to dissipate and disappear," said Dr. Relman.[82] Of course, no formal commission has yet been established.

In late 2020, the US State Department under Secretary Mike Pompeo launched an investigation into the origins of the virus. After Joe Biden was inaugurated as president, he quietly shut it down. When his termination of the investigation became public, President Biden covered himself by asking for an intelligence review by US intelligence agencies. The results were inconclusive, as most people had expected they would be.[83]

Congressional leaders have said for several years that they support further investigation, something that is clearly within their power. Congressman Adam Schiff, then the chairman of the House Intelligence Committee, said repeatedly in 2020, 2021, and 2022 that he supports further investigation. That body would be a natural place in which to conduct it. But no hearings have been held, nor was an investigation conducted until 2023, after Republicans claimed the majority in the House of Representatives.[84]

In March 2021, members of Congress sent a list of questions to the National Institutes of Health requesting information and documents about how covid-19 had started and how US taxpayer funds might have been used to support research at the Wuhan Institute of Virology. The NIH responded two months later but did not provide any of the documents that had been requested. Its response letter blandly declared that it believed there should be continued investigation into the virus's origins.[85]

Great Britain's prestigious medical publication the *Lancet* established a commission to develop "lessons for the future from the COVID-19 pandemic." The resulting report praised China for its "zero-COVID strategy" and cooperation, mentioning neither the country's cover-up of covid, censorship of doctors, nor destruction of covid samples.[86] Commission member Professor Jeffrey Sachs of Columbia University had dismissed the charges of genocide in Xinjiang province as "unjustified" and complained that the United States had a "false narrative" about both Russia and China.[87] Others, such as the South African epidemiologist Salim Abdool Karim, had scolded about "finger pointing" on the origin of the pandemic. China's Ministry of Foreign Affairs and the state press happily quoted him on the subject.[88] Other members of the commission included two Chinese academics and Susan Michie.[89]

Even after the pandemic had largely passed, Fauci continued to praise Beijing's response. In a 2021 panel discussion at the University of Edinburgh, he sat next to China's Dr. Zhong Nanshan, often referred to as "China's Fauci." Zhong explained that the lockdowns had worked and that covid had been defeated because of the repressive measures. He argued that his country had demonstrated the best response to the virus, while the United States' response had been somewhat less scientific. Fauci agreed with Dr. Zhong and seemed to endorse the "scientific" repression in China, saying he would "underscore everything that Professor Zhong said."[90]

Just a few months after President Biden shut down the State Department's investigation into the origins of covid, President Xi stood before a massive parade to mark the hundredth anniversary of the founding of the Chinese Communist Party. Thousands of soldiers streamed into Beijing's Tiananmen Square, where President Xi treated them to a rollicking speech. But embedded in the oration was a direct threat: nations who bully China will face "broken heads and bloodshed in front of the iron Great Wall of the 1.4 billion Chinese people."[91]

CONCLUSION

My research for this book has focused on actions that Beijing is taking that directly result in American casualties and the lack of concerted foreign policy response to those actions that has been typical of our leaders. Some of this may simply be due to lack of exposure to the evidence on these matters. My hope is that this book will open some eyes to the seriousness of this situation. But for many of our leaders, the benefits of personal enrichment, whether from direct financial gain or simply from not rocking the boat, outweigh the risks of challenging what is being done to our country. A growing number may even align ideologically with Marxism with Chinese characteristics and welcome the destruction that China's actions—and our inaction—have wrought.

What Beijing is doing has all the elements of a war: physical casualties (from fentanyl, illegal gun enhancements, and covid manipulation), mental casualties of indoctrination (from TikTok, Hollywood), and a clearly defined objective: the undermining and defeat of the United States. That is because it is a war—an unrestricted war that has redefined the weapons and battlefields.

Beyond the scope of this book, Beijing clearly also engages in a myriad of other actions that demonstrate a disregard for US sovereignty. In light of what I have presented here, that disregard becomes especially serious. Evidence abounds of cases on US soil of secret Chinese police stations and harassment of Chinese dissidents, the buying of farmland and other real estate assets, including near military bases, rampant corporate technology espionage and theft, the collection of Americans' identity data, K–12 school influence, and proxy lobbying to work around the Foreign Agents Registration Act, among other questionable activities. Constructive responses within the federal government and specific states have to some extent been undertaken by law enforcement personnel, journalists, and political leaders. Yet such responses have met with political resistance, such as when the Department of Justice recently challenged a Florida law restricting Chinese land ownership near military installations as unconstitutional.[1] For whom, exactly, is the DOJ working?

The scattershot and often partisan response of our country's leaders speaks not only to a range of motivations on their part but also to a division in perception about the long-range intentions of Beijing toward us. We must establish a bipartisan consensus on whether Beijing's intentions are benign, as expressed by the wishful American corporate model of "win-win," or malign. My research for this book has led me to conclude unequivocally that Beijing has demonstrated malign intent and practices toward the United States. This unpleasant truth offers the only foundation upon which US policy toward the CCP should rest. It is necessary to craft a solid strategy to defend ourselves and hold to account both Beijing and those who are willing to do its bidding.

As of this writing, there are some early signs of hope: the House of Representatives has recently passed the Stop Chinese Fentanyl Act of 2023, which would impose sanctions on Chinese entities producing, selling, distributing, or financing synthetic opioids or precursors to tackle the production of fentanyl at its source, according to Representative Andy Barr, the bill's main sponsor. Cosponsor Blaine Luetkemeyer stated the obvious: "Make no mistake—there's no fentanyl crisis without the CCP."[2] Bipartisan work on the issue in both the House and the Senate has been encouraging, even as the Biden administration's policies have not. But even if this bill becomes a law, will it be enforced? Or will present and future presidential administrations fail to use this tool because they are reluctant to call out Beijing?

Some people may hope that the challenges presented by Beijing will simply go away. They cite the problems that China faces, from demographic problems to governmental controls that place a premium on political control over economic growth. But will these problems make Beijing less aggressive or more desperate? History is unkind to those who hope that such problems will fix themselves. Moreover, what should be said to the families who have lost loved ones due to Beijing's existing aggressions?

We are well beyond the 1960s la-la land mantra of "Suppose they gave a war and nobody came?"[3] The only people who haven't shown up are the ones who should be defending us.

ACKNOWLEDGMENTS

My name may be on the front cover, but this book is the result of the labor of many hands. The late Cap Weinberger, who was a mentor of mine, once told me that the American West was not settled by cowboys—but by wagon trains. I've been fortunate to take this journey with many wonderful colleagues.

I am blessed to be surrounded by terrific leadership at the Government Accountability Institute. Our chairman, Rebekah Mercer, is fearless, allowing us to pursue whatever stories we uncover, regardless of the consequences. The other members of the board of directors, including Ron Robinson and Thomas W. Smith, share that spirit. All of them always provide outstandingly sage advice.

All my writing is research-driven, and I was blessed to have a terrific team on this book. In particular, I would like to thank Jedd McFatter, Seamus Bruner, Hunter Pease, Maggie Dowd, Price Sukhia, Peter Aagaard, Steven Richards, Tarik Noriega, Corey Adamyk, and Keegan Connolly. I am also grateful for the translation work of David Leino as well as Jonathan Ward.

I also benefited from the writings of Michael P. Senger on the covid virus. While I don't share all his conclusions, his work helped me understand more fully what Beijing was doing as we grappled with this crisis. I independently confirmed his reporting. Likewise, Michael Gray, the founder and chairman of the Fentanyl Awareness Coalition, helped me to see the opioid crisis through a different lens. I am grateful.

Once I have written the draft based on the evidence we have amassed, our editorial team helps to shape it—with terrific editorial support from Peter Boyer and Joe Duffus—and then we make sure that evidence is accurately reported. Steve Post, our vice president for content, is the ultimate fact-checker. I appreciate his precision and care.

Running GAI requires great leadership, and I am blessed to have the help of Executive Vice President Stuart Christmas, as well as Vice Presidents Eric Eggers and Steve Stewart, and Executive Vice President Peter Boyer. Catherine Baer, our operations/IT manager, makes a ship like GAI run as smoothly as possible.

Once the book goes to the publisher, Eric Nelson, my longtime editor at Harper, reads it with a clear and sober eye, and helps to shape it into the volume you now have before you. I am grateful for his professional precision and friendly spirit. I want to acknowledge the hard work James Neidhardt put into this manuscript. I also appreciate the work of my agents Glen Hartley and Lynn Chu.

Reaching a maximum audience requires a diligent and a high-caliber publicist team: Sandy Schulz and Faith Bruner, who work tirelessly, have my gratitude.

Finally, thank you again to my patient family, who tolerate late nights in front of the computer or reading yet another document, as well as constant rewrites that consume so much of my time and energy. To my wife, my children, my sister, and my mother: I love you all.

The author alone is responsible for the contents of this book.

NOTES

Introduction: Vacant Eyes

1. Dan De Luce and Darch Gregorian, "Downed Chinese Balloon Was 200 Feet Tall, U.S. Military Says," NBC News, February 6, 2023, https://www.nbcnews.com/politics/national-security/downed-chinese-balloon-was-200-feet-tall-us-military-says-rcna69371; Katharina Buchholz, "The Chinese Spy Balloon's Path Across North America," Statista, February 6, 2023, https://www.statista.com/chart/29242/chinese-balloon-flight-path/.

2. Peter Baker, "Biden Tries to Calm Tensions over Chinese Aerial Spying," *New York Times*, February 16, 2023, https://www.nytimes.com/2023/02/16/us/politics/biden-spy-balloon-ufo.html.

3. Sun Tzu, *The Art of War*, quoted in William J. Holstein, *The New Art of War: China's Deep Strategy Inside the United States* (Derring Harbor, NY: Brick Tower Press, 2019), 10.

4. Fumio Ota, "Sun Tzu in Contemporary Chinese Strategy," *Joint Force Quarterly* 73, no. 2 (April 2014): 76–80, https://ndupress.ndu.edu/Media/News/Article/577507/sun-tzu-in-contemporary-chinese-strategy. Vice Admiral Ota is the former director of Japan's Defense Intelligence Headquarters.

5. China Aerospace Studies Institute, *In Their Own Words: Foreign Military Thought*, 2013, https://www.airuniversity.af.edu/Portals/10/CASI/documents/Translations/2021-02-08%20Chinese%20Military%20Thoughts-%20In%20their%20own%20words%20Science%20of%20Military%20Strategy%202013.pdf, 331.

6. Ota, "Sun Tzu in Contemporary Chinese Strategy"; Vikrant Deshphande, ed., *Hybrid Warfare: The Changing Character of Conflict* (New Delhi: Pentagon Press, 2018), https://www.idsa.in/system/files/book/book-hybrid-warfare-vdeshpande.pdf; Erbing Li et al., *Wajie Zhan* [Disintegration Warfare] (Beijing: Liberation Army Press, 2010).

7. Ibid.

8. Ren Tianyou and Zhao Zhouxian, eds., *Strategic Support for Achieving the Great Chinese Resurgence* (Beijing: National Defense University Press, 2018), 118–19, quoted in Ian Easton, *The Final Struggle: Inside China's Global Strategy* (Manchester, UK: Eastridge, 2022), 181.

9. Michael Pillsbury, *The Hundred-Year Marathon: China's Secret Strategy to Replace America as a Global Superpower* (New York: Henry Holt, 2015), 34.

Chapter 1: The New Opium Wars

1. Agence France-Presse (@afpfr), "Joe Biden et Xi Jinping se sont retrouvés à Bali pour un face-à-face très attendu grâce auquel le président américain," Twitter, November 14, 2022, 04:03 a.m., https://twitter.com/afpfr/status /1592110973904904195.

2. Jim Tankersley and Lisa Friedman, "After Admiralty, China and the United States Agreed to Restart Climate Negotiations," *New York Times* China, November 15, 2022, https://cn.nytimes.com/business/20221115/china-us -climate-change; "U.S. President Biden Raises Human Rights Issues in Tibet During Talks with Xi Jinping," Asian News International, November 14, 2022.

3. "Readout of President Biden's Call with President Xi Jinping of the People's Republic of China," The White House, July 28, 2022, https://www .whitehouse.gov/briefing-room/statements-releases/2022/07/28/readout-of -president-bidens-call-with-president-xi-jinping-of-the-peoples-republic-of-- china; "Readout of President Joe Biden's Meeting with President Xi Jinping of the People's Republic of China," The White House, November 14, 2022, https://www.whitehouse.gov/briefing-room/statements-releases/2022/11/14 /readout-of-president-joe-bidens-meeting-with-president-xi-jinping-of-the -peoples-republic-of-china; "Readout from the Biden-Xi Virtual Meeting: Discussion with National Security Advisor Jake Sullivan," The Brookings Institution, November 16, 2021, https://www.brookings.edu/events/readout -from-the-biden-xi-virtual-meeting-discussion-with-national-security -advisor-jake-sullivan; Micaela Burrow, "In 2.5 Hour Conversation with China's Xi, Biden Mentions COVID Origins and Fentanyl Zero Times," The Daily Caller, July 28, 2022, https://dailycaller.com/2022/07/28/2-hour -conversation-china-xi-biden-covid-fentanyl.

4. "Biden, Xi 'Agreed' Nuclear Weapons Should Never Be Used," Manila Bulletin, November 15, 2022, https://mb.com.ph/2022/11/15/biden-xi-agreed -nuclear-weapons-should-never-be-used.

5. Scott Higham, Sari Horwitz, and Katie Zezima, "The Fentanyl Failure," *Washington Post*, March 13, 2019, https://www.washingtonpost.com /graphics/2019/national/fentanyl-epidemic-obama-administration.

6. Ibid.; "Drug Overdoses: Data Details," National Safety Council, https://injuryfacts.nsc.org/home-and-community/safety-topics/drugoverdoses/data-details.

7. Rebecca Morin, "Biden Is in Mexico City. His First Action? Asking the Mexican President for Help with Fentanyl," *USA Today*, January 9, 2023, https://www.usatoday.com/story/news/politics/2023/01/09/biden-mexico-lopez-obrador-immigration-fentanyl/11013731002.

8. Kacie Sinton, "Rep. Boebert Introduces Legislation to Classify Fentanyl as a Weapon of Mass Destruction," KKCO 11 News, June 13, 2022, https://www.nbc11news.com/2022/06/13/rep-boebert-introduces-legislation-classify-fentanyl-weapon-mass-destruction.

9. See, e.g., "Officer Safety: Fentanyl Mixture Appears to Be Cannabis," *Criminal Intelligence Unit* 15, no. 6 (2019), Office of the Ohio Attorney General, https://www.peaf.net/wp-content/uploads/2019/05/Fentanyl-laced-marijuana.pdf.

10. Ibid.

11. Higham et al., "Obama Officials Failed to Focus as Fentanyl Burned Its Way Across America."

12. Grant Newsham, "Cruel Truths Behind China's Killer Fentanyl Exports," *Asia Times*, December 11, 2020, https://asiatimes.com/2020/12/cruel-truths-behind-chinas-killer-fentanyl-exports.

13. Rachel Nostrant, "Man Indicted in Fentanyl Overdoses of West Point Cadets on Spring Break," *Army Times*, May 19, 2022, https://www.armytimes.com/news/your-army/2022/05/19/man-indicted-in-fentanyl-overdoses-of-west-point-cadets-on-spring-break; Teresa Dumain, "What Is Substance Abuse?," WebMD, November 28, 2022, https://www.webmd.com/mental-health/addiction/news/20220314/fentanyl-overdose-west-point-cadets-florida.

14. Anna Edney, "This Killer Opioid Could Become a Weapon of Mass Destruction," Bloomberg, December 12, 2018, https://www.bloomberg.com/news/features/2018-12-12/killer-opioid-fentanyl-could-be-a-weapon-of-mass-destruction.

15. Jon Kamp, José de Córdoba, and Julie Wernau, "How Two Mexican Drug Cartels Came to Dominate America's Fentanyl Supply," *Wall Street Journal*, August 30, 2022, https://www.wsj.com/articles/mexico-drug-cartels-fentanyl-overdose-sinaloa-jalisco-11661866903.

16. "KNR" Strategic Targeting and Analysis Group, DEA Phoenix Field Division, February 25, 2020.

17. Paul Szoldra, "The Homeland Security Department Is Considering Labeling Fentanyl a 'Weapon of Mass Destruction,'" Business Insider, April 15, 2019, https://www.businessinsider.com/homeland-security-department-dhs-fentanyl-weapon-of-mass-destruction-2019-4.

18. Michael Pillsbury, *The Hundred-Year Marathon: China's Secret Strategy to*

Replace America as a Global Superpower (New York: Henry Holt, 2015), 116–17.

19. Qiao Liang and Wang Xiangsui, *Unrestricted Warfare* (Beijing: PLA Literature and Arts Publishing House, 1999), xviii.

20. Ibid., 123.

21. David Kilcullen, *The Dragons and the Snakes: How the Rest Learned to Fight the West* (London: C. Hurst, 2020), 206–7.

22. "Counter-Unconventional Warfare: White Paper," United States Army Special Operations Command, September 26, 2014, https://www.soc.mil /Files/Counter-UnconventionalWarfareWP.pdf, 32.

23. Nathan L. Rusin, "Illicit Chinese Fentanyl—America's Next National Security Crisis," May 7, 2019, https://apps.dtic.mil/sti/pdfs/AD1077974.pdf, 5.

24. John Poole, "Unrestricted Warfare and Drug Smuggling," *The Counter Terrorist: A Journal for Law Enforcement, Intelligence and Special Operations Professionals* 7, no. 1 (February–March 2014): 32, 41, 36, https:// issuu.com/thecounterterroristmagazine/docs/ct_feb_mar_2014_ap_edition.

25. "Drug Overdose Death Rates," National Institute on Drug Abuse, June 30, 2023, https://nida.nih.gov/research-topics/trends-statistics/overdose-death-rates.

26. Celina B. Realuyo, "The New Opium War: A National Emergency," *PRISM* 8, no. 1 (2018): 133, https://cco.ndu.edu/News/Article/1767465/the-new -opium-war-a-national-emergency.

27. Paul L Schiff, Jr., "Opium and Its Alkaloids," *American Journal of Pharmaceutical Education* 66, no. 2 (2002): 188–96.

28. Frederic Delano Grant, Jr., "'A Fair, Honorable, and Legitimate Trade,'" *American Heritage* 37, no. 5 (August–September 1986), https://www .americanheritage.com/fair-honorable-and-legitimate-trade.

29. Schiff, "Opium and Its Alkaloids."

30. Karl E. Meyer, "The Opium War's Secret History," *New York Times*, June 28, 1997, https://www.nytimes.com/1997/06/28/opinion/the-opium-war-s -secret-history.html.

31. Sun Tzu, *The Art of War*, https://suntzusaid.com/book/3.

32. Greg R. Lawson, "The Fentanyl Crisis Is a Reverse Opium War," *National Interest*, December 26, 2017, https://nationalinterest.org/feature/the-fentanyl -crisis-reverse-opium-war-23812.

33. Qiao Lang and Wang Xiangsui, *Unrestricted Warfare: China's Master Plan to Destroy America* (Brattleboro, VT: Echo Point Books and Media, 1999), 26.

34. "The Opium Wars Still Shape China's View of the West," *Economist*, December 19, 2017, https://www.economist.com/christmas-specials/2017/12 /19/the-opium-wars-still-shape-chinas-view-of-the-west.

35. Barbara Demick, "Chinese President's Father Is Getting a Postmortem Revival," *Los Angeles Times*, October 15, 2013, https://www.latimes.com /world/la-xpm-2013-oct-15-la-fg-china-xi-father-20131016-story.html.

36. Evan Osnos, "Red," *New Yorker*, March 30, 2015, https://www.newyorker .com/magazine/2015/04/06/born-red.

37. *Communist China and Illicit Narcotics Traffic: Hearings Before the Subcommittee to Investigate the Administration of the Internal Security Act and Other Internal Security Laws*, 84th Cong., 1955, https://babel.hathitrust .org/cgi/pt?id=uiug.30112119649785&view=1up&seq=5, 34–91.

38. Victory Lasky, "Red China's Secret Weapon," *Freeman*, April 20, 1953, https://cdn.mises.org/Freeman53-4b_3.pdf, 515.

39. Quoted in A. H. Stanton Candlin, *Psycho-chemical Warfare: The Chinese Communist Drug Offensive Against the West* (New Rochelle, NY: Arlington House, 1973), 200–201.

40. "Deverall, Richard L.-G. (Richard Lawrence-Grace) 1911–," Social Network and Archival Context Cooperative, https://snaccooperative.org/view/31317188; Testimony of Richard Deverall, *Communist China and Illicit Narcotics Traffic: Hearings Before the Subcommittee to Investigate the Administration of the Internal Security Act and Other Internal Security Laws*, 76.

41. See, e.g., H. J. Anslinger and William F. Tompkins, *The Traffic in Narcotics* (New York: Funk & Wagnalls, 1953), 76–84. Anslinger was the US commissioner of narcotics; Tompkins was the US attorney for the District of New Jersey.

42. Sam Cooper, *Wilful Blindness: How a Network of Narcos, Tycoons, and CCP Agents Infiltrated the West* (Toronto: Optimum Publishing International, 2022), 49.

43. Joseph Kessel, *Hong-Kong et Macao* (Paris: Éditions Gallimard, 1957), 29–30, quoted in Rudolf Schermann, *The Peking Bomb: The Psychochemical War Against America* (Washington, DC: Robert B. Luce, 1975), 103–4.

44. Quoted in Candlin, *Psycho-chemical Warfare*, 110.

45. Frank Bartholomew, "Red Spying Operations Centered in Switzerland," *Detroit Free Press*, July 18, 1958.

46. 108 Cong. Rec. H4612 (1962), https://ia803400.us.archive.org/32/items /sim_congressional-record-proceedings-and-debates_march-16-april-2-1962 _108/sim_congressional-record-proceedings-and-debates_march-16-april -2-1962_108.pdf. (This is from a section of the "Congressional Record, Proceedings and Debates of the 87th Congress, Second Session, Vol. 108, Part 4, March 16, 1962, to April 2, 1962, pages 4341–5744. The quote is a *Tampa Times* editorial of Friday, March 16, 1962, "Narcotics Is Communist Weapon," entered into the record and from page 4612.)

47. T'ang Ming-Chieh, "The Maoist Production of Narcotics and Their Intrigue to Poison the World," *Issues & Studies* 9 (1973): 30–37, citing an article

in the French magazine *Histoire pour Tous*, January 1973. The incident is also recounted in Mohammed Hassanein Heikal, *The Cairo Documents: The Inside Story of Nasser and His Relationship with World Leaders, Rebels, and Statesmen* (New York: Doubleday, 1971), 278–79.

48. Quoted in Candlin, *Psycho-chemical Warfare*, 57.

49. Testimony of Lewis Walt, *World Drug Traffic and Its Impact on U.S. Security: Hearings Before the Subcommittee to Investigate the Administration of the Internal Security Act and other Internal Security Laws*, 92nd Cong., 2nd sess., 1972, 157–58, 55, 56, https://babel.hathitrust.org/cgi/pt?id=umn .31951p011500680&view=1up&format=plaintext&seq=4.

50. Among the delegation sent to Vietnam was John Steinberg, a Democratic staff member of the Senate's Subcommittee on Juvenile Delinquency. He confirmed what General Walt had reported: the heroin being sold to American GIs was 95 to 100 percent pure, compared to street heroin sold in the United States, which was normally 4 to 5 percent pure. "Because of this I am inclined to speculate that it could be part of a plot to put a large number of fighting men in Vietnam on heroin and out of action permanently." It was his "personal belief" that it "could be coming from Red China." *Hearings Before the Subcommittee to Investigate Juvenile Delinquency of the Committee on the Judiciary*, U.S. Senate, 83d Cong., 1954, 6770–71, quoted in Schermann, *The Peking Bomb*, 125–26.

51. Schermann, *The Peking Bomb*, 8.

52. "Drugs Reported Tied to Vietnam Pullout," *New York Times*, June 7, 1971, https://www.nytimes.com/1971/06/07/archives/drugs-reported-tied-to -vietnam-pullout.html.

53. Frank Faso and Paul Meskil, "Color New Drug Epidemic Hong Kong Hue," *Daily News* [New York], March 20, 1973, https://www.govinfo.gov/content /pkg/GPO-CRECB-1973-pt15/pdf/GPO-CRECB-1973-pt15-4-3.pdf, 19323–24.

54. Joseph D. Douglass, *Red Cocaine: The Drugging of America and the West* (Cambridge, UK: Edward Harle, 1999), 89.

55. Jack Anderson, "Kennedy May Help in California," *Washington Post*, May 26, 1972.

56. Jim Scott, "Jim Scott: Long Fight for Documents Reveals the Truth About CIA Wiretapping of My Father, Journalist Paul Scott," *Capital Gazette*, March 17, 2021, https://www.capitalgazette.com/opinion/columns/ac-ce -column-jim-scott-2021318-20210317-5jupuubhlzc3jja7d5auoaxwqu-story .html.

57. Paul Scott, "Peking's Drug Trade Ignored," *Indianapolis News*, March 9, 1972, https://www.newspapers.com/image/312596186.

58. Edward Jay Epstein, *Agency of Fear: Opiates and Political Power in America* (New York: G. P. Putnam's Sons, 1977), 149–50.

Chapter 2: China's Foot Soldiers

1.   The connection between the CCP and the triads made the Chinese gangs more powerful, too. As Bertil Lintner, a senior writer on crime matters at the *Far Eastern Economic Review*, put it in his masterful book *Blood Brothers: Crime, Business and Politics in Asia*, "The close relationship between the authorities in Beijing, especially the Communist Party of China and the People's Liberation Army (PLA)—and organized crime—makes the Chinese underworld very different from other ethnic mobs in North America." In return, the triads would help the CCP. "Without the criminal underworld on its side, it would be almost impossible for Beijing to extend its writ beyond its frontiers, and that is what makes the new nexus between the Triads and China's present leaders so dangerous for the rest of the world. China is, even more than North Korea, a state that feels that it has to engage in criminal activities such as drug running and the printing of counterfeit dollars to survive." See Lintner, *Blood Brothers: Crime, Business, and Politics in Asia* (Crows Nest, Australia: Allen and Unwin, 2002), 369, 379–80; Aadil Brar, "Glitz, Glamour and Gambling: Behind China's Secret Societies and Crime Syndicates," ThePrint, December 1, 2021, https://theprint.in/opinion/eye -on-china/glitz-glamour-and-gambling behind-chinas-secret-societies-and -crime-syndicates/7744483.

2.   Jim Mann, "Hong Kong Is a Top Gun in Arms Traffic," *Los Angeles Times*, January 18, 1992, https://www.latimes.com/archives/la-xpm-1992-01-18 -mn-266-story.html; Cooper, *Wilful Blindness*, 64.

3.   Catherine Wang, "Children of Late Hong Kong Tycoon Henry Fok Settle Fight over Estate Worth $1.45 Billion," *Forbes*, February 8, 2022, https:// www.forbes.com/sites/catherinewang/2022/02/08/children-of-late-hong -kong-tycoon-henry fok settle-fight-over-estate-worth-145-billion; "Top 10 Chinese Gangsters," China Whisper, https://www.chinawhisper.com/top-10 -chinese-gangsters; David Sheff, "From the Archives: *The Ninth Zero*—Part 2," Worth, March 3, 2017, https://www.worth.com/from-the-archives-the -ninth-zero-part-2.

4.   Lintner, *Blood Brothers*, 103–4, 113–17.

5.   Ian Verrender, "Is Telstra in Bed with the Wrong Mogul?," *Sydney Morning Herald*, October 21, 2000, 10, https://www.newspapers.com/image/125567348.

6.   "Chinese Intelligence Services and Triads Financial Links in Canada," RCMP-CSIS Joint Review Committee, June 24, 1997, https://www.primetimecrime .com/Articles/RobertRead/Sidewinder%20page%201.htm; Cooper, *Wilful Blindness*, 67; Anthony B. Chan, *Li Ka-Shing: Hong Kong's Elusive Billionaire* (Oxford, UK: Oxford University Press, 1997), 71, 126, 183, 199; Gerald Posner, *Warlords of Crime: Chinese Secret Societies—the New Mafia* (New York: McGraw-Hill, 1988), 175–76; Seattle Burma Roundtable, "Singapore, Malaysia Investors Urged to Cut Links to Burmese Drug Lord; Singaporean GIC 'Liquidates' Druglord Tie Under Pressure," November 22,

1997, https://www.burmalibrary.org/reg.burma/archives/199711/msg00365 .html.

7. Denise Wee, "Banking Asia's Family Fortunes," FinanceAsia, March 1, 2015. [Found in Lexis: https://advance.lexis.com/api/document?collection =news&id=urn:contentItem:5FH2-65K1-JC4B-V532-00000-00&context =1519360.]

8. Senator John Kerry, *The New War: The Web of Crime That Threatens America's Security* (New York: Simon & Schuster, 1997), 59.

9. *The New Heroin Corridor: Drug Trafficking in China: Joint Hearing Before the Committee on the Judiciary and the Caucus on International Narcotics Control of the U.S. Senate*, 102nd Cong., 1992, 1, 2, https://babel.hathitrust .org/cgi/pt?id=mdp.39015042696727&seq=1.

10. Observatoire Géopolitique des Drogues, "The World Geopolitics of Drugs, 1997/1998 Annual Report," *Trends in Organized Crime* 4 (December 1998): 77, https://doi.org/10.1007/BF02900346.

11. Lintner, *Blood Brothers*, 9–10; "Gangsterism with Chinese Characteristics," Indo-Pacific Defense Forum, February 4, 2022, https://ipdefenseforum.com /2022/02/gangsterism-with-chinese-characteristics.

12. Lintner, *Blood Brothers*, 375.

13. Ibid., 124–25.

14. Kerry, *The New War*, 52.

15. Alan Wright, *Organised Crime* (London, UK: Willan Publishing, 2013).

16. Pang Li, "Xi Jinping's 17 Years in Fujian," *Economic Observer*, November 21, 2012, http://www.china.org.cn/china/2012-11/21/content_27179199 .htm.

17. Ian Easton, *The Final Struggle: Inside China's Global Strategy* (Norwalk, CT: Eastbridge Books, 2022), 43.

18. Immigration and Refugee Board of Canada, "China: Organized Crime or Black Society Activity, Particularly in Guangdong and Fujian, Including Links with Government Officials, Repercussions Associated with Failing to Meet Demands of Criminal Gangs, and Government Efforts at Tackling Organized Crime (2005–2006)," May 5, 2006, https://www.refworld.org /docid/45f1470620.html.

19. Melinda Liu, "The Capture of a Gang Leader," *Newsweek*, September 12, 1993, https://www.newsweek.com/capture-gang-leader-192918.

20. Nicholas D. Kristof and Sheryl WuDunn, *China Wakes: The Struggle for the Soul of a Rising Power* (New York: Alfred A. Knopf, 1995), 198.

21. National Drug Intelligence Center, "New York/New Jersey High Intensity Drug Trafficking Area: Drug Market Analysis 2009," April 2009, https:// www.justice.gov/archive/ndic/pubs32/32784/32784p.pdf.

22. James O. Finckenauer, "Chinese Transnational Organized Crime: The Fuk Ching," United Nations Activities, https://www.ojp.gov/pdffiles1/nij/218463 .pdf.

23. Kerry, *The New War*, 57.

24. Olaalpha, "Chinese President's Cousin Draws Scrutiny of Australian Authorities in Money Laundering and Organized Crime Probe," Financial Crime Compliance Education, July 31, 2019, https://financialcrimewatch .com/chinese-presidents-cousin-draw-scrutiny-money-laundering.

25. Jorge Guajardo, "Is China the Next Mexico? Lessons from the One-Party Model," speech at UC San Diego School of International Relations and Pacific Studies, January 16, 2014, https://china.ucsd.edu/_files/Jorge_Guajardo _keynote.

26. For example, Kuok had a 13 percent stake in CITIC Pacific. See Sterling Seagrave, *Lords of the Rim: The Invisible Empire of the Overseas Chinese* (New York: G. P. Putnam's Sons, 1995), 343; "Are Li Ka-shing and Citic Making Rival Bets on China's Future?," Change of Guard, Week in China, January 30, 2015, accessed November 2022, https://www.weekinchina.com /2015/01/change-of-guard/.

27. "Party Capital: A Blueprint for National Security Due Diligence on China," C4ADS, September 16, 2021, https://c4ads.org/wp-content/uploads/2022/03 /PartyCapitalReport.pdf, 37, 38.

28. Dennis F. Poindexter, *The Chinese Information War: Espionage, Cyberwar, Communications Control and Related Threats to United States Interests*, 2nd ed. (Jefferson, MO: McFarland, 2018), 105.

29. Kerry, *The New War*, 52–53.

30. David Armstrong, "Kerry Urged to Pressure China to Do More to Curb Sale of Deadly Fentanyl to US," STAT, May 24, 2016, https://www.statnews.com /2016/05/24/fentanyl-china-toomey-kerry; Jeanne Whalen, "U.S. Seeks Curb on Chemicals Used to Make Fentanyl, a Powerful Opioid," *Wall Street Journal*, October 14, 2016, https://www.wsj.com/articles/u-s-asks-u-n-to-class-two -chemicals-used-to-make-fentanyl-as-controlled-substances-1476469235.

31. Maria Shao, "Mass. Firms Pursue the China Trade; Kerry-Led Expedition Trying to Connect," *Boston Globe*, November 14, 1994.

32. David Sanger, "Businessman at White House Social Has Close Ties to China's Military Power," *New York Times*, December 21, 1996, https://www.nytimes .com/1996/12/21/us/businessman-at-white-house-social-has-close-ties-to -china-s-military-power.html; *Investigation of Illegal or Improper Activities in Connection with 1996 Federal Election Campaigns*, Final Report of the Committee on Governmental Affairs, United States Senate, March 10, 1998, https://www.hsdl.org/?view&did=830259.

33. *Anne L. Weismann v. Sheldon Adelson, Cheung Chi Tai, and Ng Lap Seng*, 52 U.S. Code § 30106, complaint form, https://www.fec.gov/files/legal/murs

/current/115774.pdf; Robert Zapesochny, "Chinagate and the Clintons," *American Spectator*, October 6, 2016, https://spectator.org/chinagate-and -the-clintons.

34. The Canadian Press, "Immigration Hearing Reveals How Asian Gang Crime Works in Canada," *Maclean's*, February 26, 2013, https://www.macleans.ca /news/immigration-hearing-reveals-how-asian-gang-crime-works-in-canada.

35. Charles R. Smith, *Deception: How Clinton Sold America Out to the Chinese Military* (La Porte, IN: Pine Lake Media Group, 2004), 155; Charles Smith, "'Cash Register' Li Ka-Shing," WND, June 7, 2000, https://www.wnd.com /2000/06/7104/.

36. Observatoire Géopolitique des Drogues, "The World Geopolitics of Drugs, 1997/1998 Annual Report," 77.

37. Alain Labrousse and Laurent Laniel, eds., *The World Geopolitics of Drugs, 1998/1999* (Dordrecht, Netherlands: Kluwer Academic Publishers, 2001), 85.

38. Benjamin T. Smith, *The Dope: The Real History of the Mexican Drug Trade* (New York: W. W. Norton, 2021), 405.

39. Rusin, "Illicit Chinese Fentanyl," 5–6.

40. "Fentanyl Fact Sheet," Colorado's 17th Judicial District Attorney's Office, https://adamsbroomfieldda.org/Fentanyl-Fact-Sheet.

41. Rusin, "Illicit Chinese Fentanyl," 6; Abi Millar, "Fentanyl: Where Did It All Go Wrong?," Pharmaceutical Technology, February 27, 2018, https://www .pharmaceutical-technology.com/analysis/fentanyl-go-wrong.

42. *United States v. O'Brien*, United States District Court (E.D.N.Y., 2017), case no. 13-CR-586 (RRM).

43. Channing Mavrellis and John Cassara, *Made in China: China's Role in Transnational Crime and Illicit Financial Flows*, Global Financial Integrity, October 27, 2022, https://34n8bd.p3cdn1.secureserver.net/wp-content /uploads/2022/10/GFI-China-TOC-IFF-Report-FINAL-OCT-22.pdf, 7.

44. Ibid.

45. Bonnie Girard, "Fentanyl in America: A Barometer of the China-US Relationship," *Diplomat*, August 31, 2021, https://thediplomat.com/2021 /08/fentanyl-in-america-a-barometer-of-the-china-us-relationship.

46. "China 2022," Amnesty International, https://www.amnesty.org/en/location /asia-and-the-pacific/east-asia/china/report-china.

47. Mavrellis and Cassara, *Made in China*, 15.

48. Peter Canning, *Killing Season: A Paramedic's Dispatches from the Front Lines of the Opioid Epidemic* (Baltimore: Johns Hopkins University Press, 2021), 145.

49. *Commonwealth v. Higgs*, 237 A.3d 462 (Pa. Super., 2020).

50. Mavrellis and Cassara, *Made in China*, 7; Vanda Felbab-Brown, "The

Foreign Policies of the Sinaloa Cartel and CJNG—Part II: The Asia-Pacific," The Brookings Institution, August 5, 2022, https://www.brookings.edu/opinions/the-foreign-policies-of-the-sinaloa-cartel-and-cjng-part-ii-the-asia-pacific.

51.   Leandra Bernstein, "Drug Trade War: Chinese Fentanyl Is Fueling the US Opioid Crisis," WJLA-TV, October 2, 2018, https://wjla.com/news/nation-world/chinese-fentanyl-is-fueling-the-us-opioid-crisis-drug-trade-tensions-escalate.

52.   Cooper, *Wilful Blindness*, 44–45.

53.   Ben Westhoff, "Exploring the Growing U.S. Reliance on China's Biotech and Pharmaceutical Products," July 31, 2019, https://www.uscc.gov/sites/default/files/Ben%20Westhoff%20Written%20Testimony.pdf.

54.   Emily Feng, "'We Are Shipping to the U.S.': Inside China's Online Synthetic Drug Networks," NPR, November 17, 2020, https://www.npr.org/2020/11/17/916890880/we-are-shipping-to-the-u-s-china-s-fentanyl-sellers-find-new-routes-to-drug-user.

55.   "The 64 Chinese Companies Selling Chemicals and Machines to Mexico's Cartels to Unleash an Epidemic of Uncontrolled Fentanyl," CE Noticias Financieras English, March 7, 2021. [Found in Lexis: https://advance.lexis.com/api/document?collection=news&id=urn:contentItem:625D-4FP1-JBJN-M54F-00000-00&context=1519360.]

56.   "Xuyang Biotechnology Co., Ltd.," China.cn, https://xuyang.en.china.cn/about.html.

57.   "Skyrun Industrial Co. Limited," Chemical Register, https://www.chemicalregister.com/Skyrun_Industrial_Co_Ltd/Supplier/sid33045.htm; "Jiang Jinhua," Bloomberg, https://www.bloomberg.com/profile/person/6560656; "Annual Report 2021," Holly Futures Co., Ltd., March 29, 2022, https://www1.hkexnews.hk/listedco/listconews/sehk/2022/0420/2022042000362.pdf; "Jian Ying Wang," *Wall Street Journal*, https://www.wsj.com/market-data/quotes/SZDEF/company-people/executive-profile/137494123; "Shan Xiaomin," Bloomberg, https://www.bloomberg.com/profile/person/21714493.

58.   Mark Wilson, "US Sanctions Reveal CJNG's Grip on Mexico Port to Move Fentanyl," InSight Crime, October 8, 2021, https://insightcrime.org/news/us-sanctions-reveal-cjngs-grip-on-mexico-port-to-move-fentanyl; "Treasury Works with Government of Mexico to Sanction CJNG Members Operating Through the Port of Manzanillo," U.S. Department of the Treasury, October 6, 2021, https://home.treasury.gov/news/press-releases/jy0389.

59.   Gary Dixon, "Mexico Seizes Fentanyl on Maersk Boxship," TradeWinds, September 2, 2019, https://www.tradewindsnews.com/law/mexico-seizes-fentanyl-on-maersk-boxship/2-1-664401.

60.   In October 2011, analyst Douglas Farah had testified before the House Oversight Committee on the drug trade. "China's growing presence, including

control of four key ports in Mexico, through which extensive movement of precursor chemicals and significant money laundering operations occur, is another significant factor in transnational criminal activity in Mexico." See *The International Exploitation of Drug Wars and What We Can Do About It: Hearings Before the Subcommittee on Oversight and Investigations of the Committee on Foreign Affairs, House of Representatives, One Hundred Twelfth Congress, First Session, October 12, 2011* (Washington, DC: U.S. Government Printing Office, 2011); Zinnia Lee, "Billionaire Li Ka-Shing's CK Hutchison and Vodafone Strike Deal to Create Britain's Biggest Mobile Operator," *Forbes*, June 15, 2023, https://www.forbes.com/sites/zinnialee /2023/06/15/billionaire-li-ka-shings-ck-hutchison-and-vodafone-strike-deal -to-create-britains-biggest-mobile-operator/?sh=35b082fc3274.

61. "Who We Are," Hutchison Ports ICAVE, https://hutchisonportsicave.com /en/who-we-are/hph-group/.

62. Vanessa Neumann, "Of Chinese Snakeheads and Mexican Coyotes: The Globalization of Crime-Terror Pipelines," Foreign Policy Research Institute, August 24, 2012, https://www.fpri.org/article/2012/08/of-chinese -snakeheads-and-mexican-coyotes-the-globalization-of-crime-terror -pipelines.

63. "Chinese Billionaire Wants Global Crossing," Newsmax, February 11, 2002, https://www.newsmax.com/pre-2008/chinese-billionaire-wants-global/2002 /02/11/id/664418/.

64. George W. Grayson, "La Familia Drug Cartel: Implications for U.S.-Mexican Security," Strategic Studies Institute, US Army War College, December 1, 2010, http://www.jstor.org/stable/resrep11895, 18, 19.

65. Sam Cooper, "How China Made Canada a Global Node for Narcos and Cyber-criminals," *Sunday Guardian*, May 15, 2021, excerpt from *Wilful Blindness: How a Network of Narcos, Tycoons, and CCP Agents Infiltrated the West*, https://sundayguardianlive.com/news/china-made-canada-global -node-narcos-cyber-criminals.

66. Dan Levin, "In China, Illegal Drugs Are Sold Online in an Unbridled Market," *New York Times*, June 21, 2015, https://www.nytimes.com/2015 /06/22/world/asia/in-china-illegal-drugs-are-sold-online-in-an-unbridled -market.html.

67. Mavrellis and Cassara, *Made in China*, 8.

68. Lauren Greenwood and Kevin Fashola, "Illicit Fentanyl from China: An Evolving Global Operation," U.S.-China Economic and Security Review Commission, August 24, 2021, https://www.politico.com/f/?id=0000017e -7dee-d8d6-a3fe-ffef55460004.

69. "Counterfeit Prescription Pills Containing Fentanyl: A Global Threat," DEA Intelligence Brief, July 2016, https://content.govdelivery.com /attachments/USDOJDEA/2016/07/22/file_attachments/590360 /fentanyl%2Bpills%2Breport.pdf, 2.

70. See *U.S. v. Lyon*, 2022, U.S. District, 64847 (D. Me., April 7, 2022), no. 1: 19-cr-00169-Jaw-1.

71. *State v. Hartwell*, Tenn. Ct. App., April 24, 2018, file no. E2017-00633 -CCA-R3-CD.

72. *Commonwealth v. Higgs*; Daniel Flatley, "US Sanctions Chinese Firms over Pill-Pressing Machines," Bloomberg, May 30, 2023, https://www.bloomberg .com/news/articles/2023-05-30/us-sanctions-chinese-firms-over-machines -that-make-fake-pills.

73. "Chinese Pill Presses Are Key Components for Illegally Manufactured Fentanyl," U.S. Department of Justice, Office of Private Sector, Health Care and Public Sector, April 30, 2020, leaked document, BlueLeaks.

74. "Counterfeit Prescription Pills Containing Fentanyl: A Global Threat"; Chao Wang et al., "The Evolving Regulatory Landscape for Fentanyl: China, India, and Global Drug Governance," *International Journal of Environmental Research and Public Health* 19, no. 4 (February 2022): 2074, https://doi.org /10.3390%2Fijerph19042074.

75. Keyword searches for "pill tablet presses" and "pill press machines" on Alibaba.com and Made-in-China.com brought up over 13,000 results on February 24, 2023.

76. Sebastian Rotella and Kirsten Berg, "How a Chinese American Gangster Transformed Money Laundering for Drug Cartels," ProPublica, October 11, 2022, https://www.propublica.org/article/china-cartels-xizhi-li-money -laundering.

77. Del Quentin Wilber, "Fentanyl Smuggled from China Is Killing Thousands of Americans," *Los Angeles Times*, October 19, 2018, https://www.latimes .com/politics/la-na-pol-china-fentanyl-20181019-story.html; Vanda Felbab-Brown, "The China Connection in Mexico's Illegal Economies," The Brookings Institution, February 4, 2022, https://www.brookings.edu/opinions /the-china-connection-in-mexicos-illegal-economies; "Two Chinese Nationals Charged with Operating Global Opioid and Drug Manufacturing Conspiracy Resulting in Deaths," US Department of Justice, August 22, 2018, https:// www.justice.gov/opa/pr/two-chinese-nationals-charged-operating-global -opioid-and-drug-manufacturing-conspiracy.

78. "Two Chinese Nationals Charged with Operating Global Opioid and Drug Manufacturing Conspiracy Resulting in Deaths"; see also Sushant Lakkadwala et al., "Dual Functionalized Liposomes for Efficient Co-delivery of Anti-cancer Chemotherapeutics for the Treatment of Glioblastoma," *Journal of Controlled Release* 307 (2019): 247–60, https://www.ncbi.nlm.nih.gov/pmc /articles/PMC6732022/, which states that chemicals were "bought from Cambridge Chemicals (Woburn, Massachusetts)"; Benjamin Kirchweger et al., "*In Silico* Workflow for the Discovery of Natural Products Activating the G Protein-Coupled Bile Acid Receptor 1," *Frontiers in Chemistry* 6 (2016): 242, https://www.ncbi.nlm.nih.gov/pmc/articles/PMC6036132, which states "was purchased from Cambridge Chemicals (USA)"; "Chinese National

Living in Massachusetts Pleaded Guilty to Distributing Opioids and Other Drugs That Were Shipped from China to the U.S. and Ultimately to Ohio," United States Attorney's Office, Northern District of Ohio, https://www .justice.gov/usao-ndoh/pr/chinese-national-living-massachusetts-pleaded -guilty-distributing-opioids-and-other; City of Woburn, Regular Meeting of the City Council, minutes, August 6, 2013, https://www.woburnma.gov /public-meetings/5684/.

79. City of Woburn, Regular Meeting of the City Council, minutes, August 6, 2013, https://www.woburnma.gov/public-meetings/5684; Office of Public Affairs, "Two Chinese Nationals Charged with Operating Global Opioid and Drug Manufacturing Conspiracy Resulting in Deaths," U.S. Department of Justice, August 22, 2018, https://www.justice.gov/opa/pr/two-chinese -nationals-charged-operating-global-opioid-and-drug-manufacturing -conspiracy; *United States of America v. Fujing Zheng and Guanghua Zheng*, United States District Court (N.D. Ohio, 2010), case no. 1:18 CR 474, https://www.justice.gov/opa/press-release/file/1089101/download.

80. "Chinese National Living in Massachusetts Pleaded Guilty to Distributing Opioids and Other Drugs That Were Shipped from China to the U.S. and Ultimately to Ohio."

81. *US v. Bin Wang*, Sentencing Memorandum, Case: 1:18-cr-00123-JRA, Doc #: 45, Filed: 11/05/18. *United States v. Wang*, N.E. 284 (N.D. Ohio 2018) (defendant's sentencing memorandum with exhibits).

82. William C. Hannas, James Mulvenon, and Anna B. Puglisi, *Chinese Industrial Espionage; Technology Acquisition and Military Modernisation* (London: Routledge, 2013), 113; Bin Wang, Letter to Judge Adams, Case: 1:18-cr-00123-JRA, 1. Bin Wang Letter to Judge J. Adams, May 22, 2020, received and filed May 29, 2020, with the U.S. District Court Northern District of Ohio.

83. Cooper, *Wilful Blindness*, 303.

84. "Party Capital: A Blueprint for National Security Due Diligence on China," C4ADS, September 16, 2021, https://c4ads.org/wp-content/uploads/2022 /03/PartyCapitalReport.pdf, 15; Shannon Tiezzi, "What Is the CPPCC Anyway?," *Diplomat*, March 4, 2021, https://thediplomat.com/2021/03 /what-is-the-cppcc-anyway.

85. Daniel Garrett, "A Hard-Boiled Belt and Road: Backlash to the UN-Bribes-for-OBOR Scandals," in *Organized Crime and Corruption Across Borders: Exploring the Belt and Road Initiative*, edited by T. Wing Lo, Dina Siegel, and Sharon I. Kwok (London: Routledge, 2020), 63.

86. Lena H. Sun and John Pomfret, "China Adviser's Gift to DNC Under Review," *Washington Post*, February 25, 1997, https://www.washingtonpost .com/archive/politics/1997/02/25/china-advisers-gift-to-dnc-under-review /c4f6f2d6-c7f8-4be8-8089-9d2082375ef4.

87. Peter Beaumont, "Stanley Ho, Flamboyant 'Godfather' of Macau Casinos,

Dies Aged 98," *Guardian*, May 26, 2020, https://www.theguardian.com /business/2020/may/26/stanley-ho-the-billionaire-macao-casino-tycoon-dies -aged-98.

88. Niall Fraser, "What Has Former 14K Triad Boss 'Broken Tooth' Wan Kuok-kai Been Up to Since Leaving Prison?," *South China Morning Post*, February 21, 2021, https://www.scmp.com/magazines/post-magazine/long -reads/article/3122201/what-has-former-14k-triad-boss-broken-tooth-wan; "Gangsterism with Chinese Characteristics."

89. "The email program routed its traffic through encrypted servers located in countries and jurisdictions believed by Phantom Secure to be uncooperative with law enforcement, such as Panama and Hong Kong SAR of China." *United States of America v. Ramos*, United States District Court, S.D. Cal., June 12, 2019, case No. 3:18-CR-01404-WQH, S.D. Cal., June 12, 2019, https://sherloc.unodc.org/cld/case-law-doc/drugcrimetype/usa/2019/united _states_of_america_v._ramos_no._318-cr-01404 wqh_s.d._cal._jun_12 _2019.html.

90. Kim Bolan, "REAL SCOOP: CEO of Criminal Encryption Company Hid $80 Million," *Vancouver Sun*, April 24, 2019, https://vancouversun.com /news/staff-blogs/real-scoop-ceo-of-criminal-encryption-company-hid-80 -million.

91. Harshawn Ratanpal, "After U.S. Scrutiny of WeChat, Chinese Conglomerate Tencent Holdings Spent Millions on Federal Lobbying," Open Secrets, February 7, 2023, https://www.opensecrets.org/news/2023/02/after-us -scrutiny-of-wechat-chinese conglomerate-tencent-holdings-spent-millions -on-federal-lobbying/; Rotella and Berg, "How a Chinese American Gangster Transformed Money Laundering for Drug Cartels."

92. Drazen Jorgic, "Special Report—Burner Phones and Banking Apps: Meet the Chinese 'Brokers' Laundering Mexican Drug Money," Reuters, December 3, 2020, https://www.reuters.com/article/us-mexico-china-cartels -specialreport/special-report-burner-phones-and-banking-apps-meet-the -chinese-brokers-laundering-mexican-drug-money-idUSKBN28D1M4.

93. Ben West, "'Dark Angel' and the Mexican Meth Connection," Stratfor Security Weekly, June 14, 2012, https://worldview.stratfor.com/article/dark -angel-and-mexican-meth-connection.

94. Department of Homeland Security and Department of Justice, Joint Intelligence Report, "Chicago's New Fusion: Chinese Money Laundering Organizations Partnering with Mexican Transnational Criminal Organizations," April 2020.

95. DEA Phoenix Field Division 'KNR,' October 21–28, 2019, Strategic Targeting and Analysis Group, accessed from BlueLeaks.

96. Rotella and Berg, "How a Chinese American Gangster Transformed Money Laundering for Drug Cartels."

97. Ibid.

98. Ibid.; Lulu Yilun Chen, *Influence Empire: The Story of Tencent and China's Tech Ambition* (London: Hodder & Stoughton, 2022), 106.

99. David W. Murray and John P. Walters, "COVID-19 Isn't China's Only Deadly Export," Hudson Institute, April 12, 2021, https://www.hudson.org /domestic-policy/covid-19-isn-t-china-s-only-deadly-export.

100. Vanda Felbab-Brown, "China and Synthetic Drugs Control: Fentanyl, Methamphetamines, and Precursors," The Brookings Institution, March 2022, https://www.brookings.edu/wp-content/uploads/2022/03/FP_20221107 _drug_trafficking_felbab_brown.pdf, 32.

101. David Asher, "How to Fight the Mexican and Chinese Fentanyl Cartels Driving Biggest Money Laundering Scheme in History," Hudson Institute, August 20, 2022, https://www.hudson.org/national-security-defense/how -to-fight-the-mexican-and-chinese-fentanyl-cartels-driving-biggest-money -laundering-scheme-in-history. It is important to note that "Ninety percent of recommendation letters for Chinese applicants to Western universities are falsified," according to a study by Jon Marcus, "Barefaced Cheating in China's Bull Market for Academic Fraud," *International Higher Education* 73 (Fall 2013): 9–11, https://doi.org/10.6017/ihe.2013.73.6119.

102. Jorgic, "Special Report—Burner Phones and Banking Apps: Meet the Chinese 'Brokers' Laundering Mexican Drug Money."

103. Rotella and Berg, "How a Chinese American Gangster Transformed Money Laundering for Drug Cartels."

Chapter 3: Willful Blindness

1. Quoted in Tim Fernholz, "With China, Money Talks," *American Prospect*, July 29, 2009, https://prospect.org/departments/china-money-talks.

2. Orrin Hatch, "Downgrading of 'Drug Czar' and His Office," *San Diego Union Tribune*, March 31, 2009, https://www.sandiegouniontribune.com /sdut-lz1e31hatch194129-downgrading-drug-czar-and-his-of-2009mar31 -story.html.

3. Erika Kinetz and Matthew Pennington, "Obama Administration Lets Myanmar Sanctions List Languish," *Jefferson City News Tribune*, May 18, 2013, https://www.newstribune.com/news/2013/may/18/obama-administration -lets-myanmar-sanctions-list-l; Kyaw Min Htun and Win Ko Lwin, "Myanmar: Sanctions to Take Center Stage During Aung San Suu Kyi's U.S. Visit," Radio Free Asia, September 14, 2016, https://www.rfa.org/english /news/myanmar/sanctions-to-take-center-stage-during-aung-san-suu-kyis -us-visit-09132016160236.html; Aung Hla Tun, "Myanmar Lawmakers Want Tougher Measures to Combat Drugs," Reuters, August 3, 2016, https://www.reuters.com/article/us-myanmar-drugs/myanmar-lawmakers -want-tougher-measures-to-combat-drugs-idUSKCN10E1DU; Gibson Dunn, "United States Lifts Burma (Myanmar) Sanctions in Response to Ongoing

DemocraticReforms," October 10, 2016, https://www.gibsondunn.com/united
-states-lifts-burma-myanmar-sanctions-in-response-to-ongoing-democratic
-reforms.

4. Peter Olsen-Phillips, "Friends in High Places: Major Obama Donors with Interests in China," Sunlight Foundation, March 24, 2014, https://sunlightfoundation.com/2014/03/24/friends-in-high-places-major-obama-donors-with-interests-in-china; Rachel Abrams, "China's Film Quota Cracked," *Variety*, February 20, 2012, https://variety.com/2012/film/news/china-s-film-quota-cracked-1118050508.

5. Ben Wilson, "Biden Campaign Co-chair Has Deep China Connections, Met with Xi Jinping," *Washington Free Beacon*, April 26, 2023, https://freebeacon.com/biden-administration/biden-campaign-co-chair-has-deep-china-connections-met-with-xi-jinping.

6. "Ex-Fugees Rapper Pras Michel Found Guilty in Scheme to Help China Influence US Government," CBS News, April 26, 2023, https://www.cbsnews.com/atlanta/news/ex-fugees-rapper-pras-michel-found-guilty-in-scheme-to-help-china-influence-us-government.

7. Tom Phillips, "Barack Obama 'Deliberately Snubbed' by Chinese in Chaotic Arrival at G20," *Guardian*, September 4, 2016, https://www.theguardian.com/world/2016/sep/04/barack-obama-deliberately-snubbed-by-chinese-in-chaotic-arrival-at-g20.

8. Higham, Horwitz, and Zezima, "Fentanyl Failure."

9. Office of the Press Secretary, "FACT SHEET: Obama Administration Announces Prescription Opioid and Heroin Epidemic Awareness Week," The White House, September 19, 2016, https://obamawhitehouse.archives.gov/the-press-office/2016/09/19/fact-sheet-obama-administration-announces-prescription-opioid-and heroin.

10. Katie Zezima and Colby Itkowitz, "Flailing on Fentanyl," *Washington Post*, September 20, 2019, https://www.washingtonpost.com/graphics/2019/investigations/fentanyl-epidemic-congress.

11. Higham, Horwitz, and Zezima, "Fentanyl Failure."

12. National Committee on U.S.-China Relations, "CHINA Town Hall 2017 with Ambassador Susan Rice," October 25, 2017, YouTube, https://www.youtube.com/watch?v=N82B2ufHLHs&t.

13. "Watch Highlights from China Town Hall 2017 with Ambassador Susan Rice," National Committee on U.S.-China Relations, https://www.ncuscr.org/watch-highlights-china-town-hall-2017-ambassador-susan-rice.

14. Rusin, "Illicit Chinese Fentanyl," 8.

15. "Chinese Online Sellers Pay $40,000 to Take Pictures with Obama," CGTN, December 8, 2017, https://news.cgtn.com/news/324d7a4e30637a6333566d54/share_p.html.

16. Susan Scutti, "Drug Overdoses, Suicides Cause Drop in 2017 US Life Expectancy;

CDC Director Calls It a 'Wakeup Call,'" CNN, December 17, 2018, https://www.cnn.com/2018/11/29/health/life-expectancy-2017-cdc/index.html.

17. The Reality Check Team, "Fentanyl Crisis: Is China a Major Source of Illegal Drugs?," BBC, September 24, 2018, https://www.bbc.com/news/world-45564744.

18. "Ongoing Emergencies & Disasters," Centers for Medicare & Medicaid Services, https://www.cms.gov/about-cms/agency-information/emergency/epro/current-emergencies/ongoing-emergencies.

19. Sui-lee Wee, "Trump Says China Will Curtail Fentanyl. The U.S. Has Heard That Before," *New York Times*, December 3, 2018, https://www.nytimes.com/2018/12/03/business/fentanyl-china-trump.html.

20. Steven Nelson, "Brazen Fentanyl Sales Continue Online as China Vows Crackdown," *Washington Examiner*, December 11, 2018, https://www.washingtonexaminer.com/policy/technology/brazen-fentanyl-sales-continue-online-as-china-vows-crackdown.

21. John Pomfret, "Why Is China Refusing to Stop the Flow of Fentanyl?," *Washington Post*, March 4, 2019, https://www.washingtonpost.com/opinions/2019/03/04/why-is-china-refusing-stop-flow-fentanyl.

22. "Decreasing Fentanyl Seizures in the Air Environment Likely Indicate Changes in Fentanyl Supply Routes," Department of Homeland Security, November 4, 2019, 3, accessed from BlueLeaks.

23. Robert Spalding, *War Without Rules: China's Playbook for Global Domination* (New York: Sentinel, 2022), 71.

24. Lauren Greenwood and Kevin Fashola, "Illicit Fentanyl from China: An Evolving Global Operation," U.S.-China Economic and Security Review Commission, August 24, 2021, https://www.politico.com/f/?id=0000017e-7dee-d8d6-a3fe-ffef55460004, 5.

25. Ibid., 8.

26. Ian Spiegelman, "Fentanyl Deaths Have Risen 1,208 Percent in L.A. Since 2016," *Los Angeles Magazine*, November 30, 2022, https://www.lamag.com/citythinkblog/fentanyl-deaths-in-l-a-have-risen-1208-percent-in-l-a-since-2016.

27. "Health Alert: Counterfeit Pills Contaminated with Fentanyl Causing Drug Overdose," Burbank Unified School District, September 15, 2022, https://www.burbankusd.org/site/default.aspx?PageType=3&DomainID=4&ModuleInstanceID=5183&ViewID=6446EE88-D30C-497E-9316-3F8874B3E108&RenderLoc=0&FlexDataID=16560&PageID=1.

28. "Approximately 100,000 Fake Oxycodone Pills Containing Fentanyl Seized by DEA Los Angeles Field Division and Burbank PD," United States Drug Enforcement Administration, July 19, 2022, https://www.dea.gov/press-releases/2022/07/19/approximately-100000-fake-oxycodone-pills-containing-fentanyl.

29. Charmaine Patterson, "TikTok Star Cooper Noriega's Cause of Death Confirmed by Coroner 6 Months After He Was Found Dead," *People*, December 19, 2022, https://people.com/human-interest/TikTok-star-cooper -noriegas-cause-of-death-revealed-by-l-a-county-coroner.

30. Spiegelman, "Fentanyl Deaths Have Risen 1,208 Percent in L.A. Since 2016."

31. The keyword search of the word "fentanyl" on Adam Schiff's webpage was conducted on October 2, 2023.

32. "Fentanyl Crisis Is Out of Control," *Glendale* [CA] *News-Press*, January 11, 2023, https://glendalenewspress.outlooknewspapers.com/2023/01/11 /fentanyl-crisis-is-out-of-control.

33. Troy Anderson, "L.A.'s New Mob Threat: Ethnic Gangs Organizing into Global Problems," *Los Angeles Daily News*, March 18, 2001; Rone Tempest, "Medi-Cal Scandal Alarms Armenians," *Los Angeles Times*, December 8, 1999, https://www.latimes.com/archives/la-xpm-1999-dec-08-mn-41634 -story.html.

34. "Manhattan U.S. Attorney Charges 44 Members and Associates of an Armenian-American Organized Crime Enterprise with $100 Million Medicare Fraud," United States Attorney's Office, Southern District of New York, October 13, 2010, https://www.justice.gov/archive/usao/nys /pressreleases/index1010.html.

35. Bruce Fein, "Democratic Congressional Campaign Committee Should Return Illicit Donation," HuffPost, May 25, 2011, https://www.huffpost .com/entry/democratic-congressional_b_766162.

36. "Gang Bill Divides Lawmakers," *Inland Valley* [CA] *Daily Bulletin*, May 11, 2005.

37. Susan Crabtree, "Schiff and Boxer Form Fundraising Alliance That Could Help Boost a Senate Bid," *Washington Free Beacon*, August 15, 2017, https:// freebeacon.com/politics/schiff-and-boxer-form-fundraising-alliance-that -could-help-boost-a-senate-bid.

38. Search of FEC.gov for Schiff campaign and related PAC donations and "Allied Wallet"; "Shady Payment Processor Gave Millions to Hillary and Trump," *New York Post*, August 2, 2018, https://nypost.com/2018/08/02 /shady-payment-processor-gave-millions-to-hillary-and-trump/;   "Arizona Bank That Received TARP Funds Agrees to Forfeit Profits from Processing Online Gambling Payments," United States Attorney's Office, Southern District of New York, September 15, 2020, https://www.justice.gov/archive /usao/nys/pressreleases/September10/goldwaterbankforfeiturepr.pdf.

39. Jake Pearson and Jeff Horwitz, "Feds Probe Firm's Ties to Illegal Pharma Merchants," Associated Press, August 3, 2018, https://www.apnews.com /4a72ce1729274f80965d6e4dd2ec4bff/Feds-probe-firm's-ties-to-illegal -pharma-merchants.

40. Jake Pearson and Jeff Horwitz, "Donor Helping Fraudsters, Offshore Bettors

Backs Trump," Associated Press, August 1, 2018, https://apnews.com/article /55d30d088f8845308a6840acd5c199da.

41. "Saudi Authorities Reveal Location of Disappeared Royals, Allow Family Visits," DAWN, November 22, 2021, https://dawnmena.org/saudi-authorities -reveal-location-of-disappeared-royals-allow-family-visits.

42. Josh Rudolph and Thomas Morley, *Covert Foreign Money: Financial Loopholes Exploited by Authoritarians to Fund Political Interference in Democracies*, Alliance for Security Democracy, August 2020, https:// securingdemocracy.gmfus.org/wp-content/uploads/2020/08/ASD-Covert -Foreign-Money.pdf, 49, footnote 547.

43. "Allied Wallet and UnionPay International Make History with UnionPay Branded Prepaid Debit Card," Allied Wallet, https://www.alliedwallet.com /blog/press-releases/allied-wallet-unionpay-international-make-history -unionpay-branded-prepaid-debit-card; James Pomfret, "Special Report: How China's Official Bank Card Is Used to Smuggle Money," Reuters, March 11, 2014, https://www.reuters.com/article/us-china-unionpay-special-report /special-report-how-chinas-official-bank-card-is-used-to-smuggle-money -idUSBREA2B00820140312.

44. For example, in 2023, Alvin Chau, the boss of a notorious junket operator who "brokered the gambling activity of Chinese high-rollers," was sentenced to eighteen years in prison for racketeering and was forced to pay over $800 million in restitution. Chau is allegedly a member of the Macau faction of the 14K triad society. According to a detailed report by the Hong Kong Jockey Club, for more than two years Chau used UnionPay to launder more than a million dollars per day, which included proceeds of triad drug trafficking. In another case, the Chinese billionaire property developer Phillip Dong Fang Lee ran a scheme to launder money using UnionPay. The laundering scheme was run through an Australian casino connected to massive drug trafficking. See Philip Wang, "Macao Gambling Promoter Alvin Chau Sentenced to 18 Years— Public Broadcaster," CNN, January 18, 2023, https://www.cnn.com/2023 /01/18/business/macao-alvin-chau-hong-kong-hnk-intl/index.html; "Inquiry Questions the Star on Relationship with Chau Despite 'Unsavory Business Applications,'" *Macau Daily Times*, April 7, 2022, https://macaudailytimes .com.mo/inquiry-questions-the-star-on-relationship-with-chau-despite -unsavory-business-associations.html; Elouise Fowler and Hannah Wootton, "Dirty Dollars: How Australia's Casino Industry Became So Rotten," *Australian Financial Review*, April 13, 2022, https://www.afr.com/companies/games-and -wagering/dirty-dollars-how-australia-s-casino-industry-became-so-rotten -20220406-p5abcx; Philip Conneller, "$100 Million Slots Session at Star Sydney Led to Massive Cocaine Bust," Casino.org, July 7, 2021, https://www.casino .org/news/100-million-slots-session-at-star-sydney-led-to-massive-cocaine-bust.

45. James Bamford, "These Shady UAE Donors Gave Millions to Clinton and Trump While the Feds Dozed," The Daily Beast, January 16, 2023, https:// www.thedailybeast.com/these-shady-uae-donors-gave-millions-to-clinton -and-trump-while-the-feds-dozed.

46. Andy Nguyen, "Glendale Attorney Admits to Laundering over $500,000 as Part of $14-Million Tax-Fraud Scam," *Glendale* [CA] *News-Press*, December 21, 2018, https://www.latimes.com/socal/glendale-news-press/news/tn-gnp -me-arthur-charchian-guilty-plea-20181221-story.html.

47. "1,000 Strong Capacity Crowd Celebrates the Armenian Cause and ANCA-WR," October 18, 2018, Armenian National Committee of America, Western Region, https://ancawr.org/press-release/anca-wr-gala-coverage -2018/.

48. Fein, "Democratic National Campaign Committee Should Return Illicit Donation."

49. A keyword search of "Ed Buck" in the Donor Lookup section of OpenSecrets. org revealed this information: "Grand Jury Indicts Ed Buck on Drug Trafficking Offenses, Including Giving Methamphetamine to 2 Victims Who Suffered Fatal Overdoses," United States Attorney's Office, Central District of California, July 28, 2021, https://www.justice.gov/usao-cdca /pr/grand-jury-indicts-ed-buck-drug-trafficking-offenses-including-giving -methamphetamine-2; John Riley, "Wealthy Democratic Donor Sentenced to 30 Years in Prison," *Metro Weekly*, April 15, 2022, https://www. metroweekly.com/2022/04/ed-buck-gets-30-years-in-prison-for-injecting- gay-black-men-with-drugs.

50. Domenico Montanero, "Adam Schiff, the Surprising Face of the Impeachment Inquiry into President Trump," NPR, October 10, 2019, https://www .npr.org/2019/10/10/768048653/adam-schiff-the-surprising-face-of-the -impeachment-inquiry-of-president-trump; Jennifer Auther, "Rep. Rogan Faces Uncertain Future," CNN, September 1, 1999, https://edition.cnn.com /ALLPOLITICS/stories/1999/09/01/rogan.

51. Juliet Eilperin, "Movie Studios Still Support Rogan," *Washington Post*, March 27, 1999, https://www.washingtonpost.com/wp-srv/politics /campaigns/keyraces2000/stories/rogan032799.htm.

52. See, e.g., Finn Hoogensen, "Fentanyl Seized at Drug Mill Located Blocks Away from Bronx Day Care: 'Shockingly Brazen,'" Pix 11 News, September 28, 2023, https://pix11.com/news/local-news/bronx/fentanyl-seized-at-drug -mill-located-blocks-away-from-bronx-day-care-shockingly-brazen/.

53. On October 5, 2023, a search for "fentanyl" on Ocasio-Cortez's House site yielded zero results: https://ocasio-cortez.house.gov/search?search_api _fulltext=fentanyl.

54. "Biden: 9-Point Plan for a Clean Energy Revolution," Biden 2020 Campaign, April 23, 2020, https://news-photos-features.com/tag/biden-2020 -campaign/.

55. John Riley, "White House Names Monkeypox Czars," *Metro Weekly*, August 2, 2022, https://www.metroweekly.com/2022/08/white-house-names -monkeypox-response-coordinators.

56. Joseph R. Biden, Jr., "Memorandum on Presidential Determination on Major

Drug Transit or Major Illicit Drug Producing Countries for Fiscal Year 2023," The White House, September 15, 2022, https://www.whitehouse .gov/briefing-room/presidential-actions/2022/09/15/memorandum-on -presidential-determination-on-major-drug-transit-or-major-illicit-drug -producing-countries-for-fiscal-year-2023.

57. "Secretary of State Antony Blinken Discusses U.S.-China Relations After Beijing Trip," CBS News, June 19, 2023, YouTube, https://www.youtube .com/watch?v=ibQ6Dzltqqo.

58. Gillian Brassil, "As Fentanyl Overdoses in California Climb, Here's What Biden Said He Would Do to Stop It," *Sacramento Bee*, February 21, 2023, https:// www.sacbee.com/news/politics-government/capitol-alert/article272527500 .html; "Remarks of President Joe Biden—State of the Union Address as Prepared for Delivery," The White House, February 7, 2023, https://www .whitehouse.gov/briefing-room/speeches-remarks/2023/02/07/remarks-of -president-joe-biden-state-of-the-union-address-as-prepared-for-delivery.

59. See Peter Schweizer, *Red-Handed: How American Elites Get Rich Helping China Win* (New York: HarperCollins, 2022), 32–40.

60. "Risk Watch: What Does the Detention of CEFC Chairman Ye Jianming Signal?," SinoInsider, March 3, 2018, https://sinoinsider.com/2018/03/risk -watch-what-does-the-detention-of-cefc-chairman-ye-jianming-signal; Jenni Marsh, "The Rise and Fall of a Belt and Road Billionaire," CNN, https:// www.cnn.com/interactive/2018/12/asia/patrick-ho-ye-jianming-cefc-trial-intl.

61. "Estos son los socios chinos que han convertido al Cártel de Sinaloa en el rey del fentanilo," *El Diario de Chihuahua*, November 2, 2019, https://www .eldiariodechihuahua.mx/nacional/estos-son-los-socios-chinos-que-han -convertido-al-cartel-de-sinaloa-en-el-rey-del-fentanilo-20191102-1582316 .html; "DEA revelo organigramas de quien es quien en el Cartel de Sinaloa," *Extraoficial Periodismo digital con sentido*, November 20, 2019, https:// extraoficial.mx/dea-revelo-organigramas-de-quien-es-quien-en-el-cartel -de-sinaloa/; "In the Bowels of the Sinaloa Cartel; The DEA Revealed Who Is Who in the Criminal Organization That Led 'El Chapo,'" *CE Noticias Financieras English*, November 19, 2019.

62. John Pomfret, "The China Connection," *Washington Post*, December 31, 2000, https://www.washingtonpost.com/archive/politics/2000/12/31/the-china -connection/43d3037a-3934-4e63-8848-1436caa1db65/.

63. Neil S. Helfand and David L. Osborne, "Asian Organized Crime and Terrorist Activity in Canada, 1999–2002," Federal Research Division, Library of Congress, July 2003, https://apps.dtic.mil/sti/pdfs/ADA439619.pdf, 23.

64. Pomfret, "The China Connection."

65. Matt Viser, Tom Hamburger, and Craig Timberg, "Inside Hunter Biden's Multimillion-Dollar Deals with a Chinese Energy Company," *Washington Post*, March 30, 2022, https://www.washingtonpost.com/politics/2022/03 /30/hunter-biden-china-laptop; "Patrick Ho, Former Head of Organization

Backed by Chinese Energy Conglomerate, Sentenced to 3 Years in Prison for International Bribery and Money Laundering Offenses," United States Attorney's Office, Southern District of New York, March 25, 2019, https://www.justice.gov/usao-sdny/pr/patrick-ho-former-head-organization-backed-chinese-energy-conglomerate-sentenced-3.

66. Nick McKenzie et al., "Beijing's Secret Plot to Infiltrate UN Used Australian Insider," *Sydney Morning Herald*, November 11, 2018, https://www.smh.com.au/world/asia/beijing-s-secret-plot-to-infiltrate-un-used-australian-insider-20181031-p50d2e.html; "Macau Billionaire Sentenced to 48 Months in Prison for Role in Scheme to Bribe United Nations Ambassadors to Build a Multibillion-Dollar Conference Center," United States Attorney's Office, Southern District of New York, May 14, 2018, https://www.justice.gov/usao-sdny/pr/macau-billionaire-sentenced-48-months-prison-role-scheme-bribe-united-nations; Micah Morrison, "The Macau Connection," *Wall Street Journal*, February 26, 1998, https://www.wsj.com/articles/SB888439204883313500.

67. See Schweizer, *Red-Handed*, 18.

68. Jessica Chasmar and Cameron Cawthorne, "Eric Schwerin's Role in Hunter Biden's Chinese Business Deals Could Be Missing Key in GOP Investigations," FOX News, August 11, 2023, https://www.foxnews.com/politics/eric-schwerins-role-hunter-bidens-chinese-business-deals-missing-key-gop-investigations.

69. Kenneth P. Vogel (@kenvogel), Twitter, February 28, 2023, 4:44 p.m., https://twitter.com/kenvogel/status/1630685374619025408.

70. Bethany Allen-Ebrahimian, "China's Influence Agents Lawyer Up," Axios, September 29, 2020, https://www.axios.com/2020/09/29/chinas-influence-agents-lawyer-up; Brandon L. Van Grack, email message to Abbe David Lowell, "Re: Possible Obligation to Register Pursuant to the Foreign Agents Registration Act," April 6, 2020, https://www.documentcloud.org/documents/23692441-dojs-fara-chief-asks-abbe-lowell-about-his-work-for-foreign-principals-april-6-2020.

71. Jimmy Quinn, "Chinese Official Mocks U.S. Opioid Crisis as Biden Admin Seeks Cooperation on Fentanyl," *National Review*, February 21, 2023, https://www.nationalreview.com/corner/chinese-official-mocks-u-s-opioid-crisis-as-biden-admin-seeks-cooperation-on-fentanyl.

72. "China," Albright Stonebridge Group, https://www.albrightstonebridge.com/regions/china.

73. John Kerry, Public Financial Disclosure Report Form 278e, January 20, 2021, U.S. Office of Government Ethics, https://www.documentcloud.org/documents/20694598-john-kerry-financial-disclosure.

74. Teng Yue Partners, L.P., LinkedIn, https://www.linkedin.com/company/tengyuepartners; Josh Boswell, "EXCLUSIVE: John Kerry's Heinz Ketchup Heiress Wife Has Millions of Dollars in Chinese Investments, Leaving

Biden's Climate Change Envoy Facing an Ethical Dilemma as He Regularly Meets with the Country's Top Leaders to Cut Deals," *Daily Mail*, September 20, 2021, https://www.dailymail.co.uk/news/article-9885049/John-Kerrys -wife-millions-dollars-Chinese-investments.html.

75. See Schweizer, *Red-Handed*, 232–34.

76. "Chinese Ambassador to the US Qin Gang Takes an Interview with Newsweek on the Fentanyl Issue," Ministry of Foreign Affairs of the People's Republic of China, September 30, 2022, https://www.fmprc.gov.cn/mfa_eng /wjb_663304/zwjg_665342/zwbd_665378/202209/t20220930_10775685 .html.

77. Quinn, "Chinese Official Mocks U.S. Opioid Crisis as Biden Admin Seeks Cooperation on Fentanyl."

78. "Sweeping Two-Day Operation Targets International Organized Crime in Sacramento Area Neighborhoods," United States Attorney's Office, Eastern District of California, April 4, 2018, https://www.justice.gov /usao-edca/pr/sweeping-two-day-operation-targets-international-organized -crime-sacramento-area; Paige St. John, "The Reality of Legal Weed in California: Huge Illegal Grows, Violence, Worker Exploitation and Deaths," *Los Angeles Times*, September 8, 2022, https://www.latimes .com/california/story/2022-09-08/reality-of-legal-weed-in-california-illegal -grows-deaths; Don Thompson, "US Seizes Pot-Growing Houses Tied to China-Based Criminals," Associated Press, April 4, 2018, https://apnews .com/60e9e35eeb81482b85acce911a582266/US-seizes-pot-growing-houses -tied-to-China-based-criminals.

79. "Members of International Drug Trafficking Conspiracy Sentenced to Prison," United States Attorney's Office, Western District of Washington, June 18, 2019, https://www.justice.gov/usao-wdwa/pr/members-international-drug -trafficking-conspiracy-sentenced-prison.

80. Lester Black, "Bay Area Cannabis Grows Linked to Chinese Organized Crime," SFGATE, March 23, 2023, https://www.sfgate.com/cannabis/article /california-illegal-cannabis-grow-17856215.php.

81. Chris Casacchia, "California Report Shows Ramped-Up Crackdown on Illicit Marijuana Operators," MJBizDaily, March 3, 2023, https://mjbizdaily .com/california-report-shows-ramped-up-crackdown-on-illicit-marijuana -operators.

82. Jennie Taer, "EXCLUSIVE: Illegal Chinese Marijuana Grow Operations Are Taking Over Blue State, Leaked Memo Says," Daily Caller, August 16, 2023, https://dailycaller.com/2023/08/16/exclusive-illegal-chinese-marijuana-grow -operations-taking-over-blue-state-leaked-memo-says/; "Maine Delegation Urges DOJ to Shut Down Foreign-Owned, Illegal Operated Marijuana Businesses," August 24, 2023; https://www.king.senate.gov/newsroom /press-releases/maine-delegation-urges-doj-to-shut-down-foreign-owned -illegally-operated-marijuana-businesses.

83. nick, "Is Marijuana Stronger Now Than Ever Before?," The Freedom Center, June 12, 2023, https://www.thefreedomcenter.com/is-marijuana-stronger -now-than-ever-before.

84. Patrick Hauf, "Cases of Marijuana Laced with Fentanyl Increasing, Says Washington Doctor," FOX News, May 15, 2023, https://www.foxnews.com /health/cases-marijuana-laced-fentanyl-increasing-says-washington-doctor.

85. Bruce Schreiner, "Kentucky Shatters Its Fatal Overdose Record; Fentanyl Blamed," MyTwinTiers.com, June 13, 2022, https://www.mytwintiers.com /news-cat/health-news/kentucky-shatters-its-fatal-overdose-record-fentanyl -blamed.

86. Zezima and Itkowitz, "Flailing on Fentanyl."

87. Mel Baker, "Overdoses Have Killed More than Three Times as Many People as COVID-19 in San Francisco," *San Francisco Public Press*, December 17, 2020, https://www.sfpublicpress.org/overdoses-have-killed-more-than-three -times-as-many-people-as-covid-19-in-san-francisco.

88. Jill Cowan, "A Timeline of the Coronavirus in California," *New York Times*, June 15, 2021, https://www.nytimes.com/2021/06/15/us/coronavirus -california-timeline.html.

89. Jjsmith (@war24182236), "Today I was able to ask Gavin Newsom, the governor what is he going to do about the Fentanyl epidemic," Twitter, April 19, 2023, 12:46 p.m., https://twitter.com/war24182236/status /1648759883901317121; Kristine Parks, "Gavin Newsom Roasted for Non-answer About Addressing Fentanyl Epidemic: 'What Should I Do?,'" FOX News, April 20, 2023, https://www.foxnews.com/media/gavin-newsom -roasted-non-answer-addressing-fentanyl-epidemic-what-should-i-do.

90. John B. Roberts II and Elizabeth A. Roberts, *Freeing Tibet: 50 Years of Struggle, Resilience, and Hope* (New York: AMACOM Books, 2009), 224–25.

91. "Mayor Newsom Launches ChinaSF in Shanghai," Office of the Mayor, November 12, 2008, https://web.archive.org/web/20081114042237/http:// www.sfgov.org/site/mayor_index.asp?id=92777.

92. Chen Jia, "Bay Area a Magnet for Chinese Investors," *China Daily*, September 16, 2013, https://usa.chinadaily.com.cn/epaper/2013-09/16/content _16972583.htm.

93. Andrew S. Ross, "ChinaSF to Open Office in Beijing," SFGATE, October 1, 2010, https://www.sfgate.com/business/bottomline/article/ChinaSF-to-open -office-in-Beijing-3251345.php.

94. Jeanne Lawrence, "Shanghai Social Diary: A Green Tech Summit and a Birthday Party," Jeanne Lawrence's Travels, January 20, 2009, http:// jeannelawrence.com/wordpress1/2009/01/20/shanghai-social-diary-a -green-tech-summit-and-a-birthday-party; "Business Leaders Sign Private San Francisco Bay Area/China Pact," FreightWaves, April 29, 2007, https://

www.freightwaves.com/news/business-leaders-sign-private-san-francisco
-bay-area-china-pact.

95. Keith Wallis, "Anger at Report of Triad Role on Sites," *South China Morning Post*, May 24, 1994, https://www.scmp.com/article/75240/anger-report
-triad-role-sites; Keith Wallis, "Shui on Site Security Run by Gangs," *South China Morning Post*, May 23, 1994, https://www.scmp.com/article/75088
/shui-site-security-run-gangs.

96. Robert Olsen, "Hong Kong Elite Select City's New Leader Amid Protests," *Forbes*, March 25, 2012, https://www.forbes.com/sites/robertolsen/2012/03
/25/hong-kongs-elite-selects-citys-new-leader-amid-protests.

97. John Garnaut, "Scourge of Family Feuds Blights China," *Sydney Morning Herald*, March 30, 2013, https://www.smh.com.au/world/scourge-of-family
-feuds-blights-china-20130329-2gz2x.html.

98. "Real Estate Developers Association of Hong Kong Limited," Webb-site Who's Who, August 6, 2023, https://webb-site.com/dbpub/officers
.asp?p=762593; Rose Varrelli, "Macau Casino Mogul Stanley Ho Dead at 98," CasinoAus, updated February 14, 2022, https://www.casinoaus.net
/news/macau-casino-mogul-stanley-ho-dies.

99. Dan Levy, "Harnessing the Tiger in China/Hong Kong Developer Behind Billion-Dollar Deal for BofA Center Seeks More Territory to Conquer," SFGATE, January 1, 2006, https://www.sfgate.com/business/article
/Harnessing-the-tiger-in-China-Hong-Kong-2524366.php.

100. Paul Burton, "Planning Commission Approves 555 Howard Street Project," San Francisco Building and Construction Trades Council, March 25, 2017, https://www.sfbuildingtradescouncil.org/news/top-stories/850-planning
-commission-approves-555-howard-street-project; Michael Cole, "Ping An Trust Invests $31M in Great Eagle California Projects," Mingtiandi, March 31, 2016, https://www.mingtiandi.com/real-estate/outbound-investment
/ping-an-trust-invests-31m-in-great-eagle-california-projects/;
Executive Summary, Section 309 Determination of Compliance, Conditional Use Authorization, Variances and Exemption, San Francisco Planning Department, March 2, 2017, https://commissions.sfplanning.org
/cpcpackets/2015-008058DNXCUAVAR.pdf.

101. "China Green Energy Major Comes to S.F.," San Francisco Center for Economic Development, March 10, 2010, https://web.archive.org/web
/20100823081419/http://www.sfced.org/international/chinasf/chinasf-en
/News-Archive/2010-headlines.

102. Terry Glavin, "The Battle to Clean Up B.C.," *Maclean's*, February 7, 2018, https://macleans.ca/news/canada/the-battle-to-clean-up-b-c; Nevin Nie, "GCL-Poly Energy Aims for HK$1.2b to Buy Plants, Upgrade Production," *South China Morning Post*, October 30, 2007, https://www.scmp.com
/article/613604/gcl-poly-energy-aims-hk12b-buy-plants-upgrade
-production.

103. Cooper, "How China Made Canada a Global Node for Narcos and Cyber-criminals."

104. Brian K. Miller, "Trina Solar, China Daily to Set Up Shop," GlobeSt. com, November 12, 2008, https://www.globest.com/sites/globest/2008/11 /12/trina-solar-china-daily-to-set-up-shop; "International News," Penn Libraries Guides, University of Pennsylvania, accessed September 8, 2023, https://guides.library.upenn.edu/c.php?g=1274605&p=9400203.

105. Miller, "Trina Solar, China Daily to Set Up Shop"; Christian Roselund, "SolarWorld Testifies on Chinese IP Theft," pv magazine, October 10, 2017, https://pv-magazine-usa.com/2017/10/10/solarworld-testifies-on-chinese-ip -theft.

106. Dr. Weirde and Kevin J. Mullen, "The Six Companies," FoundSF, https:// www.foundsf.org/index.php?title=The_Six_Companies; Bob Egelko, "Las Vegas Man Charged in Notorious 2006 Slaying in SF's Chinatown," SFGATE, January 27, 2017, https://www.sfgate.com/bayarea/article/Las-Vegas-man -charged-in-2006-slaying-of-SF-10887611.php.

107. Richard Winton, Chris Megerian, and Matt Stevens, "Asian Gang Figure 'Shrimp Boy' at Center of Yee Scandal," Los Angeles Times, March 26, 2014, https://www.latimes.com/local/lanow/la-me-ln-raymond-chow-shrimp-boy -20140326-story.html.

108. See fifth mention of Gavin Newsom in USA v. Raymond Chow: Notice of Motion for Discovery and Motion to Dismiss for Selective Prosecution, filed August 4, 2015, https://www.scribd.com/doc/273554556/USA-v-Raymond-Chow-Motion-to-Dismiss-for-Selective-Prosecution.

109. "FBI Sting Shows San Francisco Chinatown Underworld," KSBW Action News, March 27, 2014, https://www.ksbw.com/article/fbi-sting-shows-san -francisco-chinatown-underworld/1053810; Emmanuel V. Pascua, Aff. in support of complaint, N.D. Cal, San Francisco Division, filed March 24, 2014, https://www.sfgate.com/file/757/757-complaint_affidavit_14-70421-nc.pdf; Matier & Ross, "Mayor Sinks 'Shrimp Boy' Market," SFGATE, June 14, 2009, https://www.sfgate.com/bayarea/article/Mayor-sinks-Shrimp-Boy -market-3229114.php.

110. Emmanuel V. Pascua Affidavit; Matt Isaacs, "Twice Burned," SF Weekly, June 14, 2000, https://web.archive.org/web/20080101211948/http://www .sfweekly.com/2000-06-14/news/twice-burned/full.

111. Veronica Rocha, "'Shrimp Boy' Gets Life in Prison," San Diego Union Tribune, August 5, 2016. [Accessed from Lexis, https://advance.lexis.com /api/document?collection=news&id=urn:contentItem:5KD1-9101-JBM5 -R10K-00000-00&context=1519360.]

112. USA v. Raymond Chow: Notice of Motion for Discovery and Motion to Dismiss for Selective Prosecution.

113. Laurel Rosenhall, "Keith Jackson Built Connections for Leland Yee, Prosecutors

Assert," *Sacramento Bee*, April 6, 2015; Phillip Matier and Andrew Ross, "Keith Jackson Emerges as Major Figure in Calif. Sen. Yee Probe," SFGate, updated April 2, 2014, https://www.sfgate.com/bayarea/matier-ross/article /keith-jackson-emerges-as-major-figure-in-calif-5368557.php; Richard Eber, "Concord's 'Partner in Development' Lennar-Urban-Five Point in Dire Financial Trouble," September 4, 2016, Granicus, City of Irvine, https://irvine.granicus.com/MetaViewer.php?view_id=68&clip_id=3901 &meta_id=73743

114. 星電視 [singtaotv], "星島日報83周年歡慶晚宴精彩花絮" [Sing Tao Daily 83rd Anniversary Highlights], August 16, 2021, YouTube, https://www.youtube .com/watch?v=2P_Zvy2I184.

115. Sam Dorman, "Gavin Newsom Praised Chinese Outlet Designated Foreign Agent, with Reported Ties to Communist Party," FOX News, August 30, 2021, https://www.foxnews.com/politics/gavin-newsom-chinese-newspaper.

116. Evan Symon, "Newsom Vetoes Bill to Prohibit Foreign Governments from Buying CA Agricultural Land," *California Globe*, September 28, 2022, https://californiaglobe.com/articles/newsom-vetoes-bill-to-prohibit-foreign -governments-from-buying-ca-agricultural-land.

117. "Our Story," PlumpJack Winery, https://plumpjackwinery.com/our-story/; "PlumpJack, CADE and Odette Estates Distributor List, Domestic (updated 10.24.2019)," PlumpJack Winery, https://plumpjackwinery.com/content /uploads/2020/10/Distributor-List-with-Addresses-10.07.20.xls.

118. Rebecca Bowe, "Newsom's Fancy Gift, Trip to China," *San Francisco Bay Guardian*, March 4, 2011.

119. "Governor Releases Master Plan for Tackling the Fentanyl and Opioid Crisis," *Lake County News*, March 21, 2023, https://www.lakeconews.com /news/75233-governor-releases-master-plan-for-tackling-the-fentanyl-and -opioid-crisis.

120. Office of the Governor of California, twitter.com, October 18, 2023, https:// twitter.com/CAgovernor/status/1714748078060908722?=20.

121. Philip Lenczycki, "Chinese Intel Service 'Affiliate' Takes Credit for Bringing Gavin Newsom to China," Dailycaller.com, October 31, 2023, https:// dailycaller.com/2023/10/31/gavin-newsom-china-trip-intel/.

122. Jeff Pao, "California Governor Visit Gets High Marks from China," Asiatimes. com, October 31, 2023, https://asiatimes.com/2023/10/california-governor -visit-gets-high-marks-from-china/#:~:text=%E2%80%9CChina%20 gave%20Newsom%20a%20high,US%20politician%20a%20rising%20 star; "明日之星"纽森州长访华，受到超高规格礼遇，为何让美媒吃?," https:// baijiahao.baidu.com/s?id=1780789381612835986&wfr=spider&for=pc.

123. Sophia Bollag, "Optics-Heavy China Trip Reveals Advantages and Pitfalls of Gavin Newsom's Image on the Global Stage," *San Francisco Chronicle*, October 30, 2023, https://sfchronicle.com/politics/article/newsom-china -optics-18455955.php.

124. https://www.gov.ca.gov/2023/10/25/governor-newsom-meets-with-chinese -president-xi-jinping.

125. 加州州長訪華會晤習近平 對中美關係釋出正面信號, https://chinatimes.com .hk/20231026/75760; Betsy Woodruff Swan and Christopher Cadelago, "Federal Prosecutor Raises Alarm About Chinese Election Interference," November 1, 2023, https://www.politico.com/news/2023/11/01/china -election-interference-california-newsom-00124716.

126. "Fentanyl Flow to the United States," Drug Enforcement Administration, January 2020, https://www.dea.gov/sites/default/files/2020-03/DEA_GOV _DIR-008-20%20Fentanyl%20Flow%20in%20the%20United%20States_0 .pdf.

127. Crawford Kilian, "Carfentanil: The Drug War Goes Nuclear," The Tyee, September 9, 2016, https://thetyee.ca/Opinion/2016/09/09/Carfentanil-Drug -War.

128. Jon Kamp and Julie Wernau, "'Tranq,' a Veterinary Drug, Is Worsening the Fentanyl Crisis," *Wall Street Journal*, February 12, 2023, https://www .wsj.com/articles/tranq-a-veterinary-drug-is-worsening-the-fentanyl-crisis -a27e7065; "DEA Reports Widespread Threat of Fentanyl Mixed with Xylazine," Drug Enforcement Administration, https://www.dea.gov/alert /dea-reports-widespread-threat-fentanyl-mixed-xylazine.

129. Nike Ching, "US Seeks Reengagement with China to Stop Illicit Fentanyl as Blinken Heads to Beijing," Voice of America, January 25, 2023, https://www .voanews.com/a/us-seeks-reengagement-with-china-to-stop-illicit-fentanyl -as-blinken-heads-to-beijing-/6933842.html.

130. Quoted in Rotella and Berg, "How a Chinese American Gangster Transformed Money Laundering for Drug Cartels."

Chapter 4: Arming Criminals

1. Stephen M. Lepore, "Revealed: Stray Bullet that Killed Accountant, 53, as He Visited His Son for Marist College Family Weekend Was One of THIRTY Fired by Ski Mask–Clad Robber in Poughkeepsie Hotel Lobby," *Daily Mail*, October 12, 2022, https://www.dailymail.co.uk/news/article-11307749 /Gunman-wearing-black-ski-mask-fired-THIRTY-ROUNDS-killed-New -York-accountant.html; Allie Griffin, "Dad Killed While Visiting Marist Student for Family Weekend Identified as Long Island Accountant Paul Kutz," *New York Post*, October 3, 2022, https://nypost.com/2022/10/03 /dad-killed-while-visiting-marist-student-for-family-weekend-identified-as -paul-kutz/.

2. Frank Main et al., "In Chicago, Handguns Turned into High-Capacity Machine Guns Fuel Deadly Violence," NPR, October 28, 2022, https:// www.npr.org/2022/10/28/1131026241/chicago-handgun-violence-auto-sear -machine-gun.

3.   Courtney Spinelli, "Chicago Area Law Enforcement Sees Rise in Machine Gun Conversion Device Recoveries," WGN-TV, March 1, 2023, https://wgntv.com/news/cover-story/chicago-area-law-enforcement-sees-rise-in-machine-gun-conversion-device-recoveries.

4.   Liang and Xiangsui, *Unrestricted Warfare*, 97.

5.   Sun Haichen, *The Wiles of War: 36 Military Strategies from Ancient China* (Beijing: Foreign Language Press, 1991), 77–87.

6.   China Aerospace Studies Institute, *In Their Own Words: Foreign Military Thought, Science of Military Strategy (2013)*, October 2013, https://www.airuniversity.af.edu/Portals/10/CASI/documents/Translations/2021-02-08%20Chinese%20Military%20Thoughts-%20In%20their%20own%20words%20Science%20of%20Military%20Strategy%202013.pdf, 31.

7.   St. John Barned-Smith, "More Houston Shootings Are Involving 'Glock Switches,' Which Turn Pistols into Machine Guns," *Houston Chronicle*, February 25, 2022, https://www.houstonchronicle.com/news/houston-texas/crime/article/More-Houston-shootings-involve-Glock-16945519.php.

8.   Krista Johnson, "Illegally, Modified Guns Turning Up in Louisville; Tiny, Easy-to-Make Devices Make Pistols Fully Automatic," *Louisville Courier Journal*, September 14, 2022, https://eu.courier-journal.com/story/news/crime/2022/09/13/auto-sears-showing-up-more-on-louisvilles-streets-police-say/66874528007/.

9.   Frank Main et al., "20 Shots in a Second: They're Not Just Handguns Anymore," WBEZ, October 28, 2022, https://www.wbez.org/stories/chicago-gun-violence-fueled-by-extended-magazines/f6657f7c-b725-47e1-bd12-d2ad89911cf1.

10.   St. John Barned-Smith, "Police 'Terrified' by Rise of 'Glock Switches'; Simple Modification Turns a Handgun into a Machine Gun," *Houston Chronicle*, April 11, 2022.

11.   Main et al., "20 Shots in a Second."

12.   Libor Jany, Richard Winton, and Kevin Rector, "Sacramento Massacre Shows Rising Dangers of Handguns Converted into Automatic Weapons," *Los Angeles Times*, April 7, 2022, https://www.latimes.com/california/story/2022-04-07/la-me-sacramento-shooting-automatic-weapons.

13.   Alain Stephens and Keegan Hamilton, "The Return of the Machine Gun," The Trace, March 24, 2022, https://www.thetrace.org/2022/03/auto-sear-gun-chip-glock-switch-automatic-conversion.

14.   Scott Glover, "ATF on the Hunt for Thousands of Illegal Machine Gun Conversion Devices Smuggled into US," CNN, May 23, 2019, https://www.cnn.com/2019/05/23/us/atf-agents-hunting-down-illegal-machine-gun-device-invs/index.html; A search for "auto sear switch" in the products section of Made-in-China brought up dozens of products, many with discounts as mentioned.

15.   Stephens and Hamilton, "The Return of the Machine Gun."

16.   Main et al., "In Chicago, Handguns Turned into High-Capacity Machine Guns Fuel Deadly Violence."

17.   "Enforcement Actions for Displaying Prohibited and Controlled Items," Alibaba.com, October 10, 2023, https://rulechannel.alibaba .com/icbu?type=detail&ruleId=2044&cId=1396#/rule/detail?cId =1396&ruleId=2044.

18.   *United States v. Charles Brent Justice*, United States District Court (D.N.M, January 29, 2021), case no. 20-1210 JAP, https://casetext.com/case/united -states-v-brent-2.

19.   See CBTForce, Facebook, https://www.facebook.com/CBTForce.

20.   Cyrus Farivar, "It's Shockingly Easy to Buy Illegal Gun Modifiers on Instagram, Facebook and Twitter," *Forbes*, June 28, 2023, https://www .forbes.com/sites/cyrusfarivar/2023/06/28/its-shockingly-easy-to-buy-illegal -gun-modifiers-on-instagram-facebook-and-twitter

21.   Matthew Corley, "Illegally Imported Glock Auto Sears from China," Chicago Crime Gun Intelligence Center, Investigative Advisory no. 2019-03 -0056, March 14, 2019.

22.   Barned-Smith, "Police 'Terrified' by Rise of 'Glock Switches.'"

23.   Ángel Hernández, "Cártel de Sinaloa Crea Pieza Que Vuelve Una Pistola en Metralleta," Milenio, July 5, 2023, https://www.milenio.com/policia/cartel -sinaloa-crea-pieza-vuelve-pistola-metralleta; Cártel de Sinaloa Le Entra a la Tecnologia, Crea Pieza Que Convierte Una Pistola en Metralleta con Impresora 3D, Revela Fuente Estadounidense," *La Opinión*, July 7, 2023, https://laopinion.com/2023/07/07/cartel-de-sinaloa-le-entra-a-la-tecnologia -crea-pieza-que-convierte una-pistola-en-metralleta-con-impresora-3d -revela-fuente estadounidense/.

24.   "Glock Switches: A Continuing Threat to Officer and Public Safety," Office of Intelligence, July 15, 2019.

25.   Bruce Vielmetti, "Agents Intercept Machine Gun Conversion Parts; Milwaukee ManCharged," *Reporter*,October14,2022.[AccessedfromLexis,https://advance .lexis.com/api/document?collection=news&id=urn:contentItem:66M5-J0N1 -JB1V-G242-00000-00&context=1519360.]

26.   John Crump, "Two Men Arrested with 117 Glock Selector Switches," AmmoLand.com Shooting Sports News, December 11, 2020, https:// www.ammoland.com/2020/12/two-men-arrested-with-117-glock-selector -switches.

27.   "Cahokia Heights Teen Indicted for Trafficking Glock Switches from China," United States Attorney's Office, Southern District of Illinois, June 5, 2023, https://www.justice.gov/usao-sdil/pr/cahokia-heights-teen-indicted -trafficking-glock-switches-china.

28. Andrew Luger, "U.S. Attorney Announces New Federal Violent Crime Strategy," Bureau of Alcohol, Tobacco, Firearms and Explosives, May 3, 2022, https://www.atf.gov/news/pr/us-attorney-announces-new-federal-violent-crime-strategy.

29. Barned-Smith, "Police 'Terrified' by Rise of 'Glock Switches.'"

30. Barned-Smith, "More Houston Shootings Are Involving 'Glock Switches,' Which Turn Pistols into Machine Guns."

31. Lester Duhé, "80+ Cases Involving 'Glock Switches' Used in Crimes over Past 2 Years in BR; DA Proposing Changes," WAFB, January 19, 2023, https://www.wafb.com/2023/01/20/80-cases-involving-glock-switches-used-crimes-over-past-2-years-br-da-proposing-changes.

32. Spinelli, "Chicago Area Law Enforcement Sees Rise in Machine Gun Conversion Device Recoveries."

33. Stephens and Hamilton, "The Return of the Machine Gun."

34. Ibid.

35. "The Miami Police Crime Gun Intelligence Detail Warns Officers of the Prevalence of Machine Guns Used in Recent Shootings," City of Miami Police Department, Crime Gun Intelligence Detail, January 29, 2020, 1.

36. Stephens and Hamilton, "The Return of the Machine Gun."

37. "Glock Handguns Modified for Automatic Fire," Situational Information Report no. SIR-00325803847, Federal Bureau of Investigation, Philadelphia Division, February 27, 2019.

38. Scott Glover, "ATF on the Hunt for Thousands of Illegal Machine Gun Conversion Devices Smuggled into US," CNN, May 23, 2019, https://www.cnn.com/2019/05/23/us/atf-agents-hunting-down-illegal-machine-gun-device-invs/index.html.

39. Crump, "Two Men Arrested with 117 Glock Selector Switches."

40. Dave Linton, "Wrentham Weapons Suspect Bought Gun Parts from China, Police Say," *Sun Chronicle* [Attleboro, MA], July 29, 2019, https://www.thesunchronicle.com/news/local_news/wrentham-weapons-suspect-bought-gun-parts-from-china-police-say/article_c3b78074-d28f-52b4-917e-3f4a5d4d8b41.html.

41. "ATF on the Hunt for Thousands of Illegal Machine Guns Sold on Amazon and Wish.com," CarbonTV, May 24, 2019, https://blog.carbontv.com/2019/05/24/atf-on-the-hunt-for-thousands-of-illegal-machine-guns-sold-on-amazon-and-wish-com.

42. Crump, "Two Men Arrested with 117 Glock Selector Switches."

43. Belinda Robinson, "Cheap Metal Part Turns Regular Guns into Automatics," *China Daily*, June 21, 2022, https://www.chinadaily.com.cn/a/202206/21/WS62b127d1a310fd2b29e67918.html.

44. "High-Capacity Machine Guns Converted from Handguns Fuel Deadly Violence in U.S. Chicago: NPR," Xinhua, November 1, 2022, https://english.news.cn/20221101/b4c40f33973d48638a9f7d470e3841d6/c.html.

45. Joshua Eaton, "Federal Operation Nabs Nearly 43,000 Illegal Gun Silencers Shipped from China," NBC News, May 13, 2022, https://www.nbcnews.com/news/us-news/illegal-gun-silencers-china-rcna28505.

46. "Happy Valley Man Sentenced for Illegally Trafficking Counterfeit Gun Parts for Use as Airsoft Accessories," United States Attorney's Office, District of Oregon, December 14, 2022, https://www.justice.gov/usao-or/pr/happy-valley-man-sentenced-illegally-trafficking-counterfeit-gun-parts-use-airsoft.

47. Eaton, "Federal Operation Nabs Nearly 43,000 Illegal Gun Silencers Shipped from China."

48. *United States v. Seamster*, 272 P.3d 247 (Wash., 2012).

49. *United States v. Hay*, 46 F. 4th 746 (8th Cir., 2022).

50. Ivan Pentchoukov, "Seizure of 10,800 Gun Parts Highlights Surge in Intercepts of Chinese Contraband Weapon Parts," The Epoch Times, July 1, 2020, https://www.theepochtimes.com/seizure-of-10800-gun-parts-highlights-surge-in-intercepts-of-chinese-contraband-weapon-parts_3407230.html; Sasha Ingber, "Customs Agents Make 'Unusual' Seizure of Nearly 53,000 Chinese Gun Parts," NPR, August 23, 2019, https://www.npr.org/2019/08/23/753687623/customs-agents-make-unusual-seizure-of-nearly-53-000-chinese-gun-parts.

51. Jelvin Jose and Kannan Reghunathan Nair, "To Honor Its Commitment to UN Arms Treaty, China Must Sacrifice," *Journal of Indo-Pacific Affairs*, August 25, 2021, https://www.airuniversity.af.edu/JIPA/Display/Article/2743926/to-honor-its-commitment-to-un-arms-trade-treaty-china-must-sacrifice.

52. "Interpreting these positions is made more challenging by the opacity of China's system for controlling SALW exports and preventing trafficking and the lack of data on the size and destinations of Chinese SALW exports. . . . The amount of information that China makes available about how the system works is far more limited than in the case of dual-use goods and technologies." Mark Bromley, Mathieu Duchâtel, and Paul Holtom, "China's Exports of Small Arms and Light Weapons," Stockholm International Peace Research Institute, October 2013, https://www.sipri.org/sites/default/files/files/PP/SIPRIPP38.pdf, vi, 1.

53. "New York Judge Frees Fok on Plea Bargain," *South China Morning Post*, November 10, 1993, https://www.scmp.com/article/51188/new-york-judge-frees-fok-plea-bargain.

54. See Richard C. Paddock and Ronald J. Ostrow, "U.S. Agents Say Chinese Tanks, Rockets Offered," *Los Angeles Times*, May 24, 1996, https://www.latimes.com/archives/la-xpm-1996-05-24-mn-7854-story.html; Lintner, *Blood Brothers*, 382.

55. Paddock and Ostrow, "U.S. Agents Say Chinese Tanks, Rockets Offered."

56. Ibid.; Fabian Dawson, "Asian Crime Targets MPs: Secret Report Hits Parliament Today Describing Triad Link with Chinese Gov't," *Province*, September 20, 2000, A6.

57. "Law of the People's Republic of China on Control of Guns," China.org.cn, February 14, 2011, http://www.china.org.cn/china/LegislationsForm2001 -2010/2011-02/14/content_21916528.htm.

58. Ted R. Bromund, "At a U.N. Meeting on Guns, the U.S. Stands Up Under Fire," The Heritage Foundation, June 8, 2015, https://www.heritage.org /arms-control/commentary/un-meeting-guns-the-us-stands-under-fire.

59. "Suppressed: CBP Seized Firearm Silencers," U.S. Customs and Border Protection, January 11, 2023, https://www.cbp.gov/newsroom/local-media -release/suppressed-cbp-seized-firearm-silencers.

60. John Tunison, "Feds Charge Multiple Michigan Men Tied to Illegally Converting Handguns to Fully Automatic," *Kalamazoo Gazette*, December 15, 2022, https://www.mlive.com/news/kalamazoo/2022/12/feds-charge -multiple-michigan-men-tied-to-illegally-converting-handguns-to-fully -automatic.html.

61. Dan Rieck, "St. Louis Officials Warn of Uptick in Attachments That Make Guns Fully Automatic," *St. Louis Post-Dispatch*, January 5, 2023, https:// www.stltoday.com/news/local/crime-and-courts/st-louis-officials-warn-of -uptick-in-attachments-that-make-guns-fully-automatic/article_d3f56870 -cc02-5281-b3d3-6f3f91b38f3c.html.

62. Travis Breese and Joseph Garcia, "Focus: Customs Agents Find More 'Glock Switches' Coming into Kentucky," WHAS-TV, March 21, 2023, https:// www.whas11.com/article/news/investigations/focus/focus-glock-switches-us -customs-police-crime-guns/417-b7769030-9799-45e7-b888-89c4a274b25f.

63. "Klobuchar, Booker Urge Justice Department to Address Dangerous Firearm Conversion Devices," U.S. Senator Amy Klobuchar, November 2, 2021, https:// www.klobuchar.senate.gov/public/index.cfm/2021/11/klobuchar-booker-urge -justice-department-to-address-dangerous-firearm-conversion-devices.

64. "Klobuchar, Peters Lead Colleagues in Introducing Legislation to Combat Increased Use of Dangerous Gun Conversion Devices," U.S. Senator Amy Klobuchar, July 25, 2022, https://www.klobuchar.senate.gov/public/index .cfm/2022/7/klobuchar-peters-lead-colleagues-in-introducing-legislation-to -combat-increased-use-of-dangerous-gun-conversion-devices.

65. Dakin Andone, "13 States Have Backed Mexican Government's Lawsuit Against Group of U.S. Gun Manufacturers," CNN, February 6, 2022, https://www.cnn.com/2022/02/06/us/mexico-lawsuit-us-gun-manufacturers /index.html.

66. Franklin Foer, *The Last Politician: Inside Joe Biden's White House and the Struggle for America's Future* (New York: Penguin Press, 2023), 313.

67.   Morgan A. Martin and Clinton J. Williamson, "Mapping Chinese Influence in Hollywood," *Indo-Pacific Security Studies* 4 (January 2023): 5–8, https://www.airuniversity.af.edu/Portals/10/AUPress/Papers/KP_04_Martin _Mapping_Chinese_Influence_in_Hollywood.pdf.

68.   Robert Kaplan, *Asia's Cauldron: The South China Sea and the End of a Stable Pacific* (New York: Random House, 2014), 23.

Chapter 5: Magnifying Social Chaos

1.   "Houston Consulate One of Worst Offenders in Chinese Espionage, Say U.S. Officials," Reuters, July 24, 2020, https://www.reuters.com/article/us-usa -china-consulate-houston-idCAKCN24P1XT; "Documents Burned on the Grounds of the Chinese Consulate in Houston," ABC 13, July 22, 2020, https://abc13.com/fire-chinese-consulate-documents-being-burned-houston -us-and-china-tensions/6328284.

2.   "【耳邊風】壓倒休斯敦領館的最後一根稻草" [Wind in the Ears; The Last Straw that Overwhelmed the Consulate in Houston], Radio Free Asia, August 7, 2020, https://www.rfa.org/cantonese/news/ear/ear-straw-0806202 0081345.html.

3.   Hongshanke, "Protests, Violence, Polarizatin [*sic*] . . . What's Wrong with the U.S.?," China Military Online, August 18, 2020, http://www.81.cn/jwywpd /2020-08/18/content_9884721.htm.

4.   Shemon Salam and Arturo Castillon, *The Revolutionary Meaning of the George Floyd Uprising* (Québec: Daraja Press, 2021), vii–viii.

5.   Martin and Williamson, "Mapping Chinese Influence in Hollywood," 2.

6.   Robin D. G. Kelley and Betsy Esch, "Black like Mao: Red China and Black Revolution," *Souls: A Critical Journal of Black Politics, Culture, and Society* 1, no. 4 (Fall 1999): 13, https://doi.org/10.1080/10999949909362183.

7.   Huey P. Newton, *Revolutionary Suicide* (New York: Penguin Classics, 2009), 350, 352.

8.   "Interview with Three Correspondents from the Central News Agency, the Sao Tang Pao and the Hsin Min Pao," September 16, 1939, *Selected Works*, vol. 2, 272, https://www.marxists.org/reference/archive/mao/selected-works /volume-2/mswv2_18.htm.

9.   Kelley and Esch, "Black like Mao," 21.

10.   Joe Pateman, "Mao Zedong, China and Black Liberation," *International Critical Thought* 11, no. 3 (2021): 358–59, https://doi.org/10.1080/21598282 .2021.1965006.

11.   Ibid., 360.

12.   Ibid., 363.

13. Todd Stein, "To Win Against China, The U.S. Must Bide Its Time," *Newsweek*, October 12, 2022, https://www.newsweek.com/win-against-china-us-must -bide-its-time-opinion-1750507.

14. Trevor Loudon, "Communists and Race," The Epoch Times, March 22, 2019, https://www.theepochtimes.com/opinion/communists-and-race-2778952 . FRSO's account of the presentation can be found in "An In-Depth Look at the Ferguson Eruption: Organization for Black Struggle Leader Lays It Out," Freedom Road Socialist Organization, August 13, 2015, https://web .archive.org/web/20150919031208/https://freedomroad.org/2015/08/an-in -depth-look-at-the-ferguson-eruption-organization-for-black-struggle -leader-lays-it-out.

15. James Simpson, "Black Lives Matter: Racist Provocation with Radical Roots," Capital Research Center, September 21, 2016, https://capitalresearch .org/article/blm-roots.

16. Max Elbaum, *Revolution in the Air: Sixties Radicals Turn to Lenin, Mao and Che* (Brooklyn, NY: Verso, 2018), 290.

17. John D. Holst, "Globalization and Education Within Two Revolutionary Organizations in the United States of America: A Gramscian Analysis," *Adult Education Quarterly 55*, no. 1 (November 2004): 26, https://doi.org /10.1177/0741713604268895.

18. Randy Furst, "2010 FBI Raid Linked to Terror," *Star Tribune* [Minneapolis], February 27, 2014, https://www.startribune.com/2010-fbi-raid-linked-to -terror/247404421.

19. Brian Becker, "The Bernie Sanders Campaign and Building the Movement for Socialism in the U.S.," LiberationNews.org, February 4, 2020, https:// www.liberationnews.org/the-bernie-sanders-campaign-and-building-the -movement-for-socialism-in-the-us; "Brian Becker," LiberationNews.org, https://www.liberationnews.org/author/brian_becker.

20. "From Rage to Rebellion—to Revolution," Liberation School, August 13, 2014, https://www.liberationschool.org/from-rage-to-rebellion-to-revolution.

21. Brian Becker, "What Do Socialists Defend in China Today?," in *China: Revolution and Counterrevolution* (San Francisco: PSL Publications, 2012), 19.

22. Brian Becker, "Tiananmen: The Massacre That Wasn't," LiberationNews. org, June 4, 2021, https://www.liberationnews.org/tiananmen-the-massacre -that-wasnt-2; "Tiananmen Square Protest Death Toll 'Was 10,000,'" BBC News, December 23, 2017, https://www.bbc.com/news/world-asia-china -42465516.

23. "China's Socialist Goals a Source of Inspiration to Those Who Seek a Humanist Alternative: Anti-War Socialist," Global Times, July 5, 2022, https://www.globaltimes.cn/page/202207/1269828.shtml.

24. See, e.g., "Global Times Interview: Brian Becker on Socialism and the U.S. Campaign Against China," LiberationNews.org, July 5, 2022, https://www

.liberationnews.org/global-times-interview-brian-becker-on-socialism-and
-the-u-s-campaign-against-china.

25. Nadeen Shaker, "'This Injustice Has Taken Genocidal Proportions': Why
Cornel West and Carl Dix Are Rising Up Against Police Brutality," Salon,
October 21, 2015, https://www.salon.com/2015/10/21/this_injustice_has
_taken_genocidal_proportions_why_cornel_west_and_carl_dix_are_rising
_up_against_police_brutality.

26. "Carl Dix—Founding Member of Revolutionary Communist Party, USA,"
NYC Media Training, https://www.nycmediatraining.org/podcast/carl-dix
-founding-member-of-revolutionary-communist-party-usa; Charlie Gillis,
"Race to the Bottom in Ferguson," Maclean's, August 27, 2014, https://
www.macleans.ca/news/world/race-to-the-bottom-in-in-ferguson.

27. "Ferguson Protesters Struggle to Keep Focus on Slain Teenager," China
Daily, October 14, 2014, http://www.chinadaily.com.cn/world/2014-10/14
/content_18734666.htm.

28. Shaker, "'This Injustice Has Taken Genocidal Proportions.'"

29. "Mao-Tse Tung 100th Anniversary" (video), C-Span, December 26, 1993,
https://www.c-span.org/video/?53368-1/mao-tse-tung-100th-anniversary.

30. Chen Weihua, "Despite Progress, Racial Issue Still Haunts U.S. Society,"
China Daily, August 18, 2014, https://www.chinadaily.com.cn/world/2014
-08/18/content_18448165.htm.

31. Pateman, "Mao Zedong, China and Black Liberation," 366.

32. Ibid., 368.

33. "Who Are the Uyghurs and Why Is China Being Accused of Genocide?,"
BBC News, May 24, 2022, https://www.bbc.com/news/world-asia-china
-22278037.

34. Pateman, "Mao Zedong, China and Black Liberation," 357.

35. Hao Cao, "Organizing an 'Organizationless' Protest Campaign in the
WeChatsphere," Big Data & Society 9, no. 1 (January–June 2022), https://
doi.org/10.1177/20539517221078823.

36. Ibid.

37. Zach Dorfman, "How Silicon Valley Became a Den of Spies: The West Coast
Is a Growing Target for Foreign Espionage. And It's Not Ready to Fight
Back," Politico, July 27, 2018, https://www.politico.com/magazine/story
/2018/07/27/silicon-valley-spies-china-russia-219071.

38. Salam and Castillon, The Revolutionary Meaning of the George Floyd
Uprising, viii.

39. Dakin Andone and Aaron Cooper, "Heart Disease, Fentanyl Contributed to
George Floyd's Death but Were Not Main Cause, Medical Examiner Says,"
CNN, April 9, 2021, https://www.cnn.com/2021/04/09/us/derek-chauvin

-trial-george-floyd-day-10/index.html; "George Floyd Was Infected with COVID-19, Autopsy Reveals," Reuters, June 4, 2020, https://www.reuters .com/article/us-minneapolis-police-autopsy/george-floyd-was-infected-with -covid-19-autopsy-reveals-idUSKBN23B1HX.

40. "The Contributions of the Chinese Revolution Have Changed the World," Free-dom Road Socialist Organization, October 29, 2019, https://frso.org/statements /the-contributions-of-the-chinese-revolution-have-changed-the-world.

41. Trevor Loudon, "Confessions of an American Insurrectionist: Communist Tells of 'Joy' at Watching Police Station Burn," The Epoch Times, October 12, 2020, https://www.theepochtimes.com/confessions-of-an-american -insurrectionist-communist-tells-of-joy-at-watching-police-station-burn _3454854.html.

42. "36 Strategies: Watch the Fire Burning from Across the River," *China Daily*, November 16, 2020, https://www.chinadaily.com.cn/a/202011/16 /WS5fb1cf11a31024ad0ba94334.html.

43. Freedom Road Socialist Organization (@freedomroadorg), Twitter, July 1, 2020, 6:00 a.m., https://twitter.com/freedomroadorg/status/12782973992 83326982.

44. Mick Kelly, "Mick Kelly: 100 Years of the Communist Party of China," Friends of Socialist China, July 23, 2021, https://socialistchina.org/2021/08 /28/mick-kelly-100-years-of-the-communist-party-of-china.

45. Ibid.

46. "About Us," Center for Marxist Parties in Foreign Countries of CCNU (MPFC), http://www.ccnumpfc.com.

47. William Engdahl, "American Color Revolution," Center for Marxist Parties in Foreign Countries of CCNU, July 23, 2020, http://www.ccnumpfc.com /index.php/View/2419.html.

48. See, e.g., "自由道路社会主义组织：庆祝中国共产党成立一百周年" [Free Path Socialist: Celebrating the Centenary of the Founding of the Communist Party of China], Center for Marxist Parties in Foreign Countries of CCNU, August 2, 2021, http://www.ccnumpfc.com/index.php/View/3082.html; http://www.ccnumpfc.com/index.php/View/2954.html; "国外共产党和工人党动" [Communist and Workers' Parties Abroad Moved], Center for Marxist Parties in Foreign Countries of CCNU, https://www.ccnumpfc.com/index. php/List/Index/type/16/p/6; "美国多个共产主义政党和左翼政党对新冠病毒的声明" [Statement on the Coronavirus from Several Communist and Left-wing Parties in the United States], Center for Marxist Parties in Foreign Countries of CCNU, April 27, 2020, http://www.ccnumpfc.com/index.php /View/2311.html.

49. "Greetings to the Closing of the Congress," Freedom Road Socialist Organization, October 24, 2022, https://frso.org/statements/freedom-road -socialist-organization-congratulates-the-communist-party-of-china-on -successful-20th-national-congress.

50. Salam and Castillon, *The Revolutionary Meaning of the George Floyd Uprising*, viii–ix.

51. Claire Goforth, "Jacksonville Activist Groups Work Together to Push Police Reform," WJCT Public Media, July 9, 2020, https://news.wjct.org/first -coast/2020-07-09/jacksonville-activist-groups-work-together-to-push -police-reform.

52. Ibid.; "FRSO Demands Justice for Ahmaud Arbery," Freedom Road Socialist Organization, May 10, 2020, https://frso.org/statements/frso-demands -justice-for-ahmaud-arbery.

53. Freedom Road Socialist Organization (@freedomroadorg), "We're here in Kenosha, WI. We're marching and fighting!," Twitter, August 24, 2020, 8:01 p.m., https://twitter.com/freedomroadorg/status/1298078013830172672; "Fight for Justice for Jacob Blake! Arrest, Charge and Convict KPD Officers for Attempted Murder!," Fight Back!, August 25, 2020, https://www .fightbacknews.org/2020/8/25/fight-justice-jacob-blake-arrest-charge-and -convict-kpd-officers-attempted-murder.

54. Jeffery Martin, "'Foreign Government' May Be Behind Looting Post on Facebook, Police Say," *Newsweek*, June 3, 2020, https://www.newsweek .com/investigation-underway-whether-facebook-post-encouraging-looting -came-foreign-government-1508561.

55. Mike Gonzalez, "Yes, a Pro-China Group in America Supports a Black Lives Matter Founder," The Heritage Foundation, October 21, 2020, https:// www.heritage.org/progressivism/commentary/yes-pro-china-group-america -supports-black-lives-matter-founder.

56. Huang Shaohua, "World Journal—舊金山華埠多個組織 聲援非裔追求正義" [Several Organizations in San Francisco's Chinatown Support African Americans in Their Pursuit of Justice], Chinese Progressive Association, https://cpasf.org/media-resources/world-journal舊金山華埠多個組織-聲援非裔追求正義/.

57. Clive Hamilton and Mareike Ohlberg, "The Ecology of Espionage," in *Hidden Hand: Exposing How the Chinese Communist Party Is Reshaping the World* (Toronto: Optimum Publishing International, 2021), 139–163, fn. 34.

58. Tsuneo Ayabe and Masaki Onozawa, *Continuity and Change in the Overseas Chinese Communities in the Pan-Pacific Area* (Tsukuba, Japan: Research Group for Overseas Studies, University of Tsukuba, 1993), 57. The CPA grew out of a radical pro-Beijing revolutionary movement called IWK whose leaders acknowledged that there were "limitations to being a Maoist group in Chinatown." Fay Wong, one of the founders of the San Francisco group, put it this way: "China was an inspiration to us, many of us were from China and those us who were not just found what China was able to accomplish, with the revolution, was very inspiring." But there were those in Chinatown who had fled the oppression of Maoist China and had no interest in praising Mao. So Wong and others established the Chinese Progressive Association as a mechanism for hiding their ideological roots and ties. See William Wei, *The*

Asian American Movement (Philadelphia: Temple University Press, 2010), 215; See also, Gonzalez, "Yes, a Pro-China Group in America Supports a Black Lives Matter Founder."

59. Charles "Sam" Faddis, "Beijing Front Money—Is China Burning American Cities?," AND Magazine, September 21, 2020, https://andmagazine.com /talk/2020/09/21/beijing-front-money-is-china-burning-american-cities.

60. Jonas Parello-Plesner and Belinda Li, "The Chinese Communist Party's Foreign Interference Operations: How the U.S. and Other Democracies Should Respond," The Hudson Institute, June 2018, https://s3.amazonaws .com/media.hudson.org/files/publications/JonasFINAL.pdf, 3.

61. Ibid., 8.

62. Gonzalez, "Yes, a Pro-China Group in America Supports a Black Lives Matter Founder."

63. Renee Nol, "Breaking: Banned Video Exposes Black Lives Matter Ties to the Chinese Communist Party (Must See)," RAIR Foundation USA, October 27, 2020, https://rairfoundation.com/breaking-banned-video-exposes-black -lives-matter-ties-to-the-chinese-communist-party-must-see; Trever Loudon, "Chinese Communist Party Ties to Black Lives Matter" (video), Rumble, https://rumble.com/vauw4j-chinese-communist-party-ties-to-black-lives -matter.html.

64. Paul Saba, ed., "Learning from the Life of Harry Wong," *Unity* 4, no. 2 (January 30–February 12, 1981), https://www.marxists.org/history/erol /ncm-7/lrs-wong.htm.

65. Ibid.; Yibing Du, "Imagining the Chinese Homeland from America in the Radical Age, 1969–1976," *Herodotus* 30 (Spring 2020): 83–106, https://ojs .stanford.edu/ojs/index.php/herodotus/article/view/1681/1314.

66. Elbaum, *Revolution in the Air*, 181.

67. "Chinese Progressive Association 10th Anniversary," *Unity Newspaper* 5, no. 29 (December 10, 1982), https://unityarchiveproject.org/article/chinese -progressive-association-looking-back-on-a-decade-of-work-looking-ahead -to-the-future.

68. See Jack Campbell, "U.S. Elites Backing H.K. Riots Snub Grassroots Protests on Their Soil," Global Times, June 2, 2020, https://www.globaltimes.cn /page/202006/1190332.shtml.

69. See Eugene Puryear, "This Is All About Trump and His Vitriol," *New York Times*, March 15, 2016, https://www.nytimes.com/roomfordebate/2016/03 /15/should-trump-be-allowed-to-kick-protesters-out-of-his-rallies/this-is-all -about-trump-and-his-vitriol.

70. Natalie DiBlasio, "#DCFerguson Protestors Take to Washington's Streets," *USA Today*, January 15, 2015, https://www.usatoday.com/story/news/nation /2015/01/15/dcferguson-protest-rush-hour/21795165.

71. "Not a Riot. An Uprising," LiberationNews.org, June 7, 2020, https://www.liberationnews.org/not-a-riot-an-uprising.

72. Andrew Seidman and Andrew Maykuth, "Protesters Again Take Over Vine Street Expressway," *Philadelphia Inquirer*, July 6, 2020, https://www.inquirer.com/news/protesters-vine-street-expressway-tear-gas-philadelphia-20200705.html.

73. See, e.g., "Racism & the Struggle for Liberation with Author Eugene Puryear," Facebook, https://www.facebook.com/events/1815527518696268; Graham Vyse, "What's Next for Black Lives Matter in D.C.? We Asked Longtime Activist Eugene Puryear," InsideSources, September 3, 2015, https://insidesources.com/whats-next-for-black-lives-matter-in-d-c-we-asked-longtime-activist-eugene-puryear.

74. Eugene Puryear, *Shackled and Chained: Mass Incarceration in Capitalist America* (San Francisco: PSL Publications, 2013).

75. Eugene Puryear, "The Truth Behind China's Charter 08 Manifesto," Liberation School, February 10, 2009, https://www.liberationschool.org/09-02-10-the-truth-behind-chinas-charter-html.

76. BreakThrough News, "Why China Will Win: Capitalism Inherently Collapses," YouTube, June 19, 2021, https://www.youtube.com/watch?v=heBcoxtobFM.

77. BreakThrough News, "Xinjiang, China: The Reality," YouTube, July 23, 2021, https://www.youtube.com/watch?v=2tCuZu_U9rk.

78. David Martin Jones and M. L. R. Smith, *The Strategy of Maoism in the West: Rage and the Radical Left* (Cheltenham: Edward Elgar Publishing, 2022), 3, 13.

79. Hannah Metzger, "Hundreds March Downtown to Demand Release of Arrested BLM Activists," *Denver Gazette*, March 25, 2021, https://denvergazette.com/news/local/hundreds-march-downtown-to-demand-release-of-arrested-blm-activists/article_3a586496-facc-11ea-bb78-976effaac290.html.

80. Shelly Bradbury, "Denver Police Union President Says SWAT Lieutenant Ignored Commander's Retreat Order During Sunday's Dueling Rallies," *Denver Post*, July 22, 2020, https://www.denverpost.com/2020/07/22/denver-police-union-apology-protest-retreat-order.

81. "Outbreaks in Africa, Asia, Latin America, and Europe: Release Organizers of the Denver Anti-Racism Movement," Center for Marxist Parties in Foreign Countries of CCNU, October 12, 2020, http://www.ccnumpfc.com/index.php/View/2543.

82. Matt Keeley, "One Dead, Two in Custody After Gunfire at Dueling Denver Protests," *Newsweek*, October 10, 2020, https://www.newsweek.com/one-shot-two-custody-after-gunfire-dueling-denver-protests-1538107; Tom

Batchelor, "Fact-Check: Are Protesters Throwing Cans of Soup and Tuna, as Trump Claims?," *Newsweek*, September 23, 2020, https://www.newsweek .com/fact-check-protesters-throwing-cans-soup-tuna-trump-claim-1533748.

83. Anna Orso et al., "Protesters March in Philly for Jacob Blake and 'Against Racist Police Violence,'" *Philadelphia Inquirer*, September 4, 2020, https:// www.inquirer.com/news/philadelphia/philadelphia-protest-blm-black-lives -matter-police-jacob-blake-20200904.html.

84. Sean Philip Cotter, "Hundreds Rally for Breonna Taylor in Boston," *Boston Herald*, September 25, 2020, https://www.bostonherald.com/2020/09/25 /hundreds-rally-for-breonna-taylor-in-boston.

85. Allison Pirog, "Hundreds Gather Saturday Afternoon to Call Out Police Violence," *Daily Free Press*, September 27, 2020, https://dailyfreepress .com/2020/09/27/hundreds-gather-saturday-afternoon-to-call-out-police -violence; Morgan C. Mullings and Yawu Miller, "Demonstrations After Grand Jury Clears Kentucky Cops," *Bay State Banner*, September 26, 2020, https://www.baystatebanner.com/2020/09/26/demonstrators-march-on -city-hall.

86. "Did 'End Bail' Movement Lead to Anisa Scott's Death?," MacIver Institute, September 3, 2020, https://www.maciverinstitute.com/2020/09/did-end-bail -movement-lead-to-anisa-scotts-death.

87. Logan Wroge, "As 'Week of Action' in Madison Closes, Groups Vow to Push for 'Abolition' of Policing Structures," *Chippewa* [WI] *Herald*, June 7, 2020, https://chippewa.com/news/state-and-regional/as-week-of-action-in -madison-closes-groups-vow-push-for-abolition-of-policing-structures /article_c7061b13-ba07-53af-b8c6-abc90a8e8236.html.

88. Chris Rickert, "Faced with Late-Night Protest at His Home, DA Ismael Ozanne Says He Won't Be Intimidated," *Wisconsin State Journal*, July 27, 2020, https://madison.com/news/local/crime-and-courts/faced-with-late -night-protest-at-his-home-da-ismael-ozanne-says-he-wont-be/article _be9ce2a8-38c0-5253-b26e-0e4c94ca5c37.html.

89. "'Free Them All' Protest Demands Release of Westville Correctional Facility Inmates," *Herald-Dispatch* [Huntington, WV], May 4, 2020, https:// www.lpheralddispatch.com/news/free-them-all-protest-demands-release-of -westville-correctional-facility-inmates/article_f06896d4-3f44-5f47-af89 -79e9fbae38b5.html.

90. Taylor Clark, "At Most Black Lives Matter Protests: Who Is PSL?," KTUU-TV, June 25, 2020, https://www.alaskasnewssource.com/content /news/The-group-behind-many-Anchorage-BLM-protests-571497501.html.

91. Ben Jacobs, "Steve Bannon's Go-To Funder Guo Wengui Just Got Indicted for Fraud," Vox, March 15, 2023, https://www.vox.com/politics/2023/3/15 /23641704/guo-wengui-fraud-charges-steve-bannon-indictment.

92. Michael Forsythe and Benjamin Weiser, "The Undoing of Guo Wengui,

Billionaire Accused of Fraud on 2 Continents," *New York Times*, March 30, 2023, https://www.nytimes.com/2023/03/30/us/guo-wengui-china.html.

93. Ciu Xiankang et al., "10 Years of Caixin: Exposing Fugitive Tycoon Guo Wengui," Caixin Global, November 5, 2019, https://www.caixinglobal .com/2019-11-05/10-years-of-caixin-exposing-fugitive-tycoon-guo-wengui -101479141.html.

94. *Eastern Profit Corporation Limited v. Strategic Vision U.S. LLC*, 368 S.D.R., (S.D.N.Y., 2021), 776.

95. Forsythe and Weiser, "The Undoing of Guo Wengui, Billionaire Accused of Fraud on 2 Continents."

96. Philip Wen, "Former Assistant Accuses Exiled Chinese Tycoon of Rape in Lawsuit," Reuters, September 13, 2017, https://www.reuters.com/article/us -china-corruption-tycoon/former-assistant-accuses-exiled-chinese-tycoon-of -rape-in-lawsuit-idUSKCN1BO0I5.

97. Forsythe and Weiser, "The Undoing of Guo Wengui, Billionaire Accused of Fraud on 2 Continents."

98. Bill Gertz, *Deceiving the Sky: Inside Communist China's Drive for Global Supremacy* (New York: Encounter Books, 2019).

99. Maggie Haberman, "Bannon's Work with Wanted Chinese Billionaire Began Shortly After He Left White House," *New York Times*, November 6, 2020, https:// www.nytimes.com/2019/12/23/us/politics/steve-bannon-guo-wengui.html.

100. Jonathan Swan and Erica Pandey, "Exclusive: Steve Bannon's $1 Million Deal Linked to a Chinese Billionaire," Axios, October 29, 2019, https:// www.axios.com/2019/10/29/steve-bannon-contract-chinese-billionaire -guo-media; Brian Schwartz, "Mystery Shrouds Nonprofit Linked to Wealthy Chinese Exile: Steve Bannon Leaves, Records Kept Secret," CNBC, August 16, 2021, https://www.cnbc.com/2021/08/16/steve-bannon-leaves -mysterious-nonprofit linked-to-wealthy-chinese-exile.html.

101. Forsythe and Weiser, "The Undoing of Guo Wengui, Billionaire Accused of Fraud on 2 Continents."

102. "After Brutal Beating of Friend, the Target of Steve Bannon's Protest Group Will Sue Police and City of Surrey for 'Failing to Protect Neighbourhood,'" *Toronto Star*, November 26, 2020, https://www.thestar.com/news/canada /2020/11/26/after-brutal-beating-of-friend-the-target-of-steve-bannons -protest-group-will-sue-police-and-city-of-surrey-for-failing-to-protect -neighbourhood.html; Mike Wendling and Grace Tsoi, "Guo Wengui: How a Chinese Tycoon Built a Pro-Trump Money Machine," BBC News, March 25, 2023, https://www.bbc.com/news/world-us-canada-65019134; Evan Osnos, "How a Tycoon Linked to Chinese Intelligence Became a Darling of Trump Republicans," *New Yorker*, October 17, 2022, https://www.newyorker.com /magazine/2022/10/24/how-a-tycoon-linked-to-chinese-intelligence-became -a-darling-of-trump-republicans.

103. Dan Friedman, "A Fugitive Chinese Tycoon Met Steven Bannon. Misinformation Mayhem Ensued," *Mother Jones*, March–April 2022, https://www.motherjones.com/politics/2022/02/guo-wengui-miles-guo -gettr-steve-bannon; Booth Moore, "G Fashion Brand Owned by Chinese Billionaire Linked to Steve Bannon Shutters L.A. Operation," *Women's Wear Daily*, May 18, 2021, https://wwd.com/business-news/business-features /guo-wengui-fashion-steve-bannon-brand-shutters-abruptly-1234824778.

104. "Ho Wan Kwok, A/K/A 'Miles Guo,' Arrested for Orchestrating over $1 Billion Dollar Fraud Conspiracy," United States Attorney's Office, Southern District of New York, March 15, 2023, https://www.justice.gov/usao-sdny /pr/ho-wan-kwok-aka-miles-guo-arrested-orchestrating-over-1-billion-dollar -fraud-conspiracy.

105. Friedman, "A Fugitive Chinese Tycoon Met Steven Bannon. Misinformation Mayhem Ensued."

106. Osnos, "How a Tycoon Linked to Chinese Intelligence Became a Darling of Trump Republicans"; Dan Friedman, "More Leaked Audio: Bannon Bragged That He Used Porn to Help Smear Hunter Biden," *Mother Jones*, July 26, 2022, https://www.motherjones.com/politics/2022/07/bannon-leaked-audio -porn-hunter-biden-laptop-guo.

107. "Highlights of Mr. Miles Guo's Live Broadcast on October 10th, 2021," GNews, October 11, 2021, https://gnews.org/articles/153112.

108. Friedman, "More Leaked Audio: Bannon Bragged That He Used Porn to Help Smear Hunter Biden."

109. Forsythe and Weiser, "The Undoing of Guo Wengui, Billionaire Accused of Fraud on 2 Continents."

110. Friedman, "More Leaked Audio: Bannon Bragged That He Used Porn to Help Smear Hunter Biden."

111. Schweizer, *Red-Handed*, 19–22.

112. David Klepper and Barbara Ortutay, "A Year After Trump Purge, 'Alt-tech' Offers Far-Right Refuge," Associated Press, February 5, 2022, https://apnews .com/article/coronavirus-pandemic-steve-bannon-technology-business -health-349c44b477cfee34bf3635160bfa74ea.

113. Dustin Volz and Sarah E. Needleman, "Chinese Propagandists Set Up Shop on Fringe Social-Media Site, Researchers Say," *Wall Street Journal*, September 7, 2023, https://www.wsj.com/world/china/chinese-propagandists-set-up-shop -on-fringe-social-media-site-researchers-say-71bebfe6.

114. Joseph Menn, "Indicted Chinese Exile Controls Gettr Social Media Site, Ex-employees Say," *Washington Post*, March 26, 2023, https://www .washingtonpost.com/technology/2023/03/26/gettr-guo-wengui-social-- media/.

115. Douglas Smith, *Former People: The Final Days of the Russian Aristocracy* (New York: Farrar, Straus, and Giroux, 2012), 241.

116. Tom Ginsburg, *Democracies and International Law* (Cambridge, UK: Cambridge University Press, 2021), 219.

117. Nick Aspinwall, "Guo Wengui Is Sending Mobs After Chinese Dissidents," *Foreign Policy*, October 28, 2020, https://foreignpolicy.com/2020/10/28/guo -wengui-sending-mobs-after-chinese-dissidents-bannon-ccp.

118. "After Brutal Beating of Friend, the Target of Steve Bannon's Protest Group Will Sue Police and City of Surrey for 'Failing to Protect Neighbourhood.'"

119. Stewart Doreen, "Fu: Hope Arrest of Alleged Protest Organizer Ends in 'Overdue Justice,'" *Midland Reporter-Telegram*, March 23, 2023, https:// www.mrt.com/news/local/article/chinaaid-s-bob-fu-midland-comments -arrest-guo-17856372.php.

120. Friedman, "A Fugitive Chinese Tycoon Met Steven Bannon. Misinformation Mayhem Ensued."

121. Doreen, "Fu: Hope Arrest of Alleged Protest Organizer Ends in 'Overdue Justice.'"

122. Friedman, "A Fugitive Chinese Tycoon Met Steven Bannon. Misinformation Mayhem Ensued."

123. Aspinwall, "Guo Wengui Is Sending Mobs After Chinese Dissidents."

124. Forsythe and Weiser, "The Undoing Of Guo Wengui, Billionaire Accused of Fraud on 2 Continents."

125. *Eastern Profit Corporation Limited v. Strategic Vision U.S. LLC*, 368 S.D.R., (S.D.N.Y., 2021), 781.

126. Ibid., 777.

127. Ibid., 778.

128. Ibid., 768–72.

129. Chen Jie, *The Overseas Chinese Democracy Movement: Assessing China's Only Open Political Opposition* (Northampton, MA: Edward Elgar Publishing, 2019).

130. *Eastern Profit Corporation Limited v. Strategic Vision U.S. LLC*, 368 S.D.R., (S.D.N.Y., 2021), 718–19, 733.

131. Ibid., 720–21, 727.

132. Guo reportedly said, "I will not make any decisions [about my public statements] before the 19th National Congress [of the Chinese Communist Party]." Guo told the vice minister, "I want to see if after the 19th National Congress, Meng Jianzhu and Wang Qishan have any positions." He added,

"If they're gone, and this generation comes into power, people like you can still survive. I will definitely announce that I'm not against the party, President Xi, the state, and the nation. I will add that I'm not against the Communist Party. Then I will close my Twitter account, and everything will turn around for the better, I'm sure. I will lead a normal life. I'm happy about this." Ibid., 730–31.

133. Ibid., 735.

134. Ibid., 727–28.

135. Ibid., 741.

136. Ibid., 718–19.

137. Ibid., 774–75.

138. Ibid., 671–72, 693–95.

139. *Eastern Profit Corporation Limited v. Strategic Vision U.S. LLC*, 273 S.D.R., (S.D.N.Y., 2020), 39.

140. Je operated a fund called the Hamilton Opportunity Fund based in Hong Kong, and the fund was revealed to be a major investor in GETTR. See Menn, "Indicted Chinese Exile Controls Gettr Social Media Site, Ex-Employees Say."

141. *Eastern Profit Corp. Ltd. v. Strategic Vision US, LLC*, No. 18-CV-2185 (LJL), Dkt. No. 273 at 45–47.

142. Rohan Gowami, "Meta Says It Has Disrupted a Massive Disinformation Campaign Linked to Chinese Law Enforcement," CNBC, August 29, 2023, https://www.cnbc.com/2023/08/29/meta-disrupts-chinese-misinformation -network-linked-to-law-enforcement-.html.

143. Nikhal Krishan, "GETTR Fired IT and Cybersecurity Teams amid Financial Problems, Former Employees Say," *Washington Examiner*, February 3, 2022, https://www.washingtonexaminer.com/policy/gettr-fired-it-and-cybersecurity -teams-amid-financial-problems.

144. Dan Friedman, "Alleged Fraudster Guo Wengui's Social Media App Was a Big Security Risk, Ex-Employees Say," *Mother Jones*, April 6, 2023, https:// www.motherjones.com/politics/2023/04/guo-wengui-gettr-miller.

145. Forsythe and Weiser, "The Undoing of Guo Wengui, Billionaire Accused of Fraud on 2 Continents"; Jennifer Gould, Joe Marino, and Jorge Fitz-Gibbon, "Cops Probe Whether Fire at Chinese Billionaire's NYC Pad Was Set Remotely," *New York Post*, March 16, 2023, https://nypost.com/2023 /03/16/fire-at-chinese-billionaire-guo-wenguis-nyc-pad-may-have-been-set -remotely-sources/.

146. Friedman, "Alleged Fraudster Guo Wengui's Social Media App Was a Big Security Risk, Ex-Employees Say."

147. Evan Osnos, "What Secrets Does the 'Donald Trump of Beijing' Know?," *New Yorker*, March 16, 2023, https://www.newyorker.com/news/daily -comment/what-secrets-does-the-donald-trump-of-beijing-know.

Chapter 6: Destabilizing Democracy

1. "Notes from a CSIS Virtual Event: Countering Chinese Espionage," CSIS, August 12, 2020, https://www.csis.org/blogs/strategic-technologies-blog /notes-csis-virtual-event-countering-chinese-espionage; Radio Free Asia, "Chinese Consulate in Houston Intervened in US Political Movement," Chinascope, http://chinascope.org/archives/24225.

2. Sinéad Baker and John Haltiwanger, "People Are Burning Documents at the Chinese Consulate in Houston, as Beijing Says the US Abruptly Gave It 72 Hours to Shut It Down," Insider, July 22, 2020, https://www.businessinsider.com /china-houston-consulate-document-burning-us-told-quickly-close-2020-7.

3. "Notes from a CSIS Virtual Event: Countering Chinese Espionage."

4. Paul Dabrowa, "Cognitive Hacking as the New Disinformation Frontier: TikTok's Links with an Artificial Intelligence Algorithm Designed to Repress the Chinese Population," Testimony Presented Before the Commonwealth of Australia Senate Select Committee on Foreign Interference Through Social Media, September 22, 2020, https://t.co/HGNHHW5yxB, 3.

5. Xiao Tianliang, ed., *The Science of Military Strategy* (Beijing: National Defense University Publishing House, 2015), translation in Nathan Beauchamp-Mustafaga and Michael S. Chase, *Borrowing a Boat Out to Sea: The Chinese Military's Use of Social Media for Influence Operations*, Policy Papers 2019, Johns Hopkins School of Advanced International Studies, Foreign Policy Institute, https://www.fpi.sais-jhu.edu/_files/ugd/b976eb _ad85a42f248a48c7b0cb2906f6398e71.pdf, 12.

6. Elsa B. Kania, "The Role of PLA Base 311 in Political Warfare Against Taiwan (Part 3)," Global Taiwan Institute, February 15, 2017, https:// globaltaiwan.org/2017/02/the-role-of-pla-base-311-in-political-warfare -against-taiwan-part-3; P. K. Mallick, *China's Cyber-influence Operations* (New Delhi: Vivekananda International Foundation, 2021), https:// indianstrategicknowledgeonline.com/web/China-s-Cyber-Influence -Operations.pdf, 9, 48, 49; Dipanjan Roy Chaudhury, "China Adopted 'Three-Warfare' Strategy Aiming to Expand Global Influence: French MoD Think Tank," *Economic Times*, January 21, 2022, https://economictimes. indiatimes.com/news/defence/china-adopted-three-warfare-strategy-aiming-to -expand-global-influence-french-mod-think-tank/articleshow/89036388.cms.

7. Lia Zhu, "Growing Global Support for US Protests over Killing by Police," *China Daily*, June 8, 2020, https://global.chinadaily.com.cn/a/202006/08 /WS5edd7ef0a3108348172515cc_4.html.

8. "Racism Kills" (cartoon), *China Daily*, May 29, 2020, https://www .chinadaily.com.cn/a/202005/29/WS5ed04c77a310a8b2411594b4.html.

9. Ian Williams, "How China Is Stoking Racial Tensions in the West," *Spectator*, May 2, 2021, https://www.spectator.co.uk/article/how-china-is-stoking -racial-tensions-in-the-west.

10. Chen Weihua (陈卫华) (@chenweihua), Twitter, June 8, 2020, 3:05 a.m., https://twitter.com/chenweihua/status/1269888308122959872; Chang Che, "The Forgotten Alliance Between Black Activists and China," *Washington Post*, September 28, 2020, https://www.washingtonpost.com/outlook/2020/09 /28/forgotten-alliance-between-black-activists-china.

11. Quoted in Frank Chung, "China's Cynical Embrace of 'Racism' to Sow Chaos," news.com.au, March 7, 2021, https://www.news.com.au/technology /innovation/military/chinas-cynical-embrace-of-racism-to-sow-chaos/news -story/d5d352f9f14826a9e91490ff8391a6cd.

12. Ben Nimmo, Ira Hubert, and Yang Cheng, "Spamouflage Breakout: Chinese Spam Network Finally Starts to Gain Some Traction," Graphika, February 2021, https://public-assets.graphika.com/reports/graphika_report _spamouflage_breakout.pdf, 4, 5, 51–52, 83.

13. Ibid., 52; Josh Taylor, "Twitter Deletes 170,000 Accounts Linked to China Influence Campaign," *Guardian*, June 11, 2020, https://www.theguardian .com/technology/2020/jun/12/twitter-deletes-170000-accounts-linked-to -china-influence-campaign.

14. Quoted in Mallick, *China's Cyber-influence Operations*, 38.

15. Quoted in Kimberly Orinx and Tanguy Struye de Swielande, "China and Cognitive Warfare: Why Is the West Losing?," NATO Collaboration Support Office, https://hal.science/hal-03635930/document, 8–3.

16. "Chinese Anti-U.S. Propaganda Videos: America Is an 'Empire of Lies' on the Verge of Collapse," The Middle East Media Research Institute, March 7, 2022, https://www.memri.org/tv/chinese-anti-us-propaganda-videos.

17. Thomas Rid, *Active Measures: The Secret History of Disinformation and Political Warfare* (London: Picador, 2020), 134–41.

18. Zhang Wei [张伟], "社交媒体在当代美国政治极化 加剧中的作用" [The Role of Social Media in the Intensification of Contemporary American Political Polarization], *Today's Mass Media* [今传媒] 6 (2019), cited in Beauchamp-Mustafaga and Chase, *Borrowing a Boat Out to Sea*.

19. Taylor, "Twitter Deletes 170,000 Accounts Linked to China Influence Campaign."

20. Jacob Helberg, *The Wires of War: Technology and the Global Struggle for Power* (New York: Avid Reader Press, 2021), 82.

21. Didi Kirsten Tatlow, "600 U.S. Groups Linked to Chinese Communist Party Influence Effort with Ambition Beyond Election," German Council on Foreign Relations, October 28, 2020, https://dgap.org/en/research /publications/600-us-groups-linked-chinese-communist-party-influence -effort-ambition-beyond.

22. Fergus Ryan et al., "Borrowing Mouths to Speak on Xinjiang," Australian Strategic Policy Institute, December 10, 2021, https://www.aspi.org.au /report/borrowing-mouths-speak-xinjiang.

23. Fergus Hanson and Elise Thomas, "Cyber-enabled Election Interference Occurs in One-Fifth of Democracies," The Strategist, Australian Strategic Policy Institute, May 17, 2019, https://www.aspistrategist.org.au/cyber-enabled -election-interference-occurs-in-one-fifth-of-democracies.

24. Denise Clifton, "Russian Trolls Stoked Anger over Black Lives Matter More than Was Previously Known," *Mother Jones*, January 30, 2018, https://www .motherjones.com/politics/2018/01/russian-trolls-hyped-anger-over-black -lives-matter-more-than-previously-known.

25. Wu Rui [吴 瑞], "警惕另类软战争" [Be on Guard Against Other Kinds of Soft Warfare], 军事记者 [*Military Correspondent*] 11 (2013): 53–54, cited in Beauchamp-Mustafaga and Chase, *Borrowing a Boat Out to Sea*, 64.

26. Nimmo, Hubert, and Cheng, "Spamouflage Breakout."

27. Arthur Kaufman, "Suspected Chinese State-Affiliated Online Influence Campaign Urged Real-World Protests in U.S.," China Digital Times, September 13, 2021, https://chinadigitaltimes.net/2021/09/suspected-chinese -state-affiliated-online-influence-campaign-urged-real-world-protests-in-u-s.

28. Chris Zappone, "#BlackLivesMatter Momentum Mostly Free of Bots," *Sydney Morning Herald*, June 14, 2020, https://www.smh.com.au/world /north-america/blacklivesmatter-momentum-mostly-free of-bots-20200611 -p551nx.html.

29. Williams, "How China Is Stoking Racial Tensions in the West."

30. Nimmo, Hubert, and Cheng, "Spamouflage Breakout."

31. Jessica Brandt and Torrey Taussig, "The Kremlin's Disinformation Playbook Goes to Beijing," The Brookings Institution, May 19, 2020, https://www .brookings.edu/articles/the-kremlins-disinformation-playbook-goes-to-beijing.

32. Alexander Reid Ross and Courtney Dobson, "The Big Business of Uyghur Genocide Denial," *New Lines Magazine*, January 18, 2022, https:// newlinesmag.com/reportage/the-big-business-of-uyghur-genocide-denial; Roy Singham, "On the Road from Detroit to South Africa: Black Radical Internationalist Traditions," MR Online, November 27, 2021, https:// mronline.org/2021/11/27/on-the-road-from-detroit-to-south-africa-black -radical-internationalist-traditions.

33. Micah Reddy and Sam Sole, "SA New Frame's Demise Shines a Light on China-Aligned Unions, Parties, and Disinformation Networks," San Francisco Bay Area Independent Media Center, July 26, 2022, https://www .indybay.org/newsitems/2022/07/26/18851267.php.

34. Saurabh Sharma, "Who Is Neville Roy Singham, Accused of Funding Chinese Propaganda in India and Abroad?," BusinessToday, August 8, 2023, https:// www.businesstoday.in/latest/story/who-is-neville-roy-singham-accused-of -funding-chinese-propaganda-in-india-and-abroad-393168-2023-08-07.

35. Jonathan Pelson, *Wireless Wars: China's Dangerous Domination of 5G and How We're Fighting Back* (Dallas: BenBella Books, 2021), 60–61, 65–68.

36. Noah Berman, Lindsay Maizland, and Andrew Chatzky, "Is China's Huawei a Threat to U.S. National Security?," Council on Foreign Regulations, February 8, 2023, https://www.cfr.org/backgrounder/chinas-huawei-threat -us-national-security.

37. Ross and Dobson, "The Big Business of Uyghur Genocide Denial."

38. David Kirkpatrick, "The Socialist State of ThoughtWorks," CNN, March 17, 2008, https://money.cnn.com/2008/03/14/technology/kirkpatrick_thought works.fortune/index.htm.

39. Reddy and Sole, "SA New Frame's Demise Shines a Light on China-Aligned Unions, Parties, and Disinformation Networks."

40. Li Xiang, "CIC Takes Position in Apax Partners," February 4, 2010, *China Daily*, https://www.chinadaily.com.cn/business/2010-02/04/content _9426287.htm.

41. See "Apax Partners' Funds and General Atlantic Agree to Acquire a Significant Interest in China's Largest Online Real Estate Portal—SouFun," Apax Partners, September 20, 2010, https://www.apax.com/news-views /apax-partners-funds-and-general-atlantic-agree-to-acquire-a-significant -interest-in-chinas-largest-online-real-estate-portal-soufun; "Guotai Junan Securities Co., Ltd.," Apax Partners, https://www.apax.com/partnerships/ guotai-junan-securities-co-ltd; "YunZhangFang," Apax Partners, https:// www.apax.com/partnerships/yunzhangfang.

42. Kirkpatrick, "The Socialist State of ThoughtWorks."

43. Ross and Dobson, "The Big Business of Uyghur Genocide Denial."

44. Drew Forrest, "Good Reasons Why We Should Fear China," *Mail & Guardian* [South Africa], August 18, 2022, https://mg.co.za/opinion/2022 -08-18-good-reasons-why-we-should-fear-china.

45. Reddy and Sole, "SA New Frame's Demise Shines a Light on China-Aligned Unions, Parties, and Disinformation Networks."

46. Ibid.

47. Allie Coyne, "ThoughtWorks Snapped Up by Private Equity Firm," itnews, August 24, 2017, https://www.itnews.com.au/news/thoughtworks-snapped -up-by-private-equity-firm-471610; *Martin Fowler* (blog), "Roy Sells ThoughtWorks," Martin Fowler, August 23, 2017, https://martinfowler.com /articles/201708-tw-sale.html.

48. Ross and Dobson, "The Big Business of Uyghur Genocide Denial."

49. Mara Hvistendahl, David A. Fahrenthold, Lynsey Chutel, and Ishaan Jhaveri, "A Global Web of Chinese Propaganda Leads to a U.S. Tech Mogul," *New York Times,* August 10, 2023, https://www.nytimes.com/2023/08/05/world /europe/neville-roy-singham-china-propaganda.html.

50. https://www.fec.gov/data/receipts/individual-contributions/?contributor _name=Singham%2C+Neville&contributor_name=Singham%2C+Roy&two

_year_transaction_period=2012&two_year_transaction_period=2014 &two_year_transaction_period=2016&two_year_transaction_period=2018 &two_year_transaction_period=2020&two_year_transaction _period=2022&two_year_transaction_period=2024&min_date=01 %2F01%2F2010&max_date=12%2F31%2F2024.

51. https://www.fec.gov/data/receipts/individual-contributions/?contributor _name=Evans%2C+Jodie&two_year_transaction_period=2012&two_year _transaction_period=2014&two_year_transaction_period=2016&two_year _transaction_period=2018&two_year_transaction_period=2020&two_year _transaction_period=2022&two_year_transaction_period=2024&min _date=01%2F01%2F2010&max_date=12%2F31%2F2024

52. Medea Benjamin and Jodie Evans, eds., *Stop the Next War Now: Effective Responses to Violence and Terrorism* (Novato, CA: New World Library: 2005), 232.

53. Ross and Dobson, "The Big Business of Uyghur Genocide Denial."

54. "China and the Left: A Socialist Forum," The People's Forum, September 18, 2021, https://peoplesforum.org/events/china-and-the-left-a-socialist-forum.

55. See, e.g., Li Jiayao, "Peace Activists Castigate Those Vilifying China," China Military Online, November 2, 2020, http://www.81.cn/jwywpd/2020-11 /02/content_9929217.htm; Chen Lufan, "Belligerent U.S.: Source of Global Scourge," China Military Online, March 11, 2021, http://www.81.cn /jwywpd/2021-03/11/content_10001798.htm.

56. Ross and Dobson, "The Big Business of Uyghur Genocide Denial."

57. Zack Budryk, "Progressive Groups Warn of Risk to Climate from U.S. Confrontational Approach to China," The Hill, July 8, 2021, https://thehill .com/policy/energy environment/562084-progressives-warn-of-risk-to -climate-from-confrontational-approach.

58. People's Support Foundation Limited, Internal Revenue Service Form 990, U.S. Department of the Treasury, https://projects.propublica.org/nonprofits /organizations/821202926/202023189349100007/full; "Businessman Neville Roy Singham Quietly Sponsors an Initiative Opposing US Assistance to Kyiv," Intelligence Online, November 11, 2022, https://www.intelligenceonline .com/corporate-intelligence/2022/11/11/businessman-neville-roy-singham -quietly-sponsors-an-initiative-opposing-us-assistance-to-kyiv,109863896 -art; "United Community Fund," Cause IQ, https://www.causeiq.com /organizations/united-community-fund,371913339/.

59. The People's Forum (@PeoplesForumNYC), Twitter, December 21, 2021, 8:22 a.m., https://twitter.com/PeoplesForumNYC/status/1473312812944531457.

60. "CubaBrief: 'Cuban Regime Cracks Down on Protesters Demanding Freedom' MSNBC | 'Cuba Repression Tactics Must Not be Repeated' Amnesty | 'How to Help Victims of Hurricane Ian in Cuba' PBS News," Center for a Free Cuba, October 4, 2022, https://www.cubacenter.org/archives/2022/10/4 /cubabrief-cuban-regime-cracks-down-on-protesters-demanding-freedom

-msnbc-cuba-repression-tactics-must-not-be-repeated-amnesty-how-to-help-victims-of-hurricane-ian-in-cuba-pbs-news-.

61. Peoples Forum Inc., Internal Revenue Service Form 990, U.S. Department of Treasury, https://projects.propublica.org/nonprofits/organizations/611844780/201933169349305308/IRS990.

62. "Solidarity with the Political Prisoners of the Anti-Racist Struggle in the US!," The People's Forum, September 23, 2020, https://peoplesforum.org/events/solidarity-with-the-political-prisoners-of-the-anti-racist-struggle-in-the-us/2020-09-23; Lori Lizarraga, "Preliminary Hearing Approaching for PSL Protestors Facing Dozens of Felony Charges," KUSA, January 3, 2021, https://www.9news.com/article/news/local/protests/psl-protestors-facing-felony-charges-approach-preliminary-hearing/73-7b37eb77-16cd-4c17-8a98-3353be17c456; "Black Liberation, Anti-fascism & the Arsenal of Democracy," The People's Forum, October 22, 2019, https://peoplesforum.org/events/black-liberation-anti-fascism-the-arsenal-of-democracy/.

63. "July 2017 China Delegation Photos," China Delegation, http://immigrantsolidarity.org/China/July07Photos.html; Ken McIntyre and Kevin Mooney, "Far-Left Antifa Agitators on the Rise in the Age of Trump," The Daily Signal, August 17, 2017, https://www.dailysignal.com/2017/08/17/far-left-antifa-agitators-on-the-rise-in-the-age-of-trump/.

64. Abdul Rahman, "The Myth-Making Around Tiananmen Square," Popular Resistance, June 5, 2022, https://popularresistance.org/the-myth-making-around-tiananmen-square.

65. Vijay Prashad, "Genocide Denier? Not Me, Pal. Try the White House Instead," CounterPunch, February 7, 2022, https://www.counterpunch.org/2022/02/07/genocide-denier-not-me-pal-try-the-white-house-instead.

66. David Klion, "What Should the Left Do About China?," Nation, January 11, 2022, https://www.thenation.com/article/world/china-left-foreign-policy.

67. Pradeep Thakur, "ED Probes Media Portal's Funding from Businessman 'Linked' to China Regime," Times of India, July 18, 2021, https://timesofindia.indiatimes.com/india/ed-probes-media-portals-funding-from-businessman-linked-to-china-regime/articleshow/84514212.cms.

68. William Bredderman, "U.S. Tech Mogul Bankrolls Pro-Russia, Pro-China News Network," The Daily Beast, May 28, 2023, May 29, 2023, https://www.thedailybeast.com/neville-singham-funded-breakthrough-news-is-pushing-moscow-beijing-propaganda.

69. Klion, "What Should the Left Do About China?"; "China and the Left: A Socialist Forum," The People's Forum, September 18, 2021, https://peoplesforum.org/events/china-and-the-left-a-socialist-forum/.

70. "Can the Chinese Diaspora Speak?," Qiao Collective, August 19, 2021, https://www.qiaocollective.com/articles/can-the-chinese-diaspora-speak; "Xinjiang: A Report and Resource Compilation," Qiao Collective, September 21 [no year], https://www.qiaocollective.com/education/xinjiang.

71. Lev Nachman, Adrian Rauchfleisch, and Brian Hioe, "How China Divides the Left: Competing Transnational Left-Wing Alternative Media on Twitter," *Media and Communication* 10, no. 3 (2022): 50–63, https://doi.org/10.17645/mac.v10i3.5345.

72. Maurice Isserman, "Congress Now Has More Socialists than Ever Before in U.S. History," *In These Times*, January 11, 2021, https://inthesetimes.com/article/democratic-socialism-dsa-aoc-bernie-sanders-congress; Democratic Socialists of America, https://www.dsausa.org.

73. Van Gosse, "Why the United States Is Not a True Democracy, Part Two," Democratic Socialists of America, October 11, 2019, https://www.dsausa.org/democratic-left/why-the-united-states-is-not-a-true-democracy-part-two/.

74. Tom Hayden, "Harrington's Dilemma," *Nation*, May 25, 2000, https://www.thenation.com/article/archive/harringtons-dilemma/.

75. Klion, "What Should the Left Do About China?"

76. Travis S., "Building a Mass Movement with No Apologism: The Left and the Communist Party of China," *Tempest*, December 24, 2021, https://www.tempestmag.org/2021/12/building-a-mass-movement-with-no-apologism.

77. "DSA Political Platform," Democratic Socialists of America, https://www.dsausa.org/dsa-political-platform-from-2021-convention/.

78. Caleb T. Maupin, "Talk of Socialism Stirs Controversy in the US," China.org.cn, August 23, 2018, http://www.china.org.cn/opinion/2018-08/23/content_59858184.htm.

79. Zhang Liyan, "自三月份以来，成千上万的美国人成为社会主义者" [Since March, Thousands of Americans Have Become Socialists], Center for Marxist Parties in Foreign Countries of CCNU (MPFC), June 12, 2020, http://ccnumpfc.com/index.php/view/2382.html.

80. Niu Zhengke, "美国共产党：走过百年，艰难谋求新的发展　牛政科" [The Communist Party of the United States: After a Century, It Is Difficult to Seek New Development], Center for Marxist Parties in Foreign Countries of CCNU (MPFC), February 4, 2021, ccnumpfc.com/index.php/view/2684.html.

81. Zhang Liyan, "美共主席乔•西姆斯：选举重要，运动更重要" [Joe Sims, Chairman of the American Communist Party: Elections Are Important, and Sports Are Even More Important], Center for Marxist Parties in Foreign Countries of CCNU (MPFC), June 21, 2020, http://www.ccnumpfc.com/index.php/View/2393.html.

82. Ryan et al., "Borrowing Mouths to Speak on Xinjiang."

83. "Roll Call 26, Bill Number: H. Res. 11," Clerk of the United States House of Representatives, January 10, 2023, https://clerk.house.gov/Votes/202326?Page=11.

84. Nikki Schwab, "Code Pink Protesters Interrupt First House China Committee Hearing—as Lawmakers Discuss Country's Role in Fentanyl Trade, the Spy

Balloon Fiasco, and a Potential War over Taiwan," *Daily Mail*, February 28, 2023, https://www.dailymail.co.uk/news/article-11805163/Code-Pink -protesters-interrupt-House-China-committee-hearing.html.

85. "Balloon Incident Reveals Stupidity of US Mainstream Media," Global Times, March 2, 2023, https://www.globaltimes.cn/page/202303/1286521 .shtml.

86. Ivana Stradner, "Russia and China Are Fueling Web Wars to Divide Americans," Foundation for Defense of Democracies, December 27, 2022, https://www.fdd.org/analysis/2022/12/27/russia-china-web-wars-divide -americans.

87. A. J. Vicens, "Chinese Influence Operation Seeks to Sow Political Discord, 'Aggressively' Targets U.S. Midterms," CyberScoop, October 26, 2022, https://cyberscoop.com/china-midterms-elections-influence-nord-hacking.

88. Joshua Kurlantzick, "China's Growing Attempts to Influence U.S. Politics," Council on Foreign Relations, October 31, 2022, https://www.cfr.org/article /chinas-growing-attempts-influence-us-politics.

89. Caroline Silva, "Communist Activists Decry Tyre Nichols Killing During Atlanta Protest," *Atlanta Journal-Constitution*, January 27, 2023, https:// www.ajc.com/news/communist-activists-decry-tyre-nichols-killing-during -atlanta-protest/4CMDQSXI2NFDPCITI3LSQ6UTTA.

90. Danny McDonald and Claire Law, "Vigil Held on Boston Common as Memphis Releases Police Video of Tyre Nichols Beating," *Boston Globe*, January 27, 2023, https://www.bostonglobe.com/2023/01/27/metro/vigil-planned-boston -common-ahead-release-memphis-police-video-tyre-nichols-beating.

91. Katherine Fung, "Tyre Nichols Protests Planned in These Cities Ahead of Body Cam Release," *Newsweek*, January 27, 2023, https://www .newsweek.com/tyre-nichols-protests-planned-these-cities-ahead-body -cam-release-1777215; "Find a Protest Near You: Justice for Tyre Nichols!," LiberationNews.org, January 27, 2023, https://www.liberationnews.org /find-a-protest-near-you-justice-for-tyre-nichols.

92. Lance Reynolds, "Protests Continue in Boston over the Beating of Tyre Nichols," *Boston Herald*, January 28, 2023, https://www.bostonherald.com /2023/01/28/protests-continue-in-boston-over-the-beating-of-tyre-nichols.

93. Nathaniel Rosenberg and Maggie Grether, "New Haveners Mourn Tyre Nichols, Challenge Police Violence," *Yale Daily News*, January 30, 2023, https://yaledailynews.com/blog/2023/01/30/new-haveners-mourn-tyre -nichols-challenge-police-violence.

94. Nick Arama, "Protests Get Violent in NYC's Times Square After Release of Tyre Nichols Video," RedState, January 28, 2023, https://redstate.com/nick -arama/2023/01/28/protests-get-violent-in-nycs-times-square-after-release -of-tyre-nichols-video-n695068.

95. "Bank Backing 'Cop City' Targeted as Hundreds Take to Streets of Atlanta Following Police Killing," Online Anarchist Federation, January 22, 2023, https://www.anarchistfederation.net/bank-backing-cop-city-targeted-as-hundreds-take-to-streets-of-atlanta-following-police-killing.

96. Adrian Silbernagel, "The Revolution Will Not Be Gender-Conforming: Trans/Non-Binary Comrades Talk About Socialism," Queer Kentucky, May 18, 2023, https://queerkentucky.com/the-revolution-will-not-be-gender-conforming-trans-non-binary-comrades-talk-about-socialism/.

97. Natalia Marques, "The Unity of Our Movements Terrifies Them: Pride and Right-Wing Backlash Against LGBTQ People," Peoples Dispatch, June 28, 2022, https://peoplesdispatch.org/2022/06/28/the-unity-of-our-movements-terrifies-them-pride-and-right-wing-backlash-against-lgbtq-people.

98. "8/13 | Becoming Numerous: Legacies of Queer and Trans Rebellion," Revolution 13/13, https://blogs.law.columbia.edu/revolution1313/8-13.

99. "New Research Partnership Unites Six Leading Academic Institutions to Transform the Science of Human Performance and Advance," Bloomberg, July 21, 2021, https://www.bloomberg.com/press-releases/2021-07-21/new-research-partnership-unites-six-leading-academic-institutions-to-transform-the-science-of-human-performance-and-advance.

100. Wu Tsai Female Athlete Program, Boston Children's Hospital, https://www.childrenshospital.org/programs/female-athlete-program/research-innovation/innovation-hub-boston-childrens; "Postdoctoral Fellowship Position: Available in the Female Athlete Program in the Sports Medicine Division of the Orthopedic Center at Boston Children's Hospital," https://static1.squarespace.com/static/5dd70115adeb0b3cce38c3dd/t/62da928d8e28606ea44e1c31/1658491541699/FAP+Postdoc+Flyer-3.pdf.

101. Nationwide Children's A/V, "Transgender Athlete Inclusion: An Update" (video), Vimeo, August 26, 2021, https://vimeo.com/589344405.

102. Jessica Chasmar, "Boston Children's Hospital Deletes References to Vaginoplasties for 17-Year-Olds amid Online Furor," FOX News, August 18, 2022, https://www.foxnews.com/politics/boston-childrens-hospital-deletes-references-vaginoplasties-17-year-olds-online-furor.

103. Kristine Parks, "Boston Children's Hospital Says Kids Know They're Trans 'from the Womb' in Now-Deleted Video," New York Post, October 7, 2022, https://nypost.com/2022/10/07/boston-childrens-hospital-says-kids-know-theyre-trans-from-the-womb-in-deleted-video/.

104. Erin Digitale, "Transgender," Wu Tsai Neurosciences Institute, Stanford University, May 25, 2017, https://neuroscience.stanford.edu/news/transgender.

105. "Autobiography of a Transgender Scientist," Wu Tsai Neurosciences Institute, Stanford University, March 19, 2019, https://neuroscience.stanford.edu/events/autobiography-transgender-scientist-book-club.

106. "Why It Is Becoming Increasingly Difficult to Find Safe Spaces for the LGBTQ Community in China," *CE Noticias Financieras*, June 13, 2023. [Accessed from Lexis, https://advance.lexis.com/api/document?collection =news&id=urn:contentItem:68FY-VT81-JCG7-842N-00000-00&context =1519360.]

107. Huizhong Wu, "Beijing LGBTQ+ Center Is Closed as China Cracks Down on Gay Organizations," *Los Angeles Times*, May 16, 2023, https://www .latimes.com/world-nation/story/2023-05-16/beijing-lgbtq-center-shuttered -crackdown-china.

108. Joyce Chediac, "300,000 Pro-Palestine Protesters in D.C. Confront Biden's and Netanyahu's Genocide," Liberationnews.org, November 5, 2023, https:// www.liberationnews.org/300000-pro-palestine-protesters-in-d-c-confront -biden-and-netanyahus-genocide/.

109. Center on Extremism, "Fringe-Left Groups Express Support for Hamas's Invasion and Brutal Attacks in Israel," ADL.org, October 14, 2023, https:// www.adl.org/resources/blog/fringe-left-groups-express-support-hamass -invasion-and-brutal-attacks-israel.

110. Simon Rios, "Hundreds march through Boston in support of Palestinians," wbur.org, October 17, 2023, https://www.wbur.org/news/2023/10/17 /palestine-rally-copley-israel-boston; Amin S. Lotfi, "Thousands Gather at Copley Square to March for Palestine," berkeleybeacon.com, November 21, 2023, https://berkeleybeacon.com/thousands-gather-at-copley-square-to -march-for-palestine/.

111. Bethany Allen-Ebrahimian, "In Claiming Neutrality, China Picks a Side in Israel-Hamas War," Axios.com, October 15, 2023, https://www.axios .com/2023/10/15/china-israel-hamas-war; "What Is China's Position on the Israel-Hamas War?" The Soufan Center, November 9, 2023, https:// thesoufancenter.org/intelbrief-2023-november-9/.

112. TBS Report, "Israel Disappears from Online Maps Run by Chinese Tech Giants," *Business Standard*, October 31, 2023, https://www.tbsnews.net /world/israel-disappears-online-maps-run-chinese-tech-giants-730466.

113. Jessica Flores, Annie Vainshtein, Sam Whiting, "S.F. Students Walk Out to Protest Israeli Airstrikes on Gaza After Hamas Attack," *San Francisco Chronicle*, October 18, 2023, https://www.sfchronicle.com/bayarea/article /sf-student-walkout-israel-hamas-war-bombing-sfusd-18433370.php.

114. "Stand with Palestine! Victory to the Palestinian Resistance!" frso.org, October 9, 2023, https://frso.org/statements/stand-with-palestine-victory-to -the-palestinian-resistance/.

115. "FRSO—Twin Cities Celebrates the Chinese Revolution with Panel Event," Beforeitsnews.com, October 22, 2023, https://beforeitsnews.com/opinion -liberal/2023/10/frso-twin-cities-celebrates-the-chinese-revolution-with -panel-event-2621824.html.

116. People's Forum Instagram Account, https://www.instagram.com/p/CyHAlskgryb/.

117. "Pro-Palestinian Events Across the U.S. Trigger Outrage from Many Politicians," *NPR Morning Edition*, October 10, 2023. (Lexis).

118. "300,000 March in Largest Pro-Palestine Action in U.S. History. Next Step: 'Shut It Down for Palestine!' on Nov. 9," peoplesforum.org, November 5, 2023, https://peoplesforum.org/blog_post/300000-march-in-largest-pro -palestine-action-in-us-history-next-step-shut-it-down-for-palestine-on-nov-9/.

Chapter 7: A TikToking Bomb

1. Beata Wallsten, "Bilden av ett Sverige i krig sprids på TikTok" [The Image of a Sweden at War Is Spreading on TikTok], *Aftonbladet* [Sweden], January 15, 2022, https://www.aftonbladet.se/nyheter/a/wO5eqo/bilden-av-ett-sverige-i -krig-sprids-pa-TikTok.

2. "War Is Coming—TikTok Used to Scare Children in Sweden," Cyber Security Intelligence, January 17, 2022, https://www.cybersecurityintelligence.com /blog/war-is-coming---TikTok-used-to-scare-swedish-children-6066.html.

3. Elisabeth Braw, "'War Is Coming': Mysterious TikTok Videos Are Scaring Sweden's Children," Defense One, January 16, 2022, https://www.defenseone .com/ideas/2022/01/war-coming-mysterious-TikTok-videos-are-scaring -swedens-children/360808.

4. "Medical Moment: Overuse of TikTok Might Lead to Neurological Issues," WNDU, February 1, 2022, https://www.wndu.com/2022/02/01/medical -moment-overuse-TikTok-might-lead-neurological-issues.

5. Caroline Olvera et al., "TikTok Tics: A Pandemic Within a Pandemic," *Movement Disorders Clinical Practice* 8, no. 8 (November 2021): 1200–1205, https://doi.org/10.1002/mdc3.13316.

6. Qiao Liang and Wang Xiangsui, *Unrestricted Warfare: China's Master Plan to Destroy America* (Panama City, Panama: Pan American Publishing, 2002), 30.

7. Matthew Brennan, *Attention Factory: The Story of TikTok and China's ByteDance* (self-published, 2020), 209; James Hale, "Jimmy Fallon's TikTok Partnership Resulted in Record Engagement Spike for the App," Tubefilter, November 20, 2018, https://www.tubefilter.com/2018/11/20/jimmy-fallon -TikTok-the-tonight-show-partnership.

8. Chris Stokel-Walker, *TikTok Boom: China's Dynamite App and the Superpower Race for Social Media* (Kingston upon Thames, UK: Canbury Press, 2021), 146–47.

9. Brennan, *Attention Factory*, 196.

10. Tiffany Hsu, "On TikTok, Election Misinformation Thrives Ahead of Midterms," *New York Times*, August 14, 2022, https://www.nytimes.com /2022/08/14/business/media/on-TikTok-election-misinformation.html.

11. Stokel-Walker, *TikTok Boom*, 186.

12. Paige Heidebrink, "TikTok on the Brain," Communicating Psychological Science, https//www.communicatingpsychologicalscience.com/blog/TikTok -on-the-brain.

13. Li Ming, "WeChat and TikTok Help the CCP Spread Its Thought Control Overseas," Minghui.org, December 30, 2020, https://en.minghui.org/html /articles/2020/12/30/189173p.html.

14. Martin and Williamson, "Mapping Chinese Influence in Hollywood," 9.

15. Mallick, *China's Cyber-influence Operations*, 4.

16. Stokel-Walker, *TikTok Boom*, 133; "Ministry of State Security of the People's Republic of China," Mapcarta, https://mapcarta.com/W690857120; "知春东里社区" [Zhichun Dongli Community], Mapcarta, https://mapcarta. com/W849088075; Richard Uber, *China's Artificial Intelligence Ecosystem* (Washington, DC: National Intelligence University, 2020), https://ni-u.edu /wp/wp-content/uploads/2021/08/Uber_Monograph_DNI2021_02261.pdf.

17. Wm. C. Hannas and Huey-meei Chang, "China's Access to Foreign AI Technology: An Assessment," Center for Security and Emerging Technology, September 2019, https://cset.georgetown.edu/wp-content/uploads/CSET _China_Access_To_Foreign_AI_Technology.pdf, 16.

18. Craig S. Smith, "U.S.-China Rivalry Boosts Tech—and Tensions," *IEEE Spectrum*, January 2020, https://read.nxtbook.com/ieee/spectrum/spectrum _na_january_2022/u_s_china_rivalry_boosts_tech.html.

19. Stokel-Walker, *TikTok Boom*, 142.

20. Since 2017, ByteDance has had a party committee that is headed by CCP secretary and company editor in chief Zhang Fuping (張輔評). Keoni Everington, "TikTok Owners Show True Colors with Communist Flag," *Taiwan News*, August 6, 2020, https://www.taiwannews.com.tw/en/news/3982027.

21. Louise Lucas, "The Chinese Communist Party Entangles Big Tech," *Financial Times*, July 18, 2018, https://www.ft.com/content/5d0af3c4-846c -11e8-a29d-73e3d454535d.

22. Salman Ahmad, "TikTok Could Be More Dangerous Than You Think," CTN News, May 9, 2022, https://www.chiangraitimes.com/opinion/TikTok-could -be-more-dangerous-than-you-think; Ben Thompson, "The TikTok War," Stratechery, July 14, 2020, https://stratechery.com/2020/the-TikTok-war.

23. "Say 'No!' to U.S. Robbery of TikTok: Global Times Editorial," Global Times, September 21, 2020, https://www.globaltimes.cn/content/1201625 .shtml.

24. David L. Sloss, *Tyrants on Twitter: Protecting Democracies from Information Warfare* (Redwood City, CA: Stanford University Press, 2022), 87.

25. Aynne Kokas, *Trafficking Data: How China Is Winning the Battle for Digital Sovereignty* (Oxford, UK: Oxford University Press, 2022), 106.

26. Chris Stokel-Walker, "We Had Experts Dissect TikTok's Algorithm, and Their Findings Reveal Why a U.S. Buyer Will Struggle to Replicate Its Magic," Insider, September 8, 2020, https://www.businessinsider.com/why-TikTok-algorithm-ByteDance-acquisition-trump-2020-9; D. Bondy Valdovinos Kaye, Jing Zeng, and Patrik Wikström, *TikTok: Creativity and Culture in Short Video* (Cambridge, UK: Polity Press, 2022), 46.

27. "Peking University," China Defence Universities Tracker, November 20, 2019, https://unitracker.aspi.org.au/universities/peking-university.

28. Eugene Wei, "TikTok and the Sorting Hat," Remains of the Day, August 4, 2020, https://www.eugenewei.com/blog/2020/8/3/TikTok-and-the-sorting-hat; "About," Remains of the Day, https://www.eugenewei.com/info.

29. Kokas, *Trafficking Data*, 112.

30. Fergus Ryan, Audrey Fritz, and Daria Impiombato, "TikTok and WeChat: Curating and Controlling Global Information Flows," ASPI International Cyber Policy Centre, report no. 37, 2020, https://www.readkong.com/page/TikTok-and-wechat-curating-and-controlling-global-5842589, 17.

31. Eva Xiao, "TikTok Users Gush About China, Hoping to Boost Views," *Wall Street Journal*, June 17, 2020, https://www.wsj.com/articles/TikTok-users-gush-about-china-hoping-to-boost-views-11592386203.

32. See e.g., Baca Berita, a social media app that is based in Indonesia and owned by ByteDance. The news aggregator banned information on orders from the company's Beijing headquarters. See Mallick, *China's Cyber-influence Operations*, 24.

33. Kristina Libby, "Is TikTok Really Spying on You?," *Popular Mechanics*, July 9, 2021, https://www.popularmechanics.com/technology/apps/a31260575/tik-tok-spying.

34. John T. Cacioppo and Richard E. Petty, "Effects of Message Repetition and Position on Cognitive Response, Recall, and Persuasion," *Journal of Personality and Social Psychology* 37, no. 1 (1979): 97–109, https://doi.org/10.1037/0022-3514.37.1.97.

35. Paul Dabrowa, "Cognitive Hacking as the New Disinformation Frontier: TikTok's Links with an Artificial Intelligence Algorithm Designed to Repress the Chinese Population," Testimony Presented Before the Commonwealth of Australia Senate Select Committee on Foreign Interference Through Social Media, September 22, 2020, https://t.co/HGNHHW5yxB, 7.

36. Kaye et al., *TikTok*, 171.

37. Ibid., 8.

38. Raymond Zhong and Sheera Frenkel, "A Third of TikTok's U.S. Users May Be 14 or Under, Raising Safety Questions," *New York Times*, September 17, 2020, https://www.nytimes.com/2020/08/14/technology/TikTok-underage-users-ftc.html.

39.   Dabrowa, "Cognitive Hacking as the New Disinformation Frontier," 8.

40.   Insikt Group, "1 Key for 1 Lock: The Chinese Communist Party's Strategy for Targeted Propaganda," Recorded Future, September 28, 2022, https://www.recordedfuture.com/1-key-for-1-lock-chinese-communist-party-strategy-targeted-propaganda.

41.   Both are in the Haidian District in Beijing. See "PLA National Defence University," Military School Directory, https://militaryschooldirectory.com/china-pla-national-defense-university; "People's Liberation Army National Defence University," Mapcarta, https://mapcarta.com/W655136680.

42.   Mallick, *China's Cyber-influence Operations*, 36.

43.   Uber, *China's Artificial Intelligence Ecosystem*.

44.   Nathan Beauchamp-Mustafaga, "Cognitive Domain Operations: The PLA's New Holistic Concept for Influence Operations," *China Brief* 19, no. 16 (September 2019), Jamestown Foundation, https://jamestown.org/program/cognitive-domain-operations-the-plas-new-holistic-concept-for-influence-operations/.

45.   Mallick, *China's Cyber-influence Operations*, 37.

46.   Scott W. Harold, Nathan Beauchamp-Mustafaga, and Jeffrey W. Hornung, *Chinese Disinformation Efforts on Social Media* (Santa Monica, CA: RAND Corporation, 2021), 18.

47.   Xu Sen, "Communicating Our Military's Advanced Military Culture to the World," *Military Correspondent*, 2012, 4–6, in Beauchamp-Mustafaga and Chase, *Borrowing a Boat Out to Sea*, 50.

48.   Mu Qingziang, "智技术视域下的现代网络媒体战浅析, 作者：穆庆生, 融媒矩阵军事记者" [Analysis of Modern Network Media Warfare in the Perspective of Intelligent Technology], China Military Online, http://www.81.cn/jsjz/2021-11/11/content_10106957.htm.

49.   Peng Zhengang, "'Z世代'国际传播策略与实践路径研究" [Research on International Communication Strategies and Practice Paths of "Generation Z"], Weixin, August 18, 2021, https://archive.ph/MgNjA#selection-1261.0-1315.21.

50.   Mallick, *China's Cyber-influence Operations*, 68.

51.   Liu Ying, "'复调'新媒体国际传播的优势、困境与进路" [The Advantages, Predicaments, and Approaches of International Communication of "Polyphony": New Media], FX361.com, October 31, 2018, https://archive.ph/LJZau#selection-403.0-407.204.

52.   Tang Jingtai and Yao Chun, "Digital Propaganda and the Digital Opinion Turn: Digital Propaganda and Opinion Manipulation in Social Media Platforms," 正明 (Zhengming) 11 (2022): http://www.tsyzm.com/CN/home.

53.   "Shen Haixiong: To Use the Multilingual Nebula Studio as a Breakthrough, to Advance 'The Spread of Favor,'" WeMP.app, June 7, 2021, https://archive.ph/m0dkf#selection-289.0-346.0.

54. Martin and Williamson, "Mapping Chinese Influence in Hollywood," 15. See also Jacques Ellul, *Propaganda: The Formation of Men's Attitudes* (New York: Vintage, 1973), 9–10, 17, 20–21.

55. Quoted in Beauchamp-Mustafaga and Chase, *Borrowing a Boat Out to Sea*, 104.

56. Ibid.

57. See, e.g., Cai Yintong [蔡印同], "留学生: 民间外宣的重要 力量" [Overseas Students: An Important Force for People-to-People External Propaganda], 对外传播[*International Communications*] 3 (2009); Harold et al., *Chinese Disinformation Efforts on Social Media*, 20.

58. Insikt Group, "1 Key for 1 Lock."

59. Quoted in Beauchamp-Mustafaga and Chase, *Borrowing a Boat Out to Sea*, 95.

60. Quoted in Ian Easton, *The Final Struggle: Inside China's Global Strategy* (Norwalk, CT: Eastbridge Books, 2022), 169.

61. Stokel-Walker, *TikTok Boom*, 19.

62. Sarah Perez, "TikTok Explains How the Recommendation System Behind Its 'For You' Feed Works," TechCrunch, June 18, 2020, https://techcrunch.com/2020/06/18/TikTok-explains-how-the-recommendation-system-behind-its-for-you-feed-works.

63. Ganesh Sitaraman, "The Regulation of Foreign Platforms," *Stanford Law Review* 74, no. 5 (May 2022): 1073–152.

64. Tina Burrett and Jeffrey Kingston, eds., *Press Freedom in Contemporary China* (Milton, UK: Taylor and Francis, 2019), 38–41.

65. Kaye et al., *TikTok*, 188.

66. Matthew Brennan, *Attention Factory: The Story of TikTok and China's ByteDance* (self-published, 2020), 87–88.

67. Emily Baker-White, "LinkedIn Profiles Indicate 300 Current TikTok and ByteDance Employees Used to Work for Chinese State Media—and Some Still Do," *Forbes*, August 11, 2022, https://www.forbes.com/sites/emilybaker-white/2022/08/10/ByteDance-TikTok-china-state-media-propaganda/.

68. Ryan et al., "TikTok and WeChat," 19. ("Beijing Internet Association, 'ByteDance Party Committee: We Must Give Priority to Stressing the Correct Guidance.'")

69. Baker-White, "LinkedIn Profiles Indicate 300 Current TikTok and ByteDance Employees Used to Work for Chinese State Media—and Some Still Do."

70. Georgia Wells, "TikTok Employees Say Executive Moves to U.S. Shows China Parents Influence," *Wall Street Journal*, September 27, 2023, https://www.wsj.com/tech/TikTok-employees-say-executive-moves-to-u-s-show-china-parents-influence-ef5ff21f.

71.　Ryan et al., "TikTok and WeChat," 18.

72.　Michael Schuman, "Why America Is Afraid of TikTok," *Atlantic*, July 30, 2020, https://www.theatlantic.com/international/archive/2020/07/TikTok -ban-china-america/614725.

73.　David Bandurski, "Tech Shame in the 'New Era,'" China Media Project, April 11, 2018, https://chinamediaproject.org/2018/04/11/tech-shame-in-the -new-era.

74.　Pandaily, "Open Apology from CEO of Toutiao Following the Ban of Neihan Duanzi," Medium, April 16, 2018, https://medium.com/@pandaily /open-apology-from-ceo-of-toutiao-following-the-ban-of-neihan-duanzi -6381000939d0.

75.　Emily Baker-White and Iain Martin, "On TikTok, Chinese State Media Pushes Divisive Videos About U.S. Politicians," *Forbes*, December 1, 2022, https://www.forbes.com/sites/emilybaker-white/2022/11/30/TikTok-chinese -state-media-divisive-politics.

76.　Fergus Ryan et al., "Borrowing Mouths to Speak on Xinjiang," Australian Strategic Policy Institute, December 10, 2021, https://www.aspi.org.au /report/borrowing-mouths-speak-xinjiang.

77.　Beauchamp-Mustafaga and Chase, *Borrowing a Boat Out to Sea*, 95

78.　Zhong and Frenkel, "A Third of TikTok's U.S. Users May Be 14 or Under, Raising Safety Questions"; Chris Stokel-Walker, "Inside TikTok's Attempts to 'Downplay the China Association,'" Gizmodo, July 27, 2022, https://gizmodo .com/TikTok-master-messaging-pr-playbook-china-music-1849334736.

79.　Maria Nolan, "Rise in Technology Use Drastically Impairs Students' Attention Spans," *Arkansas Traveler*, November 3, 2022, https://www .uatrav.com/news/article_7f2d8272-5baf-11ed-b2c2-7b804a726297.html.

80.　Aleksandra, "TikTok Is Killing Your Brain, One Short-Form Video at a Time," Social Media Psychology, August 18, 2022, https://socialmediapsychology.eu /2022/08/18/TikTok-is-killing-your-brain-right-now/.

81.　Shivali Best, "Are YOU Hooked on TikTok? Scientists Reveal the Most Definitive Signs of Addiction to the App—and Say Lonely Women Are Most Likely to be Affected," *Daily Mail*, May 9, 2022, https://www.dailymail .co.uk/sciencetech/article-10796863/Scientists-reveal-key-signs-TikTok -addiction-lonely-women-likely-affected.html.

82.　Kari Paul, "What TikTok Does to Your Mental Health: 'It's Embarrassing We Know So Little,'" *Guardian*, October 30, 2022, https://www.theguardian .com/technology/2022/oct/30/TikTok-mental-health-social-media.

83.　Lindsay Dodgson, "Why TikTok Makes the Hours Seem to Melt Away, According to Experts Who Study How Our Brains Perceive Time," Insider, July 26, 2022, https://www.insider.com/why-time-passes-so-quickly-scrolling -on-TikTok-2022-7.

84. Elena Sanz, "How TikTok Affects the Brain," Exploring Your Mind, December 21, 2022, https://exploringyourmind.com/how-TikTok-affects -the-brain.

85. Alan Blotcky, "What's TikTok Doing to Our Kids?," *Daily News* [New York], November 18, 2021, https://www.nydailynews.com/opinion/ny-oped -whats-TikTok-doing-to-our-kids-20211118-32kx365w2ja6rhnoe2aoorkbpi -story.html.

86. Sri Rahayu and Tjitjik Hamidah, "The Correlation Between Narcissistic Tendency and Subjective Well Being with the Intensity of TikTok Social Media Use on Adolescents," *Advances in Social Science, Education and Humanities Research* 655 (2021): 1755–61, https://doi.org/10.2991/assehr.k .220404.285.

87. Jessica Flores, "Destructive 'Devious Licks' TikTok Trend Prompts Bay Area Campuses to Shut Restrooms," *San Francisco Chronicle*, September 23, 2021, https://www.sfchronicle.com/bayarea/article/Destructive-devious -licks-TikTok-trend-16482573.php.

88. Addison DeHaven, "TikTok Pranks No Laughing Matter," *Brookings* [SD] *Register*, November 4, 2021, https://brookingsregister.com/article/TikTok -pranks-no-laughing-matter.

89. Christine McCarthy, "Kids Seriously Injured in Dangerous TikTok Prank Gone Viral," Boston 25 News, February 19, 2020, https://www .boston25news.com/news/kids-seriously-injured-dangerous-prank-gone -viral/BTLNMXCAHVHRTK6YEBTVPPD7FE.

90. Kaye et al., *TikTok*, 61.

91. "Some Domestic Violent Extremists and Foreign Terrorist Organizations Exploiting TikTok," Office of Intelligence and Analysis, U.S. Department of Homeland Security, April 19, 2021, https://www.justsecurity.org/wp -content/uploads/2021/09/january-6-clearinghouse-dhs-ia-domestic-violent -extremists-dves-TikTok-april-19-2021.pdf, 1.

92. Hsu, "On TikTok, Election Misinformation Thrives Ahead of Midterms."

93. Gabriele Meiselwitz, ed., *Social Computing and Social Media: Participation, User Experience, Consumer Experience, and Applications of Social Computing* (Cham, Switzerland: Springer, 2020), 121.

94. "Industry Ethicist: Social Media Companies Amplifying Americans' Anger for Profit," CBS News, November 6, 2022, https://www.cbsnews.com/news /tristan-harris-social-media-political-polarization-60-minutes-2022-11-06; "About," Tristan Harris, https://www.tristanharris.com/#about.

95. Alex Tsiaoussidis, "Joe Rogan Explains Why TikTok in China Is 'Better' than the US," Dexerto, January 15, 2022, https://www.dexerto.com /entertainment/joe-rogan-explains-why-TikTok-in-china-is-better-than-the -us-1741211.

96. "Industry Ethicist: Social Media Companies Amplifying Americans' Anger for Profit."

97. "The Content on Chinese Douyin Is Better than American TikTok. Is This True?," Quora, https://www.quora.com/The-content-on-Chinese-Douyin-is-better-than-American-TikTok-Is-this-true.

98. "Douyin vs TikTok—The Differences You Never Knew (2022)," AdChina.io, https://www.adchina.io/douyin-vs-TikTok.

99. Juares Yip, "TikTok vs. Douyin: What's the Difference," Creators Network, February 7, 2022, https://creatorsnetwork.co/TikTok-vs-douyin-whats-the-difference.

100. Alex Kantrowitz, "Five Ways China Is Trying to Unaddict Kids from Social Media," Medium, November 24, 2021, https://debugger.medium.com/five-ways-china-is-trying-to-unaddict-kids-from-social-media-3e8f0e1d707c.

101. Zak Doffman, "Anonymous Hackers Target TikTok: 'Delete This Chinese Spyware Now,'" *Forbes*, July 1, 2020, https://www.forbes.com/sites/zakdoffman/2020/07/01/anonymous-targets-TikTok-delete-this-chinese-spyware-now.

102. James Coker, "Anonymous Hacking Group Declares 'Cyber War' Against Russia," Infosecurity Magazine, February 25, 2022, https://www.infosecurity-magazine.com/news/anonymous-hacking-group-cyber-war/.

103. Clive Hamilton, "Beware the Snarl of the Dragon: His Chilling Warnings of How China Infiltrated Britain Could Hardly Have Been More Timely—But Huawei Is Finally Dead, CLIVE HAMILTON Warns We Must Brace for the Backlash," *Daily Mail*, July 15, 2020, https://www.dailymail.co.uk/news/article-8523189/Beware-snarl-dragon-CLIVE-HAMILTON-warns-brace-Huawei-backlash-China.html.

104. Helberg, *The Wires of War*, 186.

105. Megan McCluskey, "TikTok Has Started Collecting Your 'Faceprints' and 'Voiceprints.' Here's What It Could Do with Them," *Time*, June 14, 2021, https://time.com/6071773/TikTok-faceprints-voiceprints-privacy.

106. Fabian Schmidt, "TikTok, WeChat & Co: How Does Spyware Get Into Smartphones?," Deutsche Welle, August 27, 2020, https://www.dw.com/en/TikTok-wechat-co-how-does-spyware-get-into-smartphones/a-54715740.

107. Ibid.

108. Emily Baker-White, "Leaked Audio from 80 Internal TikTok Meetings Shows That US User Data Has Been Repeatedly Accessed from China," BuzzFeed News, June 17, 2022, https://www.buzzfeednews.com/article/emilybakerwhite/TikTok-tapes-us-user-data-china-ByteDance-access.

109. James Paterson (@SenPaterson), "TikTok Australia has replied to my letter and admitted that Australian user data is also accessible in mainland China," Twitter, July 12, 2022, 2:38 p.m., https://twitter.com/SenPaterson/status/1546957121274621952.

110. Kokas, *Trafficking Data*, 106.

111. Easton, *The Final Struggle*, 137–38.

112. Donald Trump, "Executive Order on Addressing the Threat Posed by Tik-Tok," The White House, August 6, 2020, https://trumpwhitehouse.archives .gov/presidential-actions/executive-order-addressing-threat-posed-TikTok.

113. Adam Gabbatt, "TikTok App Poses Potential National Security Risk, Says Senior Democrat," *Guardian*, October 24, 2019, https://www.theguardian .com/technology/2019/oct/24/TikTok-foreign-interference-chuck-schumer -tom-cotton.

114. David Ingram, "The Movement to Ban TikTok: What the Midterms Could Mean for the Future of the App," NBC News, November 5, 2022, https:// www.nbcnews.com/tech/tech-news/TikTok-ban-midterm-election-vote -china-security-rcna49533.

115. James Fontanella-Khan and Miles Kruppa, "Trump's TikTok Dance: The Politicisation of American Business," *Australian Financial Review*, September 20, 2020, https://www.afr.com/technology/trump-s-TikTok -dance-the-politicisation-of-american-business-20200920-p55xdn.

116. Chen Hongwei, "融媒矩阵军事记者" [A Comparative Study on the Construction and Use of New Media in the Chinese and American Armies], http://www.81.cn/jsjz/2021-05/26/content_10039870.htm.

117. Lauren Feiner, "Biden Revokes and Replaces Trump Executive Order That Banned TikTok," CNBC, June 9, 2021, https://www.cnbc.com/2021/06/09 /biden-revokes-and-replaces-trump-executive-orders-that-banned-TikTok.html.

118. Sarah Mucha, "Biden Campaign Tells Staff to Delete TikTok from Their Phones," CNN, July 28, 2020, https://www.cnn.com/2020/07/28/politics /biden-campaign-TikTok/index.html.

119. Josh Boswell, "How American Investors in TikTok Have Been Schmoozing and Donating Millions to Democrats: Is It a Coincidence That Joe Biden Is Pushing to Let Chinese App Continue in U.S. Despite Growing Concerns About Its Real Agenda?," *Daily Mail*, October 5, 2022, https://www .dailymail.co.uk/news/article-11259273/US-investors-TikTok-donating -millions-Dems-Biden-pushes-let-Chinese-app-continue.html.

120. Schuman, "Why America Is Afraid of TikTok"; Rolfe Winkler, Jing Yang, and Alexander Osipovich, "Secretive High-Speed Trading Firm Hits Jackpot with TikTok," *Wall Street Journal*, October 1, 2020, https://www.wsj .com/articles/secretive-high-speed-trading-firm-hits-jackpot-with-TikTok -11601544610.

121. Ingram, "The Movement to Ban TikTok."

122. John D. McKinnon and Stu Woo, "The Billionaire Keeping TikTok on Phones in the U.S," *Wall Street Journal*, September 20, 2023, https://www.wsj.com /politics/policy/jeff-yass-TikTok-ByteDance-ban-congress-15a41ec4.

123. Juro Osawa and Shai Oster, "Sequoia Capital's China Arm Employed Daughter of Politburo Member," The Information, September 9, 2022, https://www.theinformation.com/articles/sequoia-capitals-china-arm-employed-daughter-of-politburo-member; "Mr. Neil Shen," Advisors, BOCHK Science and Technology Innovation Prize, https://stip.hk/en/advisory-committee-of-hkati/advisor/mr-neil-shen; Alex Konrad, "For Top VCs, ByteDance's Historic Windfall Remains a $220 Billion Mirage," Forbes, May 4, 2023, https://www.forbes.com/sites/alexkonrad/2023/05/04/ByteDance-scrutiny-leaves-midas-investors-waiting-billions/?sh=b8567ae3ccf3.

124. Boswell, "How American Investors in TikTok Have Been Schmoozing and Donating Millions to Democrats."

125. "ByteDance in Talks with Banks to Borrow over $3 bln, Sources Say," Reuters, September 8, 2021, https://www.reuters.com/technology/ByteDance-talks-borrow-up-5-bln-information-2021-09-08/.

126. Boswell, "How American Investors in TikTok Have Been Schmoozing and Donating Millions to Democrats."

127. Fontanella-Khan and Kruppa, "Trump's TikTok Dance."

128. "Client Profile: ByteDance Inc," 2022, OpenSecrets, https://www.opensecrets.org/federal-lobbying/clients/summary?cycle=2022&id=D000073174.

129. Jerry Dunleavy, "TikTok Spends Record Amount on Lobbying Blitz Targeting House, Senate, and White House," Washington Examiner, July 27, 2022, https://www.washingtonexaminer.com/policy/technology/TikTok-record-lobbying-spend-china-joe-biden; "David Thomas, Partner," Mehlman Consulting, https://mehlmancastagnetti.com/team-member/david-thomas; Hailey Fuchs, Clothilde Goujard, and Daniel Lippman, "The Campaign to Save TikTok Has Been Years in the Making," Politico, March 30, 2023, https://www.politico.com/news/2023/03/30/TikTok-bans-government-influence-campaigns-investigation-00089256.

130. Laura Olson, "Will a Pennsylvania Native Be Donald Trump's Chief of Staff?," Morning Call, March 30, 2019, https://www.mcall.com/news/pennsylvania/mc-trump-david-urban-lobbying-20170608-story.html.

131. Theodoric Meyer, "Chinese Companies Spend Big to Fend Off Trump," Politico, June 20, 2019, https://www.politico.com/story/2019/06/20/trump-china-zte-huawei-lobby-1371456.

132. Paul Mozur and Ana Swanson, "Chinese Tech Company Blocked from Buying American Components," New York Times, April 16, 2018, https://www.nytimes.com/2018/04/16/technology/chinese-tech-company-blocked-from-buying-american-components.html.

133. Chuck Ross, "Here's How the Biden Admin Lets TikTok's Chinese Parent Company Skirt Foreign Lobbying Disclosures," Washington Free Beacon, October 25, 2022, https://freebeacon.com/national-security/heres-how-the-biden-admin-lets-TikToks-chinese-parent-company-skirt-foreign-lobbying-disclosures.

134. Kirsten Grind and Erich Schwartzel, "TikTok's Behind-the-Scenes Help in Washington: Former Obama, Disney Advisers," *Wall Street Journal*, March 30, 2023, https://www.wsj.com/articles/TikToks-behind-the-scenes-help-in -washington-former-obama-disney-advisers-6ec2d63a.

135. "Biden Campaign Director Now Drafts TikTok's Misinfo Policies," Conservative News Daily, November 16, 2022, https://www .conservativenewsdaily.net/breaking-news/biden-campaign-director-now -drafts-TikToks-misinfo-policies.

136. "The Messina Group," Wellfound, https://wellfound.com/company//the-messina -group-1; "Isabelle Frances Wright," LinkedIn, https://www.linkedin.com /in/isabelle-frances-wright.

137. "Maureen Shanahan," LegiStorm, https://www.legistorm.com/person/bio /81720/Maureen_Shanahan.html.

138. Bobby Allyn, "Biden Approves Banning TikTok from Federal Government Phones," National Public Radio, December 30, 2022, https://www.npr .org/2022/12/20/1144519602/congress-is-about-to-ban-TikTok-from-u-s -government-phones.

139. Stephen Groves, "South Dakota Gov. Noem Bans TikTok from State-Owned Devices," Associated Press, November 29, 2022, https://apnews.com/article /south-dakota-bans-TikTok-from-state-devices-f7a95dd494dab9c410ff80c5 77c609dd.

140. Stokel-Walker, *TikTok Boom*, 194, 195.

141. "Shock Reason You Need to Delete TikTok Immediately," *New Zealand Herald*, July 3, 2020, https://www.nzherald.co.nz/lifestyle/shock-reason-you-need-to -delete-TikTok-immediately/H5RRNBHCXVWRS6L2HB4P5AYRQM.

142. John D. McKinnon, "Biden's TikTok Dilemma: A Ban Could Hurt Democrats More than Republicans," *Wall Street Journal*, March 13, 2023, https://www .wsj.com/articles/bidens-TikTok-dilemma-a-ban-could-hurt-democrats-more -than-republicans-a74bcf2a.

143. Taylor Lorenz, "Inside Democrats' Elaborate Attempt to Woo TikTok Influencers," *Washington Post*, October 27, 2022, https://www.washingtonpost .com/technology/2022/10/27/TikTok-democrats-influencers-biden.

144. McKinnon, "Biden's TikTok Dilemma."

145. Brittany Bernstein, "AOC Joins TikTok to Fight Against a Potential Ban," *National Review*, March 26, 2023, https://www.nationalreview.com/news /aoc-joins-TikTok-to-fight-against-a-potential-ban.

146. Danielle Wallace, "AOC TikTok Defense Ripped After Chinese Parent Company Gave 6-Figure Donations to Hispanic Caucus Nonprofits," Fox Business, March 26, 2023, https://www.foxbusiness.com/politics/aoc -TikTok-defense-ripped-chinese-parent-company-gave-6-figure-donations -hispanic-caucus-nonprofits; Gabe Kaminsky, "TikTok Lobbyist on Board of AOC-Advised Group Funded by China's ByteDance: 'Influence Peddling,'"

Washington Examiner, April 4, 2023, https://www.washingtonexaminer
.com/news/congress/TikTok-lobbyist-board-aoc-nonprofit-funded-by-Byte
Dance-china.

147. Rachel Schilke, "Schiff Uses TikTok to Speak on His Removal from Intelligence Committee," *Washington Examiner*, January 26, 2023, https:// www.washingtonexaminer.com/news/house/schiff-TikTok-removal-intel -committee.

148. "Schiff, Trahan Request Briefing from TikTok Ahead of Midterms on Strategy to Combat Election Disinformation," press release, Congressman Adam Schiff (website), October 27, 2022, https://schiff.house.gov/news/press -releases/schiff-trahan-request-briefing-from-TikTok-ahead-of-midterms-on -strategy-to-combat-election-disinformation.

149. Lara Korte, Jeremy B. White, Matthew Brown, and Ramon Castanos, "The Box That Hasn't Been Tik'd," Politico, March 24, 2023, https://www.politico .com/newsletters/california-playbook/2023/03/24/the-box-that-hasnt-been -tikd-00088696; Nikki Davidson, "Governors Love Using TikTok Even as States Ban It," Governing, April 23, 2023, https://www.governing.com /security/should-state-governors-delete-their-TikTok.

150. "Rubio Joins Hawley, Scott in Introducing Legislation to Ban TikTok from Government Devices," Marco Rubio, April 15, 2021, https://www.rubio .senate.gov/rubio-joins-hawley-scott-in-introducing-legislation-to-ban -TikTok-from-government-devices/.

151. Matthew Knott, "Trump Was Right on TikTok Threat: Leading Democrat," *Sydney Morning Herald*, October 25, 2022, https://www.smh.com.au /politics/federal/trump-was-right-on-TikTok-threat-leading-democrat -20221024-p5bsd3.html.

152. Shi Anbin Tongtong, "世界主义视域下的平台化思维：后疫情时代外宣媒体的纾困与升维" [Platform Thinking in the Context of Cosmopolitan View: The Relief and Promotion of the Media in the Post-epidemic Era], Recorded Future, no. 9, November 24, 2020.

153. Molly Roecker and Carol E. Lee, "White House Posts Video Created Using an App Owned by TikTok's Parent Company," NBC News, March 29, 2023, https://www.nbcconnecticut.com/news/national-international/white-house -posts-video-created-using-an-app-owned-by-TikToks-parent-company /3004250.

Chapter 8: Digital Entertainment

1. Salvador Rodriguez, "TikTok Parent ByteDance Sees Losses Swell in Push for Growth," *Wall Street Journal*, October 6, 2022, https://www.wsj.com /articles/TikTok-parent-ByteDance-sees-losses-swell-in-push-for-growth -11665071238.

2. Andy Robinson, "Tencent Is Reportedly Refocusing on 'Aggressively Seeking' Full Games Company Acquisitions," VGC, October 1, 2022, https://www.videogameschronicle.com/news/tencent-is-reportedly-refocusing-on-aggressively-seeking-full-games-company-acquisitions.

3. Kokas, *Trafficking Data*, 120.

4. Ibid., 132, 133, 135.

5. Ibid., 121.

6. Dalton Cooper, "Report Reveals Most-Played Games Ever Made," Game Rant, September 11, 2020, https://gamerant.com/fortnite-most-played-game-ever; "Epic Games," Giant Bomb, https://www.giantbomb.com/epic-games/3010-149.

7. Kokas, *Trafficking Data*, 129.

8. Ibid.

9. Tyler Job, "John Cena Character Outfit Coming to Popular Video Game Fortnite," NBC 26 WGBA-TV, July 26, 2022, https://www.nbc26.com/news/national/john-cena-character-outfit-coming-to-popular-video-game-fortnite.

10. Matt Perez, "Tencent Buys Majority Stake in 'Clash of Clans' Developer Supercell," *Forbes*, October 23, 2019, https://www.forbes.com/sites/mattperez/2019/10/23/tencent-buys-majority-stake-in-clash-of-clans-developer-supercell.

11. Kokas, *Trafficking Data*, 117.

12. Sam Shead, "Chinese Tech Giants Are Snapping Up Gaming Studios Around the World," CNBC, July 28, 2021, https://www.cnbc.com/2021/07/28/chinese-tech-giants-are-snapping-up-gaming-studios-around-the-world.html.

13. David Leino, translation of cadet handbook.

14. Yujie Xue, Jane Zhang, and Josh Ye, "Trump's Latest Moves Against Xiaomi, China Tech Will Have Little Immediate Impact, Experts Say," *South China Morning Post*, January 15, 2021, https://www.scmp.com/tech/policy/article/3117928/trumps-latest-moves-against-xiaomi-china-tech-will-have-little.

15. Joseph Cox, "AI-Generated Voice Firm Clamps Down After 4chan Makes Celebrity Voices for Abuse," Vice News, January 30, 2023, https://www.vice.com/en/article/dy7mww/ai-voice-firm-4chan-celebrity-voices-emma-watson-joe-rogan-elevenlabs.

16. Kokas, *Trafficking Data*, 121.

17. Stella Chen, "Gaming for the China Story," China Media Project, January 25, 2022, https://chinamediaproject.org/2022/01/25/gaming-for-the-china-story.

18.   Ibid.

19.   David Leino, translation of cadet handbook.

20.   Chen, "Gaming for the China Story."

21.   Will Jarvis, "Chinese Genshin Impact Is One of the Most Profitable Video Games on Earth. It Balances Mass Appeal with Beijing's Blessing," The World, June 21, 2022, https://theworld.org/stories/2022-06-21/chinese -genshin-impact-one-most-profitable-video-games-earth-it-balances-mass.

22.   "Top Free Games," App Store, https://apps.apple.com/us/charts/iphone /adventure-games/7002.

23.   Jarvis, "Chinese Genshin Impact Is One of the Most Profitable Video Games on Earth."

Chapter 9: The People's Republic of Hollywood

1.   Martin and Williamson, "Mapping Chinese Influence in Hollywood," 21–23.

2.   Ibid., 22–24.

3.   Ibid., 20–21.

4.   Julie Makinen, "Why Captain America's Keepers, the Russo Brothers, Are Turning to China for Inspiration," Los Angeles Times, April 28, 2016, https://www.latimes.com/entertainment/herocomplex/la-et-hc-marvel-civil -war-china-joe-russo-20160427-story.html.

5.   David Thompson, "Russo Brothers Say Avengers: Infinity War and Endgame were Political Tools," The Direct, March 5, 2021, https://thedirect.com /article/avengers-endgame-infinity-war-russo-brothers-marvel-political.

6.   Michael Nordine, "As China Dominates the Global Box Office, a Look at the Movies Giving Hollywood a Run for Its Mondy," IndieWire, April 30, 2018, https://www.indiewire.com/features/general/chinese-box-office-wolf -warrior-2-1201956049/.

7.   Zheping Huang, "China's Answer to Rambo Is About Punishing Those Who Offend China—and It's Killing It in Theaters," Quartz, August 8, 2017, https://qz.com/1048667/wolf-warriors-2-chinas-answer-to-rambo-and -about-punishing-those-who-offend-china-is-killing-it-at-the-box-office.

8.   Sarah J. Clifford and Scott N. Romaniuk, "*Wolf Warrior II* (战狼2) and the Manipulation of Chinese Nationalism," *The Palgrave Encyclopedia of Global Security Studies*, 2021, 1–5, https://doi.org/10.1007/978-3-319 -74336-3_657-1.

9.   "Chinese Embassy Holds a Movie Reception of 'Wolf Warrior 2,'" Embassy of the People's Republic of China in the Republic of South Africa, November 17, 2017, http://za.china-embassy.gov.cn/eng/sgxw/201801/t20180130_6096420 .htm.

10. Makinen, "Why Captain America's Keepers, the Russo Brothers, Are Turning to China for Inspiration."

11. Patrick Brzeski, "'Wolf Warrior II' Star Frank Grillo on How China's $780M Blockbuster Was Made," *Hollywood Reporter*, August 22, 2017, https://www.hollywoodreporter.com/news/general-news/wolf-warrior-2-star-frank-grillo-how-chinas-780m-blockbuster-was-made-1031929.

12. Ben Travis, "Russo Brothers Tackling Non-Marvel Projects and Setting Up Studio After Avengers 4," *Empire*, April 27, 2018, https://www.empireonline.com/movies/news/russo-brothers-tackling-non-marvel-projects-setting-studio-avengers-4.

13. Erich Schwartzel, "Hollywood's Latest Power Brothers Hunt for the Next China-Backed Blockbuster," *Wall Street Journal*, March 12, 2018, https://www.wsj.com/articles/hollywoods-latest-power-brothers-hunt-for-the-next-china-backed-blockbuster-1520852400.

14. Patrick Brzeski, "Russo Brothers Launch Studio to Produce Chinese-Language Films," *Hollywood Reporter*, March 13, 2016, https://www.hollywoodreporter.com/news/general-news/russo-brothers-launch-studio-produce-874955.

15. Makinen, "Why Captain America's Keepers, the Russo Brothers, Are Turning to China for Inspiration."

16. James Politi, "Hollywood Mogul Pledges 'All the Resources' Joe Biden Needs to Win in 2024," *Financial Times*, May 11, 2023, https://www.ft.com/content/43bf35f8-e000-41a4-848e-272dd71f3930.

17. Joshua Kurlantzick, *Beijing's Global Media Offensive: China's Uneven Campaign to Influence Asia and the World* (Oxford, UK: Oxford University Press, 2022), 302.

18. Martin and Williamson, "Mapping Chinese Influence in Hollywood," 29.

19. Ibid., 35, 41.

20. Kurlantzick, *Beijing's Global Media Offensive*, 301.

21. Manuel Hermosilla, Fernanda Gutiérrez, and Juan Prieto-Rodriguez, "Can Emerging Markets Tilt Global Product Design? Impacts of Chinese Colorism on Hollywood Castings," Carey Business School Research Paper No. 17-13, Johns Hopkins Carey Business School, October 2017, https://dx.doi.org/10.2139/ssrn.3047403, 1.

22. Ibid., 8.

23. Martin and Williamson, "Mapping Chinese Influence in Hollywood," 36.

24. "DreamWorks China Venture to Produce First Animation in 2016," Xinhua Economic News Service, March 20, 2012; Martha Bayles, *Through a Screen Darkly: Popular Culture, Public Diplomacy, and America's Image Abroad* (New Haven, CT: Yale University Press, 2014), 52–53.

25. Martin and Williamson, "Mapping Chinese Influence in Hollywood," 39–40.

26. Kurlantzick, *Beijing's Global Media Offensive*, 303.

27. Ralph Jennings, "China Launches Propaganda for Recognition of Disputed Maritime Claims," Voice of America, July 27, 2020, https://www.voanews .com/a/east-asia-pacific_china-launches-propaganda-recognition-disputed -maritime-claims/6193497.html.

28. Tim Brayton, "Over the Moon (2020)," Alternate Ending, October 30, 2020, https://www.alternateending.com/2020/10/over-the-moon-2020.html.

29. Nancy Tartaglione, "China's Alibaba Takes Stake in Steven Spielberg's Amblin; Will Team on Global Pics," Deadline Hollywood, October 9, 2016, https://deadline.com/2016/10/amblin-alibaba-china-deal-equity-stake -steven-spielberg-marketing-distribution-1201833550.

30. Bob Tourtellotte and Paul Eckert, "Steven Spielberg Quits as Adviser to Olympics over Darfur," Reuters, February 12, 2008, https://www.reuters .com/article/us-olympics-spielberg/steven-spielberg-quits-as-adviser-to -olympics-over-darfur-idUSN1231478420080212.

31. Martin and Williamson, "Mapping Chinese Influence in Hollywood," 21.

32. Hermosilla et al., "Can Emerging Markets Tilt Global Product Design?," 8.

33. Martin and Williamson, "Mapping Chinese Influence in Hollywood," 41.

34. Song Hwee Lim, "Soft Power and Cinema: A Methodological Reflection and Some Chinese Inflections," in *Cinema and Soft Power: Configuring the National and Transnational in Geo-Politics*, edited by Stephanie Dennison and Rachel Dwyer (Edinburgh: Edinburgh University Press, 2023), 21, 22, https://doi.org/10.3366/edinburgh/9781474456272.003.0002.

35. "What Video Games Teach Us About Politics," Political Science at Haverford College, November 1, 2022, https://pols.sites.haverford.edu /studentvoices/what-video-games-teach-us-about-politics; Xu Fan, "China's Role in 'Midway' Success," *China Daily*, November 13, 2019, https://www .chinadaily.com.cn/a/201911/13/WS5dcb9b9da310cf3e35577187.html.

36. Lucas Shaw, "Fearing Chinese Censors, Paramount Changes 'World War Z,'" TheWrap, March 31, 2013, https://www.thewrap.com/fearing-chinese -censors-paramount-changes-world-war-z-exclusive-83316.

37. Martin and Williamson, "Mapping Chinese Influence in Hollywood," 41.

38. Ibid., 45.

39. Ibid., 46.

40. Sen-Lun Yu and John Hazelton, "Co-production: How to Solve a Chinese Puzzle," *Screen International*, June 12, 2008, https://www.screendaily.com /co-productionhow-to-solve-a-chinese-puzzle/4039379.article.

41. Martin and Williamson, "Mapping Chinese Influence in Hollywood," 47.

42. Chris Homewood, "The Limits of Hollywood as an Instrument of Chinese

Public Diplomacy and Soft Power," in *Cinema and Soft Power: Configuring the National and Transnational in Geo-Politics*, edited by Stephanie Dennison and Rachel Dwyer (Edinburgh: Edinburgh University Press, 2023), 100.

43. David S. Cohen, "'Transformers': A Splendidly Patriotic Film, If You Happen to Be Chinese," *Variety*, July 3, 2014, https://variety.com/2014/film/columns /transformers-age-of-extinction-patriotic-for-china-1201257030.

44. Homewood, "The Limits of Hollywood as an Instrument of Chinese Public Diplomacy and Soft Power," 100.

Chapter 10: Social Engineering a Pandemic

1. *State of Missouri, et al., v. Joseph R. Biden Jr., et al.*, 293 So. 169 (W.D. La., 2022), deposition of Dr. Anthony Fauci, https://ago.mo.gov/docs /default-source/press-releases/135885afauci112322_full_redacted.pdf; Nick Brown and Jonathan Allen, "New York City Crematories Work Overtime as Coronavirus Brings Backlog of Bodies," *Reuters*, April 2, 2020, https:// www.reuters.com/article/us-health-coronavirus-usa-bodies/new-york -city-crematories-work-overtime-as-coronavirus-brings-backlog-of-bodies -idUSKBN21K27D.

2. Alastair Gee, "Texas Doctor, 28, Dies of COVID: 'She Wore the Same Mask for Weeks, if Not Months,'" *Guardian*, October 7, 2020, https://www .theguardian.com/us-news/2020/oct/07/texas-doctor-adeline-fagan-covid -coronavirus.

3. Li Shenming, "The World Landscape and the China-U.S. Relations in the Wake of the COVID-19 Pandemic," in *China's Fight Against the COVID-19 Epidemic: Its International Contribution and Significance in the Eyes of the World*, edited by Jiang Hui (Reading, UK: Paths International, 2020), 7, 9.

4. Sarah Al-Arshani, "Supreme Court Justice Neil Gorsuch Calls COVID-19 Response 'The Greatest Intrusion on Civil Liberties in Peacetime History,'" Business Insider, May 20, 2023, https://www.businessinsider.com/supreme -court-justice-neil-gorsuch-pandemic-covid-reponse-civil-liberties-2023-5.

5. Elaine Okanyene Nsoesie et al., "Analysis of Hospital Traffic and Search Engine Data in Wuhan China Indicates Early Disease Activity in the Fall of 2019," Harvard University, 2020, http://nrs.harvard.edu/urn-3:HUL .InstREpos:42669767, 1.

6. Katherine Eban, "The Lab-Leak Theory: Inside the Fight to Uncover COVID-19's Origins," *Vanity Fair*, June 3, 2021, https://www.vanityfair.com/news /2021/06/the-lab-leak-theory-inside-the-fight-to-uncover-covid-19s-origins.

7. Michael Houston, "More Athletes Claim They Contracted COVID-19 at Military World Games," Inside the Games, May 17, 2020, https://www .insidethegames.biz/articles/1094347/world-military-games-illness-covid-19.

8. Diane Francis, "Diane Francis: Canadian Forces Have Right to Know if They Got COVID at the 2019 Military World Games in Wuhan," *Financial Post*, June 25, 2021, https://financialpost.com/diane-francis/diane-francis -canadian-forces-have-right-to-know-if-they-got-covid-at-the-2019-military -world-games-in-wuhan.

9. Eban, "The Lab-Leak Theory."

10. Josephine Ma, "Coronavirus: China's First Confirmed Covid-19 Case Traced Back to November 17," *South China Morning Post*, March 13, 2020, https:// www.scmp.com/news/china/society/article/3074991/coronavirus-chinas -first-confirmed-covid-19-case-traced-back.

11. Mike Stobbe, "More Evidence Suggests COVID-19 Was in US by Christmas 2019," Associated Press, June 15, 2021, https:// apnews.com/article/more-evidence-covid-in-us-by-christmas-2019 -11346afc5e18eee81ebcf35d9e6caee2; Kate Kelland, "Italy Sewage Study Suggests COVID-19 Was There in December 2019," Reuters, June 19, 2020, https://www.reuters.com/article/us-health-coronavirus-italy-sewage /italy-sewage-study-suggests-covid-19-was-there-in-december-2019 -idUSKBN23Q1J9.

12. Sandip Sen, "How China Locked Down Internally for COVID-19, but Pushed Foreign Travel," *Economic Times*, April 30, 2020, https://economictimes .indiatimes.com/blogs/Whathappensif/how-china-locked-down-internally -for-covid-19-but-pushed-foreign-travel/.

13. "The Origins of Covid-19: An Investigation of the Wuhan Institute of Virology," House Foreign Affairs Committee Report, 117th Cong., August 2021, https://foreignaffairs.house.gov/wp-content/uploads/2021/08 /ORIGINS-OF-COVID-19-REPORT.pdf, 13.

14. Gao Yu et al., "In Depth: How Early Signs of a SARS-like Virus Were Spotted, Spread, and Throttled," Caixin, February 29, 2020, https://www .caixinglobal.com/2020-02-29/in-depth-how-early-signs-of-a-sars-like-virus -were-spotted-spread-and-throttled-101521745.html; Monika Chansoria, "Biological Weapons the Focus of China's Military Research in the Last 20 Years," JAPAN Forward, March 25, 2020, https://japan-forward.com /biological-weapons-the-focus-of-chinas-military-research-in-the-last-20 -years.

15. Jasper Becker, *Made in China: Wuhan, Covid and the Quest for Biotech Supremacy* (London: C. Hurst, 2021), 225.

16. *Biden Jr., et al.*, 293 So. 169 (W.D. La., 2022), deposition of Dr. Anthony Fauci, 34.

17. Eban, "The Lab-Leak Theory."

18. Becker, *Made in China*, 187–88.

19. Alina Chan and Matt Ridley, *Viral: The Search for the Origin of COVID-19* (New York: HarperCollins, 2021), 53.

20. "New Analytic Technique Indicates China Likely Hid Severity of COVID-19 from the International Community While It Stockpiled Medical Supplies," U.S. Department of Homeland Security, May 1, 2020, https://www.scribd .com/document/459791553/New-Analytic-Technique#.

21. Ibid.

22. Ibid.

23. World Health Organization (@WHO), "Preliminary investigations conducted by the Chinese authorities have found no clear evidence of human-to-human transmission of the novel #coronavirus," Twitter, January 14, 2020, 4:18 a.m., https://twitter.com/WHO/status/1217043229427761152.

24. Scott Gottlieb, *Uncontrolled Spread: Why Covid-19 Crushed Us and How We Can Defeat the Next Pandemic* (New York: HarperCollins, 2021), 56, 59–60.

25. Ibid., 43.

26. Shannon Molloy, "China is Infiltrating Australia on Multiple Fronts, from Politics to Business, via Its Powerful and Covert United Front Agency," news.com.au, June 11, 2020, https://www.news.com.au/finance/economy /australian-economy/china-is-infiltrating-australia-on-multiple-fronts-from -politics-to-business-via-its-powerful-and-covert-united-front-agency/news -story/9318c7799e540164dd0b985b9e8969c2.

27. Cooper, *Wilful Blindness*, 357.

28. Sam Cooper, "United Front Groups in Canada Helped Beijing Stockpile Coronavirus Safety Supplies," Global News, April 30, 2020, https:// globalnews.ca/news/6858818/coronavirus-china-united-front-canada -protective-equipment-shortage; Sheridan Prasso, "China's Epic Dash for PPE Left the World Short on Masks," Bloomberg, September 17, 2020, https://www.bloomberg.com/news/articles/2020-09-17/behind-china-s-epic -dash-for-ppe-that-left-the-world-short-on-masks.

29. Keith Bradsher and Liz Alderman, "The World Needs Masks. China Makes Them, but Has Been Hoarding Them," *New York Times*, April 2, 2020, https://www.nytimes.com/2020/03/13/business/masks-china-coronavirus .html.

30. Clifford D. May, "Did Chinese Communist Party Intend for COVID-19 to Destabilize a Disunited United States?," *Washington Times*, June 2, 2020, https://www.washingtontimes.com/news/2020/jun/2/did-chinese-communist party-intend-for-covid-19-to.

31. Prasso, "China's Epic Dash for PPE Left the World Short on Masks."

32. Myah Ward, "15 Times Trump Praised China as Coronavirus Was Spreading Across the Globe," Politico, April 15, 2020, https://www.politico.com/news /2020/04/15/trump-china-coronavirus-188736.

33. U.S. Mission China, "The United States Announces Assistance to the

COVID-19," U.S. Embassy & Consulates in China, February 7, 2020, https://china.usembassy-china.org.cn/the-united-states-announces-assistance-to-the-novel-coronavirus.

34. "New Analytic Technique Indicates China Likely Hid Severity of COVID-19 from the International Community While It Stockpiled Medical Supplies."

35. Warren Fiske, "Fact-Check: Did Fauci Say Coronavirus Was 'Nothing to Worry About'?," *Austin American-Statesman*, April 29, 2020, https://www.statesman.com/story/news/politics/elections/2020/04/29/fact-check-did-fauci-say-coronavirus-was-nothing-to-worry-about/984113007; Stephen Sorace, "Fauci, Who Opposed China Travel Ban and Praised Their Transparency, Criticizes Trump Response," FOX News, March 11, 2021, https://www.foxnews.com/politics/fauci-china-travel-ban-coronavirus-transparency-criticizes-trump-response.

36. Quint Forgey, "Fauci Endorses National Stay-at-Home Order: 'I Just Don't Understand Why We're Not Doing That,'" Politico, April 3, 2020, https://www.politico.com/news/2020/04/03/fauci-endorses-national-stay-at-home-order-162794.

37. Xi Jinping, "坚持和完善中国特色社会主义制度推进国家治理体系和治理能力现代化" [Insist On and Improve the System of Socialism with Chinese Characteristics and Advance the Modernization of the National Governance System and Its Governance Capabilities], Qiushi, January 1, 2020, http://www.qstheory.cn/dukan/qs/2020-01/01/c_1125402833.htm.

38. Ian Easton, *The Final Struggle: Inside China's Global Strategy* (Norwalk, CT: Eastbridge Books, 2022), 57, 58.

39. Ibid., 61–62.

40. The author owes a debt to Michael P. Senger for his writing in *Tablet* and his book *Snake Oil: How Xi Jinping Shut Down the World* (New York: Plenary Press, 2021), on how lockdowns came to the West. Though I do not agree with all his conclusions about the virus, his insight into the politics of lockdowns is very illuminating. I have independently confirmed all the sources he used in his reporting.

41. "China: Events of 2020," Human Rights Watch, https://www.hrw.org/world-report/2021/country-chapters/china.

42. Noreen Qualls et al., "Community Mitigation Guidelines to Prevent Pandemic Influenza—United States, 2017," *Recommendations and Reports* 66, no. 1 (April 2017): 1–34, http://dx.doi.org/10.15585/mmwr.rr6601a1.

43. Thomas V. Inglesby et al., "Disease Mitigation Measures in the Control of Pandemic Influenza," *Biosecurity and Bioterrorism: Biodefense Strategy, Practice, and Science* 4, no. 4 (December 2006): 366–75, https://doi.org/10.1089/bsp.2006.4.366.

44. Michael Senger, "The Deeper History of 'Social Distancing'—The Western

Term for Lockdown," Brownstone Institute, September 13, 2022, https://brownstone.org/articles/real-story-of-social-distancing.

45. John Fund, "'Professor Lockdown' Modeler Resigns in Disgrace," *National Review*, May 6, 2020, https://www.nationalreview.com/corner/professor-lockdown-modeler-resigns-in-disgrace; The Editorial Board, "Worst-Case Coronavirus Science," *Wall Street Journal*, March 27, 2020, https://www.wsj.com/articles/worst-case-coronavirus-science-11585351059.

46. Kylie E. C. Ainsley et al., "Report 11: Evidence of Initial Success for China Exiting COVID-19 Social Distancing Policy After Achieving Containment," Imperial College COVID-19 Response Team, March 24, 2020, https://spiral.imperial.ac.uk/bitstream/10044/1/77646/11/2020-03-24-COVID19-Report-11.pdf.

47. Katherine Rushton and Daniel Foggo, "Neil Ferguson, the Scientist Who Convinced Boris Johnson of UK Coronavirus Lockdown, Criticised in Past for Flawed Research," *Daily Telegraph*, March 28, 2020, https://www.telegraph.co.uk/news/2020/03/28/neil-ferguson-scientist-convinced-boris-johnson-uk-coronavirus-lockdown-criticised.

48. Gottlieb, *Uncontrolled Spread*, 206.

49. Andrew Scheuber, "Chinese President Sees UK-China Academic Partnerships at Imperial," Imperial College London, October 21, 2015, https://www.imperial.ac.uk/news/168497/chinese-president-sees-uk-china-academic-partnerships.

50. Chai Hua, "Tsinghua Signs Cooperation Agreements with Five Global Universities," *China Daily*, October 18, 2018, https://www.chinadaily.com.cn/a/201810/18/WS5bc86f7da310eff30328335c.html.

51. Hannah Devlin, "Imperial College to Shut Joint Research Ventures with Chinese Defence Firms," *Guardian*, September 11, 2022, https://www.theguardian.com/world/2022/sep/11/imperial-college-to-shut-joint-research-ventures-with-chinese-defence-firms.

52. "They claimed to have flattened the curve. I was sceptical at first. I thought it was a massive cover-up by the Chinese. But as the data accrued it became clear it was an effective policy." Tom Whipple, "Professor Neil Ferguson: People Don't Agree with Lockdown and Try to Undermine the Scientists," *The Times*, December 25, 2020, https://www.thetimes.co.uk/article/people-don-t-agree-with-lockdown-and-try-to-undermine-the-scientists-gnms7mp98.

53. *Biden Jr., et al.*, 293 So. 169 (W.D. La., 2022), deposition of Dr. Anthony Fauci, 139; Becky Kark, "Fauci Assistant: Mixed Messages Hurt U.S. Pandemic Response," *South Haven Tribune*, February 28, 2021, https://www.heraldpalladium.com/southhaventribune/localnews/fauci-assistant-mixed-messages-hurt-u-s-pandemic-response/article_1919910d-d992-5868-9272-cfe60afde709.html.

54. Bob Woodward, *Rage* (New York: Simon & Schuster, 2020), 250.

55. *Biden Jr., et al.*, 293 So. 169 (W.D. La., 2022), deposition of Dr. Anthony Fauci, 164.

56. John Power, "Why China's COVID Figures Don't Add Up," Aljazeera, December 9, 2022, https://www.aljazeera.com/economy/2022/12/9/why -chinas-covid-figures-are-hard-to-take-at-face-value.

57. *Biden Jr., et al.*, 293 So. 169 (W.D. La., 2022), deposition of Dr. Anthony Fauci, 165.

58. Ibid., 263.

59. Ibid., 166.

60. Anthony S. Fauci, H. Clifford Lane, and Robert R. Redfield, "COVID-19— Navigating the Uncharted," *New England Journal of Medicine* 382, no. 13 (March 2020): 1268–69, https://doi.org/10.1056/NEJMe2002387.

61. Doug Gollan, "COVID-19 Travel Update: Fauci Says Cruising Is OK If You Are Healthy," *Forbes*, March 9, 2020, https://www.forbes.com/sites /douggollan/2020/03/09/fauci-says-cruising-is-ok-if-you-are-healthy.

62. Associated Press, "Fauci Open to a 14-Day National Shutdown to Stem Coronavirus," *Los Angeles Times*, March 15, 2020, https://www.latimes .com/world-nation/story/2020-03-15/fauci-open-to-a-14-day-national -shutdown-to-stem-virus.

63. Anthony Fauci, email message to Melinda Haskins, "RE: Please Review: House Oversight Letter on Coronavirus Diagnostics," March 6, 2020, https:// s3.documentcloud.org/documents/20793561/leopold-nih-foia-anthony-fauci -emails.pdf, 345.

64. Jason Horowitz and Steven Erlanger, "Italy Gives Xi, and China's Vast Infrastructure Project, a Royal Welcome," *New York Times*, March 22, 2019, https://www.nytimes.com/2019/03/22/world/europe/italy-china-xi -road.html.

65. Michael P. Senger, "Neil Ferguson, China and a Fanatical Socialist Health Minister: The Untold Story of How Lockdowns Came to Italy and the West," The Daily Sceptic, August 5, 2022, https://dailysceptic.org/2022/08/05/neil -ferguson-china-and-a-fanatical-socialist-health-minister-the-untold-story -of-how-lockdowns-came-to-italy-and-the-west.

66. Michael P. Senger, "China's Global Lockdown Propaganda Campaign," *Tablet*, September 15, 2020, https://www.tabletmag.com/sections/news /articles/china-covid-lockdown-propaganda.

67. Deborah Birx, *Silent Invasion: The Untold Story of the Trump Administration, Covid-19, and Preventing the Next Pandemic Before It's Too Late* (New York: HarperCollins, 2022), 138.

68. Jason Hahn, "City Fills Skatepark with 37 Tons of Sand to Keep Kids and Parents Away amid Coronavirus," *People*, April 17, 2020, https://people

.com/human-interest/city-fills-skatepark-with-37-tons-sand-coronavirus/; Hannah Fry, "Paddle Boarder Chased by Boat, Arrested in Malibu After Flouting Coronavirus Closures," *Los Angeles Times*, April 3, 2020, https:// www.latimes.com/california/story/2020-04–03/paddle-boarder-arrested-in -malibu-after-flouting-coronavirus-closures.

69. Anjalee Khemlani, "Coronavirus Update: New York, California, and Illinois Take Drastic Measures as US Cases Skyrocket," Yahoo! News, March 20, 2020, https://www.yahoo.com/now/coronavirus-update-new-york-california -take-drastic-measures-as-us-cases-skyrocket-171823088.html.

70. Michael P. Senger, "The Masked Ball of Cowardice," *Tablet*, August 29, 2021, https://www.tabletmag.com/sections/news/articles/masked-ball-cowardice.

71. Kate Conger, "Twitter Removes Chinese Disinformation Campaign," *New York Times*, June 17, 2020, https://www.nytimes.com/2020/06/11/technology /twitter-chinese-misinformation.html.

72. Senger, "China's Global Lockdown Propaganda Campaign."

73. Io Dodds, "China Floods Facebook with Undeclared Coronavirus Propaganda Ads Blaming Trump," *Daily Telegraph*, April 5, 2020, https://www.telegraph .co.uk/technology/2020/04/05/china-floods-facebook-instagram-undeclared -coronavirus-propaganda.

74. Quoted in Steven W. Mosher, *The Politically Incorrect Guide to Pandemics* (Washington, DC: Regnery Publishing, 2022), 146.

75. Mary Meisenzahl, "'We Are Trying to Save Lives, Not Be Big Brother': U.S. Police Are Facing Backlash for Using 'Dystopian' Drones to Ask People to Stay Home," Insider, April 23, 2020, https://www.businessinsider.com/us -police-drones-enforce-coronavirus-stay-at-home-orders-2020-4; Zachary Evans, "Chinese Company Suspected of Spying on U.S. Citizens Donates Police Drones to 22 States," *National Review*, April 20, 2020, https:// www.nationalreview.com/news/chinese-company-suspected-of-spying-on -u-s-citizens-donates-police-drones-to-22-states; Mercy A. Kuo, "Pentagon Blacklists Chinese Drone Maker DJI for PLA Links," *Diplomat*, November 15, 2022, https://thediplomat.com/2022/11/pentagon-blacklists-chinese -drone-maker-dji-for-pla-links.

76. Kiran Stacey and Patrick McGee, "California Police to Use Drones to Patrol Coronavirus Lockdown," *Financial Times*, March 20, 2020, https://www.ft .com/content/c7d0dee1-6125-475c-9cc7-78f4671d7cea.

77. Susan Wood, "Northern California Citizens Call Tip Lines on Mask, Social Distancing Offenders," *North Bay* [CA] *Business Journal*, August 24, 2020, https://www.northbaybusinessjournal.com/article/industrynews/northern -california-citizens-call-out-mask-social-distancing-offenders.

78. Cheryl K. Chumley, *Lockdown: The Socialist Plan to Take Away Your Freedom* (West Palm Beach, FL: Humanix, 2022), 53–54.

79. Anna Fifield, "As Coronavirus Goes Global, China's Xi Asserts Victory on

First Trip to Wuhan Since Outbreak," *Washington Post*, March 10, 2020, https://www.washingtonpost.com/world/asia_pacific/chinas-xi-attempts-a -coronavirus-victory-lap-with-visit-to-wuhan/2020/03/10/ca585ddc-6281 -11ea-8a8e-5c5336b32760_story.html.

80. Peter Hessler, "How China Controlled the Coronavirus," *New Yorker*, August 10, 2020, https://www.newyorker.com/magazine/2020/08/17/how -china-controlled-the-coronavirus.

81. Geremie R. Barmé, "The Good Caucasian of Sichuan and Kumbaya China: Viral Alarm," China Heritage, September 1, 2020, https://chinaheritage.net /journal/the-good-caucasian-of-sichuan-kumbaya-china.

82. Talha Burki, "China's Successful Control of COVID-19," *Lancet* 20, no. 11 (November 2020): 1240–41, https://doi.org/10.1016/S1473-3099(20)30800 -8.

83. Chris Mooney and Gerry Shih, "The U.S. Has Absolutely No Control over the Coronavirus. China Is on Top of the Tiniest Risks," *Washington Post*, November 10, 2020, https://www.washingtonpost.com/health/2020/11/10 /us-has-absolutely-no-control-over-coronavirus-china-is-top-tiniest-risks.

84. Javier C. Hernández, "U.S. Says Virus Can't Be Controlled. China Aims to Prove It Wrong," *New York Times*, November 17, 2020, https://www .nytimes.com/2020/10/30/world/asia/china-covid-coronavirus.html.

85. Renee DiResta et al., "Telling China's Story: The Chinese Communist Party's Campaign to Shape Global Narratives," Stanford Digital Repository, 2022, https://stacks.stanford.edu/file/druid:pf306sw8941/sio-china_story_white _paper-final.pdf, 34.

86. Ibid., 33.

87. Ibid., 34.

88. Steerpike, "Sage Scientist Claims Social Distancing Should Remain 'Forever,'" *Spectator*, June 10, 2021, https://www.spectator.co.uk/article/covid-professor -claims-social-distancing-should-remain-forever; Angela Dewan, "This Pandemic Risks Bringing Out the Worst in Humanity," CNN, March 15, 2020, https://www.cnn.com/2020/03/15/world/coronavirus-humanity-global -response-intl/index.html; Ivana Kottasová, "The Muddled Public Message on Coronavirus Isn't Just Confusing. It's Harmful," CNN, July 16, 2020, https:// www.cnn.com/2020/07/16/health/coronavirus-pandemic-communication -intl/index.html.

89. Ben Ellery, "BBC 'Lacking Balance' in Interview with Hard-Left Scientist Susan Michie," *The Times*, November 29, 2021, https://www.thetimes.co .uk/article/bbc-lacking-balance-in-interview-with-hard-left-scientist-susan -michie-jdsxcfrqt.

90. Professor Susan Michie (@SusanMichie), "Exemplary response to home confinement of children due to #COVID19 in China. Could UK Government do this?," Twitter, March 3, 2020, 7:52 a.m., https://twitter

.com/SusanMichie/status/1234854069392625664; Steerpike, "Sage Scientist Claims Social Distancing Should Remain 'Forever'"; Jordan Lancaster, "COVID Lockdown Zealot Gets into Testy Exchange When Host Asks About Her Membership in Communist Party," Daily Caller, July 7, 2021, https://dailycaller.com/2021/07/07/covid-lockdown-susan-michie-host -richard-madeley-membership-communist-party.

91. Mallory Simon, "Over 1,000 Health Professionals Sign a Letter Saying, Don't Shut Down Protests Using Coronavirus Concerns as an Excuse," CNN, June 5, 2020, https://www.cnn.com/2020/06/05/health/health-care-open-letter -protests-coronavirus-trnd/index.html.

92. Email message to Marion Rosenke, "Informationsfreiheitsgesetz: Strategiepapier des Bundesinnenministeriums 'Wie wir COVID-19 unter Kontrolle bekommen'" [Freedom of Information Act: Strategy Paper of the Federal Ministry of the Interior, "How We Can Get COVID-19 Under Control"], June 9, 2020, https://clubderklarenworte.de/wp-content/uploads /2020/06/BMI-Dokument-incl.-Autoren.pdf; Anette Dowideit, "Germany's Ministry of the Interior Hired Scientists to Justify 'Tough Corona Measures,'" Global Research, https://www.globalresearch.ca/germanys-ministry-of-the -interior-hired-scientists-to-justify-tough-corona-measures/5736941.

93. Otto Kolbl, "Hong Kong—An Extreme Example of Parasitic Development," Rainbowbuilders, http://rainbowbuilders.org/china-development/hong-kong -economy; Otto Kolbl, "Have Tibetans Benefited from Recent Economic Development?," Rainbowbuilders, http://rainbowbuilders.org/tibet-development -tibet-development-aid; "Otto Kolbl, Short CV," Rainbowbuilders, https://www .rainbowbuilders.org/team/otto-kolbl-e.

94. "Prof. Dr. Maximilian Mayer," Center for Advanced Security, Strategic and Integration Studies, Rheinische Friedrich-Wilhelms-Universität Bonn, https://www.cassis.uni-bonn.de/en/about-us/all-employees/mayer.

95. See, e.g., Tong-Wen Sun, Xi-Jing Zhang, Zhui Yu, and You Shang, "Chinese Expert Consensus on the Diagnosis and Treatment of Severely and Critically Ill Patients with Coronavirus Disease 2019," Chinese Medical Journal 133, no. 24 (December 2020): 2963–65, https://doi.org/10.1097%2FCM9 .0000000000001264.

96. Madeleine Carlisle, "Gov. Cuomo Says Chinese Government Delivering 1,000 Ventilators to New York," Time, April 4, 2020, updated April 6, 2020, https://time.com/5815687/cuomo-ventilators-china-coronavirus.

97. Michael Biesecker and Tom Krisher, "Becoming 'King of Ventilators' May Result in Unexpected Glut," Associated Press, May 10, 2020, https:// apnews.com/article/donald-trump-ap-top-news-mi-state-wire-politics-virus -outbreak-e08621567fd8758c89b0c5aed5ac5d72.

98. "Mortality rates for those who received mechanical ventilation in the 18- to-65 and older-than-65 age groups were 76.4% and 97.2%, respectively. Mortality rates for those in the 18-to-65 and older-than-65 age groups who did not receive mechanical ventilation were 1.98% and 26.6%, respectively."

See Safiya Richardson et. al, "Presenting Characteristics, Comorbidities, and Outcomes Among 5700 Patients Hospitalized With COVID-19 in the New York City Area," *Journal of the American Medical Association* 323, no. 20 (April 2020): 2052–59, http://jamanetwork.com/article.aspx?doi=10 .1001/jama.2020.6775; Sharon Begley, "New Analysis Recommends Less Reliance on Ventilators to Treat Coronavirus Patients," Stat, April 21, 2020, https://www.statnews.com/2020/04/21/coronavirus-analysis-recommends -less-reliance-on-ventilators.

99. Andrew Jacobs, "A Glut of Chinese Masks Is Driving U.S. Companies Out of Business," *New York Times*, May 29, 2021, https://www.nytimes.com/2021 /05/29/health/us-china-mask-production.html.

100. Brian E. McGarry, David C. Grabowski, and Michael L. Barnett, "Severe Staffing and Personal Protective Equipment Shortages Faced by Nursing Homes during the COVID-19 Pandemic," *Health Affairs* 39, no. 10 (August 2020): 1812–21, https://doi.org/10.1377/hlthaff.2020.01269.

101. "New Survey Findings from 21K US Nurses: PPE Shortages Persist, Re- use Practices on the Rise amid COVID-19 Pandemic," American Nurses Association, September 1, 2020, https://www.nursingworld.org/news /news-releases/2020/new-survey-findings-from-21k-us-nurses--ppe-shortages -persist-re-use-practices-on-the-rise-amid-covid-19-pandemic.

102. "Shortage of Personal Protective Equipment Endangering Health Workers Worldwide," World Health Organization, March 3, 2020, https://www.who .int/news/item/03-03-2020-shortage-of-personal-protective-equipment-- endangering-health-workers-worldwide.

103. Bonny Lin et al., "China Is Exploiting the Pandemic to Advance Its Interests, with Mixed Results," Center for Strategic & International Studies, September 30, 2021, https://www.csis.org/analysis/china-exploiting-pandemic-advance -its-interests-mixed-results.

104. Song Guoyou, "US Soft Power Declining Because of Its COVID-19 Pandemic Bungling," Global Times, May 26, 2020, https://www.globaltimes.cn /content/1189596.shtml; Song Luzheng, "Many Western Governments Ill- Equipped to Handle Coronavirus," Global Times, March 15, 2020, https:// www.globaltimes.cn/content/1182661.shtml.

105. Larry N. Gerston, Mary Currin-Percival, and Garrick L. Percival, *California's Recall Election of Gavin Newsom: COVID-19 and the Test of Leadership* (Milton, UK: Taylor & Francis, 2022), 75–77.

106. Alexander Smith, "British Doctors Warn Some Chinese Ventilators Could Kill If Used in Hospitals," NBC News, May 1, 2020, https://www.nbcnews .com/news/world/british-doctors-warn-chinese-ventilators-could-kill-if-used -hospitals-n1194046.

107. Iulian Chifu and Dumitru Saranuta, "Coronavirus Pandemic and the Changes of the World," Editura Institulului De Stinte Politice si Relatil Internationale "Ion I. C. Bratianu," https://web.archive.org/web/20220625011325/https://

ifspd.org/wp-content/uploads/2020/12/Coronavirus-Pandemic-and-the
-Changes-of-the-World.pdf, 36; Josiah Case, *Telling China's COVID-19
Story Well: Beijing's Efforts to Control Information and Shape Public
Narratives Regarding the 2020 Global Pandemic*, CNA, https://apps.dtic.
mil/sti/pdfs/AD1145617.pdf, 37, 43.

108. Mike Pompeo, *Never Give an Inch: Fighting for the America I Love* (New
      York: Broadside Books, 2023), 290–91.

109. Gottlieb, *Uncontrolled Spread*, 51.

110. Josh Rogin, "How China Is Planning to Use the Coronavirus Crisis to Its
      Advantage," *Washington Post*, March 16, 2020, https://www.washingtonpost
      .com/opinions/2020/03/16/how-china-is-planning-use-coronavirus-crisis
      -its-advantage; Barnini Chakraborty, "China Hints at Denying Americans
      Life-Saving Coronavirus Drugs," FOX News, March 13, 2020, https://www
      .foxnews.com/world/chinese-deny-americans-coronavirus-drugs.

111. Zhang Tengjun, "张腾军：2020年美国大选中的民主社会主义浪潮： 表现、
      原因及走势" [The Wave of Democratic Socialism in the 2020 US General
      Election: Performance, Causes and Trends], December 11, 2020, https://brgg
      .fudan.edu.cn/articleinfo_3210_4.html.

112. Christian Bjørnskov, "Did Lockdown Work? An Economist's Cross-Country
      Comparison," *CESifo Economic Studies* 67, no. 3 (September 2021): 318–
      31, https://doi.org/10.1093/cesifo/ifab003.

113. Virat Agrawal et al., "The Impact of the COVID-19 Pandemic and Policy
      Responses on Excess Mortality," working paper no. 28930, NBER Working
      Paper Series, June 2021, https://www.nber.org/system/files/working_papers
      /w28930/w28930.pdf.

114. Scott W. Atlas, *A Plague upon Our House: My Fight at the Trump White
      House to Stop COVID from Destroying America* (New York: Bombardier
      Books, 2021), 299–302.

115. Elise Gould and Melat Kassa, "Low-Wage, Low-Hours Workers Were Hit
      Hardest in the COVID-19 Recession," Economic Policy Institute, May 20,
      2021, https://www.epi.org/publication/swa-2020-employment-report.

116. Lei Zheng et al., "Is Lockdown Bad for Social Anxiety in COVID-19
      Regions?: A National Study in the SOR Perspective," *International Journal
      of Environmental Research and Public Health* 17, no. 12 (June 2020): 4561,
      https://doi.org/10.3390/ijerph17124561.

117. University of Bath, "UK Public View COVID-19 as a Threat Because of
      Lockdowns, New Study Suggests," Phys.org, July 7, 2021, https://phys.org
      /news/2021-07-uk-view-covid-threat-lockdowns.pdf.

118. Atlas, *A Plague upon Our House*, 299.

119. "Wanted by the FBI: China MSS Guangdong State Security Department
      Hackers," Federal Bureau of Investigation, https://www.justice.gov/opa
      /press-release/file/1295986/download; "Two Chinese Hackers Working with

the Ministry of State Security Charged with Global Computer Intrusion Campaign Targeting Intellectual Property and Confidential Business Information, Including COVID-19 Research," Office of Public Affairs, U.S. Department of Justice, July 13, 2022, https://www.justice.gov/opa/pr/two -chinese-hackers-working-ministry-state-security-charged-global-computer -intrusion; Roger Faligot, "Book Excerpt: How Coronavirus Could Be Part of China's Biological Attack Programme," Outlook Weekender, June 25, 2022, https://www.outlookindia.com/magazine/international/book-excerpt -how-coronavirus-could-be-part-of-china-biological-attack-programme -weekender_story-204651.

120. Mark Moore, "Rick Scott Accuses China of Trying to Sabotage Coronavirus Vaccine," *New York Post*, June 7, 2020, https://nypost.com/2020/06/07/sen -rick-scott-accuses-china-of-trying-to-sabotage-coronavirus-vaccine.

121. Sarah Fitzpatrick and Kit Ramgopal, "Hackers Linked to Chinese Government Stole Millions in COVID Benefits, Secret Service Says," NBC News, December 5, 2022, https://www.nbcnews.com/tech/security/chinese -hackers-covid-fraud-millions-rcna59636.

Chapter 11: A Cover-Up for China and Themselves

1. *Biden Jr., et al.*, 293 So. 169 (W.D. La., 2022), deposition of Dr. Anthony Fauci, 153–54.

2. Ibid., 156.

3. Ibid., 106.

4. Ibid., 102.

5. Fauci, email message to Melinda Haskins, "RE: Please Review: House Oversight Letter on Coronavirus Diagnostics."

6. Attachments to James Comer and Jim Jordan, letter to Xavier Becerra, January 11, 2022, https://s3.documentcloud.org/documents/21177759 /house-oversight-letter-and-email-transcriptions.pdf, 4.

7. Ibid., 8.

8. Select Subcommittee on the Coronavirus Pandemic, "The Proximal Origin of a Cover-Up: Did the 'Bethesda Boys' Downplay a Lab Leak?," Interim Majority Staff Report, July 11, 2023, 20, https://oversight.house.gov/report /interim-staff-report-the-proximal-origin-of-a-cover-up-did-the-bethesda -boys-downplay-a-lab-leak/.

9. Batao Xiao, Lei Xiao, and Matthew Elvey, "The Possible Origins of 2019-nCoV Coronavirus," preprint (February 2020), http://dx.doi.org/10.13140 /RG.2.2.23421.03047; Batao Xiao and Lei Xiao, "The Possible Origins of 2019-nCoV Coronavirus," ResearchGate, February 2020, https://img-prod .tgcom24.mediaset.it/images/2020/02/16/114720192-5eb8307f-017c-4075 -a697-348628da0204.pdf.

10. Fan Wu et al., "A New Coronavirus Associated with Human Respiratory Disease in China," *Nature* 579 (2020): 265–69, https://doi.org/10.1038 /s41586-020-2008-3, mentioned in Becker, *Made in China*, 183.

11. *Biden Jr., et al.*, 293 So. 169 (W.D. La., 2022), deposition of Dr. Anthony Fauci, 188, 190.

12. Emily Kopp and Karolina Corin, "Emails Show Wuhan Lab Collaborator Played Central Role in Public Messaging About COVID-19 Origins," U.S. Right to Know, December 8, 2022, https://usrtk.org/covid-19-origins/emails -show-wuhan-lab-collaborator-played-central-role-in-public-messaging -about-covid-19-origins.

13. Hongying Li et al., "Human-Animal Interactions and Bat Coronavirus Spillover Potential Among Rural Residents in Southern China," *Biosafety and Health* 1, no. 2 (September 2019): 84–90, https://doi.org/10.1016/j .bsheal.2019.10.004.

14. Becker, *Made in China*, 163.

15. Katherine Eban, "The Lab-Leak Theory: Inside the Fight to Uncover COVID-19's Origins," *Vanity Fair*, June 3, 2021, https://www.vanityfair .com/news/2021/06/the-lab-leak-theory-inside-the-fight-to-uncover-covid -19s-origins.

16. Ibid.

17. Charles Calisher et al., "Statement in Support of the Scientists, Public Health Professionals, and Medical Professionals of China Combatting COVID-19," *Lancet* 395, no. 10226 (March 2020): e42–43, https://doi.org/10.1016/S0140 -6736(20)30418-9.

18. Paul D. Thacker, "Former CDC Director Robert Redfield on Inside Battles with Anthony Fauci, and Why Classified Information Will Point to a Lab Accident in Wuhan," *The DisInformation Chronicle* (Substack), September 15, 2022, https://disinformationchronicle.substack.com/p/former-cdc-director -robert-redfield.

19. "Anderson Cooper 360 Degrees," transcript, CNN, April 17, 2020, http:// www.cnn.com/TRANSCRIPTS/2004/17/acd.01.html.

20. Ibid.; *Biden Jr., et al.*, 293 So. 169 (W.D. La., 2022), deposition of Dr. Anthony Fauci, 198.

21. Nicholas Wade, *Where COVID Came From* (New York: Encounter Books, 2021), 8–9.

22. Eban, "The Lab-Leak Theory."

23. Mara Hvistendahl, "I Visited a Chinese Lab at the Center of the Biosafety Debate. What I Learned Helps Explain the Clash over Covid-19's Origins," The Intercept, June 19, 2021, https://theintercept.com/2021/06/19/lab-leak -covid-origins-virology.

24. Peter Daszak, email message to Rita Colwell, "RE: Coronavirus Statement,"

February 8, 2020, https://usrtk.org/wp-content/uploads/2020/11/The_ Lancet_Emails_Daszak-2.8.20.pdf.

25. Paul D. Thacker, "Former CDC Director Robert Redfield on Inside Battles with Anthony Fauci, and Why Classified Information Will Point to a Lab Accident in Wuhan," *The DisInformation Chronicle* (Substack), September 15, 2022, https://disinformationchronicle.substack.com/p/former-cdc -director-robert-redfield; Rand Paul, *DECEPTION: The Great Covid Cover-Up* (Regnery, Washington, DC, 2023), 20–21, 31–32.

26. "The Origins of Covid-19: An Investigation of the Wuhan Institute of Virology," House Foreign Affairs Committee Report, 117th Cong., August 2021, https://foreignaffairs.house.gov/wp-content/uploads/2021/08/ORIGINS -OF-COVID-19-REPORT.pdf, 55.

27. Kopp and Corin, "Emails Show Wuhan Lab Collaborator Played Central Role in Public Messaging About COVID-19 Origins."

28. Eban, "The Lab-Leak Theory."

29. Sainath Suryanarayanan, "EcoHealth Alliance Wanted to Block Disclosure of COVID-19-Relevant Virus Data from China," U.S. Right to Know, January 10, 2022, https://usrtk.org/covid-19-origins/ecohealth-alliance-wanted-to -block-disclosure-of-covid-19-relevant-virus-data-from-china.

30. Nidhi Subbaraman, "'Heinous!' Coronavirus Researcher Shut Down for Wuhan-Lab Link Slams New Funding Restrictions," *Nature*, August 21, 2020, https://www.nature.com/articles/d41586-020-02473-4.

31. "党支部" [Party Branch], Wuhan Institute of Virology, http://www.whiov .cas.cn/djkxwh/dqzz/dzb; "The Origins of Covid-19: An Investigation of the Wuhan Institute of Virology," 15.

32. "纪委" [Commission for Discipline Inspection], Wuhan Institute of Virology, http://www.whiov.cas.cn/djkxwh/dqzz/jw; "The Origins of Covid-19: An Investigation of the Wuhan Institute of Virology," 16.

33. "所长致辞" [New Year's Speech by the Director in 2021], Wuhan Institute of Virology, January 2022, http:/www.whiov.cas.cn/gkjj/szzc_160220; "The Origins of Covid-19: An Investigation of the Wuhan Institute of Virology," 17.

34. Peter Daszak at C-SPAN forum event, "Pandemics" (video), C-SPAN, https:// www.c-span.org/video/?404875-1/pandemics.

35. Anthony S. Fauci, "Research on Highly Pathogenic H5N1 Influenza Virus: The Way Forward," *mBio* 3, no. 5 (September–October 2012): e00359–12, https://doi.org/10.1128%2FmBio.00359-12.

36. Eban, "The Lab-Leak Theory."

37. Becker, *Made in China*, 127.

38. "The Origins of Covid-19: An Investigation of the Wuhan Institute of Virology," 30.

39. Ibid., 35.

40. Sharon Lerner and Mara Hvistendahl, "NIH Officials Worked with EcoHealth Alliance to Evade Restrictions on Coronavirus Experiments," The Intercept, November 3, 2021, https://theintercept.com/2021/11/03/coronavirus-research-ecohealth-nih-emails.

41. Becker, *Made in China*, 165–66, 175–76.

42. "Fact Sheet: Activity at the Wuhan Institute of Virology," U.S. Department of State, January 15, 2021, https://2017-2021.state.gov/fact-sheet-activity-at-the-wuhan-institute-of-virology/index.html.

43. Becker, *Made in China*, 175–76.

44. Eva Fu, "Wuhan Lab Allowed to Destroy 'Secret Files' Under Partnership with U.S. National Lab, Agreement Shows," The Epoch Times, May 10, 2022, https://www.theepochtimes.com/wuhan-lab-allowed-to-destroy-secret-files-under-its-partnership-with-us-national-lab-agreement-shows_4417444.html.

45. Eban, "The Lab-Leak Theory"; Becker, *Made in China*, 170.

46. Becker, *Made in China*, 180.

47. Josh Rogin, "State Department Cables Warned of Safety Issues at Wuhan Lab Studying Bat Coronaviruses," *Washington Post*, April 14, 2020, https://www.washingtonpost.com/opinions/2020/04/14/state-department-cables-warned-safety-issues-wuhan-lab-studying-bat-coronaviruses.

48. Yuan Zhiming, "Current Status and Future Challenges of High-Level Biosafety Laboratories in China," *Journal of Biosafety and Biosecurity* 1, no. 2 (September 2019): 123–27, https://doi.org/10.1016/j.jobb.2019.09.005; "The Origins of Covid-19: An Investigation of the Wuhan Institute of Virology," 19.

49. Eban, "The Lab-Leak Theory."

50. *Biden Jr., et al.*, 293 So. 169 (W.D. La. 2022), deposition of Dr. Anthony Fauci, 147–48.

51. Quoted in Becker, *Made in China*, 48, 50.

52. Roger Faligot, "Book Excerpt: How Coronavirus Could Be Part of China's Biological Attack Programme," Outlook Weekender, June 25, 2022, https://www.outlookindia.com/magazine/international/book-excerpt-how-coronavirus-could-be-part-of-china-biological-attack-programme-weekender_story-204651.

53. Becker, *Made in China*, 123.

54. Elsa B. Kania and Wilson VornDick, "Weaponizing Biotech: How China's Military Is Preparing for a 'New Domain of Warfare,'" Defense One, August 14, 2019, https://www.defenseone.com/ideas/2019/08/chinas-military-pursuing-biotech/159167.

55. Jared B. Hirschkorn, *Pandemics and Paradigms of Conflict* (Fort Leavenworth, KS: School of Advanced Military Studies, 2021), 22, 24.

56. Becker, *Made in China*, 169.

57. "The Origins of Covid-19: An Investigation of the Wuhan Institute of Virology," 23.

58. Javin Aryan, "A Look at China's Biowarfare Ambitions," Observer Research Foundation, June 2, 2021, https://www.orfonline.org/expert-speak/a-look-at-chinas-biowarfare-ambitions; Eban, "The Lab-Leak Theory."

59. Eban, "The Lab-Leak Theory."

60. Becker, *Made in China*, 166.

61. Eban, "The Lab-Leak Theory."

62. Billie Thomson, "China 'Appoints Its Top Military Bio-warfare Expert to Take Over Secretive Virus Lab in Wuhan,' Sparking Conspiracy Theories That Coronavirus Outbreak Is Linked to Beijing's Army," *Daily Mail*, February 14, 2020, https://www.dailymail.co.uk/news/article-8003713/China-appoints-military-bio-weapon-expert-secretive-virus-lab-Wuhan.html.

63. Sakshi Piplani et al., "In Silico Comparison of SARS-CoV-2 Spike Protein-ACE2 Binding Affinities Across Species and Implications for Virus Origin," *Scientific Reports* 11, no. 13063 (2021), https://doi.org/10.1038/s41598-021-92388-5; "The Origins of Covid-19: An Investigation of the Wuhan Institute of Virology," 38.

64. Daniel Wrapp et al., "Cryo-EM Structure of the 2019-nCoV Spike in the Prefusion Conformation," *Science* 367, no. 6483 (March 2020): 1260–63, https://doi.org/10.1126%2Fscience.abb2507; "The Origins of Covid-19: An Investigation of the Wuhan Institute of Virology," 37.

65. "SARS Basics Fact Sheet," Centers for Disease Control and Prevention, https://www.cdc.gov/sars/about/fs-sars.html.

66. "Geographical Distribution of Confirmed Cases of MERS-CoV by Reporting Country, April 2012–February 2023," European Centre for Disease Prevention and Control, April 5, 2023, https://www.ecdc.europa.eu/en/publications-data/geographical-distribution-confirmed-cases-mers-cov-reporting-country-april-2012-2.

67. "WHO Coronavirus (COVID-19) Dashboard," World Health Organization, https://covid19.who.int.

68. "Proposal: Volume 1—Project DEFUSE: Defusing the Threat of Bat-Borne Coronaviruses," EcoHealth Alliance, March 24, 2018, https://drasticresearch.files.wordpress.com/2021/09/main-document-preempt-volume-1-no-ess-hr00118s0017-ecohealth-alliance.pdf; Sharon Lerner and Maia Hibbett, "Leaked Grant Proposal Details High-Risk Coronavirus Research," The Intercept, September 23, 2021, https://theintercept.com/2021/09/23/coronavirus-research-grant-darpa/.

69. Lawrence A. Tabak, letter to James Comer, October 20, 2021, https://int.nyt
     .com/data/documenttools/nih-eco-health-alliance-letter/512f5ee70ce9c67c
     /full.pdf; Sharon Lerner, Mara Hvistendahl, and Maia Hibbett, "NIH
     Documents Provide New Evidence U.S. Funded Gain-of-Function Research,"
     The Intercept, September 9, 2021, https://theintercept.com/2021/09/09
     /covid-origins-gain-of-function-research/.

70. Qiong Wang et al., "A Unique Protease Cleavage Site Predicted in the Spike
     Protein of the Novel Pneumonia Coronavirus (2019-nCoV) Potentially
     Related to Viral Transmissibility," Virologica Sinica 35, no. 3 (June 2020):
     337–39, https://doi.org/10.1007%2Fs12250-020-00212-7.

71. "The Origins of Covid-19: An Investigation of the Wuhan Institute of
     Virology," 6.

72. Jeffrey A. Tucker, "The Lab Leak: The Plots and Schemes of Jeremy Farrar,
     Anthony Fauci, and Francis Collins," Brownstone Institute, January 13,
     2022, https://brownstone.org/articles/the-lab-leak-the-plots-and-schemes
     -of-jeremy-farrar-anthony-fauci-and-francis-collins; "Sir Jeremy Farrar,"
     Wellcome Trust, https://wellcome.org/who-we-are/people/jeremy-farrar.

73. Eban, "The Lab-Leak Theory."

74. Ibid.

75. Ibid.

76. Hvistendahl, "I Visited a Chinese Lab at the Center of the Biosafety Debate."

77. Ibid.

78. Eban, "The Lab-Leak Theory."

79. Ibid.

80. Ibid.

81. Jim Garamone, "President Remembers Those Lost on 9/11, Says Day
     Changed America," U.S. Department of Defense, September 11, 2022,
     https://www.defense.gov/News/News-Stories/Article/Article/3154596
     /president-remembers-those-lost-on-911-says-day-changed-america;
     National Commission on Terrorist Attacks upon the United States, Thomas
     H. Kean and Lee Hamilton, The 9/11 Commission Report (Washington,
     D.C.: U.S. Government Printing Office, 2004).

82. Eban, "The Lab-Leak Theory."

83. Kylie Atwood, "Pompeo-Led Effort to Hunt Down Covid Lab Theory Shut
     Down by Biden Administration over Concerns About Quality of Evidence,"
     CNN, May 26, 2021, https://www.cnn.com/2021/05/25/politics/biden-shut
     -down-trump-effort-coronavirus-chinese-lab/index.html.

84. See e.g., Christa Case Bryant, "Lab Leak? Why Congress Is Split on
     Investigating COVID's Origins," Christian Science Monitor, June 7, 2021,
     https://www.csmonitor.com/USA/Politics/2021/0607/Lab-leak-Why

-Congress-is-split-on-investigating-COVID-s-origins; COVID–19 ORIGIN ACT OF 2023, S. 619, 118th Cong. (2023).

85.   Ibid.

86.   Jeffrey D. Sachs et al., "The *Lancet* Commission on Lessons for the Future from the COVID-19 Pandemic," *Lancet* 400, no. 10359 (October 2022): 2–3, https://doi.org/10.1016/S0140-6736(22)01585-9.

87.   Jeffrey D. Sachs, "The Xinjiang Genocide Allegations Are Unjustified," Jeffrey D. Sachs, April 20, 2021, https://www.jeffsachs.org/newspaper-articles /apfjc5yg352d554k2ar2wwwkk8ryw9; Jeffrey D. Sachs, "The West's False Narrative About Russia and China," Jeffrey D. Sachs, August 22, 2022, https:// www.jeffsachs.org/newspaper-articles/h29g9k7l7fymxp39yhzwxc5f72ancr.

88.   "An Interview Conducted with Prof. Salim Abdool Karim, Epidemiologist on Sinovac's Coronavirus Vaccine and the Issue of COVID-19 Source-Tracking," Embassy of the People's Republic of China in the Republic of South Africa, July 23, 2021, https://web.archive.org/web/20220117015606/https://www .mfa.gov.cn/ce/cezanew/eng/sgxw/t1894678.htm; CGTN, "COVID-19 Origins: SA Scientist Says 'No Time for Finger-Pointing,'" Global Times, August 2, 2021, https://www.globaltimes.cn/page/202108/1230376.shtml.

89.   Sachs et al., "The *Lancet* Commission on Lessons for the Future from the COVID-19 Pandemic."

90.   Eva Fu, "Beijing Seizes Upon Fauci's Calls for Solidarity to Push COVID-19 Propaganda," The Epoch Times, March 16, 2021, https://www .theepochtimes.com/beijing-seizes-upon-faucis-call-for-solidarity-to-push -covid-19-propaganda_3731620.html.

91.   "Threat of 'Broken Heads, Bloodshed' as China's Communist Party Marks 100 Years," RFI, January 7, 2021, https://www.rfi.fr/en/international /20210701-threat-of-broken-heads-and-bloodshed-as-china-s-communist -party-celebrates-100-years.

Conclusion

1.   Julia Shapero, "DOJ Argues Florida Law Restricting Chinese Land Ownership Is 'Unlawful,'" The Hill, June 28, 2023, https://thehill.com/homenews/state -watch/4072675-doj-argues-florida-law-restricting-chinese-land-ownership -is-unlawful/.

2.   Jamie Joseph, "House to Consider Bipartisan Bill to Crack Down on Chinese Opioid Manufacturers," FOX News, July 25, 2023, https://www.foxnews .com/politics/house-consider-bipartisan-bill-cracking-down-chinese-opioid -manufacturers.

3.   Marco den Ouden, "Suppose They Gave a War and Nobody Came," Foundation for Economic Education, November 9, 2017, https://fee.org /articles/suppose-they-gave-a-war-and-nobody-came.

INDEX